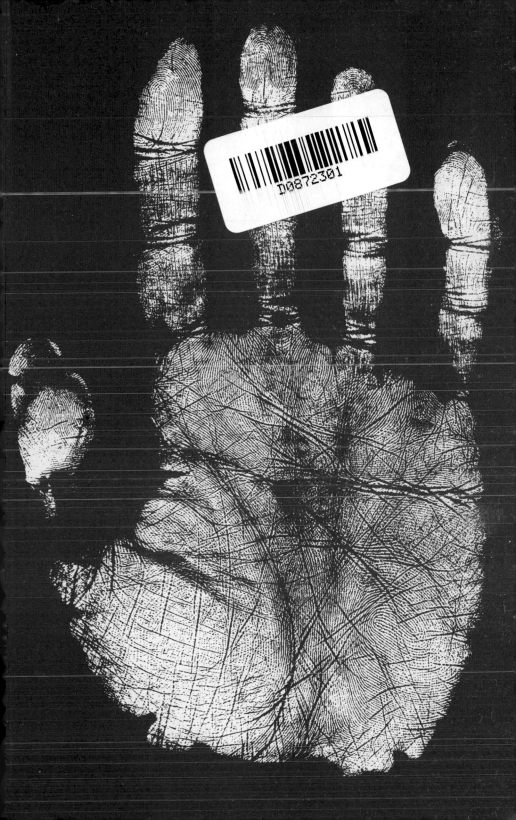

D0872301

9/6

L. Popper.
October 47.

THE SCARLET TREE

LIST OF WORKS BY OSBERT SITWELL

Published by Macmillan & Co.

PENNY FOOLISH. A Book of Tirades and Panegyrics
MRS. KIMBER. A Poem
THOSE WERE THE DAYS. Panorama with Figures
ESCAPE WITH ME ! An Oriental Sketch-Book
TWO GENERATIONS. A Double Biography
OPEN THE DOOR ! Short Stories
A PLACE OF ONE'S OWN. A Ghost Story
SING HIGH ! SING LOW ! A Book of Essays
LEFT HAND, RIGHT HAND An Autobiography

With Edith and Sacheverell Sitwell

TRIO. Dissertations on Some Aspects of National Genius

With R. J. Minney

GENTLE CAESAR. A Play in Three Acts

Published by Gerald Duckworth & Co.

ARGONAUT AND JUGGERNAUT. Poems
TRIPLE FUGUE. Short Stories
OUT OF THE FLAME. Poems
BEFORE THE BOMBARDMENT. A Satirical Novel
WHO KILLED COCK ROBIN ? Reflections upon Modern Poetry
DISCURSIONS. An Illustrated Book of Travel
THE MAN WHO LOST HIMSELF. A Novel
MIRACLE ON SINAI. A Novel
WINTERS OF CONTENT. An Illustrated Book of Travel
COLLECTED POEMS. (Ordinary Edition, and Limited Edition
signed and numbered)
DUMB ANIMAL. Short Stories
SELECTED POEMS, OLD AND NEW

With Sacheverell Sitwell

ALL AT SEA. A Social Tragedy in 3 Acts

With Margaret Barton

SOBER TRUTH. An Anthology of Strange Occurrences in the
Victorian Era
VICTORIANA. An Anthology of Strange Sayings in the Victorian Era

With Nina Hamnett

THE PEOPLE'S ALBUM OF LONDON STATUES

THE AUTHOR (*æt.* 9) WITH SACHEVERELL SITWELL (*æt.* 4)

THE SCARLET TREE

BEING THE SECOND VOLUME OF
LEFT HAND, RIGHT HAND!

An Autobiography by
OSBERT SITWELL

LONDON
MACMILLAN & CO. LTD
1946

COPYRIGHT

PRINTED IN GREAT BRITAIN
BY R. & R. CLARK, LIMITED, EDINBURGH

To

MAYNARD HOLLINGWORTH

" . . . the blood, that fragile, scarlet tree
we carry within us. . . ."

LEFT HAND, RIGHT HAND!

ACKNOWLEDGEMENTS

My thanks are due to the Proprietors and Editor of *The Times* for allowing me to reproduce from the columns of their paper the long extracts at the end of this book, entitled "Appendix E : The Camorra Trial", and, similarly, to Miss Emily Anderson for permitting me to quote, as "Appendix C : The History of the Cold ", a passage from *The Letters of Mozart and His Family*, and to my publishers, Messrs. Macmillan, for agreeing to the reprint, as Appendix D, of a portion of a chapter, "Paters' Match ", from my novel *Those Were the Days*. Messrs. Gerald Duckworth have been most kind in allowing me to use, in the course of this volume, various poems by Miss Edith Sitwell—whom I must also thank for giving her consent —and by myself. And I would like once more to express my sense of obligation to my friend Mr. Thomas Mark for the help he has given me in seeing this second volume of my autobiography, as he saw the first, through the press.

OSBERT SITWELL

CONTENTS

BOOK III
CHAMBERS OF THE EAST

BOOK IV
THE HAPPIEST TIME OF ONE'S LIFE

LIST OF ILLUSTRATIONS

Book Three :: Chambers of the East

Chapter One   THE RUNNING SHADOW

It was the following year. A shadow had come to live among us, and it was growing thicker and darker. Suspicion, conjecture and fear now plainly took substance to themselves. A vein of indefinable sorrow and uneasiness threaded the air of the rooms, and affected the persons in them, so that at once other shadows could rush in to join their grey precursor, projected as they were from the warm palpitating twilight that lives beneath men's ribs or in the dreaming hollows, vast caverns, of their skulls. The air, I say, was disturbed and jarring, with hints of dire futures more than of a lengthy and tragic past, but old talk revived that the house was haunted, and the maids, white as milk, walked hand in hand down long corridors. To us, it was difficult to trace the outline of the shadow, for it was still ill-defined, if opaque, bearing about it something loutish and lumpish, yet it was showing more audaciously every day, coming out into the light, altering and distorting the outlines of familiar things so that they could be seen through it but dimly. It seemed to be there all the time, the shadow, the forerunner, mixing itself up now with the beauty of what it was trying to obscure and degrade. Some days it tainted even the finest morning with a feeling of uncertainty that hid far down beyond the midriff. Often the sun, the heat of the spring days, seemed, because of their truth, their splendid directness, to make this feeling worse. Though we loved the house, we were yet eager to be out of it and beyond reach. Thus we would choose now the longer, cooler way to the lake below, through the wooden gate between the stone warrior and amazon, whose plumy, characteristic images floated, glittering upon the surface of the leaves, with a kind of melancholy and solemn panache. Then we would run along the sheltered alleys of the Wilderness, with their tall holly hedges caught in dewy cobwebs, on through the parabolas made by the young trees, and down under the high vaulting of the old beeches, their pillars grey like smoke, down the steep paths, that lay, narrow strips, deep in leaf-mould, upon the rocky sides of the hill, past cliffs and clefts and the negro's cave, down precipices, as they seemed, and stony chasms, towards the water. Looking up, the sides of the hills were lighter and more blue than the sky, for the hyacinths were out, and their breath, sweet, evasive, unlike any other scent, permeated the entire countryside.

The house above, out of sight from this point, was so sensitive that it took on the ambience of those who dwelt under its roof and even communicated this atmosphere to the immediate surroundings ; thus, now that the shadow was growing worse, it offered during the daytime the living counterpart to the ghostly terrors of the night. . . . But here below, at the Sawmill — as much a place of arrival as is a quay or the platform of a station —, though it, too, may have been haunted, we were at last beyond the reach of the shadow. In spite of the noise of machinery, the dominating sound was that of water, water turning, falling, gently swirling and murmuring, and the being, if there was one, whom you would have found here, rising from the damp mould where she had been hiding under the branches of green willow, soft as feathers, beside the clear, smoke-blue water of the spring — which flowed through a little channel to the lake — would have been the nymph of a fountain ; some rustic, northern Arethusa, clad in tangled green weed that matched in shade her lank, flat tresses, and wearing fresh-water mussel-shells as her jewellery and for her crown. There, by the side of the little stream, must formerly have stood some primitive wooden temple, you would have thought, for all round its banks were lying, stacked or singly, the fallen drums of pillars, of every size, columns and sections and cones and cylinders of wood ; a dry, geometric world, cushioned in thorns and splinters, that yet possessed a certain beauty of its own, for its aridity was everywhere tempered by the sound of water flowing. Even the huge gold and sepia dragon-flies seemed made of varnished wood, brittle, clever inventions, as they darted and turned, first to the stream, then to the lake, that lay fringed with its trees, dull-green and sage-green and grey-green, like the background of a picture by Fragonard. It extended, vast and misty, beneath

its shroud, made of steel and silver and the fins and scales
of fishes.

Up on the hill, the house stood in a sullen dream, and the
clustered blossom of apple and pear showed pink and white
clouds, very pale and strange in their illumination, against a
sky darker than the stone, for a Sheffield blight was passing
over, and the light seemed to come from the ground of the
blue glades, odorous and idyllic. The birds, disorientated in
their sense of time by this false dusk, had stopped singing and,
instead, gave shrill calls, and flying, as it were, with all the
feeling of an augury, darted in a sudden flutter of darker wings
across the foreground, across the green-vaulted upper air of
these vistas. . . . Indoors, my father was superintending the
general rearrangement of the pictures occasioned by the
arrival of the Sargent group. It was difficult work, and he
was determined not to make it less difficult — *everything* must
be moved. But it was dark — it looked as if there was going
to be a thunderstorm, he said to himself, for though Sheffield
blights were proverbial as Sheffield steel, and came our way
several times a year, he would not admit their existence ; they
had not occurred in 1341 — or, at any rate, had not been
mentioned —, so why allow their presence ? Such a mistake !
. . . Yes, there it was ! They were carrying the Sargent past
him now ; but the coming storm was making it impossible for
him to see the picture clearly — one thing, though, he could
see : they were carrying it all wrong, so he called out in an
exasperated voice, " No, no, no ! Put it down ! ", and then
added, "Not like that ! Of course not ! "
Yes, it was a fine thing, he thought, as he gazed at it.
How right he had been to go to Sargent — a pity, of course,
that the painter had not consulted him more often, but artists
were notoriously pig-headed and always thought they knew
more about their own work than anyone else could tell them.
Self-opinionated. . . . All the same, it was an interesting
group. . . . And looking back, I, too, am obliged to allow
that this portrait focussed and summed up personalities and
things, and the ways to which life had been pointing. It
cut across our lives. After it was finished, everything, so far
at least as I was concerned, was noticeably different.
Now that I was a little older, I began to comprehend

3

more fully the world round me ; people said, and I understood what they said, though even now saying and understanding were only the brittle crust that formed over the deep chasms and gullies of feeling. But the surfaces of the earth were cooling for me ; the sunrise, with the mysterious hints which it had carried from the darkness out of which it came, was over, and its intimation of a glory beyond the ken of man was fading. The light, though still strange and beautiful, and peculiarly clear, was fast becoming daylight. . . . Nevertheless, life was full, so full. Its force bubbled and brimmed over, and our voices, like those of all children, ceaselessly lifted up in enquiry, were, I suppose, the expression of this sense of chronic elation, as much as of any particular desire for knowledge. The air, indeed, was loud with a continual demand for enlightenment, and an irritation that for once, though repressed, was most fully justified, could be observed in my father's patient and perpetual phrase, "Not so many questions just now ". And, in spite of the shadow to be felt, there were whole periods, apparently sempiternal, of sunlight and flowers and all the singular detail that goes to make a child's day.

Life was so full — but, nevertheless, since the painting had been executed, a twist seemed to have come upon the lives of the persons represented. It was possible to perceive now that the childish impression of permanence as a thing in itself was false ; it proved to be but a slow-motion section of something in progress. Even the Boer War, and the British disasters that had seemed the enduring part of it, were drawing to their close. Then there were illnesses, too, and my grandfather Londesborough had died, and there were the lawsuits in which my father was engaged, against the lessees of the coal-mines. Large sums of money were at stake in these, and though I did not understand the facts, I understood what they portended. One case had already been lost and, consequently, talk of poverty had for months fallen, like a miraculous shower of pebbles, among the peaches and the silver. My father spoke both of personal privation and of a doubtful future for Englishmen — and though this latter view, in such utter contradistinction to the popular forecast of a golden age of Empire, may at the time have been ill-founded, yet the future for our race, which included two major wars within forty years, was indeed

4

harder than any fate he can have foreseen.

As for our new-found indigence, to me — and I often felt bothered about it — it seemed to be of an odd sort. I had not known poverty, but I had seen its face very clearly as a child. I had heard the bitter whining, " Rags and Bones ! Rags and Bones ! ", insinuated against the glare of the winter dawn by the battered scarecrow who slunk down back alleys ; later I had examined the collections he made. I could, from him and from the tattered clothes and mouldering goods he piled upon his barrow, deduce the gesticulating automatons whom want drove to every action, to thieving and every kind of crookedness and crankiness, even to killing themselves or the slaughter of others. I had beheld the poor in London, that other nation that lived pressed into the narrow spaces between the houses of the rich. . . . But this brand of poverty I could neither recognise nor comprehend ; though now I can see it possessed the same sort of reality as pertained to those problem pictures that so fascinated the public of the same epoch every year at the Royal Academy : a man, let us say, sat sighing at a table in his study, with his head in his hands, and a pile of bills — yes, they were bills, they *must* be bills — on the table in front of him, where also were depicted the plush interior of an empty jewel-case, an overturned silver mustard-pot, a silver-backed hair-brush, a pawn-ticket and an empty bottle, labelled " Sleeping Draught ". Just outside the window, a tree was being cut down ; and in the room itself, a pet spaniel, so thin as to appear afflicted, was endeavouring to eat a mouse (it *looked* like an india-rubber mouse). Ox-eyed with wonder, a little crowd concentrated its attention for a full hour on these tell-tale details. It scarce stirred, though from time to time an individual would murmur. . . . What could it mean ? this picture, in which everything was yet so real as to make even the most obtuse believe in a meaning. What *could* it mean ? . . . *Poverty !* . . . Of course, that was it. Poverty !

Our poverty, then, signified chiefly that we were no longer allowed to throw down pennies, done up in screws of paper, to the conductors of German bands,[1] in their peaked caps,

---

[1] I find in my governess's account-book for 7th November 1901, " German Band 1/4d. ", " Dec. 12, 1901 1/3d. ". . . . By 1910, the German bands, the symbol of former German poverty and subservience, as Italian waiters and

or to the Italians, childishly gay and childishly melancholy, who turned the handles of barrel-organs, and that Stephen Pare's wages were cut down to a figure I cannot bear to think of ; indeed, how furnished with sadness was his life, with his wife, to whom he was devoted, mad, and himself condemned to a lifelong solitary confinement in darkness.

The chief difference, however, which my father's alleged loss of fortune made to us was that in future, so our governess told us, we were only to be given " useful presents ". This deceptive phrase formed cover for a device which, even then, I considered as unworthy, and which Davis — all the more on our side because of her hatred of governesses, and because Miss King-Church had been chosen to break the news of it to us — characterised as " downright mean ". It meant that, when it became plainly necessary for us to have new hair-brushes, or a piece of soap, these articles now reached us, not as a natural fulfilment of our needs, but disguised as a Christmas or birthday present. No self-respecting child could possibly like to have his stocking on Christmas Eve filled magically with such prosaic objects as toothbrushes and boot-laces, instead of tangerines done up in silver paper, chocolates and toys. My mother, with the indulgence and generosity of her temperament, tried always to circumvent such prophetic experiments in austerity, but my father, his relations and the governess were in league, and now Davis, who had always stood ranged on the other side, behind my mother, was suddenly snatched away from us and could no longer offer us support.

We had taken a house in London, 17 Lancaster Gate, a tall yellow house, of which, except that it seemed built up of fog, I remember little : for it contained much less in it to catch the fancy of a small boy than had the interior of our temporary home the previous year in Chesham Place. It was here, though, that after a violent quarrel with my father, Davis gave notice, never surmising, I believe, for an instant that it would be accepted. During the month before her going, we organised, as a demonstration, a great deal of

organ-grinders of Italian, had completely disappeared from English life, were no more to be seen in London or at the seaside. New and megalomaniac conceptions were suppressing them. . . . The last instance I know of Bohemians leading a bear round on a chain occurred just before the 1914 war, when my brother saw such a group at Eton ; it being part of the great Gypsy coppersmith invasion of those years.

weeping, in which my mother joined freely : but my father was resolute. We needed a " modern, scientific nurse ", he said, and our governess agreed with him. And so I used to lie awake in my small room, hearing Miss King-Church and a friend talking about Stephen Phillips's *Ulysses* — just produced at His Majesty's Theatre, a few days before, by Beerbohm Tree — and it seemed to me that the remarkable scene in Hades, which, stationed just outside my door, they went on to describe, a grey world wherein shadows moved dimly, very much resembled our life as it would be without our dear old nurse.

A few days before Davis left, she took Sacheverell and myself for our first sightseeing expedition to Kensington Palace. In the future, when the achievements of architecture, and indeed all forms of beauty, had become our chief resource and means of recreation, Sacheverell and I were destined in each other's company to visit many palaces and examine together many colonnaded vistas, painted rooms and gardens : the palaces of Venice coruscating in their own decay, the lights fluttering upon their gothic arcades, pillared balconies and marble quatrefoils, or upon the later out-thrust heads of warriors, feathered as Incas, and of tritons and amphibian beings carved in Istrian stone, as though mermaids were flashing their mirrors at them, the hard-edged, lily-towered palaces of Florence or those that seem built of sea boulders, the gilded galleries of Rome and Naples, full of furniture of tortoiseshell or inlaid with marble, of busts and urns, the rich and intricately carved fronts of Lecce, with their special swirls of cabbage-leaf cut in golden stone, the pure and flower-like beauty of the vaulted halls at Urbino, the fantastic forms that raise themselves, with the bravest fanfares of rhetoric, into the soft air of many lesser Italian cities, the palaces of Sicily, with their coved ceilings of looking-glass and their garden walls upon which strut stone dwarfs, the Arabian pavilions, with their alveolate roofs, that grace the lands of Spain and Portugal, the correct taste exemplified in the proportions of the great rooms of France, the baroque extensions into Bohemia, Germany and Austria, where upon wall and dome the limbs of gigantic plaster saints and cupids seemed modelled of the placid summer clouds outside, the elaborate tents, lined with tiles, of Turkey and North Africa ; in Venetian saloons we were to look up at heavens afloat with fair-haired goddesses, painted by the hand of Tiepolo, and at walls on which Veronese had set feasts for them ; we were to walk down the long vistas, cut alleys, past the proud fountains of peruked kings, and, in distant Marrakesh, to wander through trellised passages in which played, ever and again, a burning wind from the desert, in order to regard the flat water-lawns created by black-faced princes ; we were to wonder at the austere and grand apartments of sixteenth-century Spanish monarchs tortured by their faith, and the gay, lustrous rooms built of china, and full of birds that fluttered artificial wings and warbled arias by Mozart and Haydn, of their heirs a hundred years later, the elephantine essays in grandeur of neurasthenic sultans, and the pagan chambers, painted with gods and goddesses who nonchalantly posed as saints, that had been created for the Popes, the various dreams, half-dreamt, of Ludwig of Bavaria, the domes and dragons and palm-trees of George IV ; but still I remember as vividly as any of these — and with as much pleasure — the sedate good manners of the old brick palace. And I recall, too, the obvious interest that Sacheverell, though only four years old, took in everything he saw, the State Apartments with their suites of panelled rooms and decorous furniture and pictures, the dark staircase painted by Verrio, and the orangery, outside, at once so bold in its design, and yet so full of repose, with its stone-cornered façade built of bricks in two colours.

By this expedition, Davis, indeed, helped to influence our future more than she can have known, and far beyond her own departure — which left us desolate. . . . I had been for several months now in the charge of a red-haired young tutor from Cambridge, who tried his best to make me forget my loss. He would tell me for many hours about Rome, a city he had visited, and for which, naturally, he had conceived the greatest veneration. He even took me to Bumpus's bookshop and encouraged me to invest ten shillings of my savings (during the whole of my life this seems to have been the only period in which I ever possessed savings) in an illustrated book upon its grandeurs ancient and modern. (I remember distinctly his explaining to me at some length that most people called it the Eternal City.) But his talk of catacombs and Colosseums could not compensate me for Davis's tales of the former places she had held, of earlier charges, and of their parents. She had built up for me, through her conversation, a whole mythology, and I knew each of the children and their relatives as well as I knew those round me, I knew the nurseries, and the houses in which they were situated, and the gardens outside : it was the first world of the imagination in which for a minute or an hour at a time I could exist, though, in the very year of her leaving, it was beginning to yield place a little to the more highly-coloured panoramas of Harrison Ainsworth and Dickens. My tutor realised, it may be, that he was making no headway, and, as compensation, I was now offered a drive with him round the City on the top of an omnibus, should my father give his consent.

Eventually it was all arranged, and I recall the extraordinary sensation of importance that this concession afforded me. Only grown-up persons, I was aware, engaged in their mysterious businesses, clutching bags, hanging on straps, their eyes glazed by urgency to an almost trance-like condition, were allowed to travel thus. I looked forward to my experience for days beforehand. The whole tour would take two hours, and the same bus was to bring us back to our starting-place. My tutor laid stress on the necessity of obtaining the two top seats on the left-hand side, for that was the best vantage-point. Muffled immensely against the east wind, we made our way by 9.30 to Oxford Street, and were fortunate enough at once to obtain the places we wanted. The buses of those days had two large wheels in front and two smaller ones behind ; they were painted, as they are today, in reds and whites, but were not so metallically bright and flashing, depended on the paper placards they carried more than upon enamel, and the seats on the roof resembled garden seats. Our vehicle was drawn by two fine horses and travelled eight miles an hour. It carried about fourteen persons on the top, which was much lower than that of the motor-bus of today. And I recall, when motor-buses first came in, the fear of many passengers, as they swept under arches and viaducts at great speed and on so much higher a level, that they would be decapitated, and how, when approaching them, they involuntarily ducked their heads. But though the old horse-drawn bus may have been wanting in the feeling of prodigious power that the present conveyance imparts, though indeed this may compare as skating with walking where speed and impetus are concerned, nevertheless it atoned for that by a sense of companionship, and a wealth of cockney fun, for the driver sat only just beneath, with no shelter above his head, and he would often turn round and address remarks up at you. He would, for example, comment on other drivers who passed him, and tell you their histories. And you, for your part, could question him about the buildings and vehicles you were approaching.

The London through which we drove was very different from that of today in colour, shape and rhythm. Already, of course, it was beginning to take on the cosmopolitan, nondescript air of the modern international metropolis, but the old London of the eighteenth and early nineteenth centuries still preponderated. In the impression of overwhelming size that it conveyed — a feature upon which I have commented before, and which has characterised this particular city increasingly for the last two centuries — resided, doubtless, its peculiar and most obvious fascination. Its other charms were more subtle. And I think it was upon the morning in question, a fine winter's morning with a tattered edge of rosy and golden fog which clothed Wren's spires in a lovely opalescence — making them somehow not ethereal in any way, but beautiful with the perfection of a neat, clean fact or a calculation adroitly executed — that I first realised, besides its giant proportions, and the fogs and excitement born of them, other qualities which it possessed. These factors in its aspect, new to me, made one wonder, indeed, at the vast population of house-painters that the capital must support. Consider Regent Street, down the graceful curve of which we were now driving, think of the domes and balconies and balustrades of that one street alone ; a battalion of men would be required to haul it back from the deep, fog-like colour which in so short a time it acquired, to the creamy shade wherewith it started its run of every two or three years. To the cult of the permanent — of stone and concrete and marble — London opposed an ideal of smartness, essentially temporary by its nature, of varnish and enamel and brass-plates and railings and prettily shaped shining shop-windows, and shields with the royal arms, and the delicate, finical pointing of the brick-work. And everywhere we saw vehicles and horses ; vehicles

that belonged to and were the very flower of the same transient
civilisation of paint and patent-leather ; horses, glossy and
well-fed as nowhere else in the world, but yet, as it were,
prancing, unaware of their doom, on the edge of a volcano,
for the horse-age was within a few short months of the outbreak
of the revolution that was to destroy it utterly, curbing entirely
equine power, and leaving to our sacred national animal only
a trivial life of amusement in the hunting-field and on the
racecourse at Ascot and Goodwood : reserved for it, too, was
that epitome of every kind of retrogression, the cavalry. . . .
In the course of a decade, only a score of hansom-cabs were to
be left in the whole of this assemblage of cities, of which at
the moment they were the pride, while a new race of hard-
featured, sharp-tongued mechanics was to replace the old,
husky race of cabmen and drivers of buses, in the same way
that the conquering horde of burgesses had ousted the aristocrats in the France of a hundred years before.

For the moment, however, London still made the carriages,
and England supplied the horses, for the whole world. In
the thoroughfares we traversed, we saw chiefly buses, four-
wheelers and hansoms — hansoms that with each year of the
past half-century had become more elegant, the very perfect
expression of the wealth of London, its luxury and its particular understanding, that I have tried to indicate, of shining,
clean surfaces, of gloss and nap. This cab, too, imparted to
London streets a sense of idiosyncrasy, of dash and style ;
(just as the tandem gave it to the countryside — and here,
though I abhor horses, and love motors, I must admit that no
racing-motor has ever exhaled the same air of elegance as a
tandem, nor afforded its owner such an appearance of dandiacal
grace and swagger). The whole equipage possessed a frail
and brittle elegance, every single thing about it, from the
top-hat and red buttonhole of the driver, down to the two
sliding glass panes of the front, even down to the tail, shoes
and hoofs of the horse, had polish, finish and ingenuity. This
was essentially the vehicle that had been perfected, through
more than a century or two, for — and by — a continuing
line of fops, beaux, macaronis, dudes, bucks, blades, swells,
bloods and mashers. . . . Occasionally other conveyances
would pass us, a private omnibus, it may be, filled with a
county family, its dogs and retainers, on the way from one

terminus to another. (If there were no dogs, this signified Victoria Station and that the family was *en route* for Dover and hydrophobic foreign parts). Gone already from the scene were chariots (known on the Continent, where they survived for cabs, as " Mi-Lords "), gone were the pilentum, the britzska, the Clarence (ancestor of the surviving, trundling " growler "), the phaeton (demi-mail, spider and Beaufort), the dioropha and the barouche ; but broughams, landaus, coaches, waggonettes (Portland and Lonsdale), drags, victorias and sociables, with imitation cane-work on their panels, all these could still be seen turning out of the endless residential quarters and heading for Hyde Park.

Horses — horses and carriages even more than people — gave London, as I remember it then, its particular distinction, for it was the capital of an island where the horse was still god, where stables were often finer than houses, and race-courses better than parks. The staccato tapping of hoofs, and not the sound of a river flowing, was the appropriate and jaunty music of London. . . . As for the people, the general run of them that you saw in the streets were both more smart and more shabby than they are today ; whole crowds were clothed in frock-coats and top-hats, entire armies were crowned with bowlers ; moustaches were long and upturned, often the ends were waxed, and there were more, and fuller, beards in evidence. Fewer women were hurrying or sauntering in the streets, but those we passed were both more elaborately dressed and, at the same time, more untidy ; their hair, then billowing out into puffs and curls, and creeping into fringes, was never as steely neat and tight as it is today, and their figures were more ample. The rich and the middle classes sported greater quantities of lace, bows, frills, tucks and trinkets ; while the poor, men equally with women, showed their distress more plainly. There were mobs, unkempt, their clothes and boots torn, the men with red noses, the women with faces blue and pinched ; from these the contemporary gangs of tramps and pedlars and street-walkers, types that vary little through the centuries in dress or appearance, were patently recruited.

Our journey was an endless jolting rumble, broken continually by sudden halts : but I can only dimly recall the changing of horses which I suppose took place. The Bank of England and the Mansion House were two of the chief objects

Rischgitz

ST. PAUL'S FROM FLEET STREET, 1903

ST. PAUL'S, 1945

by John Piper

of our pilgrimage, but they proved a great disappointment
to me, seeming much too black and quiet for the wealth they
represented ; St Paul's, our other lodestar, justified, on the
contrary, every hope that I had formed of it. Here, even
a small boy could see, was a complicated building of genius
that, for all its restraint, could make no secret of its greatness,
and of a magnificence that was English to the core — yet
have I heard a high-church cleric condemn it as a " foreign-
looking edifice " !

We returned home on the same bus, down Fleet Street,
the Strand and Piccadilly and, regarding them attentively,
some of the buildings looked almost too modest for their size
and importance, almost ostentatiously unpretentious. Devon-
shire House, that yellow-brick Venetian villa with its stone
facings and vases, its spacious forecourt and plain, stout
wooden doors (the wrought-iron gates from Chiswick House
had not yet been re-erected here), exhibited a certain non-
chalant grandeur, as of one who brings the country to town,
and refuses to bend to the conventions. But many of the other
great London houses appeared, to a small boy, who had no
sense of dignity, to be merely quiet ; graceful, perhaps, but
dull. It was the general effect that was overwhelming; where
else could there exist so many miles of square and crescent,
continually repainted, as the climate enforced ; where else,
such a cluster of mean cities, composed of two-storey houses
of dirty brick, never washed, their ledges and woodwork never
painted : and round these, circling them in ring after ring,
the innumerable houses of the suburbs, sunk in a heavy,
atrocious boredom of their own, where, in the drab and
airless stillness of their sitting-rooms smothered behind dusty
curtains, a yawn turned to a sigh, scarcely remarked, and then
to a groan, and the prosaic, out of the very depths of its want
of soul, attained to the romantic and the morbid ; cities in
which love, entrancing dentists, or greed, blinding insurance-
agents and the dealers in second-hand clothes to the fate in
store for them by making them so sure of their invincible
cleverness, so certain of escaping detection, drove them towards
strange acts, to giving away poisoned chocolates, to drowning
their wives in greasy tin baths, or murdering their lodgers with
the poison off fly-papers, or to mixing prussic acid with the
morning glass of effervescent salts so widely advertised, together

with other wares of the time, with Pears' Soap, Mazawattee Tea and Van Houten's Cocoa, on the hoardings that edged these roads ? Here, in these null mazes of brick, where, however, spring came for a few days every year with a heart-sick and unutterable beauty of its own, decking out the grimed trees for a week or so in its brightest green or loading them with its most fragile and honeyed treasures that seemed to bring the sky right down into these streets ; even here, where life felt so safe, because so dull as not to be credible to those who had not experienced it, its intensity reaching to the force of a cult, the crimes that took place were often more passionate, and in nearly all cases more curious and involved, than any that occurred in Naples or Baghdad. But, at the time, I had not seen these wildernesses of the spirit, except from the train, when, approaching London in the evening, you would note a lighted window in a row of shuttered houses, and a single figure standing, with a curious, pleading solitariness, outlined in the glow.

Today was the furthest I had gone ; though a week or so later, Edith and I went to see the Tower of London, and loved its grandeur, so bleak in its black and grey, so incisive in its saw-edged crenellations, the perfect setting, it seemed, for its chief treasure, the crown jewels, those small objects of unparalleled value, hidden somewhere within this vast and fortified bulk. Moreover, the clothes of the Beefeaters, and the very names of the gates, carried me back to the Harrison Ainsworth world in which I liked to exist during every evening. . . . Here, in the Tower, I was in the future to spend many months as a young officer in the Household Brigade ; just as I was to spend many nights on guard in the Bank of England, which I had passed on the journey I have described, and thus be given the opportunity to learn to know its garden-courts and to come to appreciate Soane's ingenuity as an architect ; but of this, that long, delicious, exciting ride afforded me no inkling ; I did not even know what career I wanted to follow when I grew up — though I was certain in my mind as to what I did not want to be : a soldier.

Even the joys of this ride could not, though, divert my affection away from Davis towards this new friend and teacher, Mr. Keigwin. I was permitted one or two more excursions of the same kind, but then a great smallpox epidemic began to rage, we were caught in a festering orgy of vaccination, and by my father's orders were allowed to go to no public places. . . . My tutor, however, continued to be clever in his treatment of me, consulting me on many points of adult life, and finally won me round by asking me to come to his room and drink cocoa with him, made in the same way as he had made it at what he called " the Varsity ". . . . I much preferred the cocoa to the catacombs ; but, though I liked him, it took me many months to recover from losing our old friend, and to forget my jealousy of the fortunate children upon whom she was now attending. It seemed, too, as though, with her going, all instinctive wisdom had been withdrawn from us, and that " trying to do the right thing " had taken its place. In token of this change, schoolroom and nursery were now filled on days of festival with horrid utilitarian objects, long overdue, " A nice sponge, just what you've been wanting ", or " Look ! What a lovely piece of new Pears' soap ! " . . . It was at about this period, too, that there entered into my life that round collar-box made — I recollect the strong feeling of inner repulsion I had to master on first being told of this derivation — of pig-skin. Upon its smug face it bore, in the large uncompromising writing of our governess, my full initials, F. O. S. S. ; initials belonging, as it were, to my left hand, as opposed to O.S., my sign manual, belonging to my right hand and to my life as I have made it. Always — even then — I have felt a stranger to my full initials, and, in addition, I much resented the large full stops, placed in so forthright a fashion after each letter. This hard-featured, unprepossessing box later seemed to me to have constituted a sort of foretaste of school ; from it could have been deduced the horrors lurking there, the boredom, the bullying, the want of all except sadistic imagination ; a time during which I was lost in the initials F. O. S. S., marked, under fear of punishment, so clearly on everything I owned, playbox, books, clothes. But throughout boyhood, though I lost everything else that belonged to me, I could never get rid of this unattractive chattel : nor could I ever catch sight of it without being reminded of that process of a pig being killed to which it owed its existence. Far into adult life, it dogged — or should I write pigged ? — my footsteps. A hundred times I hid it and lost it, but always it would appear in my room again, whether I was abroad or in England.

Besides, then, the new kind of presents that were given us, many other changes in our intimate lives had come in the interval since Sargent had finished the family group ; changes which, in their turn, affected the way in which I regarded my fellow men. Thus the consequences of my grandfather's death certainly altered my view of life, because I observed that the sycophantic reverence and adulation which had hitherto been reserved for my grandmother Londesborough was now transferred suddenly to her daughter-in-law and successor. Not only did the old lady lose her husband, but, in addition, nearly all her belongings, being obliged to pursue hereafter the dolorous manner of life decreed by tradition for an English dowager ; not only were horses and carriages and grooms and gardens and houses and jewels and plate, and, indeed, the whole luxurious decoration of life by which she had been so long surrounded, snatched from her at a single grab, but she also forfeited — commensurately, it seemed, — the love of the majority of those who had pretended to be her friends. She felt, I apprehended, peculiarly desolate, though as a rule she would not admit it. Thus in a letter to my sister, written on the first anniversary of her husband's death, she says : " It was very dear of you writing to me, it touches me very much to know how tenderly and affectionately you and Osbert remember your Granpapa. You saw so much of him and he was so fond of you both and always so gentle and kind. I have been feeling very sad these last few days — indeed I feel sad always though I try to be cheerful." Few people now went to see her. Especially, I noticed, the younger members of the fun brigade, mentioned in the first volume, deserted her in a body. Their extravagantly expressed infatuation ceased with the last notes of the funeral march, for it transpired now that, without their having been conscious of it, it had really been to my aunt, and not to my grandmother, that these people, with their easy, affectionate natures, had the whole time been devoted ! No longer did the air resound with their tittering denunciations of this same aunt's extravagances, their diatribes against her style in dress or the ways of her house. No, they had fallen in love with them, as much as with the woman herself. Nor, even, did they tremble before my grandmother's caustic tongue, for they never went to see her, and so avoided the risk of encountering it. While she, dispossessed, shorn of all but her sorrow and her rage, had become to them " old Edith ", my aunt's name, on the other hand, showed new modifications, because, to express the discovery of their love for her, they had soon invented pet names and affectionate diminutives, " Gracie " and " Gus " and " Gussie " ousting the former *Grace*. In the world of the housekeeper's room, even, to which, being a child, I was admitted, the mystic syllables " Her Ladyship " now signified another, and even Miss Vasalt mocked her to her relatives as she travelled from station to station along the line, distributing small portions of the latest family news, served out with her familiar light giggle, the token of that perennial youth which cost her in secret so severe a struggle. . . . Contemplating this revolving of the wheel, it all seemed part of the system — at any rate, of *some* system, but one difficult to focus as a whole. . . . Nevertheless, my grandmother continued to terrify and override those near and dear to her who came within her range, and the visit, particularly viduous in character, paid to us at Renishaw the previous summer, had left its mark upon the others present. Indeed, whenever my father had shown her a new vista of which he was proud, she had responded vaguely, " Yes, isn't it a pity ! ", or had, at the least, countered with " Why, do you suppose ? "

The singular twist, which had come upon life since the portrait was finished, applied most of all to those depicted in it. Edith had withdrawn, as it were, still further to one side and into the background. With a room of her own and a guardian governess to teach and guide her, she was receiving the peculiar education reserved for young girls of her time and class. My father, of course, would have liked her to learn typewriting and prepare for a business career ; she evinced a considerable disinclination for it and lack of ability in that direction, which was the main thing, for one must always, he said, concentrate on the things one was bad at, try to make up one's weak points, and do at least one disagreeable thing each day : (he had been reading Nietzsche). But my mother, weak in so many ways, was here a rock. She insisted that Edith should have the usual " advantages ", or what would people say ? . . . So they compromised by agreeing to cut off some of the time she gave to the piano — she seemed to like playing it —, and it was decided for her that, after the manner of a geisha, she must learn to charm by means of esoteric accomplishments, such as 'cello-playing — there were others who thought the guitar would be more effective —, scarf-dancing, water-colours, recitation and small-talk. (The great thing, my father said, was to be bad at nothing and good at nothing. In conversation an unending flow of remarks, to which they need pay no attention unless they wished, was what men liked. "It kept the ball rolling.") . . . And sometimes, thinking over such an education, I have wondered whether the furious outbreaks of injured propriety on the part of mothers, when some fashion, jazz or roller-skating, or whatever it may be, strikes the town, may be due less to purely moral shock than to the fact that these new crazes relegate to the background the daughters' accomplishments, always couched — like the preparations of the War Office for battles — in the idiom of the previous generation.

My sister's hours and days were most fully taken up by her dedication to these attractions of long ago; to them she was obliged to add the prevalent rites of the gymnasium, the antics in which would, she was told, be as useful to her as the obsolete dances, lancers and the rest, which she was learning : "Nothin' a young man likes so much as a girl who's good at the parallel bars "). To this curriculum was also added, in the name of health and beauty, a good deal of plain physical torture, invented by my father in consultation with a children's surgeon, who had been introduced to him by my Aunt Grace and specialised in such things. Dr. Grabbe — for such was his name — designed and planned his own orthopedic devices, thumb-screws, nose-slams, ankle-twisters and all sorts of boards, flat or sloping, on which the young patients could be bound, a thousand little clever dodges for giving pain and taking money. Alas, my sister's nose was still not of the shape for which my father had bargained, so the reign of iron and manacles began. The harm inflicted both on her nervous system and her physique proved to be costly though fortunately not irreparable ; a few years later it took many months to break down by electric treatment the adhesions that had formed as a consequence of the use of these instruments. It was the result, on my father's part, of good intentions, coupled with a belief that he could understand the principles, and advise on the practice, of any art. Meanwhile, Dr. Grabbe had been let loose upon the family in general ; our cousins were martyred as much — or nearly as much — as ourselves. Already the same enterprising doctor was looking forward to slicing me about as well, — and to the fresh fees he would obtain for it. No trouble or expense — and certainly no pain — was to be spared. Very soon he had snatched from me my tonsils, which I have missed ever since.

In general, I was not nearly so far advanced as Edith, and was only just beginning to be instructed in the masculine counterpart to feminine accomplishments, riding and cricket and tennis and, even, rounders and ping-pong. Ping-pong was, in a sense, the very opposite of the obsolete attainments which I have discoursed upon ; it had only just made a triumphant appearance in the world, but was deemed to have arrived for ever, so that I remember my father expatiating to me on what a big part it must of necessity play in my life. He talked in a strain of great seriousness about it, and wound up with the words, " Unless you learn to play ping-pong properly, you can never hope to be a Leader of Men."

Alas, I showed as little aptitude for it as for riding ; I was by nature a nervous and clumsy rider — unfortunate, in a family to which horses had meant so much. It was true that my father himself had never been remarkable for his skill in the saddle, but he could certainly ride better than I ever could, and he would have liked me to have excelled at it — though, no doubt, had I done so, fault would eventually have been found with my methods. In those days, it must be remembered, riding was a useful thing ; for motors did not yet exist generally, and few people guessed that within a few years a horse would have sunk from being a god to being just one more animal, like a giraffe or rhinoceros, or that the four-in-hand, nay, the hansom cab itself, would have been consigned to the same limbo as the Roman war-chariot and the stage-coach. . . . As it was, I hated horses, slobbering, sweating creatures that they were, and disliked riding. Only the name of the owner of the livery stables from whom, when at Scarborough, we hired our horses, exercised a powerful fascination over my mind. " Mr Bearpark " . . . I saw the bruins grunting and hugging happily in their enclosures, under the green pennons of rugged and antlered trees.

The sole accomplishment, then, that Edith and I learnt jointly was dancing : but of a form, again, that made no attempt to compromise with reality. The classes, which we regularly attended at Scarborough twice a week for several years, were held usually in the morning, and were rather small, being composed of the children of the local *noblesse*, Willoughbys, Cayleys, Ledgards and Johnstones, who drove in from the countryside with their parents, come to do a day's shopping. All of these children were, superficially, of the same type as ourselves ; they had the same straight fair hair, the same fair skin and blue or grey eyes, and yet between them and us was set some difference for which I could not, at the time, account, but to which I will recur in a moment. . . . Our teachers were Madame Augustin and her daughter. Madame Augustin was a small Frenchwoman, very old and impressive, who always wore a tightly waisted dress of mauve silk, with a great deal of embroidered ornament and spidery jewellery, a high collar of lace, stretched upon whalebones, and an elaborate wig. She possessed lovely manners and was very kind, though very strict, and the classes were the better attended because all the parents of her pupils united in considering it a great shame that she should have come down in the world to such an extent as to have to do something for a living. Indeed, the old lady herself felt it so deeply that she had assumed a false name rather than sully her own with work. And when I understood Miss King-Church to inform me that Madame Augustin had fled hither from the horrors of the French Revolution, I could well believe it, and was at once and enthusiastically convinced that it was from the cataclysm of 1789 that she had escaped. . . . In a dim way, perhaps I recognised how secure a retreat this part of the world, so steady and assured, must have offered to someone forcibly familiar with revolutionary songs, and the tumbrils and the guillotines of Parisian mobs : (an impression that would have been strengthened had I only been old enough to read then, as I read subsequently, the memoirs of Madame de Boigne, who had spent many months staying with the Ledgards, at Ganton, near by). It was a great disillusionment to me when I found out later that I had misinterpreted what I had been told, and that it was only from the fury of the Commune that Madame Augustin had here taken refuge.

EDITH, COUNTESS OF LONDESBOROUGH, THE AUTHOR'S
GRANDMOTHER, 1908

HOTEL AND CASTLE, SCARBOROUGH

by John Piper

At the time, however, my surmise seemed almost certainly correct, and part of the admiration and respect in which I held our old instructress was founded upon it. The slowness, the grace and dignity of the dances that she taught us — for my eyes were always fixed upon her, and not on her daughter, whose face, even, I cannot see, for in my memory she is constantly bending down, correcting the attitude of one of her small pupils — seemed, as it were, deliberately opposed to the vulgar frenzy of the Carmagnole, and could have belonged to no period later than the eighteenth century. It was in the very manner of the *Vieille Cour*. And, had we performed in London ballrooms, when we grew up, these dances as we here learned them, we should, I believe, have caused so great a sensation among the jostling crowds of those executing and enjoying the dances of the contemporary world, one-steps and two-steps and the long, quick, deep-hearted waltzes of the time, that we, too, would probably have been guillotined or, at the least, lynched. Quadrilles, minuets and, I suspect, gavottes — but, at any rate, lancers and waltzes that were quite as stately —, all these we acquired laboriously, taking one slow, hesitant and painful step, after the manner of a performing poodle, about every ten minutes.

Sometimes the mothers of the children taking part would come and sit on chairs placed round the edges of the room, watching our ceremonious and rhythmic convolutions with that sort of uneasy-eyed concentration that parents show when they want in reality to talk to one another and yet have to pretend to follow the actions of their children with at least a modicum of pride and pleasure. To the accompaniment of a real seaside piano, which compared in tone with the normal instrument as the face of a swimmer who has swallowed a lot of sea-water compares with that of an ordinary human being, we bowed and curtseyed, pointed a toe or slowly twirled on it, or swept one hand down to the ground, or gave or took an arm with the consummate dignity of supreme boredom. . . . How much I was delighted with the surprise visits of my mother, who would come in unexpectedly and sit behind me at the side of the room !

I could always detect her arrival, even if I did not see it, by the scent of the gardenias or tuberoses she would be wearing, and her presence afforded me a warm feeling of support in the ordeal that classes, pleasant though they were, constituted. For, somehow or other, I, who was conscious of such a sense of accord with my brother and sister, felt out of harmony with these children, who yet, as I have said, so greatly resembled us in appearance and manner — though I could not tell why, or what the difference could be. . . . Perhaps the skeleton of Anne Brontë, lying a mile from us across the bay in its grave in the churchyard [1] merging, beyond a broken stone wall, into rough sea-meadow, the headstone at an angle now and the inscription often indecipherable because of the black and bulky shadow thrown down by the huge, ragged Norman castle on the rock above ; perhaps this skeleton, alone in the vicinity, had it but been able to clothe itself in human raiment again after the passage of fifty years, could have explained to us the nature of this difference, which was the same as that which separated her bones from those lying more at their ease round her. . . . There was no-one nearer to us in space, I apprehend, who could have shared and elucidated the secret of this feeling. Indeed it was not for another fifteen years or so that I was to find it out ; that we three were artists, or at any rate artists in embryo, belonging to a type as different from others as it is possible to be, special beings — often, it is true, much more difficult and disagreeable — with nerves and brains created for the one purpose of a certain kind of sensitive perception, and for the gathering and selecting of impressions. . . . As it was, I merely suffered this feeling of being cut off, divided from those round me, without being able in any way to understand it ; but my mother seemed to act as a link, for I realised how well and easily she got on with the other mothers, and that they all admired her beauty, and were glad to see her and talk to her, as she sat there, with her short astrakhan coat and a hat with a mauve feather in it. . . . It can be imagined, therefore, that it was a shock to me to find out that my sister, whom I loved dearly, did not share this sense of comfort and, indeed, dreaded my mother's appearance in the room, for my mother was always cruelly finding fault with her in front of other people, and behaving to her in a way in which she would never have acted to a son. Herself had been treated in just the same manner by my

---

[1] Anne Brontë (1820–1849) is buried in the cemetery of the parish church at Scarborough.

grandmother, and this fact perhaps made it both more difficult and more easy to account for ; it may have been a process of unconscious but sad compensation.

Some of the most pleasant moments in those schoolroom days were during wet afternoons, or if we were convalescent from some illness, when Miss King-Church would read aloud to us. How exciting were those romances, chiefly the novels of Rider Haggard, which reflected to perfection the Cecil-Rhodes-Boer-War materialism, tinged with both idealism and I.D.B., of that strange epoch, just as Rudyard Kipling supplied the inspired part of it — though, of course, Kipling was a genius and Haggard was not. If only one could find those hidden kingdoms, with their wealth of emeralds and diamonds and vast gold nuggets, at present wasted on the natives and guarded from their rightful owners, the British, by occult and deathless enchantresses ; if only one could find them, and " open the country up " ! And, as if to bring this same feeling of romance right into the schoolroom itself, there were the visits paid to my parents, both at Scarborough and Renishaw, by Cecil Sitwell, my father's first cousin. A most charming and handsome man, tall and fair - haired, with enough of the hero about him to appeal to the schoolroom, he looked as if he had walked straight out of the pages of one of these books, and yet offered, too, a strong feeling of kinship. He would always come to us for part of his leave, still sunburned from West Africa — in some region of which he held the post of Commissioner —, and would bring with him presents of spears, shields, hats, powder-flasks and objects of native basket-work. Indeed, the things, even when he gave them away, formed a sort of aura for him ; we saw him against a background of them. And he would talk to us of lion cubs, playful as kittens, and promise to bring one back for us. Alas, before long, the news came that he had been murdered in Africa. Singularly fearless, he had gone out unarmed to quell a dispute, and the mob had turned on him. Few people remember him today ; all that remains are some rusting spears and assegais, and useless bright-coloured basket-work, now grey with dust, in the lumber-room at Renishaw. Occasionally visitors find their way up there, and peer curiously at the rusty implements, and torn wicker hats and powder-flasks, lying among pikes' heads and stags' heads and fossils and old photographs and cracked china and broken Chippendale chairs, and wonder what they can be, and why they should be here.

Even Sacheverell will scarcely remember him, probably, for my brother was only just emerging from babyhood, but already his personality was most marked, already it was possible to divine the strength, generosity and fire of his disposition. A sturdy child, broad for his years, he seemed bursting with life and health, and, even at this early age, with intellectual curiosity. He never stopped asking questions, that wonderful form of self-education which intelligent children evolve for themselves. The questions were, naturally, on every subject within his range — or, as for that, outside ; there was no sign of specialisation, or of the direction in which his interests would lie when he was older — except perhaps the delight he took in the visit to Kensington Palace that I have described. But I remember that when a friend of the family's, for something to say, asked him what he would be when he grew up, he shifted the responsibility by replying, " *My father* wishes me to be an engine-driver." . . . Apart from the fact that he did not yet attend the classes to which Edith and I went, he entered now enormously into my life, sharing with me every hour of the day. At Renishaw and Gosden, we occupied a room together, and often in the mornings we would wake up early and talk : it seemed always such a long time before we were called, for each minute was then vast and roomy, each day an unfathomable span of time.

Let me tell you for a while of the early mornings, and of Gosden.

We visited Gosden many times, indeed almost every year, until my grandmother gave up her lease of the house towards the end of her life. . . . The first occasion must have been during the Spanish-American War, for I remember Edith and myself fighting, in a rather impersonal but extremely impassioned manner, for the possession of the island of Cuba. My sister invariably represented the United States of America, a country towards which her innate love of liberty and hatred of oppression made her feel a tremendous attachment — and one, indeed, which never wavered until it came into conflict with her esthetic sense some years later, when, at the age of fourteen, she was taken to hear Sousa conduct his own band, and, after a march of his composition had been played, was violently sick and had to be led out of the Albert Hall. . . . Equally, I was as whole-hearted in my championship of Spain, partly, I think, because of monarchist principles, and partly, perhaps, because, even then, I knew that the result of such a struggle was a mathematical problem and could only end in a victory for the American Republic, and all my life I have loved the losing causes until they won.

That year, then, I remember for its disturbed atmosphere of caps and wooden swords and war-cries, and also on account of an accident that occurred. Henry had taken my mother's maid out for a long bicycle ride, and when they returned, very late, I was told that she had " broken her leg ". It was the first time I had ever heard the phrase and it horrified me, for I interpreted " broken " in the sense of snapped off, and fully expected to find her carrying a severed limb.

Notwithstanding, the mornings, even of that year, and certainly of all the others, merge from this distance into a single golden hour, and it must be placed, by the law of averages, in the first years of the new century, the period of which I am now writing. . . . Sacheverell and I lay in our beds in an upper room in the butter-yellow dawn of a May day. No doubt, outside, taking this room as the hub of a wheel, the golden lawns and level spaces, fringed by green trees, encompassed us in their ring ; no doubt, beyond them and above, the mountains of snowy clouds that in the spring-time sheltered this landscape reared their bulk, and even towered high above the white and glittering churches of chalk and stone which stood upon the white downs. It was difficult to know the time, and at first we did not speak, for here we lay in a sort of hallucination composed of a dim glow, suffusing the darkness — for the thick curtain had been pulled across the windows so that the light should not wake us —, and of silence. It is true that the birds already chanted ceaselessly their duets and trios or sang boldly in whole choirs, and that the African doves purred softly from the roof, but these sounds seemed only to add to the silence, as the music of fountains emphasises the quiet of a garden, rather than diminishes it.

Every moment this hallucination seemed moving towards a new climax — but now the darkness of the room was breaking up, as ice melts, and in the same way that the silence outside was altering, and becoming its other aspect, sound. At first the darkness which had held within it all space, so that to reach its ultimate boundaries had seemed impossible, became faintly streaked with light, as though it were some gigantic body, cat or tiger, whose markings were just beginning to be visible, and, as this happened, the various, enormous vaulted halls of darkness and silence that he who is awake, waiting for light, always erects for himself within the limited space of his room, crumbled and came down, the ruins of them to be enclosed by its ordinary daylight dimensions, at last to be perceived ; that vast, velvety stretch of blackness upon which had floated patches of steel-grey and green, like the circles of water-leaves upon the surface of the lake, proved to be one panel of the familiar polished front of a mahogany cupboard, and the perspective of forest trees turned to the bevelled edges of a mirror. Then a glow gradually blossomed within the room, as the light penetrated the curtains more strongly — the blinds were white —, a general glow that seemed built up of mounds and mountains of roses, and in its turn revealed hundreds of patterned blossoms upon wall and sofa and chair, for all the bedrooms that my grandmother Sitwell arranged resembled boxes padded with flowered papers and flowered stuffs. Finally, sunbeams pierced through a chink or two, and within the segments of light to which they gave birth began a race and whirl of motes, moving up and down in their slow, wayward but rhythmic rise and fall ; a phenomenon that, as one watched it, seemed to hold in itself some meaning ; an instinctive, childish comprehension, one may suppose, of the mysteries of the construction of the atom or even of the universe. As with the darkness, so with the silence. The birds sang more loudly now, and, spraying and playing upon the silence as jets of water upon ice, had further melted the solid, hard nothingness of it. Various compartments were beginning to be filled with the warm domestic sounds of the early morning ; one with the gobbling of white or lavender turkeys (we knew their colour), a second with the bleating of lambs (small piebald lambs of a special breed introduced into England from Spain by my great-grandfather at the time of the Peninsular wars), a third with — I had nearly written the " lowing of kine ", for even in the nurseries my grandmother's religious interests produced a biblical atmosphere ; (everything in the house was kind and good, and no shadow lurked in its pretty rooms, unless it were the azure shadow of goodness). Across the feathery tapping at the windows of the knotted, crinkled buds of banksia roses, across the deeper sounds, the talk of the lazy old groom as he watched a younger man brush the staid old carriage horses, and the voices of gardeners, the drifts of bird-song now passed as rain sweeps over a window-pane.

It must still be the very early morning, and it seemed to last for ever, to be an instalment of that heavenly bliss — or at any rate its expectation — to which my grandmother's favourite clergy so eloquently, and so frequently, testified. Already my mind was working up towards the only religious crisis which, so far, it has ever suffered ; but the notion of heavenly bliss only brought to me the idea of its reverse, eternal damnation. I was wicked, I felt sure, a son of Beelzebub (we had heard a lot about him the previous Sunday), and my eyes, abandoning the dance of motes, turned inward to seek infinity and eternity. I tried to picture for myself eternal flames. Nor did this feat prove difficult, for when I had been about four, Edith and I had been taken for an industrial tour. We had watched china being made in Derby — and had helped to make it —, we had gilded the inside of a silver bowl — a joy never to be forgotten —, and then we had gazed on the blazing furnaces used for refining steel. Therefore now, this scene, which had made so great an impression upon both of us, came to my mind : a never-ceasing roar and glare and grumble and flicker, great walls and torrents of flame in an incandescent chamber, and outlined against this, the figures of men working, their faces black as though dyed in the waters of the Styx, their arms and chests and backs glistening, the muscles shining, while the flames still mount, shooting out tongues that are golden and rose and tulip-green, surrounding the rhythmic bodies with a glowing aureole, or placing them against cascades of golden sparks. . . . But the flames had themselves been beautiful, as well as terrible, and, to my dismay, as I tried to picture them through eternity, they became interesting in their form, in their violent raging, instead of merely horrible. . . . Beelzebub, again ! . . . Better then, to try to think of eternity, which cannot be imaged, than of its fires. I tried to make my mind concentrate upon the idea of a river that never stopped flowing, and then of waves that never ceased pounding a desolate shore : but this new effort only brought in its wake the wrecked ships and winter skies of Scarborough, where, on days of storm, everything was ragged and opaque, and grey and white and bitter green, the spray, the clouds — hanging like tattered banners from the edge of the sky —, the snow, the sleet and through the pounding and thunder of the breakers only the cruel, thick cries of the seagulls could be heard, as they hovered and swooped over something in the seething water ; a body, perhaps, newly washed in.

It seemed now as if I was in bed again at Scarborough, lying beside Davis in the early morning, and could hear the creaking of the barrow, laden with bits and edges of things, as it passed below, outside, and the cry that went up with it. (It carried, in its very rhythm and words, a protest against life itself, or the ends to which it brings us. But what, I have often thought since, was the use of crying to those skies, to those fathomless, piled-up layers of cloud and rain and snow, made for no Christian God, but for Odin, the one-eyed god

whose memory survived so long in the oath " Great Harry ",
or " By the Lord Harry ! "

> Harry, Harry, hobbillschowe !
> Se quha is cummyn nowe,
> Bot I wait nevir howe,
>   With the quhorle wynd ?
> A soldane owt of Seriand land,
> A gyand strang for to stand,
> That with the strenth of my hand
>   Beres may bynd.
> Yit I trowe that I vary,
> I am the nakit Blynd Hary,
> That lang has bene in the fary
>   Farleis to fynd.[1] . . .

For Blynd Hary would never listen.)   I was asking Davis,
in my dream, why we were there, and then I heard the cry
itself in my ears, and this woke me up and brought me back
again.   I *must* fix my mind upon eternity.   I thought now of
the desert, it was more biblical ; but whether there or by
northern seas, the idea of eternity, you will notice, came in
the guise of pain rather than of pleasure.   Even then one
knew that every delight had an end, that the rose dies but the
thorn endures, that the crocodile lives for centuries and the
butterfly was said, perhaps in tribute to its beauty, only to
live for a day.   The pleasures of the wicked last so short a
time, but their punishment endures for ever ; flesh, and the
raiment that decks it, perish, to leave behind them only rags
and bones, rags and bones, or, in southern lands, the bitter
whining, the white flaunting, of dust in the market-places.

I was still thinking, long and stoutly, of the desert.   But
my lack of experience eventually (for I continued involuntarily to think of it in terms of the sands at Scarborough)
asserted itself. . . . So I tried to pass to the nature or essence
of eternity itself, grappling with it until the immense and
overwhelming feeling of physical nausea which this process
inevitably provokes, impelled me to desist.   But the very idea
that trying to grapple with eternity could thus affect one
physically, frightened me, and seemed in itself to suggest that
an eternity of bodily torture was possible, so I lay still, and
let my surroundings impinge upon my mind again. . . . The

---

[1] " The Manere of the Crying of ane Playe ", by William Dunbar.

darkness had now caught light, as a fire does, and we were suddenly, for those few minutes, inhabiting a world composed of roses and amber. It was impossible to remain depressed. . . . I stretched a hand out toward Sachie to see if he were awake, but he still slept gently. I could see the outline of his head, his golden curls sweeping his face, and its expression of rapturous intentness.

I was tired of the whole idea of eternity, no less than I was of this particular instalment of it. Would it never end ? . . . I realised now that while I had been trying to imagine *eternity*, here it had been, all the time, caged within me, and I prisoned within it. Would the nursery-maid never come to release us, still bound here, though outside the wings of the spring sun fluttered in the air, and flowers were coming to life every moment, the petals bursting through the dry bonds that clamped them together ? Now, too, the noises of the morning were louder and reached us from beyond the domain as well as from within it. Surrey was then still a very rural country. We were bounded by a wall, so that house and grounds represented an island floating, as it were, upon surrounding commons ; wherefrom at this hour arose the quacking of ducks and hissing of geese, and the quavering of goats — modelled, you would have said, upon the talk of their owners, smocked and fringed peasants, today only to be seen upon the stage of a revived musical comedy. From beyond, from the leafy Surrey lanes, deep set in the rich soil, on the green banks of which grew a profusion of primroses and flowering nettles, and delicate clusters of violet and speedwell, were wafted the guiding cries of the carters and ploughmen as they directed their horses to the right path or encouraged them to climb the steep hills. Nearer, just outside the house, I could distinguish a sound of clinking, of water being poured or sprayed, and of voices. I could, too, most distinctly hear Henry, wallowing lustily in a hymn. . . . But alas, he was not popular here, in this house of women. The race of church-goers shunned him, for it was plain to them that even out of his singing of hymns he obtained a pagan enjoyment, and so he was not even encouraged to attend the great rite of every day here, Family Prayers. But Henry sang none the less unctuously. . . . At the moment, for he liked those hymns connected with the sea, he was favouring the world with a most depressing but fairly accurate rendering of " Eternal Father, strong to save ". The lines " O hear us when we cry to Thee For those in peril on the sea ", bore a rolling and almost intolerable note of empty menace. . . . Evidently, judging from all these various indications, the sane day was beginning, and, while I was thinking of this, and as, in consequence, an overwhelming sensation of sleepiness attacked me, Martha came in and pulled the curtains back, so that, all of a sudden, the vast territories that not so long ago I had been inhabiting through a section of eternity were utterly annihilated, no vestige of them left, and I was secure in the daylight for which I had so much longed but by which I was now blinded.

As soon as I could see, I rushed to the window to look out, and at once the light interpreted the various sounds that had reached me, verifying or falsifying them : birds in their cloaks of silver and russet and fawn and black traced their arcs of flight across the space of vision and I could see the clustered buds of the banksia roses, tightly curled though just opening, and looking as though ready to be tied to shepherds' crooks ; on the other hand, the hissing I had heard proved not to have been made by the geese on the common, as I had concluded, but by my grandmother's old coachman, in smoothing the coats of his fat and decorous horses. The clinking proved to come from pails that were being carried by the farmer's boys, to feed various pets and domestic animals, while the voices I had heard were those of Williams, the gardener, who was leaning, in an easy attitude born of long practice, on a spade, and of the friend to whom he was talking. An under-gardener was watering the roses in the new small formal garden, box-edged, which my father so much condemned because it bore no relation to the house. (It was a charming house, he allowed, but the grounds *needed* laying out ; a stretch of canal with a Palladian bridge at the far end, and a group of statues, would look well. There was no reason such a scheme should be expensive. Any good garden-architect could run up a thing of that sort cheaply, especially with his help ; the bridge could be of rubble, with stone corner-work.) . . . Thus the outward world became visible again. Soon there would be breakfast, and I would have to be downstairs for it, and afterwards take part with my assembled elders in family prayers under the chairmanship of my grandmother and aunt. . . . Of that I shall have more to say in a moment, when I return to Gosden, but now I must leave Gosden, and pass to other dawns in other places, for they are of more significance to my story than can at first be gauged.

So many small details, assets and handicaps, go to the making of a writer ; things that have not been suspected save by the person concerned. For example, the very bad hand-writing with which nature and my ancestors endowed me (for it is said to be the most hereditary of all physical traits), but which was such a constant cause of friction in later years between my father and myself — for when I was twenty I wrote with the unformed hand of a boy of ten, but a hand that was illegible as well as childish, and this naturally dis-tressed him, while I, on the contrary, did not like being taught the making of pot-hooks when I was twenty and more serious matters, as I thought, were beginning to claim my attention — this atrocious handwriting, which never improved in spite of all my own efforts and those of other people, has certainly been one of the main formative causes of my style. Just as a stammer, such a hindrance to many careers, seems to be of help to an author — there have been several notable writers who stammered —, making him choose and love this other means of expression more than talking, as well perhaps as obliging him to assemble his thoughts more neatly than does an ordinary man, so the fact that I had to copy and re-copy every page I had written several times before any typist could read it, was in the end of aid to me, because as I went, I revised, emended and improved, expanding or contracting a passage, and thus I learned, incidentally and gradually, the benefits to be derived from this continual process of transcrib-ing. It led me, too, to rate the essential clarity of a sentence, the structure of it, high above all other virtues ; it did not matter if the flesh clothed the bones in a Rubens-like abun-dance, so long as the skeleton was there to support it. Similarly, many other things, great and small, accidents of birth, heredity and environment, go to the fashioning of an artist ; the vivid changes and joys, even, of the kaleidoscope with which he has played as a child influence him, the creative energy fostered by building with bricks, the hypnotic reveries induced by the art of the soap-bubble (how clearly I can feel, as I write, the stem of the hard clay pipe between my lips, and the bitter taste of soap that sometimes lay upon the palate after it) : but of all things, I believe the most important factor is to be found in those long stretches of wakefulness I am attempting to describe, in the course of which darkness gradually turns to daylight.

Few authors sleep well regularly, and many of them no doubt regard those hours of lying awake from four or five onward, in the same way that I consider them, as part of the creation of the book upon which they happen to be engaged. In this unlike members of other professions, an author — especially perhaps a novelist — can never take a holiday. It is impossible for him to become another sort of person ; he must absorb and reflect and observe the whole time ; in addition, he can never be sure what, exactly, is going to turn into work, or when it is going to do so. Even while he is asleep, the writer's subconscious mind is always busily occupied in preparing various ideas or technical problems to lay before him when he wakes : sometimes, on the other hand, he lies there working more directly, waiting for a flame to catch the fire he is building — though it may not take light for many days still —, or reviewing what he has written, word by word ; a work similar to that of the railwayman who tests the wheels of a train with a hammer. He may, even, get up, in order to work at some point in a book that is giving him trouble ; because, as H. G. Wells once remarked to me, " If you are in difficulties with a book, try the element of surprise. . . . Attack it at an hour when it isn't expecting it." . . . And certainly I, for one, would know that I was working badly, if I had not to wrestle for some hours out of several nights in the week with my creative angel. It is a necessary, albeit tiring, process, and these long childish hours of which I am telling you were no doubt a kind of natural preparation for it.

So let us hark back once more to an early morning. I am at Renishaw again, on a level with the cumulous green tops of the tall trees, beech, elm and lime, for we are on the north side of the house, away from my father's lay-out. Even in the shelter of the darkness of the North Bow Room — as the night-nursery was called — you would have known that you were near the roof of a high old house standing upon a lofty hill. Here, unlike Gosden, every window has a wooden shutter, and so the darkness reigns for long absolute, and is at most a faintly streaked and never a glowing darkness. Yet, in spite of all this extra muffling and fastening, the feel of the air is very different. If there is a wind, though it is full-blown summer, the blinds and their wooden ends will bluster and flap against the shutters of the open windows, making the noise that a gale makes in the sails and rigging of a ship : if it is calm, the light, when at last it penetrates the cracks of one of the shutters, will be much whiter, because, as always on fine early mornings, a cocoon of white mist envelops the house and trees, hiding everything in a kind of gleaming, white negation. The light also comes down the chimney, tracing the outline of a woman's head upon the floor. And, though I know this outline is really but an accidental likeness, lacks substance and reality, does not move or breathe, I am frightened, for here the darkness — and even an August dawn — is frightening. It is so dark that I cannot see my brother at all, though a rapier of light points at a mirror, so I turn over on my other side. . . . Now I try to think back through the darkness, so that I may guess how long it is since my mother came to say good-night. A whole world must have revolved since then, for though there is little light, merely needle-scratches and pin-pricks upon the surface, I know now that it is morning outside, summer morning. The mist, no doubt, bars all prospects (the trees, the hills and the long vistas of park will later look all the more superb as they re-create themselves out of it), and separates us from the world beyond, but I long to see even this interposing veil, because, after the manner of all children, rich or poor, still illusioned, I long for the advent of every day and find the strain of waiting for it intolerable ; only less horrible indeed than resting, when in addition all a child's vital forces are in full tide and have to be checked. I comfort myself with the thought that while the light outside Gosden makes the morning seem always more advanced than it is, and whole hours of waiting may therefore stretch deceptively before one, the shuttered windows of Renishaw may mean that it is later than it seems.

On the other hand, though the machinery of life is here so much bigger, there are fewer sounds by which to judge how far the night has receded. The height of the room above the ground, and the older, more lethargic, and yet wilder, beating of the pulse here makes it more difficult. . . . So I lie still, trying to catch some sound that will guide me ; there is nothing, nothing — though some instinct helps me to sense very surely the atmosphere of the whole house in darkness. . . . In spite of the shadows, living and dead, this house is more alive than Gosden. Goodness is, perhaps, not to be felt here, but a mysterious and indefinable excitement invests its old walls and broods in its chambers, the same in kind as that ferment in the blood of its owners, a feeling of excitement that some seek to explain by saying it is haunted, while a few call it poetry outright. . . . But the moment the word " haunted " passes through the mind, it occupies the imagination, and helps to raise the alleged spectres.

The servants, as I have said, had been forbidden to mention ghosts to me, but, occasionally, all the same, murmurs reached me, or I heard Davis and the nursery-maid talking of them, when they thought I was not in the room. My mother, too, often replied to me, when I went into her room in the morning to ask her how she had slept, " Oh, fairly well, but the ghosts were about again ", treating them as if they were a nightly matter of course, in the same way as might be owls or bats or mice. But she never said what they were, nor, indeed, appeared to entertain much curiosity concerning them, so I pestered Henry to tell me about them. He tried to refuse, but eventually was driven by my importunity to invent stories for me. He developed, I remember, a circumstantial tale concerning a jumping dwarf — a black mannikin who would leap suddenly out of a clothes-basket or a dark cupboard. But this did not frighten me, for I could tell he was only joking. Not for another thirty years did he relate to me any of the stories actually current. I knew already, nevertheless, from the servants' gossip that had reached me, how it was supposed that my great-great-grandfather, Sir Sitwell Sitwell, could still be heard from time to time calling for his wife, as he lay dying downstairs in one of the immense curtained and plumed four-posters that stand in the suite of rooms he built ; I knew, too, that the most celebrated of the ghosts, a boy of fourteen, was said to wake people from their sleep by giving them the cold kisses he had brought from his grave. And I knew, further, what he looked like, for a portrait painted by Verelst,[1] and hanging in the dining-room, showed him in a pink velvet coat and breeches against the background of an avenue of poplars. This was Henry Sacheverell,[2] who, since his parents had died young, was brought up at Renishaw by his grandfather, George Sitwell. It was believed in the neighbourhood that he had met his death by drowning in the River Rother, at the edge of the park, though my father, when he showed me this picture, said the boy had been drowned at Wakefield, forty miles away. He was the last of his race, heir to a great estate, for the Sacheverells, ever since they had come over from Normandy, had held large stretches of land in Derbyshire and Nottinghamshire, so that the extinction of his family, intermarried as it was with my own, had caused a considerable stir in the neighbourhood, and to this, no doubt, were due the stories of the youth who haunted Renishaw. He was alleged to walk in the part of the house built after his death, as well as in the older core which he knew so well. There were still many persons who would not go near the river on the day in November on which tradition maintained he had been drowned. But the most picturesque of all the tales, and one that I had already heard, was that when the ballroom had been finished in the early days of the Regency, its owner had given a great rout here. All the guests had been asked to come masked and in fancy dress, and a youth, whom nobody seemed able to identify, had attracted particular attention by the beauty of his costume, which belonged to the period of George II. His partners, however, as they danced with him the new waltzes which were just then coming into fashion, had been surprised by the pallor of his forehead and lips and by the startling coldness of his hands, which he seemed able to communicate to theirs, even through the gloves he wore. . . . Only the next day, in the

---

[1] It is difficult to know which member of the Verelst tribe painted this picture. A contemporary reference just records a payment to " Mr Varelse ". But there were so many of them, that there may be still others, who have been forgotten. They seem to have been especially patronised by county families from the north of England, who, as will be seen from Appendix A, p. 296, eventually absorbed them into their ranks.

[2] Henry Sacheverell was drowned at Wakefield, through an accident, on the 26th of August 1724, in his fifteenth year. His mother was Alice Sitwell, daughter of George Sitwell of Renishaw ; and his mother and father were first cousins, Katherine Sacheverell having married Francis Sitwell, and being the mother of George. . . . The families were also connected in other ways.

dining-room, some of the girls who had danced with him recognised his likeness, hanging on the wall. They enquired who it might be, and were told that it was the drowned boy of long ago.

There were other stories, too, of a duller and more material order, concerning him, and how his coffin had been found under a floor during some repairs to the house. Sometimes, indeed, the story varied, and the boy was said to have been a baby. The tale, in fact, cropped up again lately, with the publication of *Lord Halifax's Ghost Book*,[1] making its appearance in those pages under the title of " The Renishaw Coffin ". As told there, it is circumstantial, if not particularly exciting : but it is not true. " The Renishaw Coffin " should read " Coffer ", for a coffer, about three and a half foot long, fashioned from wood with the rough bark still adhering to it, and with iron clamps and hinges, was found under a floor during some alterations, not long before my birth. I well recall its being shown to me when I was a small boy, and my father telling me it had been made during the Civil Wars as a receptacle in which to hide treasure. The box has now disappeared. Many years later, I asked him whether by any chance a body could have been buried in it, but he assured me it could not have been so. I believe some documents, lists of silver, were found near by at the same time, but there was nothing inside the box. . . . As for the kissing, which, too, is mentioned in *Lord Halifax's Ghost Book*, these same stories have recurred in my own day, and certainly some persons who had never heard of this haunting, woke up under the impression that a child had kissed them. . . . Among those woken in this fashion by the dauntless Boy in Pink — though this was before my birth — was that very strong-minded lady, that champion of Water, Tea and Women's Rights, Rosalind Countess of Carlisle.

I was not then aware of all these details, but I knew from what my father had said — because I had heard him repeat the story, amused at the phraseology employed and for once forgetful of my presence — that my old Aunt Puss, when she

---

[1] *Lord Halifax's Ghost Book*. A Collection of Stories of Haunted Houses, Apparitions and Supernatural Occurrences made by Charles Lindley, Viscount Halifax, with an introduction by Viscount Halifax, K.G. (Geoffrey Bles, London, October 1930.)

had come to stay a year or two before, had arrived late one evening and had sent for him the following morning, recording her impressions in these words : " George, last night I awoke, and was distinctly cognisant of a presence by my bedside. It was a woman, with a long dress, and as she left the room, she shut the door, but had to open it to release her train." . . . And this I could understand by daylight as peculiar melodrama : but, as I remembered it in the darkness, it was nevertheless frightening.

And now, again, as I think of it, I am lying there in the North Bow Room, and past has become present once more. . . . What can I do to occupy my mind, and so fortify it against the fear of darkness ? Though familiar with every inch of this top floor, I know nothing of it at this early hour, blotted out as it is, so I try first to chart the rooms on this side : day nursery, night nursery, maids' room, the kitchen-maids' room, and so on, until one comes to the barracks, a large room, now given up to lumber, in which, during the eighteenth century, the visiting footmen had slept. . . . The passage itself is broad, the oak floor rising and sinking at improbable angles under the weight of its centuries, and at intervals there are doors, blocking the way. . . . Opposite, on the other side, furthest away and next a staircase, my mother's maid's room comes first. This room has details to remember, a piece of panelling that survives unexpectedly, hidden away in a large wall-cupboard, a dressmaker's dummy — a headless, red bust upon which clothes could be fitted —, a special bell which sounds when my mother rings it from her bedroom. Next, is a small chamber which retains the kind of cement floor that was a speciality of this neighbourhood in Tudor and Jacobean times : a room now full of china ; it is usually locked, but sometimes, as I pass, the door has been left open and I see large blue and white vases standing on the floor, and shelves loaded with porcelain figures and oriental bowls and cups and plates. Outside the door of the next room, towards the end of the passage and in a corner by the old staircase, stands the most notable object of the whole corridor : a huge wooden rocking-horse, its body beautifully dappled, but with one ear missing. It must be ten hands high, almost as big as a real pony, and still moves beautifully, though it is over a hundred years old and, indeed, figures in a water-colour group of my grandfather and his sisters as children, painted in 1826 by Octavius Oakley.[1] Moreover it constitutes a comforting presence by the door of the room opposite to that where I am now lying.

There was nothing about this room ostensibly to frighten one ; it was not large and was simply furnished. It had a flat marble chimney, and on the wall hung a delightfully ridiculous water-colour of the blue-stocking Lady Sitwell driving a pony-chaise : yet, a year or two later, when I was ten or eleven, and slept here, I certainly went through some singular experiences. . . . For instance, every night in my dreams during a long period, my Sitwell grandfather, whom I had never seen, since he had died thirty years before I was born, would come and sit by me in my room, talking as a grown-up person would to a small boy, and talking, too — and this, which I clearly noted in my dream, was the most curious part of it —, as though he were trying by his presence to prevent my being frightened — the very sensation, of course, which his being there inevitably entailed. But it showed, as well, that he was not aware that he was dead, and I was too polite to give him an intimation of this fact or to let him see that he was terrifying me by his continued existence. . . . These dreams were very real and I have often wondered what was the cause of them, for I had heard so little of him, my father having been two at the time of his death, and so only just able to remember him at all. (When, eventually, I told my father of these dreams, he remarked, " *My* children would naturally interest him.") . . . The noises in the room, too, the interior cracking and tapping and rapping and knocking and sudden shifting of weights, filled me with uneasiness and alarm, while the sounds from the garden below, even a whirr of distant machinery that often pervaded the entire air, the trains' hooting that could be heard loud above that of the nearer owls, flapping wanly about in the avenue, did nothing to dispel such feelings. Indeed, the slow loud puffing of the

[1] Octavius Oakley (1800–1867), one of the most charming of the minor and local English portraitists of the early nineteenth century. He first worked at Leamington, and then moved to Derby, from where he drove round the county, executing groups and single figures in water-colour. He worked in the neighbourhood for some ten years, moving to London in 1842. He exhibited at the Royal Academy from 1826 to 1860, and was elected a full member of the Water-Colour Society in 1844.

trains, when it woke one up suddenly, resembled the sound of a huge figure of bronze, striding inexorably, with an immense clang and reverberation, making the heart stop beating for an instant, and formed, I realised later, the perfect rendering for the footsteps of the statue of the Commendador, as he climbed the stairs on his way to find Don Juan. . . . These various sensations, experienced at intervals through the hours of darkness during a long period of childhood, later found vent, no doubt, in *Night* — one of my first poems, which I here reproduce :

> All the dim terrors dwelling far below,
> Interr'd by many thousand years of life,
> Arise to revel in this evil dark :
> The wail forlorn of dogs that mourn for men ;
> A shuffling footfall on a creaking board ;
> The handle of a door that shakes and turns ;
> A door that opens slightly, not enough ;
> The rustling sigh of silk along a floor ;
> The knowledge of being watched by one long dead,
> By something that is outside Nature's pale ;
> The unheard sounds that haunt an ancient house ;
> The feel of one who listens in the dark,
> Listens to that which happened long ago,
> Or what will happen after we are dust ;
> The awful waiting for a near event ;
> Or for a crash to rend the silence deep
> Enveloping a house that always waits —
> A house that whispers to itself and weeps ;
> The murmur of the yew, or woodland cries,
> A sombre note of music on the breeze ;
> A shudder from the ivy that entwines
> The horror that is felt within its grip ;
> The sound of prowling things that walk abroad,
> The nauseous flapping of Night's bat-like wings ;
> These are the signs the gods have given us
> To know the limit of our days and powers.

But I am anticipating again, for we are still charting the darkness. . . . Beyond the rocking-horse outside is a door, leading to a small wooden staircase ascending to the roof — at the top of it is always a huge wooden spade, left there for clearing the snow, which often lies in its season on stone gables and flat leads for months together ; then come two lumber-rooms, draped — if they are not locked and you can enter them — with cobwebs, and their old concrete floors covered with sand from the decaying walls. One room is panelled, and the other has its paper hanging on the still and dusty air in rent strips, like the remnants of ancient banners, — the army of rags and bones again, an advance post of it within the house itself, for here a great-uncle had died nearly a century ago at the age of eleven, and the place has never since been inhabited by the living. The room nearest the high, slender staircase has, looking onto it, a tall, gracefully shaped eighteenth-century window, with a rounded top, and from the door of the day-nursery opposite you could see, across the stairs, this window, with, floating behind its dark, discoloured panes — for there was very little light in the room — the drowned face of a statue. The day-nursery itself is a thick-walled, plain, seventeenth-century room. . . . It is clear, then, that this house is one that makes no concession to children. They are part of it, and it is not considered necessary to pander to them, as elsewhere, with special silly wall-papers and books — only with such vivid and terrifying volumes as *Struwwelpeter*.

Now I begin to chart the darkness of the night-nursery itself, the wide bow, which gives its name to the room and has three windows in it, on the pane of one of which an inscription of three generations before, written in French, glitters, when daylight comes, like the diamond that had carved it, the high lattice and wood commode, stepped like a ladder; the prints of " Silver-Tongued " Hely-Hutchinson and Lord Wensleydale ; the walnut chest of drawers, some ugly bits of pewter ; the tall-backed, very plain, oak chairs that had been here since the time of the Commonwealth when they were made. The room was rather bare for its size, and I soon had exhausted the contents ; so, in place of this cataloguing, I repeat to myself the names of the rooms in the house, as they occur downstairs, where they are painted, outside the servants' hall, under various large old-fashioned bells now obsolete. (Occasionally, one of these, long disused, would ring suddenly of itself, probably because a mouse had nibbled its wire. The sound could be heard distinctly in the dining-room, and if it happened during luncheon or dinner my mother would call, " Henry ! Why is that bell ringing ? " And he would always reply, very respectfully with great dignity, " Sign of Death, my lady.") These names were printed in large white letters on large black labels, and must be a hundred years old. . . . What odd names they are, I think to myself : Assembly Room, Duke's Room, Great Parlour, Cocked Hat Room, Tapestry Room, Lady Margaret's Room (Who could Lady Margaret have been ? I try to imagine what she was like), Oak Room, North Bow Room, Pine-apple Room. . . . I repeat the names mechanically over and over again, until I fall asleep. . . .Only for an instant, though, or so it seems, for I am woken by the clatter of the flat iron bar that clamps together the shutters, as it drops down, swinging, and like the fall of a knife in a guillotine, decapitates night at one blow. This is always the first sound if I am asleep, for the nursery-maid enters, according to the secret rules that govern her profession, noiselessly, but then proceeds to make a tremendous din unfastening the shutters and snapping up the blinds. . . . I sit up and try to look out of window. You can still see nothing outside, however, but white clouds, white mist hanging round the trees. In the intervals between their indistinct shapes there is a vague appearance of brilliance, of light made lighter by the surrounding vapour.

My brother's new nurse now enters the room in a business-like manner, and the nursery-maid says, " Good morning, Miss Smith, it's going to be a lovely day." (It is typical of the new scientific nurse that she is not, after the manner of Davis, awarded the courtesy title of " Mrs.") This information is important to Smith, because Mrs. Selby, my mother's old nurse and Davis's former chief and subsequently my grand-mother's housekeeper, has come to pay us a state visit. Smith does not like her, since the old woman shows that she regards her as an interloper and one who knows nothing of " The Family " ; but all the same it is necessary to receive her as fits the dignity of the house. As for me, I respect her greatly, for she was responsible for the chocolate cakes I have mentioned in the first volume.

In accordance with her dowager status, Mrs. Selby is always encased in black silk when in public. When out of doors, she wears over her dress a mantle decorated with jet, and a black bonnet on the top of her flat grey hair. She is well over eighty now, and has to wear very strong glasses, that make her eyes vast and staring as those of a Pacific Island god, and her upper lip is fringed with a fairly heavy moustache, the skin beneath the hair being always damp from incessant drinking of black tea. She talks through the summer days with a husky voice, pitched loud enough to sound above the humming of a sewing-machine, which turns ceaselessly as a prayer-wheel. Her stories are mostly concerned with my grandmother, for so long her revered mistress, though even she now finds a certain melancholy satisfaction in contemplating her former employer's almost biblical downfall. . . . " How are the mighty fallen " : one could almost hear it being warbled, as she talked with a characteristic melody that symbolised inner contentment.

Chapter Three
THE MOUNTAIN ASH BERRIES

I THINK everyone — except, formerly, Davis, who had thoroughly enjoyed them — felt the strain of these long visits. Domestic etiquette, so strict in its laws, demanded that Mrs. Selby should be waited on hand and foot, given the best food — nor did she hesitate to make moan, were it not good enough — and allowed to talk without interruption. And after a time chatter about the old days, especially to those who had not known them, became tedious. Further, Mrs. Selby did not seem interested in the idea of the Coronation of King Edward, which was due to take place the following June, but harped on and on, about how, as Prince of Wales, he had contracted typhoid fever, thirty years before, at Londesborough Lodge (you would have thought, Smith remarked later, that she would have preferred not to mention it, if it were *true*), and always turned the conversation back to Queen Victoria. . . . However, she finally went so far as to admit that the ceremony would be " a wonderful sight for them as could see it ", . . . and then changed her course, as it were, so as to speak of my father. . . . She was afraid of him and did not like him (and he strongly disapproved of her in return : she had, he said, " all the wrong ideas "), but she did not state this explicitly, contenting herself with insinuating that " Sir George did not seem at all himself at present ".

My father had decided to give up politics. He showed symptoms of being unwell, and he and my mother and a friend went to Germany for a holiday that year, hoping that a sojourn in the ancient cities of Nuremberg and Rothenburg, with their gothic character, their toys and torture-chambers, would soon put him right.[1] For a while he seemed better, but the improvement did not last, until gradually the theme that Mrs. Selby had announced became the central fact of our

[1] A letter he had written to me during this visit, when I was eight years of age, forms Appendix B on p. 298. The first part of it parodies a current guide-book.

44

family life ; *he was not himself.* He was ill. . . . It was the month of May that I was trying to describe at the beginning of this book, and the woods and the Wilderness had their smoke-blue carpet spread throughout every glade, perfuming the air, through and through, with a faint and hungry sweetness, while in their green retreats, high up in beech and ash and oak, the choirs of birds were singing as though they had no other purpose but to praise creation. Inside the house, my father was engaged on one of the innumerable tasks he set himself. The effort of finding a balanced hanging in one room for the three large family groups of himself, his grandfather and great-grandfather — and consequently of being obliged to shift every picture in the house — was making him more irritable than he had ever been in his whole life. He admitted to himself that he was not feeling well ; it had begun two days before, when there had nearly been that thunderstorm, and he had been trying the pictures in their various places —, as he was doing again today.

Generally, this sort of thing suited him : but now he had to confess he felt overdone. In addition, as he had decided to leave Belvoir House, there was all the furniture from Scarborough to arrange, for he had moved it hither. But the hanging of the pictures must be settled first. Three joiners were on duty all day, carrying the various things. He still had not found the proper place for the Sargent. . . . Here it was again ! . . . Almost before the picture had been hoisted tentatively, and with difficulty, into the space he had last chosen for it, he would shout, " No, no, no ! ", and give orders for it to be held up once more in the position from which the men had just brought it. Backwards and forwards they tramped, seeming figures come to life from an Assyrian frieze of conquest, plodding slowly, their backs bent. (They ought to . wear special felt shoes, my father reflected, so as not to scratch the stone floors with their nailed boots. . . . He would make a note about that in his book labelled " General Advice ", and would himself design a pair later on, if he had time). Dear, dear ! Here they were again. . . . No, no, no ! *All* wrong !

The young sub-agent had to be present, too, to oversee the three joiners and take the blame. In a letter dated 10th May 1902, he writes to his friend the agent : " I find that if I allow him, Sir G. will take up the whole of my time. We have been very busy moving furniture every moment he has been here and have got practically nothing done yet. . . . Another time I must arrange to be missing, or busy elsewhere as much as possible."

My father had other troubles, besides ; he had called in allies. He had asked an old friend, Major Viburne, to " keep an eye on the household bills ", and had imported him to Renishaw for that purpose. . . . We children had made his acquaintance the previous summer in Scarborough, when there had broken out one of those recurrent attacks of charity matinées, which always afflict towns of this sort in times of national emergency. The entertainment to which I allude had been presumably organised on behalf of some Boer-War good cause — if such existed —, and included tableaux in which my mother and my Aunt Londesborough, together with various friends they had invited to assist them, took part. Edith, Sacheverell and myself attended as many rehearsals as possible within the schoolroom limits of time, lost in admiration at the pictures presented to us, and trying in vain to identify in them our friends and relations ; who could they be, these inhabitants of another and more beautiful world, these languorous but deeply breathing ladies, wearing peasants' straw hats, carefully tilted over one eye, and clasping sheaves of golden corn as though they were favourite Aberdeen terriers, held there to be admired ; the solitary, soulful form of an Athenian girl, wearing sandals and a white robe, with a pitcher by her side, and leaning against an already ruined pillar of white marble under the amber sunlight, or, finally, the Tennysonian-gothic figures, floating, in a static golden moment, in their barge, amid flaxen tresses, wild flowers, and harps ? Who, *who*, could they be ?

Sometimes we were allowed to wait in the theatre to see the other items — and it had been thus that we first were introduced to Major Viburne, who was stage-manager. Amateur theatricals could not, indeed, take place in Scarborough, without his playing this part — for such it was. Never did a man more thoroughly act a role. No sooner did he enter the door than his entire character changed and he became temperamental in the best histrionic tradition, as against the matter-of-fact view which he usually upheld and embodied. Bald, with white, close-cropped hair running round the back of his head from ear to ear, a polished mirror-like cranium of the same colour as his rather reddish face, and with two white, down-turned moustaches, he was something of an anachronism ; a miniature Blimp, stranded before his time. Yet his appearance and his way of talking were misleading, for they disguised a deep, if narrow, sense of humour.

Just as one of the most celebrated of our local actresses was trying out her best effect, polishing in her own inimitable manner her wittiest lines, a sharp word of command would ring out from the back, like the crack of his own musket, and Major Viburne, rushing forward, would forget that the hair round his bald head was closely cropped and tear at it with his hands as though he were a French critic. He would roar and rave for minutes together, military and dramatic mingling in his style. Probably he sounded more ferocious than he felt ; most of it was bravado and, even, clowning, the fury being assumed, at any rate to a limited extent, in order to amuse certain people,— my mother, who would sit enchanted by these transports, among them. All the same, his mock rages occasionally took root, and he would become genuinely angry ; so angry that a fit of dizziness would ensue — blood-pressure, I suppose, though the word was then unknown —, and he would have to be led away to rest for a while.

As for his " keeping an eye on the household bills ", nothing could have been more disastrous. To begin with, his knowledge of them was entirely theoretical ; himself was always on a diet. The regime varied but it could usually be summarised by a medieval formula, such as

> Shun things that run,
> Eat things with wings,

or

> Foot and fin
> Go ill within,
> Fruits of earth
> Will prove their worth.

(Usually these inane little rhymes had a catch concealed in them ; for example, with reference to the first, the Major could eat partridge, but not French partridge, because that bird *runs* for long distances in the stubble.) At the moment, moreover, he had, as it were, altogether lost touch with his teeth, being confined by his doctor to a total diet of Plasmon biscuits, a health food which, though altogether admirable and sustaining, was one that, as an only form of nourishment, no medieval couplet or quatrain could romanticise. My father, however, had formed the opinion that he was a *bon vivant*, and had run an army mess, and, in the face of every evidence to the contrary, always consulted him on the ordering of dishes and of wines for the cellar, as well as on the paying of the bills, a subject upon which he was no less ignorant. In reality Major Viburne had never held a commission in the Regular Army, though for a time he had been in the Volunteers, but this only rendered him the more military, ideally military, in bearing and outlook. One of the results of it was that, though the most good-natured of men, he now treated the Chesterfield tradesmen — with some of whom we had dealt for several generations — as he imagined, in a mind permanently inflamed with imperialism, that an officer in the Regular Army would treat a low-caste Hindu accused of chicanery. First of all he would write a brusque, orderly-room letter, but one that was at the same time full of subtle insinuations and menaces, and then, receiving no answer, he would take a train to Chesterfield for the day, " to have it out with them ". . . . The rich tradesmen, now knighted or holding civic dignities, had no time for these long arguments, but most of all they resented his battlefield language and arbitrary conduct. In fact, a great deal of unpleasantness arose. . . . But my brother and I delighted in him. In a year or two, he became Sacheverell's tutor, and after that, when we were both at school, he always came to us for the holidays. Indeed he was the best possible foil that could be found for an imaginative boy, and with us would always be good-tempered and, in his way, amusing. Sacheverell would continually ask him questions that seemed impossible to answer : " Do people live on the moon ? " and " Why not ? ", or " Where did the Greeks come from ? ", or " Why is the sun larger than the earth ? ", and would always receive in reply a concise, polite and matter-of-fact — though no doubt often a wrong — answer. While making these enquiries, in which he was genuinely interested, Sacheverell would none the less be engaged in drawing pictures with an indelible pencil on the flat scarlet surface of the

Major's head. It would always take the old man a long time to discover the trick played upon him ; nor would he be angry, for he was conscious that we liked him. And he knew he could lull us into quiet by recounting his military experiences to us. We used, both of us, immensely to enjoy listening to his braggadocio stories of the 'sixties, of how formerly he had commanded at Scarborough Castle, and quelled a mutiny, or how the War Office experts had consulted him, while he was still a boy, on the running of the Crimean War.

Major Viburne, then, was one of the chief allies upon whom my father had called for counsel. . . . Another was Mr. Coppinger, whom he had persuaded to come here and advise him on the hanging of pictures. Mr. Coppinger owned a fashionable photographer's shop in London, with a branch in Scarborough ; he was so thin as to be almost invisible except for his long moustaches, and nothing except those, together with so much style that it animated — or, on the contrary, starched — what would otherwise have been a bundle, not of bones, but of clothes, and a drawl that kept people perpetually on the *qui vive* and perpetually disappointed, differentiated him from a phantom. He knew nothing about pictures, and was obviously dreadfully startled when asked for his opinion on them, and how they should be placed : however, he did his best, with the help of his drawl, to get through a difficult time. . . . But to my father, in spite of his gifts, a picture was a picture, just, as we shall see in a moment, paint was paint. Portraits and photographs had much in common : they both, for instance, had frames ; and a portrait, like a photograph, should be a " pleasant likeness ". One did not *want* to see the worst side of people, or of things. . . . (Such a mistake, the way Velasquez painted dwarfs, a most unpleasant subject !) And if a man knew how to " place " the subject of a photograph, then he *must* know how to hang a picture. . . . Many there are who hold identical views with equal conviction ; but usually they are persons of little education and considerable simplicity — Davis, our former nurse, for one, would at least have agreed with my father in these matters.

Perhaps the most perfect concrete example of what I am trying to convey is to be found in an incident that took place twenty years later, when Gino Severini, one of the first and most celebrated of the Futurists, was occupied in frescoing a room at Montegufoni, where for a long time he resided with us. My father was employing him under the misconception that he was Mancini, who had been dead for some years. The error had occurred thus. . . . My brother and I admired Severini's work and were anxious to help him and please ourselves by obtaining commissions for him, but we realised that my father might not like his designs. . . . One day, however, some time after we had in vain urged him to write to Severini, my father suddenly asked us (as it turned out afterwards, confounding the names of the two painters), " What sort of work does *Mancini* do ? " We replied truthfully, " Sargent has always admired Mancini's paintings tremendously ", and on this recommendation my father engaged Severini to decorate some walls for him. . . . Then, one Saturday a friend of my father's who lived in Florence came to stay with us at Montegufoni. Upon his temple he bore a large birth-mark, of which he was so conscious that he used every morning to camouflage it with grease-paint. On Sunday morning, he came downstairs with the blemish for once in evidence, and said :

" Oh, Sir George, I'm so sorry that this thing shows. It looks so dreadful . . . but I've forgotten to bring my paint."

" But we have an artist staying in the house," my father replied at once, with a little flourish of his hand. " I'm sure he'll be delighted to paint it out for you."

Similarly, at the moment of which I am writing, my father had brought over to Renishaw from the office of the local Scarborough paper, which he owned, his chief printer, Stubble. Stubble printed books, therefore books were his territory, and my father accordingly set him to the uncongenial task of cataloguing the books in the library. I liked the man, for, since he did no work at all, he spent much time in talking to me, and he was, indeed, a lively companion. I remember when I said one day to my mother, " I like Stubble. He seems to enjoy himself so much," she laughed and replied, " Yes, that's just his trouble." . . . I wondered at the time what she meant, but I found out later. My father, however, observing Stubble's idleness, would grow very angry at finding himself obliged to pay him for doing nothing, and would decide to send him away. Accordingly he would give him his journey-money and tell him to go home to

Scarborough. But it was obvious that Stubble regarded his journey-money, literally, as *pourboire*. He would catch the local train to Sheffield, where he was obliged to change, and in that black but riotous city would spend on drink every single shilling he possessed, and would then proceed to roar his way back to Renishaw on foot — eight miles at least — in the early hours. The look of him, back in the library again the next day, plainly suffering from what we have since learned to call a " hangover ", enraged his patron. But it seemed no good giving him his journey-money again . . . and so he would be there for another two days, until once more he obtruded his lack of energy too clearly, and once more my father dismissed him, and the whole jolly process would repeat itself. In short, it was apparently impossible to get rid of the man.

Last night had been the sixth time it had happened. . . . There he was, in the library again ! Better not to look at him, my father thought, it would only annoy one. . . . Where were the joiners ? And where was Hollingworth ? There was a lot to do, such a lot, things that *had* to be done. . . . All the furniture from the ball-room at the far end of the house must be taken to the upper drawing-room, and all the furniture from the upper drawing-room moved down to the ball-room, and then, if it did not look right — and he was by no means convinced that it *would* look right —, back again. . . . There the Sargent was, being carried past once more. But he had never told them to do that ! And why must they carry it upside-down ? And why weren't they doing it as he had instructed them ? How often had he ordered them never to touch the frame without wearing gloves ? So inconsiderate. . . . What was that ? No gloves ? *Certainly not.* Why should he pay for them ? He had never heard such a suggestion. (It was extraordinary the way that nowadays people expected one to do everything for them, though the income tax was a shilling in the pound.) Very sorry, *he* couldn't afford it. (That reminded him, he must tell his secretary to write to the lawyers about raising money on mortgage, and Viburne must insist on a contract for jam ! The catering ought to be run on the same lines as an army mess.) There was the Sargent again. No, no, of course not. . . . That would never do !

It was not only the intense activity of my father's mind, and the amount and variety of tasks that he set himself, which rendered him just at this time in a peculiarly exacerbated condition of irritability. These traits were his, as they are mine, by heredity and nature, but ordinarily his temperament could cope with them. Now, however, he was unhappy in his own life. The great political career for which, conscious of his own remarkable talents, he had hoped, did not materialise of itself, and he seemed unable to command it. He saw, instead, fools preferred. The second lawsuit had been lost, though himself had been in the witness-box for two days, a very great strain. In addition, he was crushed, he felt, by a mountain of debts for which there was nothing to show, neither reason nor result, since my mother bought objects because she liked them, or, at any rate, liked buying them; then she would give them away — or she would buy them in order to give them away. With her, spending money was an expression both of the enjoyment of life and of its opposite : if she felt well and happy, she would order every sort of thing, that neither herself nor anyone else could want. If she felt miserable, then she chose things at random in order to cheer herself up.

I do not know how long my father and mother had been married before he realised the extravagance of her nature. Perhaps the episode of The Learned Pig may have put him wise to it. Certainly this had been one of her earliest and most ill-fated purchases. . . . A few months after her marriage, when she was not yet eighteen, she had been asked to open a Conservative bazaar at Scarborough. There she had seen an animal known as The Learned Pig, which told fortunes, and had been greatly impressed by its uncanny knowledge of character and grasp of the future. I am not sure by what method, whether by horoscope, tea-leaves, palmistry, clairvoyance or rapping on tables with its cloven hoof, the creature made its prognostications, nor how it published them to its clients or the world. . . . At any rate my mother had been unable to resist bidding for the remarkable creature when it was offered for auction at the end of the bazaar. Sure enough she obtained it, but for a very considerable amount of money. . . . This was bad enough, but once the erudite porker was on her hands, its psychic gifts deserted it, and at the same time she realised she dare not tell my father what she had bought. Nor did she mention it to *her* father ; but, since she could not let the poor brute starve, she arranged for it to be boarded at one of his farms, and told the farmer on no account to divulge the animal's existence. . . . However, after a year or two, the farmer, finding that he was not paid, rendered an enormous account for feeding and grooming the beast to my grandfather. Though he was furious at having to pay, my mother succeeded in persuading him not to mention the matter to my father. My mother agreed that the pig must be killed, but the idea of killing such an unusual animal — or, as for that, of killing any animal at all — upset her so much, that secretly she took steps to have it sent, instead, by rail to Renishaw. . . . Here she contrived for it to be farmed out again — on this occasion, of course, on one of my father's farms, and again it refused to tell fortunes. This time, after a long period, the farmer wrote to the agent to demand payment, the agent, not understanding at all what had happened, forwarded the letter to my father, and the true story came out. . . . My father paid the bill, not with the best of grace, and ordered the animal to be destroyed. . . . But The Learned Pig could never be mentioned in front of him, for not only was he annoyed at having to find the money for it, but in addition he was angry because, hating super-stition as he did, he found that he had become a vicarious victim of it.

I do not know whether this opened his eyes at all, but, in any case, in spite of his strength of character, he appeared incapable of preventing or putting a stop to such expenditure. He would never recognise any fact which he did not want to recognise, neither the tendencies of the time, nor even the more visible processes of nature, least of all the actions of human beings. . . . And here, too, I must stretch again for a moment to a period some twenty years later, for in a symbolic sense the fragment of conversation I wish to record sums up the respective attitudes of my mother and father. . . . We were having luncheon one hot August day at Renishaw, and there had been a silence of some minutes, when my mother suddenly said, across the table :

" George ! . . . The mountain ash berries have turned already. . . . It means an early autumn."

" Well, I haven't seen them."

" That doesn't prevent their being there, George."

To which my father replied finally, and with an air of triumphant virtue :

" I don't *allow* myself to see things like that ! "

This last remark was particularly true. He had learnt to mask his sensitiveness and to barricade himself behind the multiplicity of his interests, so that he would only see the end of a process, when, indeed, it naturally, by the appearance of violent change that it offered, since he had noticed none of the intermediate steps, forced itself upon his attention. Then, when he could no longer avoid seeing, he could still nevertheless avoid comprehending ; and, further, what he now saw, suddenly, he perceived far too large — an exaggerated vista of ruin, of empty, desolate houses and penniless children. . . . " If it were not for me," he would sometimes remark, with an air suitable to the pathos of the situation, " we should all be living in lodgings on three thousand a year ! "

Notwithstanding, it was true that he exhibited in his character streaks of intense foresight, and was undoubtedly a clever business man, though apt to want to strike too hard a bargain. Immensely extravagant after his own fashion, he knew the value of money, but he could never understand or excuse extravagance in others. . . . You see, it was not necessary for *them* to spend money or buy things : he could do it for them *so* much better. . . . He noticed that Miss King-Church, admirable in so many ways, had bought the wrong kind of sponge for Edith. . . . If only people would come to him for his advice ! If only, *if only*, Ida would consult him about her clothes, instead of getting those expensive fashionable dresses ! He could put her on to something interesting at a tenth of the price ! Or he could order the dresses himself — she should make more use of his taste —, pay for them, and then deduct the money every other fortnight from her quarterly allowance (it was called an allowance, but was, in fact, the income from her own small capital). Or he might give it her ; let her pay for it, and then let her have the money back, so much every ten days. Or again he might set off part of the cost of it against what she had paid for his share in that bazaar — though he felt sure it could not come to so much as she made out : there were lots of ways of ringing the changes. He had a passion for rather complicated transactions of this kind. . . . Such a mistake to leave him out of it, he could so easily run her up one of those charming medieval things. It would be original and friends would want to copy it. He had lots of notes somewhere, for the reformation of clothes. It was only necessary to get back to the old lines (they understood these things so much better in the Middle Ages!). There was, for example, that delightful old leper's gown at Naples, a thing anyone would be glad to wear! Probably, if he asked him, the curator, Professor Roselli, would be only too pleased to lend one a piece of it, so as to have the pattern copied. And himself would give her a necklace or pendant to go with it ; perhaps one of those beautiful old bits of lead jewellery. He could easily have it imitated, if he could find the right person to do it. It was just as beautiful in design as any piece decorated with emeralds or diamonds, and far less expensive ; and it would look splendid with a sackcloth jerkin ! If he decided on a pendant, he could have it copied from one of the examples in the Musée Cluny in Paris. He had made full notes on them when he was there, with little drawings, rough but serviceable enough. (He drew such things on the spot, with a stump of pencil on the back of an old envelope, and then, when he got home, entered a facsimile of them — inscribed with one of the special pens he always used and constructed for himself out of three long holders and fine nibs (nib and holder being made in one piece) dovetailed together — into the right — or, it might be, the wrong — notebook.)

By this time he had worked himself up and was growing really excited about the idea ; (though underneath, somewhere deep inside him, lay the haunting, bitter certainty that his advice was not wanted, would not be asked for and, if it were, most certainly would not be taken : but he did not allow this knowledge to come to the surface). Where was that book ? *The Beauty of Dress at the Time of the Black Death* : it bore its name on its back in large letters. . . . No, that was not it ! Where could it be ? . . . No, nor that. . . . (These house-maids would tidy everything up ! Or it might be Henry, though he pretended never to move anything.) It was annoying that he could not find it at the moment, but the real beauty of the system he had evolved for keeping such things was, that though you might not find a particular note when you looked for it, you would be sure to find it some other time.

. . . Of course it might be in one of the boxes upstairs in his study, together with the loose notes. He went up to search for it. . . . The boxes of notes, all with their names pasted on the front, were arranged in a wooden case he had designed for them. . . . He ran through the list of names :

> *Schedules for Re-settlement* (. . . no, it would scarcely be in that)
> *Reresby and Normanville*
> *The Young Pretender's Court in Rome*
> *Sacheverell Miscellaneous*
> *Design in Brocades*
> *The Origin of Surnames*
> *Rotherham in the Dark Ages*
> *Lepers' Squints* (could it have got in there by mistake ?)
> *The Romances*
> *Sweet Preserves in the Fourteenth Century*
> *Wool-Gathering in Medieval Times and Since*
> *The Eckington Dump*
> *Court-Life in Byzantium*
> *Estate Miscellaneous*
> *Heraldry*
> *Introduction of the Peacock into Western Gardens*
> *John Brown & Co.*
> *The History of the Fork*
> *Landscape Notes*
> *On the Colours of Flowers*
> *Sheffield in the Eighteenth Century*
> *Nottingham Guilds* (1328–1384)
> *Trust Accounts*
> *Heber — Hiccock — Hely-Hutchinson*

No, it could be in none of those. He would look for it again tomorrow. . . . Disappointed, his mind reverted to what had originally started the trail of thought. *What* a pity Ida did not consult him ! . . . It was especially difficult to curb these outbreaks of extravagance in London, for, when there, he worked much at the British Museum, had business to do, with lawyers and banks, and so he only saw her in the evenings. The source of all this trouble, he deduced — and in this perhaps he was right — was to be traced to having friends.

Now, however, all these various interests and worries and troubles came together and coalesced to overwhelm him, and

FROM UPSTAIRS, RENISHAW

by John Piper

SACHEVERELL SITWELL, *æt.* 2

by their timing appeared to quadruple their power. And the final touch was added, I was always given to understand, by the literary strain imposed upon him by the writing of an essay, entitled " The Origin of the Word Gentleman ", for a quarterly of luxurious format called *The Ancestor*. His serious illness came on with great suddenness.

Only a week or two before he had been staying with my godfather, Ernest Beckett,[1] for a house-party, and had found time, directly he returned, to write a typical letter to Turnbull, still, it will be noticed, with esthetic and archaeological threads running through the fabric of it.

RENISHAW, May 21

MY DEAR PEVERIL,

The wooden covering mantel [2] to protect the marble mantelpiece in the drawing-room has been made and fitted before I was

---

[1] Ernest William Beckett, 2nd Lord Grimthorpe (*b.* 1856, *d.* 9th May 1917). Conservative member for the Whitby Division 1885–1905, partner in Beckett & Co. — connoisseur and patron, man about town, and politician. He inherited two vast sums, from his father and uncle the bankers ; commonly said to amount to seven millions. He lost a large part of his money the year after he had inherited his second fortune, having invested largely in San Francisco, it was supposed, before the disastrous earthquake and fire. He then retired to Ravello, near Naples, where he lived in the Villa Cimbrone. He was interested in modern French art, and commissioned George Moore, who was a friend of his, to buy a Manet for him. When he saw it, he would not pay the price of a thousand pounds asked for it, and in this way Moore was lucky enough to have it left on his hands, and ultimately to acquire it himself.

[2] *Extracts from Estate Correspondence*
(From my Father to Turnbull

29 Nov. 1901

The damage has been done by the fire smoking. . . . A sheet of glass can be prepared to fit, but neither this nor Hollingworth's cover for the drawing-room mantelpiece should be fitted unless I am there to see it done. The workmen are quite capable of drilling holes in the marble or any other folly. Maynard H. should send me the plan of his cover as it may not suit my ideas at all. Have you any acquaintances who could tell you whether to " plaust " for to cart hay or corn, and " sord " for the rind of bacon or cheese are still used in Peak dialect ? They are said to be derived from the Latin *plaustrum* and *sordes*. They were in use 70 years ago, as Glover states.

(From Hollingworth to Turnbull)

5 Dec. 1901

I enclose a sketch of the wooden mantel. We have not touched the marble in any way, simply fitted it up to and fastened it with hooks into the frame of the tapestry. . . .

I have asked several people about the word " plaust ", but nobody has ever heard of it. *Sord* is very commonly used here for rind of bacon and we never use anything else. I have not heard any but Derbyshire people use it.

consulted. This is not as it should be. What was the cost of it ?

Many thanks for your notes re *sord*. But can you ascertain for me whether *plaust* is still used in the Peak District for carting hay or corn ?

Rodin is a strangely impressive man with a head expressing daemonic force. He talked little at Ernest Beckett's, but the place to meet him is in his own studio, where he explains and makes you feel everything. Sargent was interesting as always. It was a strange party — Phillips,[1] who is Keeper of the Wallace Collection,

---

[1] Sir Claude Phillips, art critic and connoisseur (*b.* in London the 29th of January 1846, *d.* 1924), the second son of Robert Abraham Phillips, court jeweller, by his wife Helen, daughter of Moses Lionel Levy, and sister of the founder of the *Daily Telegraph*, and aunt of the 1st Lord Burnham. Sir Claude was for many years attached to the family paper as art critic ; a position for which his knowledge and talent eminently fitted him. In 1900, he was appointed Keeper of the Wallace Collection on its opening at Hertford House. The author of several monographs, he was a learned and polished writer, who took great pride in his weekly essays, which appeared every Friday morning in the *Daily Telegraph*. It was said that his editor — to whom, as if a Red Indian, he always referred as "My Chief", had given him strict orders to refer at least once in each article to Raphael. Such was Sir Claude's single-mindedness, that a phrase or two would swiftly compensate — as, indeed, it should — for national, international and even esthetic disaster. In example of this trait, I recollect meeting him at a concert during the First World War, when the fortunes of the Italian armies, allied to us, were at a particularly low pitch, and it had seemed, a week previously, that, with the capture of Padua by the Germans, Venice must follow within a few days, and the whole peninsula be on the verge of collapse. . . . The scene was the *foyer* of the Queen's Hall, in the interval, and I went up to him and said :

" Sir Claude, I must congratulate you on your splendid article a little while ago on the Fall of Padua."

" I'm glad you liked it," he replied, adding, in a tone of great melancholy, " but *alas*, the *best* I *ever* wrote — and my Chief agrees in thinking it so — is never likely to be published now."

" And what is the subject ? "

" The Fall of Venice — it should have appeared last week."

In reality, however, no one was more disturbed than was Sir Claude by any damage done to works of art. Thus, I was driving with him in a taxi one day in 1913 or 1914, I remember, when he looked out of the window, and read on a poster that a suffragette, in an attempt to demonstrate that women were worthy of the vote, had slashed a Bellini in the National Gallery — of which he was a trustee at the time. I shall never forget the physical effect of the announcement upon him, and I feared that he might undergo a heart attack at any moment. . . . And, great as was his love for the masterpieces of the golden age, he possessed, too, an understanding, rare in a critic belonging to an epoch tainted with a pre-Raphaelite bias, for the beauties of later Italian painting, and in his house hung several remarkable pictures by such masters as Salvator Rosa and Domenico Feti. He was a delightful and charming talker, and his short, round body, sleekly dressed, his bald head and carefully curled grey moustaches, were to be seen at every theatre where a play of interest was being produced, and at every concert, for his knowledge and appreciation of music almost rivalled in intensity his connoisseurship of pictures.

Lord Rosslyn, one or two M.P.'s, Frank Harris [1] (of all people !) and three or four leading musicians, Spanish, Italian and American. Beckett has just sold his collection of old French objects, and has brought back from China a good deal of jade, bronze and lacquer.— Yrs. v. sincerely, GEORGE R. SITWELL.

At the end of May, he felt he would like to return to Scarborough, though previously he had just decided to leave it. Accordingly, having a few months before given up his old house, he took from his brother-in-law a lease of Londesborough Lodge. There, in the following month, he fell alarmingly ill ; presumably with a nervous breakdown, though people scarcely knew the term then, and certainly did not understand the misery that it connotes. Whatever the nature of his affliction, it entirely prostrated him, so that he could attend to no business. He became convinced that he was a dying man, and the knowledge that his father had died at precisely the same age — a fact of which his mother kept reminding him by inference, saying to him, for example, " You look just like your poor father did, today " — persuaded him of it still more surely. And members of the medical profession could do — or at any rate did — little to help him.

Here, having watched the development of a character, as seen by a child, a son, the reader may ask why my father so continually insisted on being in the right, to the extent that if events proved to him that he had been wrong, and he could no longer avoid such a conclusion, he had to fall ill. . . . The reason, I deduce, must be sought a long way back, in the 'sixties of the previous century when he was a small child. . . . I used to think that his disposition and his whims, sometimes so delightful and removed from reality, at others so harsh and, indeed, hateful, were the result of his having been

[1] Frank Harris (*b.* 1856, *d.* 1931), the celebrated writer and editor, and one of the chief figures of the " 'nineties."

My father had known Frank Harris fairly well. For part of the time that Harris was editor of the *Saturday Review*, my father was chairman of the board of directors, but resigned, he told me, on observing that the policy of the paper was calculated solely in order to blackmail a celebrated public man (I have never found out who he was). . . . Harris, when editing a paper in America in 1919, wrote asking me to send him an essay for publication in it. At the end of his letter — in case, one supposes, I might already have heard of his behaviour in the matter just referred to —, he added as postscript : " I used to know your father well, when he was Chairman of the *Saturday* at the time that I was editor, and Wells and Shaw were regular contributors. I rejoiced in his quaint ideas."

brought up entirely by women since the age of two, when, as we have seen, he succeeded his father ; were rooted in the circumstances that he had never been controlled or disciplined or contradicted, and that, further, he had inherited an ample fortune at the age of twenty-one, finding himself, in fact, one of those local princes of whom Meredith tells us in *The Ordeal of Richard Feverel*. But my father had always maintained that his mother, though, by the time I knew her, gentle and on occasion almost indulgent, had not — for she was one of a family of five daughters — understood how a boy should be managed, and had treated him — of course, without meaning to do so, for she was utterly devoted to him — with severity, and sometimes almost with cruelty. . . . And I have come to believe that this was true, since I found in 1938 in the library at Renishaw a forbidding-looking account-book, short and thick, with an ecclesiastical clasp of brass. I opened this volume at random, and my eye lit on a page, not devoted to figures, on which were written, in a round, childish hand, very different from that which I knew, and yet even then recognisable, the words " George naughty again Jan 20th ". From the character of the letters, he plainly could not have been more than six or seven when obliged to enter that sentence. Underneath was inscribed in my grandmother's beautiful, flowing hand, " George naughty a second time Jan 20th ".[1]

For how much subsequent suffering, for himself and others, may not these simple words have been responsible ! The insistence on *always* being right, on never being in error, sprang, probably, from that or some similar slight and trivial occurrence, too harshly corrected. When I first read the words, I felt a pang at my heart for him, and for his mother.

To return to the epoch of which I am writing, just as my father's illness began, preparations were in progress throughout the land for local displays of loyalty to the throne, for King

---

[1] The only other entry, except those that dealt with money, was headed *Children's Books*. Under it were the following names :

> The Shepherd King
> Rescued From Egypt
> Babylonish Captivity
> Pride and Its Prisoner
> Idols of the Heart
> The Young Pilgrim.

A depressing list, it seemed, for infants.

Edward VII was to be crowned on 26th June. Not least did
our loyal borough resound with shouting and hammering,
which must have been most trying for a nervous patient. It
was impossible to escape the noise and bustle. And even for
us children, who loved this sense of bustle and happy energy,
nevertheless the bright colours of the bunting outside and the
general feeling of cheerful anticipation only served to emphasise
the atmosphere of illness and unhappiness within the house.
Moreover, there were other contrasts to be observed ; although
the keenest sense of patriotism and rejoicing seemed to inspire
everyone, so that even the strange being from whose example
I had first learnt to speak, the whining, hoarse-voiced collector of rags and bones, this summer, sported a miniature
union-jack in the buttonhole of his scarecrow's frock-coat, and
although, indeed, I could not help wondering what particular
cause he found to be thus jolly and excited, for a kind of mad
sense of frolic now gleamed from his eyes, nevertheless I noticed
that others were absent or had disappeared. Lousy Peter had
vanished from his summer haunts, where he was wont to
lounge in the plazas of the noon with an almost southern
nonchalance ; or perhaps he had only been suppressed by
the bunting, and reclined under it somewhere, wrapped, after
the fashion of Merlin the enchanter within his thorn-bush,
in a long sleep. But no voice spoke. Indeed a fresh wave of
conquering matter-of-fact seemed to be flooding the new century
and to have swept away many of the useless figures on this world's
edge. . . . Yet another and more enormous form was to replace
them, at any rate temporarily. It was this very summer that
a whale, the first I ever saw, was stranded upon the shore,
on the sands near the old harbour. A colossal, shapeless and
primeval carcase, it reared its useless bulk there for weeks,
and seemed in its immensity, that was yet lost against the
golden sweep of the bay, to hold in it some symbolism difficult
to seize upon ; to herald, perhaps, the wrecking of an empire
or of a civilisation.

At first gangs of small boys could be seen cutting their
initials on its soft, responsive rind, and could be heard uttering,
with the ferocity that those who are little like to be able to
show to fallen giants, whoops of triumph as they dug their
penknives into its dark flanks. . . . One morning, however,
Edith and I were taken to look at Leviathan. The hour was

very early, it was a peculiarly low tide, and at the sands' edge showed a line of rocks which was hardly ever uncovered. The whole scene was deserted, there were no groups of riders to dapple the sands with their passing shadows, no donkey-boys, no pierrots, no children ; the expanse lay untrodden as a desert, but fresh from the waves, so that a shimmering sheen of palest water-white lay in long stretches over the golden surface. The light itself, though feathery and soft, was of a kind to bring out every tone, even the bold grey projections of the castle above seemed today to bear a mysterious suggestion of colour, of lilacs and blues and whites, and the red-ribbed roofs of the fishermen's houses glowed like beds of roses. We approached the whale, and there, standing beneath its looming bulk, looking at its immense and wrecked shape, we found Count de Burgh,[1] in his usual surfeit of glory, frock-coat over tightly-laced stays, silk facings with an illegitimate papal decoration sewn upon the lapel, braided and striped trousers, and a tall top-hat with his fringe of curls affixed to it. But he did not take his hat off, or even appear to see us at all, but remained gazing at the whale with an expression of rapt melancholy, in a sort of dreamy, trance-like condition of mournfulness. Perhaps in its predicament, stranded in a world of which it had no knowledge and in which it was of no use, able to exert, for all its strangeness, not the minutest fraction of influence, he identified something akin to his own fate.

It was a long time before the now plainly rotting corpse of Leviathan was removed, and for many days the townspeople avoided the part of the sands upon which it lay, while visitors from the industrial towns sniffed the breeze with relish and remarked upon the unusual strength of the ozone in Scarborough air. It felt, it even smelt, quite different from that of Leeds or Bradford. . . . The whale presented altogether, it seemed to us, an unhappy episode : yet we did not remain saddened by it for long. The Coronation was drawing nearer, and banners, shields and wreaths were being everywhere erected. Fresh from reading Harrison Ainsworth, I was disappointed that there were not to be on this occasion, as his books had led me to expect, fountains spouting red wine, but, on the other hand, the municipal authorities had planned

[1] See *Left Hand, Right Hand!* vol. i, p. 165-6.

for the fireworks — which in Tudor times, I felt sure, had been of a very rudimentary kind, — to be on a scale and of a splendour never before attempted in Scarborough. There were to be set-pieces of King Edward and Queen Alexandra, and John Bull shaking hands with South Africa, a large helmeted female, and unusually explosive portraits of Lords Kitchener and Roberts, as well as all the usual Roman candles, golden fountains, " whirling silver wheels " and " ruby and diamond cascades ". And my mother had arranged that we children were to be allowed to sit up — indeed, the banging and spluttering would have made it impossible to remain asleep — and watch the rockets coruscating up into the sky from the Spa below. . . . Then, only two days before the ceremony in the Abbey, came the shattering news that King Edward had been obliged to undergo an operation for appendicitis, and that his crowning — and, with it, our fireworks — was to be postponed. . . . The King himself could hardly have been more disappointed than was I.

Apart from the atmosphere at home, caused by my father's illness, it seems to me, looking back, that a new sense of space, of leisure, and even of excitement, surrounded us ; we were in the Edwardian Age now, the transition was complete, and even if some of the revellers scarcely deserved their place, even if it were difficult to know why others of them revelled at all, nevertheless those of them who *were* prosperous were entering on a period of prosperity greater than had ever been known. As for the excitement, albeit, when viewed from the present Age of Violence, it may seem, compared with the sensations experienced by those who destroy whole cities or are destroyed in them, to have been tame as the feelings of a visitor at an exhibition about to revolve in a wheel or enjoy the miniature thrills of a switchback, it was, notwithstanding, at least a pleasurable emotion, embodying that peculiar yet delightful suspense that one undergoes before embarking upon some gratification of the senses.

Thus I recall, and associate with this period — though it may, perhaps, have taken place a year later — a short but memorable journey on which I was taken by my mother and one of her sisters. . . . An enterprising firm of cab proprietors had put on the road, to ply between Scarborough and Filey, almost the first service of motor charabancs in England, and

this at a date when private motors were as yet scarcely introduced. They accomplished the journey of nearly twenty miles
in a breath-taking hour and a quarter. The whole world was
already divided into two halves, those who believed that
motors would in the end oust other equipages, and those who
regarded them as a temporary whim, a swift path that led
nowhere except to damnation. My mother's strong family
feeling — for her brother was one of the first private owners
in England of a motor-car, a machine to which I shall revert
in a later chapter — and her love of fresh air, speed and
pleasure made her a partisan of the internal combustion
engine. She had, moreover, been obliged to hide from my
father all knowledge of our proposed trip, for, in addition to
his invariable disapproval of people enjoying themselves, he
would have regarded it as an unnecessary and perilous adventure. But even more than this, the fact that my mother,
who usually only got up in time for luncheon, was willing to
be ready to leave the house at half-past nine and, still more
surprising, to be punctual, made me realise the importance
of the occasion ; it must, I knew, if that were so, rank high
as pleasure.

My aunt called for us. She and my mother wore on their
heads enormous cloth caps, several layers of thick veils fell
over their faces, and all three were enclosed in layer after
layer of coats and mufflers. We drove to the appointed
starting-place in a cab, and arrived several minutes before
the charabanc was due to leave. . . . I shall never forget
climbing up the several steps into that very high, open conveyance, and waiting with a tremulous sense of expectancy
for it to start. What made, I think, both the waiting and the
starting seem yet more strange was the rudimentary character
of such a vehicle. It was built as though to be drawn by
horses, it was the same height from the ground and, as one
looked over the dizzy gap that hung above the almost invisible
bonnet of the engine into space, one suffered the most violent
feeling of disproportion, as though in a boat that ended flat,
without a prow, for one missed the glossy animal extension
of the carriage . . . Now an intense excitement succeeded to
this vertigo, for two men were with some difficulty winding
up the dangerous machine. Soon, with a new sense of freedom
and lightness, we were speeding down the steep streets, up

the long hills, and out of the town, along the narrow, dusty country roads of those days. The Filey Road was flat, and lay like a ribbon above the abrupt cliffs, between them and stepped table-lands, the strange primitive hills of this country, covered with heather and with tumuli, the burial-place of unknown kings with crowns of iron and bone. Here and there we passed a tree, blasted by the salt wind, driven backwards from the waves towards the land, its arms stretched out in flight, as though trying with all its immobility to escape inland from the pounding breakers below and the decaying shores. We passed many familiar landmarks : we could see where the grass of Parnassus grew, and farms of my grandfather's, where we used to go for tea as a treat, and then we sped past Caton Bay, which belonged to the Londesboroughs too, and where they possessed, down by the shore, a wooden house in which we spent many happy moments, tired from finding shells and scrambling for wild flowers, or from going to the rocks far off to search for new sea-gardens of anemones and weeds wherein small crabs sidled or dug laterally into the rippled gold sand. . . . In a few moments, though, we were in country we had not known, and after that — but before we could have dreamed it possible — we had arrived in Filey and were congratulating ourselves, rather carefully and without saying too much — for the return journey still loomed in front of us — on our safety. We discussed the dust, the noise and the vibration, and declared our enthusiasm for this method of travelling. . . . Certainly not even a first ride in an aircraft could have been more exciting. A new age had, indeed, arrived.

We began, however, as we neared Scarborough, to feel guilty at having been away, and at not having told my father what we were doing. . . . He was no better ; on the contrary, he seemed still to be getting worse. And as his illness grew more severe, doctors multiplied. Of a now extinct species, impressive and momentous men, who wore frock-coats and who carried top-hats as though in homage to the undertakers with whom they were in league, would drive round at all hours of the day and night in broughams that resembled abbreviated, one-horse hearses ; family doctors, other people's family doctors, specialists from Leeds, Liverpool and London, fashionable doctors and doctors of whom no one had ever heard, all these different healers would be summoned and appear — but always at different houses, for my father could not sleep and would move from the Lodge to some other house he had taken in the town, and then back again. Often he would sleep in a new house every night in the week. A letter from my grandmother Sitwell to Turnbull, dated the 22nd of July 1902, says : " . . . Thank you also for your kind enquiries after our poor Patient. I think he is a *little* better in spite of adverse circumstances. He went on Monday to the very pretty house which had been lent him in Fulford Road, and left it the same evening, as he could not sleep. The doctors then said that if I put in a hundred workmen, I must get Wood End [1] ready the following night. We just got his, Lady Ida's, the nurses' and the valet's rooms ready. In spite of his not having had a good night, he seems calmer and more at rest."

Two days later, in a letter to Turnbull, Henry Moat writes : " I am rather confused and have spoilt this page as we have moved twice in three days ".

Ill and sleepless as he was, nevertheless the intense activity of my father's mind remained unabated, and — for was I not his eldest son, soon due to go to school ? — he was much occupied with the problem of education. . . . It was wrong, all wrong (they had managed these things so much better in the Middle Ages ; archery was splendid training). It should be different. He did not feel well enough now to think it out, but if he survived the present year, which he doubted, and when he had time, he would turn his attention to it and try to get it right — at any rate in theory. However, he could not get on with the matter now, so the system remained unreformed and it was understood that I should have to put up with it as best I could.

The winter before his collapse, he and my mother had succeeded in picking out a school that they thought suitable for me, and one which was known to pay much attention, by

---

[1] Wood End had been my grandmother's residence in Scarborough before she had moved to Hay Brow. My father had lived there a great deal from his childhood until his marriage, but it had, at the time this letter was written, stood empty for some years, and a special effort, therefore, was needed to get it ready. She now gave him the house ; in which my mother and father were to spend a good many months of every year, until the Bombardment of Scarborough dislodged them in 1914. It then remained empty until I returned there to fight an election in 1918.

means of the generally accepted combination of brutality, boredom and slow torture, to preparing its pupils for their time at Eton. . . . The boys were not mollycoddled — that was the great thing, everyone agreed — and the school team was notorious for its proficiency at football, which was held in some mystic manner to be — I could never quite make out *why* — supremely important. (Since I showed no aptitude for them, my father was especially keen that I should be good at games.) In London I had heard him discussing this school with my mother ; that which finally converted both of them to it, I had gathered, was their discovery that the headmaster was " the most famous dribbler in England ". This recommendation bewildered me, because I had never hitherto observed that dribbling was considered a meritorious accomplishment at home, and I was quite unaware of its place as a technical term in the vocabulary of Association football — and, for aught I know, of Rugby football and cricket. . . . My mother liked the school because the head-master's sister seemed so fond of flowers.

My father was as full of original theories as ever — indeed they tended to grow still more erratic — and I was now, alas, doomed to become the victim of one of them. Before going to the place of trimensual internment they had chosen for me, he decided that I had better attend a day-school. Herein, no doubt, he was right, for I had encountered few children except my cousins. I preferred the company of people older than myself, or of my sister and brother, and had always detested boys of my own age. The school, however, which he chose was situated in Scarborough and mainly supported by superior tradesmen and rich farmers. But my father knew the head-master, who was on the Town Council, and from hearing him hold forth mercilessly on several subjects, had formed a high opinion of his abilities as a teacher ; a fine, all-round man, possessed of his own ideas.

Accordingly, one heartless, sunny morning — it was a Monday — , I experienced when I was called the sinking feeling in the pit of the stomach that always accompanies for the imaginative a new adventure of this order, for Henry was in two hours' time to conduct me to the school and there hand me over to the headmaster. . . . He told me as many stories as he could, to divert me on my way to the scaffold.

. . . But all too soon we arrived, Henry left me, and the headmaster, a bearded man with the happy but puzzled expression of a resolute and vigorous bore, spoke " a few words " to me in an absent-minded way, as though occupied with affairs of moment. I think, really, that he had forgotten I was due to appear that day and was taken aback, annoyed at having missed the opportunity for a long and excruciating speech of welcome and exhortation. But the few words increased like the Israelites in the land of Canaan, and it seemed a long time before he had finished, and had sent for a boy to take me to the dreary asphalt torture-yard, known euphemistically as " playground ". The boy arrived : his head, I noticed, was fitted into a round cap that bore on its front a device resembling a skull and crossbones. He listened patiently to the headmaster, and then, as soon as he had left the room, broke into a run, whistling like a steam-engine as he went, and at each step hitting out regularly at every thing and every person he passed with his right hand. Even the iron railing and the stone wall did not seem to hurt it. I followed him, panting.

In an instant we had reached the yard. Not a blade of grass, not a leaf, broke the grey-mauve monotony of asphalt, stone walls and slates. Only a few odd instruments, bits of rope and wood clamped to the wall by iron rings and joints, and suggestive of torture, fair and square, stood in one corner ; though, as I found out later, they were in fact the furnishings of a poorly stocked outdoor gymnasium. At this moment, however, I had no time to examine the yard, or indeed anything but the jostling, screaming mob that occupied it, for it teemed with shouting, whistling, roaring schoolboys of different ages and sizes, though all covered with spots, and all wearing caps with the same skull and crossbones I had noticed proudly blazoned upon them. I looked round, and felt rather out of it — but not for long. Evidently I had been expected, for about half of the larger boys, directly they saw me, set on me with whirling fists and yells of " *Don't think you're everybody just because your father's a bloody baronet !* " Now this was, as matter of fact, something which had not occurred to me heretofore, because my mother made no secret of her view that a baronetcy was a disgrace, and that she regarded baronets in general as the Ishmaels of the British race, and no one else had ever mentioned it to me. . . . None the less, I returned from my first encounter with victorious British Democracy suffering from two black eyes, an aching body and a sore heart. And I fear, too, that I gave a very poor account of myself, since I did not know how to fight, hated pain and was tremendously surprised by the onslaught.

My family pretended not to notice the black eyes, and said nothing about them, except that I " looked tired ", Perhaps, indeed, they were proud of them, saying to each other, " The boy will go far, he begins fighting the very first day he goes to school." . . . I went back every morning to the school, where I displayed no ability, no aptitude of any sort for work or play. Even when I was shown how to play rounders, a game confined to the youngest boys — that is to say to those of my own age —, even at that I was a failure. Perhaps a precocious instinct for words and their meanings may have been at the root of it, for I felt that the word *play* [1] denoted something you enjoyed, and since I did not enjoy these dull runnings to and fro, I did not expect to have to go on with them. At other times, while the bigger boys were listlessly continuing their studies within, we smaller ones, eight to ten of us, were turned into the yard to play by ourselves, with no master present. Then my companions were wont to indulge in an exhibitionistic and obscene game, known by them as " horses " ; rites perhaps akin, by some strange atavistic trait, to the hobby-horse exploits of primitive races such as the Mongols and Manchus, who staged this same kind of orgy in yourtals and even in the great courts of the Imperial Palace, on the marble platforms, beneath the immense shadows of yellow-tiled roofs. Perhaps these miniature orgies, also, would have been of interest to the anthropologist ; but, unfortunately, the scene was neither so savage as in the one place, nor so splendid as in the other. Here the setting was appropriate to the squalor of the game. . . . I refused to take part in it, and grew still more unpopular in consequence.

Moreover, I was now unhappy at home as well as at school. . . . Miss King-Church had begun, very naturally, to be bored with my plaintiveness in the evenings when I returned from school. She disliked, too, I expect, my obvious want of success, which reflected no credit on any person concerned.

[1] It derives from the Middle Dutch *plegen*, to be glad or dance.

And my nights, occupied with my private problem — of which, of course, she knew nothing —, nights filled with my picturings of hell flames, my efforts to overcome my terror of them, or to think, equally, of some way of avoiding them through virtue, became an absolute torment. . . . Eventually, since my mother and the governess both saw that I was learning nothing, and in danger of losing what little I knew and of deteriorating generally, I was withdrawn, after about a fortnight or so, from the scene of my father's experiment.

During the course of this brief school career and its immediate aftermath, my self-respect had sunk extremely low, and might have vanished altogether and for ever, but for my dear old friend Miss Lloyd, and for her tea-parties which ministered to it. By some system of telepathy, or just through her loving-kindness, she knew immediately if I felt depressed — and, I suppose, examining my character at that time, that I was a moody child, prone to pass from a state of intense and almost unnatural exaltation to a leaden lowness of spirit ; in which condition I could find no pleasure in anything, though I could soar as easily and swiftly out of it, if someone tried to help me. . . . At any rate, when I felt at my most dejected, without a moment's delay she would appear in the house, in order to invite us children, accompanied by Miss King-Church, to tea the following afternoon. We were all well aware that for Miss Lloyd neither my father nor my mother, together or singly, could do wrong — an attitude from which, even when in future years it became most difficult to maintain, she never departed : but, once in her house, she made it clear, although without ever saying so explicitly, that, while she esteemed my family above the rest of mankind, she esteemed myself proportionately above the rest of my family. Further, the affection, and almost the respect, with which she treated me in front of our small world, strengthened my position in it, made my grandmother, for example, wonder whether I could really be so selfish as she had deemed me, and even induced poor Miss King-Church, who had, during recent days, most certainly suffered from my temperamental behaviour, to regard me once more with a new eye, divested of prejudice.

Partiality of this kind constitutes, I am sure, a most valuable ingredient in the upbringing of an artist, if it may not, indeed, be a necessity for every child. A child, especially a boy, longs for adult dignity, to which fondness such as this temporarily promotes him. In the same way that no gambler at roulette can win on any particular occasion, if he once allows his intellect to assert itself, to tell him coldly that the odds are steeply tilted against him by the mechanism, and that there is every reason to suppose he will lose ; in the same way that, if this occurs, he should immediately leave the rooms, since the capacity to win proceeds from some kind of psychic intoxication, no less than from what men call good luck ; in the same way that no artist, using that term in its fullest sense, can produce good work unless he suffers from the artist's proper hallucination, that everything he writes or paints or composes is of the utmost importance, and that at which he is at work at present, the most significant of all (it is admittedly possible to find an artist with this same hallucination whose work is bad, but it is never possible to find one without it whose work is good); in the same way, then, I suggest, a child, in order to progress, must be persuaded that he is doing well, and is of the utmost moment to his elders. . . . And it is here, indeed, that the cult of games enters to injure English education ; for the clever boy is often bad at games and hates them, and this makes him feel unpopular, and lose interest in what he is doing. This, as will be seen, very much affected me when I was at school.

The subtle flattery of such attentions as Miss Lloyd's, on the contrary, helps personality to take root — or is it only my individual weakness which renders me responsive to the degree that if I am conscious of being regarded as a miracle-worker, I can work miracles ? I do not know. But I must own that regard of this order is not all I need, and that to me the grossest and most rancid flattery does not come amiss. I can recognise it, certainly, for what it is, but in some manner it recharges the stores of energy upon which I have drawn. In order to achieve my best work, I require it today, as much as forty years ago at school, and, were I an oriental potentate, how willingly would I not pay a professional sycophant the highest possible fee for the measure of his praise !

There was no taint, however, of sycophancy in Miss Lloyd's composition. It was merely that she cared for me especially, and that, although I was still too young to formulate my troubles or express them in words, she appeared to be able at once to divine and dispel them. . . . As I have indicated, her house resembled a tower, with one room on each landing. The bottom floor was let to a doctor, her other favourite and thus my rival. I remember always climbing up the stairs, past this door, with the sense that doom might be — indeed, was sure to be — in course of being pronounced behind it at that very moment upon some unfortunate patient. The dining-room came next, and then, above it, on the third storey, the drawing-room. Perhaps in the winter, with the curtains — which herself had cut out, sewn, and further ornamented with a combination of needle and brush — drawn across the wide bay of the window, to hide the flocculent mass of the sky that had just caught fire, and was burning with the bitter, frosty redness of a northern sunset, the comfortable atmosphere she distilled here was more evident ; perhaps then, under the light of the shaded lamp, always dimmer than that of the firelight which pervaded and gave its tone to the room and everything in it, the furniture, which she had covered with pale yet gay designs, but which seemed to belong to an eighteenth century that had continued and never died, and the whole flickering world created by her brush and needle, of embroidery and ribbon work, and all kinds of work of which I shall never know the technical category, existed most typically. The china, decorated and baked by herself — the rarest of all her arts —, shone with a peculiar glossy lustre, the birds so softly painted upon it appeared to move, the flowers to blow. An odour of new bread, which was to this house as incense to a church, scented the room, and even the intertwining flames of the fire, to which the frost, coming down the chimney, gave the plumage of a macaw, seemed made of vermilion and green and blue ribbons, plaited together by her hand. Nevertheless, now in the summer, with yellow canariensis trained to climb up the sides of the window, and the broad window-boxes blazing with the orange and red fires of nasturtiums, instead of being hard, frosty deserts wherein birds picked at the bits of bone and hairy half-coconuts exposed for them all through the winter with such loving care, now, with a gold-green cumulus-top of a sycamore visible, like a green mound, just level with the eye, and the rest all light, light from the sea and light from the sky, light from above and all round and beneath, light

SACHEVERELL SITWELL (*æt.* 6) IN THE CRESCENT,
SCARBOROUGH

SACHEVERELL SITWELL (*æt.* 10) WITH MISS LLOYD,
RENISHAW

blown and hurled through the tree-tops by the summer wind, the room was more startling. Everything glittered and glistened, as though it were wet, everything was soaked in the intensity of it and shone. The huge white clouds that tumble above this coast in these months (clouds to which Henry Moat used to refer, in a phrase of forgotten derivation, but presumably used by the sailors always in passage to and from the countries immediately opposite, as " them great big Norwegian bishops ") seemed, by their passage across the sky, in front of the window, to intensify still further, rather than to diminish, the quality of these rays. The light modelled very clearly the soft white contours of Miss Lloyd's face, shaped like that of an exquisite cat, with her wide-open green eyes, but it in no way coarsened the greeny whiteness of her skin, which had no pink in it, but resembled the powdery whiteness of a certain kind of peach, or the texture of the curls which surged in a circle round her head and appeared to be spun of the finest white silk.

As soon as we entered, and she had met us at the door, she would go to the table and prepare to mix with the blend of Ceylon tea she always favoured a teaspoonful of green tea, taken out of a tortoise-shell caddy which she kept locked. Then she would begin talking to us, but in a rather desultory manner until the tea was made. She proceeded to pour the water into the teapot, and a feather of grey steam would tremble up into the dry, bright air of the room. She had baked for us the small loaves we loved, their crusts white with flour, and had made some chocolate caramels, crumbling and melting. In the centre of the table, though, and its chief attraction, stood a Lowestoft bowl full of enormous strawberries. She had ordered this fruit a day or two beforehand in the market from an old woman, whose first husband had been cousin to her servant's mother, and whose reliability was thus guaranteed, and Miss Lloyd herself had been down with a basket to the stone temple of Ceres, decorated at this season with bunches of moss-roses and of sweet-williams and bouquets, now obsolete, of multi-coloured country flowers — arranged in concentric circles, each ring differing in colour and in the texture, lace-like or velvety, or diapered, and stuck in stone jam-jars —, as well as with mounds of fruit and vegetables, to inspect the berries before bringing them home. She had also bought the large bunch of pinks, which scented the air of the entire room, and had paid sixpence for it. As for the strawberries, they cannot have disappointed even her wish to prepare a treat for us ; each enormous scarlet fruit, freckled and showing indented slopes, like those of a model mountain in relief where a river runs down it, possessed a character of its own, and the bowl, with its precious load, as it glowed in the marine light, might have been the central theme of a Dutch still life.

But if Miss Lloyd had expended much thought and cleverness over each smallest detail — as she did, indeed, with anything connected with her or our lives —, she always made me aware that she had taken this trouble chiefly for me. Yet there was no danger of such affection rendering a child conceited, for he could see plainly that any symptom of vanity would destroy her trust in him. . . . All this time she was talking away quietly, as if to herself, with a smile of contentment over her face. Her conversation dealt at first, as it usually did, with people we did not know, for, in the manner of all simple people — and in spite of her cleverness, she was simple —, she invariably presumed that everyone, the world over, and of whatever age, was intimately acquainted with her friends and enemies. Then it passed to my father's aunts, and dealt with that period, to a child the most mythical of all, far more remote than the age of centaurs, satyrs and nymphs, when the static, as it were, had been dynamic, and when the old people he knows and sees round him had been young and pretty, full of youth's fire. It was more difficult for me, as an example, to picture my grandmother Sitwell, handsome and graceful old lady though she was, as the pretty, winning young widow with two small children, that she had been, or Lady Hanmer as a bride, dressed as Miss Lloyd described her, in white and silver brocade with a lace veil and with a wreath of orange-blossom, than to imagine Diana changing Actaeon into a stag. To the young, the old remain unchangingly old, and therefore unchangeable. But when Miss Lloyd added, after describing to me some scene in the past, " I think Lady Hanmer wants to see you, but I'm going round there again tomorrow, and will make sure . . . I shouldn't be surprised if it was that she has a present for you," these words conjured up in my mind an image of my Aunt

Puss as a donor, an aspect of her with which I was familiar :
an old lady, swathed in lace and velvet, with a cap, and
painted eyebrows eccentrically disposed, a stick by her side,
and, in her hand, a golden sovereign shining through its one
layer of tissue paper, like the sun through clouds, ready for her
to proffer it to me when I had advanced near enough. . . .
Even then, though, I doubt if I gave enough credit to Miss
Lloyd for the part she played in " reminding ", or, more accurately, in prompting my aunt towards this act of generosity.

No, it was far easier to picture Dickens — of whom she
talked, for as a child she had known him — than to strip my
grandmother and my great-aunt of the accretions with which
the years in their passage had endowed them. . . . I listened
eagerly to every detail of the great author's appearance, oi
the red waistcoat he liked to wear and the check coat, of his
voice, and of how, when he used to read one of his novels
aloud, he would by its intonations summon up for the audience
the traits, the moral and mental atmosphere, and even the
physical likeness, of the various characters : (of whom, indeed,
Miss Lloyd herself might have been one). To all this I paid
the closest attention, because I had already read most of
his novels, and was then, as now, an enthusiastic admirer of
them. It proved, however, a cruel disappointment to me to
find that my friend had not known Cruikshank, in whose
illustrations I took no less delight ; for I had formed, I think,
a sort of conception of Dickens and Cruikshank as inseparable
beings, destined, after the manner of the Siamese twins, to be
born contemporaneously, to live together by the force of com-
pulsion, and then to die at the same gasp, as though two
flowers upon a single stem.

At times, too — but this began to take place later, next
year, when we had a new governess who was a remarkably
fine pianist, but of whose influence over us our old friend was
somewhat jealous —, she would romance a little, telling us how,
when she was a girl of sixteen being educated in a convent in
Paris, Gounod would come round to give her a lesson and,
paying tribute to her precocious talent as a musician, would
say as he left, " Miss Lloyd, I'd rather hear you render my
Ave Maria with one finger, than the whole of the Conservatoire
play it with both hands." . . . Or she would describe to us
the country of the Riviera and the towns of Cannes and Nice

and Grasse as they had been in the halcyon days of the
'seventies, when she had lived there for some time, learning
to paint the convex or concave shapes of china, and to bake
them. As she talked, the country teemed with silken waterfalls, anemones and roses : Grasse was a city built of candied
fruit, with the delicious aroma of the flowers it distilled floating
down every street ; Nice and Cannes were full of brightly
painted villas, encircled by the fronds of palm-trees and buried
under canary-coloured cascades of mimosa ; and from their
doors, under the permanently blue dome of heaven, walked
crocodiles of English couples, ladies in crinolines, clasping
prayer-books in their hands, accompanied by the stern, tall
figures of their husbands, with their whiskered countenances ;
a South of France I never recovered until Diaghileff presented
Massine's and Derain's vision of the Boutique Fantasque at
the Alhambra theatre in 1919. . . . So she talked on, while
with red-stained mouths we occupied ourselves with the strawberries : the light, streaming down on her from the windows,
showed a sort of ecstatic glaze upon her eyes, and a colour
mounting, unexpectedly, to her cheeks as she continued. . . .
And then, suddenly, she would stop, and the look of pleasure
would fade. For, though she talked so freely, there were
certain reserves, I came to see later, in her conversation, and
these made her sad. She was afraid of something in the
background, some cruel fact or person, some story — of which,
perhaps, my grandmother alone, with her sympathy, and with
her steely discretion, was aware. . . . We never found out the
nature of this mystery.

Thus, through Miss Lloyd, my self-esteem was soon
re-established, albeit even the short span I had endured at
the day-school had been sufficient to inspire me with a well-
founded distrust concerning the traditional " happiest time of
my life ", now fast approaching. . . . My mother, noticing
this, used to tell me how sure she was that I should enjoy my
time at the boarding-school they had chosen for me, and in
which I was to be incarcerated the following year. She knew
the parents of many of the boys, and I should find them quite
different ; their fathers were sportsmen, and several of them
were friends of my uncle's — the highest award of praise that
she could bestow on anyone. . . . My father, though I saw
him so seldom, when we did meet, went further and drew

positively enchanting pictures of the life before me, and of how deeply I should enjoy it ; a real, fine, healthy life which put one in a glow. Schools had, apparently, improved beyond recognition since his day. Then the boys had learnt nothing except bad language and bad habits, and had been beaten and half starved ; all that bad old tradition had been swept away. . . . He only wished he could have my time in front of him, as his own, all over again.

Alas, though, this source of comfort diminished, for I saw him less and less. He was growing no better, it appeared. . . . The nurses changed as often and as rapidly as the doctors and the houses ; sometimes of their own accord, after my father had asked them not to stare at him for long together — a trick, out of a rather limited repertory, which many nurses like to test upon their patients —, but, instead, to sit with their backs to him ; sometimes, not of their own volition.

The doctors continued to arrive, and each of them recommended at least one new cure, and more probably returned, after its failure, to prescribe a further experiment. The invalid tried them all, one after the other, in good faith and in swift rotation : continual fresh air (he was sent lumbering round the woods in heavy old cabs), no fresh air, to lay his head on hop pillows, to take exercise, to give up exercise, to stop smoking, to smoke special cigarettes, to live on meat, to touch no meat, to give up alcohol, to drink champagne and port, to walk, to run, to sing, to lie down for long periods without moving, never to keep still, to take up golf, and to abandon it, " not to use his mind ", and to " think of other things ". . . . For all these pieces of advice the doctors charged ample fees, and his payment of them aggravated the financial worry which had largely caused his illness, and so rendered his condition yet graver.

Nobody seemed, even now, to know what was the matter with him or just how ill he was. . . . The sub-agent went over to Scarborough, and on his return to Renishaw the next day wrote to Turnbull the following report :

" *July 10, 1902.* Yesterday we went to Scarborough. I found Sir G.'s printer, Stubble, who took me to Londesborough Lodge. Lady Ida sent for me and told me the doctor will not allow Sir G. to come to Renishaw this summer.

I tried to find out how Sir G. really is, but did not manage it. Lady Ida says he gets no better and is quite ill, but on the other hand the nurse told me that the doctor says he is quite well if he would only think so. Sir G. comes downstairs and can sit about in the garden. Stubble says he is much worse than reported. Lady Ida says he is incapable of doing any business at all. . . .''

Finally (but this is anticipating by half a year), as he showed no sign of mending, the general practitioner who had first attended him asserted himself, and got him away from the other doctors. He advised change. He must travel with a friend. . . . But *where* was the friend to be found ? . . . In the end, the doctor himself went with him. . . . Thus it was that my father began to spend so much of his life abroad in France and Germany and Italy, but chiefly in Italy, and that we children came to hear so much of it, of Italian houses and gardens and ways of life. At first, my mother would only occasionally, or for part of the time, go abroad with him, and, in her absence, an acquaintance of his mother's, or " somebody suitable ", of whom she or my mother had heard, was chartered to keep him company ; but Henry, of course, was always in attendance as well, and soon learnt to talk Italian, though with a broad Yorkshire accent. . . . He was much struck, I recollect his confiding in me, by the palpable resemblance between the languages of Whitby and Italy, respectively : for example, in Whitby, the ordinary greeting in the streets, when you passed a friend, was " 'Ow ist tha ? " : while in Italy the counterpart was " *Come sta ?* "

In various stages of severity, my father's illness continued for several years, and left its mark upon him for life, making him realise how insubstantial a division existed between apparently good health and complete misery. From this period, too, started his custom of resting every day for many hours ; a habit which amazed Sacheverell and myself, to whom no torture was comparable with the drag of that single hour after luncheon in which we were compelled to lie down. . . . Yet here was a man, master of his fate, who rested voluntarily, and at shorter and shorter intervals ; a habit that continued and intensified. In a typically robust but disrespectful letter, written to me, in answer to one that I had sent him from Hyères, and dated January 1938, Henry Moat alludes to this idiosyncrasy of his master's, and also to his sojourns abroad with him : [1]

Poor Sir George, he really is an hero for his bed. I have known him often being *tired* of laying in bed, get up to have a rest, and after he had rested get back again into bed like a martyr. . . .

Curious the first time I went abroad with Sir George we stayed at the Costabelle Hotel Hyères, about 1900 I suppose. . . . Sir George would send me out to buy fresh butter and eggs for breakfast which I had to boil and cakes for tea I sometimes had to walk miles all to save him about 1 franc on the hotel bill a Mr Peyron kept the hotel then. . . .—I remain Your obedient servant HENRY MOAT.

P.S. I once told Sir George when he complained he was seeing things before his eyes that he eat too many eggs per day and gave him the number 5. He fairly bit my head off.—H. M.

While my father flitted so erratically from house to house, my mother, as a rule, remained at the Lodge, for it was too much of a strain on the household if she also were to move her home every day. . . . And during part, at any rate, of the general post that was always in progress, Sacheverell and I lived with her. Nevertheless, looking back, it seems to me that I was in her company less than usual. For one thing, I had only learnt that spring to climb trees, and, in consequence, spent as much time as I could in the garden, up in the branches. These trees, it is true, were low, cut flat at the top, but, because of that, they had spread laterally, and were all the more comfortable and roomy. But, proud as I was of my new accomplishment, I had to yield the palm in this direction to another child and — what was more humiliating — a little girl at that. She and her younger sister, the daughters of Lady Chelsea, were staying in Scarborough and used to come to play with me nearly every day. The elder was about my age, a year younger I think ; but, young though she was, possessed plenty of character. She was always up the tree first, but when there, would yet induce — for she was not supposed to climb trees — an air of icy sang-froid. Extremely hard-headed and practical, she enjoyed talking, though perhaps she liked listening less. She seemed, as she talked, to be shut

---

[1] As in the first volume, the original spelling of these letters has been retained.

up in her own mind with a thousand others of her own age, just like her, and by her conversation she would make one feel that one was not in the tree-tops at all, but with feet securely planted on the earth, or at any rate in some compound of drawing-room and stable, yet essentially " the right thing ". . . .

To return, though, to my mother ; in spite of her real concern for my father, I think that at the same time she rather appreciated the immunity from criticism that her expenditure enjoyed now that his constant wish to economise had brought on a costly illness, which necessitated a complete rest from all business. Scarborough would be more full than ever of visitors this year. Lawyers could not — though they did — argue with her about household bills, so there were many parties at the Lodge, until she moved to the new house my grandmother was preparing for us. " No wonder ", a correspondent states, in a letter to Turnbull, " that Sir George's expenses are heavy. I hear of Lady Ida providing luncheon for forty, unknown to him ! "

But the worst domestic effects of his illness were to be experienced in the future ; although his direct influence on my mother, headstrong and impulsive, had always been small, his indirect influence had been considerable. By his preoccupation with the gothic age and consequent aloofness from the day, by his formal, frosted manner, the reader has seen how he always, hitherto, even perhaps without wishing it, exercised a chilling process of restraint upon those friends of hers who sought to live upon her. Her many genuine and devoted friends, it was to be noticed, liked my father ; but the others were frightened of him, for, besides his alleged " cleverness ", of which they were not in a position to judge, their sense of guilt, their inner knowledge that they were out for all they could get, made them mistake his remoteness for percipience, and his unsureness of himself, caused by his ignorance of the times in which he lived, for a thoroughly justified mistrust of themselves. Now that he was temporarily no longer to be reckoned with, now that there were, even, some doubts existing in their minds concerning the likelihood of his recovery, this control was removed. They behaved just as they liked. They encouraged my mother in every folly. They led her in any direction that could harm her, by flattering her in every way possible, by urging her on to lose her temper, telling her that she had been " splendid ", and by trying to make her do it again, by persuading her to insult some of my father's relations who disapproved of them, by leading her on to find fault with my sister in public and to mortify her — because Edith's interests, even when a child, were in poetry, painting and music, the enemies of the frivolous and dull-minded —, but, above all, by plundering my mother and sponging upon her. They would be gay — for they were not dull personally, only in their minds — and silly, and " such fun " ; they would induce her to take them on shopping expeditions, single out a dress or a piece of jewellery, a hat or a fur coat, and then, remembering dramatically of a sudden that they could not afford it, owing to a husband's stinginess or a father's cruelty, they would begin to pout and look wistful. . . . My mother hated to see anyone in distress and would at once want to help them. She would give them the objects they had admired, and, in all probability, would add several other presents as well. A pound or a hundred pounds, it was all the same to her. At once they would recover their lost spirits, and be wreathed in winning smiles. The world was bright again. But they must not tell George, she would remind them ; it was better not to worry him. How could they? they replied ; they never saw him. *How* was he? . . . All the same, he could not mind, could he, his wife being so generous and charming? He ought to be delighted. After all, people said he was a rich man. And they thought, they said, that her spending money like this must help him politic-ally. When she reminded them that he had given up politics, they replied lightly, no doubt he would take them up again when he was better, and then he would be pleased at what she had done for him, and that she had not pinched herself and made enemies for him. It would be *brutal* of him to object. . . . I do not think my father ever regained his former control ; they had gnawed it away for good. The shadow grew and darkened ; it was already beginning to totter down-hill towards the blackness that gathered beneath. . . . But there was no sign of darkness in the street outside, where a cab waited in flooding sunshine to take them home. Jockey-carts were jingling along, and a barrel-organ was playing a new tune, which the composer of its words and music had dedicated to my mother ; a tune called " How Easily Things Go Wrong ! ".

It seemed as if August, and the postponed Coronation, would never come : but at the end of July, the same bunting, the same emblazoned shields and artificial laurels, the same crowns in pasteboard and in fairy-lights, began to be looked for in dark sheds, and then to be dusted, put together and re-erected. Plans for giving expression to the sense of public rejoicing were once more reviewed — and this time reached fruition, though a certain sense of uneasiness and of anticlimax lay just under them. . . . At last the day itself, the ninth of the month, arrived, and in the morning, at an early hour, we children were taken to the balcony of the Pavilion Hotel outside the station, there to watch the contingents of troops form up for a procession. . . . Indeed, this balcony, facing the stone belfries and turrets of the station — built in Luxemburg late-Renaissance —, is inextricably mingled with all my early impression of pageantry ; from it, for example, I had witnessed, at the age of four, the first display of national or civic pomp I can remember, the rejoicings that took place in celebration of Queen Victoria's Diamond Jubilee — and I recall how my delight at the exotic appearance of the Indian troops assembled eventually overcame my disappointment, even my fury, at the lack of the diamonds I had been led, by the name of the occasion itself, so confidently to expect. . . . And now I must say a word about this hotel, thus always associated in my mind with things of interest, and with pleasure, and of the family who owned it, for they produced a man of whom the town of Scarborough is extremely proud.

Many years later, after I had stood — and been defeated — as Liberal candidate for the division, and while I was still prospective candidate at the next election, I spent a considerable time every year in the constituency. In 1922, I was staying at Wood End, but, since there was no cook there, used to walk to the Pavilion for my meals. One evening, a rather substantial young man, a son of the house, came up to me from behind his desk in the office, and enquired if I would like him to show me the improvements that had been recently effected in the hotel. . . . I had not met this member of the family before, though I had known his father and mother all my life. As he took me round, I noticed how marked a personality he possessed ; moreover, in spite of an appearance entirely opposed to the conception of him as a sleek young foreigner in a tail-coat, he was so much the smart young hotel director that it scarcely rang true, and made it seem as though he were giving an interpretation of the part. . . . The next time I saw him he was playing in Komisarjevsky's production of *The Cherry Orchard* : for this was Charles Laughton, soon to be a world celebrity, and a man whose delightful qualities of mind and humour I was to come to appreciate so intensely in a few years' time. He and his wife — whose character and wit matched his own, and were embodied in an outward aspect full of charm, and as unlike that of anyone else as was her individual style in clothes and conversation — used to stay at Ravello every winter, for several years running, while I was a mile or so away, downhill, at Amalfi. . . . Often I wondered why it was that these seas, so different from those of the East Riding, made this equally intense appeal both to him and me ; as formerly they had to my godfather Lord Grimthorpe, whose family had come from Whitby, near by. . . . Perhaps this coast, with its mountains and caves and buttresses, its waterfalls and groves of orange and lemon protected by walls of rocks, its idyllic woods of chestnut trees, every branch covered with feathery lichen, its blue skies and mountainous clouds, and the long sweeping shore sacred to pagan divinities, may have realised some ideal formed in childish years. Certainly Charles Laughton, like myself, found here some attraction that he could not define or resist. . . . If the landscape had a fault, it was that the ruins of its ancient towers and castles and Saracenic palaces rendered it a little dead, a little morbid ; but the spectacle of Charles and Elsa, with her flaming red hair, and their friend John Armstrong, the painter, who often accompanied them, climbing up the rocks and among the crenellated grey walls like goats and, however tired, triumphing with a worthy ardour over every obstacle, added as much to the liveliness of it as did their talk of an evening.

At the time of which I am writing, however, Charles Laughton, though doubtless somewhere in the hotel, was a child of three, and we are still watching the Boer War veterans, just returned after victory long delayed, arriving outside the station, and forming up with their bands, preparatory to a march round the town. There is a tremendous feeling of excitement in the air, at that moment, before the voices of brass and parchment break out, loud in their rejoicing. . . . In the evening, too, we were allowed to sit up and watch the fireworks, which blossomed into stars and fiery splinters in front of our balcony — for we had now been installed, just above the Spa, in a separate establishment. My father could no longer bear the sound of children in the same house, not even of Sacheverell, who was so young, and of whom he was particularly fond. . . . And so his illness much affected our lives, cutting us off for a time from family influences.

All this while, in the new house, my mind was more than ever occupied with the struggle I have described earlier in this chapter ; my lone tussle with the idea of a conventional hell. Perhaps nervous attacks are infectious ; I have often in after years thought that they were catching, and have on two occasions developed insomnia and nervous anguish after going to see friends who were ill with it. Certainly I now betrayed symptoms of intense neurasthenia. It was caused by the first emergence in my life of a recurrent and apparently insoluble problem, a species of problem that holds within itself a kind of fascination, similar to that exercised by a recurrent decimal, because the mind — at any rate my mind — cannot let go of it, and this prolonged grappling, not to be terminated at will, with one particular question, presents the greatest possibilities for self-torture. . . . After all, if the Christian religion was true, then hell existed ; and if hell existed, as it was so elaborately and even exultantly described in various passages in the Bible, and if I was as wicked as I was frequently told I was by my mentors, then I ought to take the whole matter with the utmost seriousness. . . . Yet none of those round me — except my Aunt Florence — seemed to be excessively worried about it. Alas, the more I thought of it, the worse became the torments of my nights, and the worse, in consequence, my conduct, willy-nilly, the following day. I was treated continually to a review of my sins, my temper and selfishness — and could not, and did not want to, explain my difficulties.

Before many months had gone by, we were living in my grandmother's house, Wood End, which she had prepared for my father and given him. (He had already moved out.) It became one of our two homes for many years ; a singular, oblong house, built in 1820 of orange-yellow stone, in what I believe was known as the Incised Bœotian Style. In the middle of it was an enormous conservatory, the roof of which had continually to be raised to allow room for a palm-tree, then some thirty feet in height, and said to be one of the tallest in England. . . . To me, the house had always something rather evil about it, and I was often frightened there at night. . . . My bedroom was cut off from the main body of the house by the conservatory, through which you had to pass to reach the library — which had been built by my father on the model of the library at Renishaw, some twenty years before — and then climb up a small staircase to the room over it. I was so nervous at times, and felt so distant and alone, that I often used to creep quietly out of bed at ten or eleven, and stand in my night-clothes on this staircase I have mentioned, so as to hear the companionable sound of the voices in the room downstairs, in which it was customary for our governess and tutor to sit after dinner. Usually I could not hear what they said, and I certainly did not want to ; I heard enough of their talk in the daytime. But on one occasion I, in fact, overheard what they were saying, when they were discussing my father and his illness without much apparent sympathy, and remarking how extraordinary it was to have a nervous breakdown just because you could not get your own way in everything. . . . I was amazed at this revelation of their feelings, for neither of them had ever committed themselves, in front of me, to any personal opinion of my parents, and so I concluded that they had formed none. I was so intensely surprised, that I was no longer afraid of being caught and was still there when they opened the door and found me, as they naturally thought, eavesdropping.

In those days, I suppose, I was really devoted to my father, and possessed great faith in him and his wisdom. As I have said, he played for this and the following year or two a rather indirect part in our lives, affecting us more by the atmosphere induced by his illness than by the little we saw of him. But it was, notwithstanding, he who rescued me from my purgatory of religious fear. One day, when he happened to feel better, he sent for me and took me out for a drive. We had not met for some weeks, and though he was so ill himself, he noticed, directly he saw me, that something had gone wrong, and contrived to persuade me to tell him my secret agony. And I have always been grateful to him for the triumphantly clever and subtly imaginative manner in which he dealt with it. He realised at once that it would be no good to enter upon long theological discussions with a small boy, and that the whole matter must be tackled from a different angle and with a different point of view. On the other hand, it would not do to dismiss the matter too lightly. So he said, in serious tones, " My dear boy, if you go to hell, you'll certainly find all the people you most admire there already — Wellington, Nelson and the Black Prince —, and they'll discover a way of getting you out of it soon enough ! "

This answer completely disposed of my childish terrors, and every night I would think of my favourite heroes organising the powers of hell, disciplining their ranks, and in the course of eternity recalling them — if only in a moderate form — to virtue.

In the first years of my father's illness, my mother, as I have said in the previous chapter, would only sometimes accompany him abroad. More usually, she would remain in London ; for Gosden, which, for the space of my father's absence abroad during the winter and spring months, became for that period our home, bored her profoundly. As it was only an hour away from London, near Guildford, she continually promised, however, to come down and remain with us for a week or two. Day after day I looked forward confidently to her arrival, and would drive into the country town to buy tuberoses or gardenias or lilies with which to welcome her, only to find, when I returned to the house, that in my absence a telegram had come announcing that she had again been obliged to postpone her visit. . . . At the time I was consumed with jealousy, though now I can so well understand the disinclination to join us that she felt.

Of a superstitious but not of a religious bent, every year she was growing more impatient of the frieze of clergymen, and their smug-faced, pug-faced satellites, that stretched from the neighbouring villages, past the geese on the commons, and up the drive, to the door. Though herself charitable and kind in an impulsive and disorganised way, she hated the regularity of the kindness here, the prayers, the sympathy, spoken or unspoken, the Bible-reading and reading aloud of " good " books. . . . This last infliction, certainly, does not at first sound seem of too severe an order, but was otherwise than it appears. If anyone in the house said that he — or more probably she — had been reading, my Aunt Florence at once enquired, in a voice meekly vibrating with virtue and kindness, whether it was " a good book or a funny book ", for " good " was used extrinsically and not intrinsically, being applied here to no literary virtue. . . . But even had " good " maintained its fortunately more general significance in this connection, it would, indeed, in no way have mollified my

mother. Her criterion was of a different order. She read one
novel after another, reading them at night, and sometimes in
the morning instead of playing patience. She would obtain
them from Mudie's, whither occasionally she would go in
person, to demand from her favourite attendant literary
advice, asking what novel he could recommend, and always
further enquiring, " Is it just out ? " or " Is it new ? ", as
though a book were liable to grow stale after the manner of
a cake, or, indeed, go bad like fish. . . . Sometimes, too, she
would add, " But are you *sure* I haven't read it before ? "
And herein, I think, is to be found the essence of her previous
questions ; the books were much the same in plot and dialogue
and title, and she read them late at night and so, after they
were finished, could remember little of them and their contents. Only, perhaps, as she read them a second time, a faint
disturbing echo would arise from the page.

As for " reading aloud ", she disliked the whole conception
of it, which to her held a suggestion of priggishness and
" showing off ". . . . But above all, it was the order and
painstaking routine of Gosden that she hated, the absence of
extravagance in ways or in thinking, the prevailing ambience
of virtue, the humour, as opposed to savagery, of the little
jokes, the cleverness and caution of the well-founded good
works ; for my mother's charities, like her processes of thought,
welled up from the blood and the heart, and came not from the
brain. This perpetual *effort* to do good, all the mass of detail
connected with it, all the calculations and little plans, were
repugnant to her pagan and pleasure-loving soul. She preferred to stay in London, go to trivial musical comedies, with
their sun-bonnet tunes and shrill gay voices, or to concerts
at which she could soak herself in the overwhelming and sensual
genius of Wagner, or to the opera where she would be sure to
enjoy the melodies of Puccini, full of the leaves of palm-trees,
lying motionless on the southern air, of the scent of orange-
blossom, sure to be moved by the catch, laden with a sense oi
grief and expectancy, in the warm, southern voice of the tenor.

I think there can never have been a place better organised
and better run than Gosden, but, throughout the house, albeit
there were grooms and gardeners, butler and footmen, the
feminine principle reigned supreme. And every woman in
every room was fully occupied for every moment of the day

in setting or following an example — sometimes, as with Leckly, in doing both. The Christian resignation on each face was visible, nearly palpable, indeed. Upstairs, Louisa, the sewing-maid, toiled at her oily machine hour after hour, and the housemaids in their print dresses went most quietly and methodically about their work. With the aid of her fifty years' experience and the prestige attaching to it, Leckly kept a far from indulgent eye upon the inmates, their comings and their goings. And over all their activities dwelt the shadow of Stepmother Church, in her black mantle.

No one was permitted to be idle for an instant. . . . Thus my Aunt Florence's Journal for June 1901, when she had reached the age of forty-four, has the enlightening entry, headed " Daily Occupations ", which follows : " Tea brought me at seven, dressing and reading quietly, then Bessie to do my hair while I read good book to her. Then breakfast, about ten minutes to nine ; letters and papers, and afterwards family prayers. From quarter to ten to ten-fifteen, I practise, and after that water the flowers, tidy newspapers, see Mother again, and perhaps read her a chapter of that delightful new book on The Revelation. Later a walk, and most probably visit and read to dear old Mrs. Ralph (except for her, I have done no poor visiting lately and must get some more in). Then journal, account-books, little lists, typewriting for Mother, any letters, or notes or necessary seeing to things, and, just now, a regular reading in English History. Luncheon at one-fifteen and afterwards change into nicer dress, and drive with Mother or Aunt Mary. I am also trying to get a short time after luncheon for reading something *nice*, like Tennyson's Life, but that depends on circumstances. At tea we usually have visitors ; this afternoon we had Lady Legard and a friend from Cairo whose name I did not catch, and Miss Fosse and her friend Miss Crew, the latter a charming person, enthusiastic about flowers. About six, put out my painting things and sketch till time to dress for dinner at seven-thirty. After dinner, except when Ida is here, reading aloud. My *Twentieth Century New Testament* has arrived and I find it quite difficult to stop reading it. . . . Last Saturday night with the Gypsies,¹ and church three times on Sunday." . . . Let me

¹ " With the Gypsies ", which sounds so debonair and raggle-taggle-O !, refers to her endeavours, mentioned in the last chapter of the first volume, to

now copy my aunt's example in summarising the activities of the day. Already, in a previous chapter, the sounds of the morning during those long waking hours before being called have been described. . . . At half-past eight, Edith and I came down to breakfast in the dining-room, and no sooner was it over, no sooner was the swinging, burnished, still faintly purring coffee-machine with its aromatic plume of steam, removed, and the remains of fish, eggs, kidneys, scones, together with the glass jars of quince jelly and marmalade — at which preserves, even in her old age, Wilkinson excelled —, than a complete metamorphosis took place. As the chairs were drawn away from the table, and arranged in a line with their backs to the windows by Frank the butler, and an insubordinate young footman named George (who was supposed to have "come under Henry Moat's influence", and whose pagan and irrepressible temperament provided a continual source of worry to the Zenana), the early-morning gaiety of a religious household faded suddenly off every dining-room face. Frank left the room, shut the door and then, almost at once, but with a mask of piety now clamped down over his former expression of service, ceremoniously threw the door open again, holding it wide with his arm. At this, the Samoyede dogs, asleep in front of the fire, immediately awoke, rose and marched out in a marked manner, as though to say " We know we are only brutes without souls ", and the servants, after an instant's pause, entered in single file, marshalled in strictest order of precedence, led by the veteran Leckly, with something of the air of an abbess, something of that of a witch, her knotty hands clasped together, her mauve lips mumbling half-formed intonings or incantations. Next came Wilkinson, a good-natured nun, hobbling and slow, and then the girls, seeming well-drilled as a *corps de ballet*, as, at a word of pious command, they moved their chairs back and revolved round, falling lightly upon their knees. At another word, they rose, wheeled round, sat for a while, sank down again for prayer, then up once more, round and out. It must have been particularly difficult to execute all this business with conventionally downcast eyes, for, during these several exercises, they must at all costs never so much as bestow a single glance upon the men,

" help " some Gypsies — the Symes — by giving them religious instruction. They lived in caravans upon the neighbouring commons.

who wound up the procession, Frank coming last and shutting the door upon the secular world beyond. Only he, of all the members of the male sex here gathered together, seemed at ease ; the rest were constrained, awkward in their movements, and, further, allowed a wild longing for escape to show in their eyes. The girls, then, who must have felt sorry for them, as for some animal caught in a net, must yet never so much as acknowledge the presence of these intruders into a feminine sanctuary : it must have been far from easy, but the effect was convincing.

My grandmother presided. Sometimes, it might be, a visiting star clergyman, acclaimed the previous year by the hot tents of Keswick, would be persuaded to give a turn, or sometimes a furry-faced deaconess, stifled in black, would be allowed to read a prayer : but, as a rule, my Aunt Florence was made to conduct the whole ceremony because it was felt that the effort and exertion of it " brought her out ". As she read, her voice developed a note of Christian entreaty, as of angels wrestling with men, that was often both touching and persuasive, though sometimes its meekness, as when obliged by the gloomy nature of the prophet Isaiah to declaim of lions and eagles or engage in immense threats and denunciations, extended beyond humility into the region of the absurd.

Now, however, the troupe was prancing out again, and the sights and sounds of an English spring once more banished the precepts and example of Ancient Judaea — for it was always spring here, or seemed to be, even in the winter. Nor was it the frozen spring of snowdrops, virginal, green-veined flowers of ice, with all the winter's brittle, hidden fragrance in their breath, but of violet and anemone, of many-eyed polyanthus, of all stippled and striped and dotted spring flowers like fritillary and grape-hyacinth, of coral-petalled *Pyrus japonica*, and of those branches with soft, furry, animal buds that children carry to church on Palm Sunday. The light, too, donned at morning and evening a golden coat of mist, warm tigrine, different from the cold-eyed light of the north to which I was used, and at midday the air was balmy, the sun strong enough to make each dappled flower seem to blossom under its own prismatic halo of rays. Nor can this impression of spring climate be altogether due to youth and the lapse of time, for looking again at my Aunt Florence's diary for these years I find it full of such entries as this — which well exemplifies, in addition, that curious twist of which she so often shows herself the master : " April 20th. Weather now exquisite, and fine enough for me to sit on the branch of a tree and read George Adam Smith's book on Isaiah, lent by kind old Mrs. Dibdin."

In the morning, after prayers, there were lessons with Miss King-Church : but even lessons here — for we were staying away, and so need not follow, it was felt, the exact schoolroom routine of ordinary times — were less disagreeable than at home. We were encouraged to go out more and my grandmother had planned, we knew, a treat for us almost every afternoon. Moreover there were some lessons that I came near to enjoying : English history, with its crowned and bearded kings striding with their long legs from legendary mists towards the beacon of present progress inaugurated by Queen Victoria ; or geography — so long as it was not represented, in a frenetic attempt to " make it attractive " to children, by arrangements of flags, barred and striped and starred in the most hideous manner ; a sort of foretaste, I can see now, of those horrible little flags, stuck on pins and dug into war maps, that seem to have haunted the whole span of my life so far. . . . Still more, I liked being taught elementary French from books with coloured plates that illustrated life upon an Alsatian farm, and showed the whole existence of red-roofed, black-and-white-walled farms, and of the cows, pigs, sheep, turkeys, guinea-fowl and hens. These came to possess for me a singular reality. I could feel the hot, sweet breath of the cows, the soft wool of the sheep ; I could touch the prim, chequered neatness of the guinea-fowls. Most of all, I marvelled at the storks flying from their nest on a neighbouring steeple, and wondered why they should never come to the farms here.

After these hours were over — and how long the airy vistas of the morning then seemed — our governess would conduct Edith and me for a long walk. In this county, we owned no land, and I learnt here to trespass, instead of being continually trespassed against. Sweet were its joys, the excitements of snatching kingcups with their super-glazed, rich yellow chalices from the marsh, all the time in fear lest a foot should sink into the squelching ground, and still more terrified of the harsh voice of authority ; even the bluebells, in reality not nearly so lovely or profuse as those which grow at Renishaw, and the lords-and-ladies, with the Lincoln-green hoods transparent in the deep yellow light of spring, acquired a fresh value if grabbed from under the unseeing eyes of old Mr. Eastwood's keepers. No one, we felt sure — and Miss King-Church, whom we so much loved and revered, finally agreed with us — no one, *could* mind our taking just a few simple wild flowers ; and we were, accordingly, much hurt and surprised when one day we were seen and chased out of the woods by an old man shouting " No trespassers '*ere* ! " . . . After that, for a considerable period, I used to feel very uncomfortable when the word " trespass " occurred in the Morning Service, which I was here compelled to attend every Sunday. It was, then, with a peculiar transport of righteous feeling that I loudly reiterated the passage from the Lord's Prayer which runs " As we forgive them that trespass against us. . . ."

Sometimes, again, Miss King-Church would take us to continue the building of a house of twigs in a copse in the grounds. Here, to the singing of regiments of birds engaged on similar tasks, we spun, of our useless ingenuity, a house, the symbol of an instinct now demoded. The weather inside this grove seemed always to be grey and soft and cloudy — I suppose because we only went there when our governess did not wish us to go too far away, thinking there might be rain —, the trees were coming into leaf, but still were bare enough for us to follow their flimsy tracery, and through the middle, under the shadows of the twigs that, if the sun struggled through, lay like a crackle upon the surface of the ground, flowed a little stream. The damp earth near it was covered with starry clumps of primroses and anemones, only their heads showing out of the thick golden-green moss — indeed, every stone in this countryside, whether it rolled or not, seemed to gather rich velvet moss and feathery lichen, grey and green and orange and silver. But our governess would not bring us to this spot as often as we should have liked, indeed would only conduct us here in the morning or early afternoon, for she did not altogether care for it ; a smell reached us at this particular point from a distant tannery, embowered in inappropriate, Watteau-like mists of yellow- and pink-stalked osier, and she was apt, furthermore, to see a bearded tramp, watching us — or her — from over a distant hedge with an expression that clearly manifested too much interest in us and our affairs. When this occurred, however, she congratulated herself that there was no need for alarm ; she knew how to treat it, paid no attention, and talked in a loud matter-of-fact voice. Indeed Edith and I never saw this vagabond, and only the sudden and peculiar alteration in our governess's tone when she spoke made us aware at times of his presence. One morning, withal, in earnest of his existence, I remember that we found a broken, discarded and infinitely old boot lying among the primroses ; a sort of foretaste of the assorted beauties of surrealism.

Generally, when we returned to the house, I had time before luncheon to escape for a quarter of an hour or so to the kitchen-garden, to have a chat with Williams. And at this particular moment I would find him in a very good mood, for he would just have finished his dinner. . . . It was not that he talked much, or as fascinatingly as Ernest de Taeye, nor was he as original in his quiet modes of thought, but he also was versed in the ways of nature, human, animal and floral, and could, as it were, feel the pulse of all green things. He possessed, too, a sort of rustic steadiness and calm, as do so many gardeners ; for theirs is a profession which combines the best qualities both of those dedicated to the arts and of those engaged in manual labour. If it is difficult for a croupier or a pander to take an agreeable view of human endeavour, so, in the same way, it is not easy for a gardener to be anything but benevolent ; his activities never harm anyone, contain no trace of worldly — as apart from professional — ambition, and often he can obtain esthetic satisfaction from them as well. Moreover, Williams had an enchanting voice, with a burr to it, and, further, expecting my visit, he would nearly always have by him a marvel of some kind to show me, a freak blossom, some vegetable curiosity, a new plant in the hothouse, or some morels that a friend had found growing under a beech-tree a few miles away ; this last would most surely lead to an enjoyable discussion concerning edible fungi (for, in the manner of all small boys, I loved best, next to asking questions, a discussion, — so long as it was not of too abstract an order — concerning things about which I knew nothing). And at any rate I was able to compare the morels with the blue-stalks that grow at Renishaw and were not found here ; lovely fawn-coloured toadstools, shaped like a mandarin's umbrella, with amethystine interior linings, as full of colour as if their pleatings had been dyed in Tyrian purple — and an exact transposition into different terms of that other Derbyshire speciality, bluejohn. Sometimes he would grow almost angry as he extolled, in counter-attack, the merits of the brown and crumbly fungus of which he had constituted himself champion.

These arguments took place in the potting-shed ; the morels, done up in a red-and-yellow bandana, lay on a shelf near by. From nails on the wall great golden beards of bast rippled down to the floor, and the atmosphere seemed to contain in it the very secret of green growth, the very germ of life, a scent of sacking and bulbs and earth and warmth. . . . Now, he would take me to see the violets in their frames, Parma violets, and great heads of purple, white, magenta, mauve, blue, brick-red and almost pink, which resembled large sweets glowing behind their misty panes of glass. Along the borders of the bisecting paths in the kitchen-garden anemone and daffodil and narcissus were out, and cascades of purple and mauve aubrietia poured in a sort of luminous suburban frenzy over walls and paving-stones. . . . But I must get back to the house for luncheon : I had to run, and even then was reproved for the untidiness of my hair and the earthiness of my fingers — which must in some way, I began to think, have been infectious, for I had touched nothing. . . . And I went through luncheon experiencing the usual small boy's sense of grievance about the dirt of his hands.

After luncheon came a rest. . . . But this enforced period of quiet was not as obnoxious at Gosden as elsewhere, for my grandmother herself voluntarily sought a similar period of repose, and one could see that she looked forward to it, so that Edith and I did not feel in the same way that life was cheating us. No doubt we tired the old lady, and no doubt she was fretting herself about my father's condition ; he was still so far from his usual self, she knew, prostrated by illness, and so far away, in Italy. After the pattern of all good mothers, she worried about his health almost perpetually from the time of his birth in 1860 until her own death in 1911 cut short her opportunity of indulging, at any rate in this world, in this particular form of self-torture. But, further, she seems to have been able to inspire in her sisters the same concern. Thus Lady Hanmer — my Aunt Puss — gives in a diary the following slight but comforting glimpse of herself in a day more ample than the present, together with a hint of that preoccupation which all five sisters shared.

" *Scarborough. January 10, 1878.* My cold and cough still troublesome. Felt much better in the evening after roast partridge, scalloped oysters, apple pudding and mulled claret. Heard of Mrs. Smith's end — how peaceful and happy ! She repeated the hymn ' Safe on the Other Side '. George Sitwell a cause of grave anxiety to us because of his delicate health and frail constitution. . . ."

Yet I copied out this entry in the autumn of 1942, and my father, though he must have undergone considerable hardships as an alien in an enemy country, that lacked food and supplies even for its own people, still survived. He had outlived by several decades his contemporaries, Sir Willoughby Patterne and Sir Austen Feverel, had been a baronet for over eighty years, and Lord of the Manor of Eckington for a longer period than any of his predecessors since the Conquest. In the neighbourhood of Renishaw, though of late years he had spent so little time here, he had become an almost legendary figure, so that the miners and countrymen of the district, perhaps with some dim memory stirring in the furthest, darkest recesses of their minds, of Prester John or of the Old Man of the Mountains, would refer to him, with a jerk of the thumb from the plains below, as " *T' Owd Mun a' Top o' Hill* ".

For years and years and years, however, my grandmother and her sisters continued to distress themselves about his health ; long before he had ever been ill, indeed. . . . No doubt, even now, when she lay resting upstairs in the dwindling golden hours of winter, when each day sheds a few moments, letting them fall down into the darkness as a tree sheds its leaves, or during the spring afternoons, when the hours, together with the whole plan of Nature, begin to expand like a flower, she would be thinking of him and his delicacy of constitution. This time, she must have reflected, he was seriously ill, and at the same age as that at which his father had been attacked by his fatal illness. Something in his expression, since his nervous breakdown had begun, reminded her often of Sir Reresby ; and when she had commented on this resemblance, my mother had asked her afterwards rather crossly not to say that sort of thing, as it " only makes George worse ". All the same, she could not help wondering darkly, behind the coating of religious resignation in which she encased herself, whether her son, too, might not be following his father to an early grave. . . . You could not judge by looks. It was true that he stood over six foot, and looked so strong and healthy, with his fair colouring ; but that meant nothing. And it seemed so sad his being so far off. . . . She longed to be able to help him.

Though these, and other sad thoughts, allowed her no repose, they were not the only things that made her weary. No doubt the organising activities of the morning had exhausted her : but, further, I could not but sometimes think that she was taking refuge in her room from the mirror held up to herself by the continued pious parodying of her by my Aunt Florence — not that they were the least alike to look at, but my aunt regarded the same things in the same way, only that the vision had become distorted ; while, too, the inflections in the voice, the ways of saying things, the things said, were identical, yet with an infinite difference dividing them.

At any rate, in order to obtain this period of calm, she would tell my aunt to go and rest, would abandon her favourite reigning clergymen — there were two of them, Mr. Bartlett and Canon Groucher — and even her heart's young friend, Mr. Alan Gramble, who, though not ordained, ranked by appearance, by the very glands of his nature, the very hair of his eyebrows, as a curate. He was short and broad in build — if such a term may be used of it, and his eyes of a disproportionate blue glared uneasily, though with a disconcerting sweetness, from a pale face to which a heavy, creeping moustache conspired to give a semblance of heartiness : notwithstanding, the whole effect indubitably recalled that of one of those nameless things that haunt dimly the dark upper air of mediocre English parish churches, or of a countenance hastily improvised out of cheese-cloth at a séance. Tweeds, references to a pipe — though never a sight of it, for this my grandmother forbade even to him —, and talk of Oxford, introduced into his conversation a man-of-the-world theme ; but it was known that in reality he regarded himself as one of O'Shaughnessy's secret super-Dreamers-of-Dreams, and he was supposed to be at work on some demonstration, too remarkable for him to be able to explain it, of this faculty. But this effort never reached fruition, for two or three years later, his glands insisted, and he took Holy Orders : an occasion I well remember, for it provided the entire household at Gosden with the excuse for a prolonged non-alcoholic bacchanal. From basement to attic sounded praise and rejoicing, and a distant tintinnabulation, as of Salvation Army tambourines. Moreover, the event was fixed in my mind by a tragic sequel : for shortly after — in 1906 —, poor Mr. Gramble, in order to cope with the parochial work deputed to him (he had obtained a curacy not far away), learnt to ride a bicycle. Alas, his experiment coincided in time — and, as it proved, in space — with one conducted by his vicar, who, also with an extension of activity in view, was learning to drive a motor. But the elder man had not yet mastered the machine, and one day, meeting Mr. Gramble in the drive, near the lych-gate, in an effort to put on the brakes, instead accelerated, and ran over and killed poor Mr. Gramble. . . . But this was in the future : for the present he was alive, excruciatingly kind and depthlessly charitable, doing good by effort and in the open. . . . " I hate these goody-goody young men of your grandmother's," my mother used to say to me during her brief, all too infrequent, visits from London, and would then give, immediately afterwards, a brilliant moment-ary impersonation of Mr. Gramble as, with hands clasped, he implored the old lady "Mayn't I, oh, *mayn't I*, go and read a *little* of *Pilgrim's Progress* to dear old Mrs. Brown this afternoon ? . . . She is not strong enough yet for *serious* reading."

Nevertheless, and in spite of her worries and fatigue, I suspect that during her rest my grandmother encouraged her mind to dwell on ideas and prospects that were pleasant to it — and chief of these, no doubt, would be the summer excursion to the Keswick Convention. On this pilgrimage she was always accompanied by my Aunt Florence, Mr. Bartlett and Canon Groucher. Mr. Bartlett, a fiery and martyred widower, was the rector of a neighbouring parish, and a habitual of the house. His lean and inspired form displayed an ascetic energy and power that were unusual, his sermons were those of a man impelled to speak, and glowed with feeling, so that on his calves the eye of faith could already descry the voluptuous curve of the episcopal gaiter. His rival in my grandmother's affections, the douce but humble Canon Groucher, on the other hand, was making his way through no spectacular gifts, but by the observation of a greasily rolling eye, coupled with an immense capacity for mischief-making and an infinite patience in devising and declaiming impromptu prayers, flat as a pancake and with no leaven in them of other-world. He, too, my grandmother felt sure, "would go far". (And in the end he did — but not in the direction she meant.)

These, then, were her companions at Keswick; and now I must again make a quotation from my Aunt Florence's Journal to give the atmosphere of this earthly instalment of the Low Church Heaven: "*Sunday: 21 July.* Reached Keswick yesterday via Darlington very hot and tired. Mr. Higgins has also arrived, coming from Italy, and Mr. Bartlett and Canon Groucher; so we are five again in the same dear little house. Mother has brought George the footman (we hope it may do him good, he may be drawn in without knowing), but no maid. We were out this morning at seven for prayer, and then a meeting in the tent. (This year there are two tents.) Mr. Inward spoke exceedingly well on the Lowering of Moral Tone by Fiction of the present day, and the spiritual witnessing of God that should take its place. A Thunderstorm later. . . . *Monday: 22nd.* Special prayers for Ireland and India. A most excellent address by Mr. Griffith Thomas on the 'I must' 'ye must' in St. John's Gospel, and a splendid Bible reading afterwards on 'Ye are a chosen generation', and a delightful little talk, rather than an address, by Mr. Evan Hopkins. . . . *Wednesday: 31st.* Back again after a wonderful, beautiful, helpful time at Keswick. I hope we may all walk worthily of God's blessing. . . . Keswick seems to me, and I think to Mother, a little bit like Heaven. It reminds one of the early chapters of the Acts of the Apostles; the enthusiastic crowds, eager for divine things, with one heart, one soul, and the beautiful, thrilling singing of the great hymns. One special meeting stands out in my mind, Mr. Webb-Peploe's earnest and stirring words about Ittai's devotion to his earthly king, and then after the meeting, the soft chanting of 'Anywhere with Jesus', and the invitation to all to stand who could truly give themselves up to follow. . . . Intensely interested by dear old Lord Rocheby, who seemed to have grown much older and more weary-looking since he saw us last. He has taken up with a Roman ecclesiastic, Bishop Miraglio, who has been excommunicated for indulging in certain practices, and who came to the Convention too."

Such were the joys, and such the company, to which my grandmother and aunt aspired. And the discerning may already have deduced from my aunt's words that the artificial paradise which the two ladies created for themselves by prayer was one wherein Catholics — or " Romans " as they were termed — were far from welcome, unless they had contrived to get themselves anathematised. . . . And circumstances from time to time occurred to make this feeling still stronger. For example, during one of my mother's fleeting and infrequent visits to Gosden, I remember that she brought with her for a few days' country air a friend, a woman of her own age whom she had known since childhood. Camilla, as she was named, was exquisitely pretty and elegant and, though a Catholic, seemed to live only for things of this world. My grandmother, I think, always disapproved of her guest's frivolity, but something now occurred to render her yet more uneasy concerning the possibility of any ultimate reclamation. Camilla, on the Saturday afternoon of which I speak, had gone into Guildford to make her confession. My grandmother guarded her own views about such observances, but still, she had to admit that they were of a religious order, however much mistaken, so it was better to say nothing. . . . Besides, the child was a friend of Ida's, and still young. But, before leaving the house herself to go for an expedition to Guildford — where, incidentally, while she was doing some shopping, the carriage was to wait outside the Roman Catholic church for Camilla so that they could drive back together — my grandmother took up a piece of paper with some jottings on it, under the impression that it was a " little list " prepared for her by my Aunt Florence, and put it in her bag.

It was not until she was well on her drive that she thought she had better take it out, so as to plan how to fit her various tasks into one short afternoon. . . . Alas, she had read it before she realised what it was : a list of the sins Camilla had lately committed, and of which she was, at that very moment, being shriven ! . . . The worst of it was that my grandmother, now fully conscious of the moral serpent she was harbouring, made aware by, as it might be, the direct intervention of her own schismatic deity, of the kind of life Camilla was leading, could yet enter no protest. . . . All she could do was to hand the list back, and say, " I think you have forgotten something, child." . . . And, as the old lady said to herself rather grimly, she longed to *help* the poor soul. To think ANY ENGLISH LADY should regard these things so lightly in her own mind as to leave a list of them in the hall, for the servants to read ! . . . The drive back to Gosden, during which the list was returned to Camilla, can have been far from comfortable, because, in spite of these wishes to help her, my grandmother could hardly bring herself to look at her guest, far less to speak to her. She sat there nodding her head, in a cold, rhythmic shudder of disapprobation. Later Canon Groucher and Mr. Gramble were in constant session with her. In the evening the doctor had to be sent for, and prescribed rest. She should try not to take so much out of herself, he said.

Even without such shocks, which rendered it a necessity, my grandmother liked to have a time for repose, in which to recall the joys of the last Keswick pilgrimage, and to dwell on the possibilities of the next. And if she were willing, in order to obtain this period of peaceful meditation, to forfeit the company of those she loved, still less reluctantly, I imagine, did she part for a while from the tireless, effortless conversation of my Aunt Mary, Lady Osborn. . . . Aunt Mary was, for some reason best known to herself, *determined* to stay at Gosden every year for long periods, two or three months at a time, and my grandmother, with her highly developed family feeling and sense of duty, did not like to refuse her sister-in-law. . . . Of course there was a certain small patch of tribal ground, as it were, on which for a time they could meet, to talk with mutual pleasure. For instance news would come of the preferment of Randall Davidson — whose wife, though so much younger, was a first cousin of my Aunt Mary's — and this would delight both of them equally. I had not yet made the acquaintance of the Davidsons, but in years to come, in spite of the dissimilarity of our interests, they always treated my sister and myself with marked kindness. And, even at this time, I, for my part, regarded them with favour ; for the reason that I will give. Looking back, it seems as though, until his ultimate preferment to the archiepiscopal throne, in February 1903, never a week went by except that my grand-mother or great-aunt received a letter from some other member of the family, containing the information that Davidson had been offered another see — that of London, for example. And this caused a glow of excitement throughout the pious household and even warmed schoolroom walls, so that Edith and I would be offered some special treat, being read to by Miss King-Church, instead of having lessons — some chapter, perhaps, from *She* by Rider Haggard, or from *The Jungle Book* (for which we did not care nearly so much) — an extra chocolate or two, or being taken for a drive. And though it is true that two or three days later another letter would come, explaining that the information had been incorrect, merely an untimely expression of family enthusiasm, or that on grounds of ill-health Randall Davidson had declined the offer, yet the cheerfulness caused by the first good news always exceeded in intensity the feeling of dullness caused by the ensuing disappointment. After all, we could not very well be docked of a chocolate, or be forced to stay indoors and do lessons, because the news had proved false.

Apart, though, from subjects such as the Davidsons, my grandmother and great-aunt had not very much in common. . . . And though I seldom observed between them evidences of open friction, I learnt later that during the course of an evening, and long after I had gone to bed, terrible crises were wont in an instant to arise over the question of whether my Aunt Mary should or should not have a second glass of rum and water. It was true that the rum was hardly perceptible in it, but my grandmother, who never drank alcohol except as a medicine, regarded a second glass as an excessive, while my great-aunt considered it as a minimum, demand. Lady Osborn was very old now, and in every direction gentle and inclined to give way ; but on this one point she was ready to go to the furthest extremes, and although to us she babbled in infantile fashion of Balmoral during her childhood, notwith-standing, when these storms in a grog-glass arose, she used, apparently, language of such biblical strength, forthrightness or originality as on each fresh occasion to take my grand-mother aback.

I have sometimes wondered whether Aunt Mary did not

come to Gosden simply in order to keep an eye on us children.
I think, in her own mind, she very unfairly condemned my
grandmother as too unworldly to be trusted with the super-
vising of a child's education : for to the older woman *education*
signified being brought up to use the right shibboleths, wear
the right clothes, ride in the proper way and hold your riding-
crop correctly. It was impossible to exaggerate the importance
of these things — and my mother would have agreed with her
in this view. To pronounce *girl* as *gurl*, or to wear patent-
leather pumps, for example, at breakfast — either of these
would have constituted a sin far worse than any purely moral
misdemeanour. She liked to take us aside, when my grandmother was not in the vicinity, and examine us herself in the
Things That Mattered, asking one to repeat the word *waistcoat*
(wescot) after her, and urging upon us the necessity of saying
Mama, and not *Mummy*. (In any case, we said neither, but
Mother.) Partly, of course, this concern with superficialities
arose from a feeling for elegance — and she was, indeed, in
her own way, a very elegant old woman, both in appearance
and manner ; partly, since herself had no sons or daughters,
from a wish to see that the younger members of her own
family continued in the way they should go. Because to her,
as to everyone interested in them, the shibboleths of her own
generation seemed immutable, framed to endure for ever, and
she never guessed that the *haut ton* of one age inevitably
becomes the shabby vulgarism of the next, or that old fashions
descend, until, for instance, only the dealers in rags and bones
or the mutes at a funeral will wear the top-hat, once England's
glory. . . . But even when she disapproved our ways, yet she
championed us ; if anyone complained of the noise we made
overhead, running about and shouting, she would always say
commendingly, "Dear little feet, poor young people !" On
the other hand, when contemporary cousins of ours, on my
grandmother's side of the family, came to stay, she was the
first to register an energetic protest against any single sound
that happened to reach her. She and my mother got on well
together, enjoyed a common detestation of Mr. Gramble,
and were in league against him. . . . But her favourite, her
greatest friend, and perhaps the real attraction to her in this
house, was Toby, my grandmother's pet monkey.

Toby lived in a large, comfortable cage that filled the

whole back of a little room on the ground floor, behind the staircase. This capering creature appealed to my grandmother, no doubt, because he seemed, as it were, part of a traveller's tale, and she had throughout her life longed to follow the example of her father and journey to distant parts, but Germany and Italy had always bounded her world, and she had never been able to gratify this inclination. . . . To my Aunt Mary, however, who had been brought up, both at Renishaw and in the Highlands, with many strange pets, wild cats and eagles and red deer, the monkey was simply a most fascinating and friendly animal. Indeed, she seemed as devoted to him as my grandmother was to Mr. Alan Gramble. They would gaze at each other through the bars with, as it appeared, the uttermost admiration. Certainly they were very unlike in appearance.

From this distance I cannot accurately name Toby's species, but he was young, large, dark, bright-eyed and blinking ; hirsute, but not hirsute enough. His most striking physical feature was the pouch, between chin and throat, with which Nature had equipped him, so that he might therein deposit anything he wished to hide or swallow. He was very active, but only at times, when he would be seized by bouts of paroxysmal energy ; during other long periods he would remain meditative as Buddha, and, one would hazard from his expression, dejected. . . . My Aunt Mary, on the other hand, was very pale, and, albeit her eyes of harebell blue blinked fondly back at his, her hair was sparse and white, except for a tail, darker and more thick, which lay coiled at the back, just under the cap that crowned her head in the now obsolete fashion of the women of her era. For the rest, she wore a black silk dress, gold-rimmed spectacles, and round her neck hung a long gold chain, on which was suspended a gold locket containing a miniature of her late husband. In her hand she carried a reticule, wherein, among other treasures, reposed, I recollect, a small gold vinaigrette ; a very pretty object of French workmanship, made to ward off the vapours of her Byronic youth.

Every morning Aunt Mary visited Toby, either after or during family prayers ; from which, in order, I think, to assert her independence, she liked to absent herself. (My grandmother could not fail to notice and disapprove such truancy, but would find it difficult to make any remonstrance.) For half an hour at a time the old lady would stand in front of the cage, watching the monkey's antics or strange quietude. At intervals she would offer him morsels of food, fruit or nuts, repeating to herself " Poor boy, poor little feller ! " And once a day for many months, and at whatever hour it might be that she came to see him, he would throw a brick out of his cage, and she, muttering terms of endearment, would pick it up, and return it to him. She was " training " him, she told me. . . . But eventually it became plain that he, looking through the bars into what must have seemed to him her larger cage, had, on the contrary, been intent during the whole of this period on training her.

To give an account of this episode, we must go back to the mainspring of the day, family prayers. . . . On the mornings upon which Lady Osborn was not present, those gathered together could often hear, through my Aunt Florence's twitterings concerning the prophets, the screech and chatter of the ape as he talked to his visitor. It was as though he were trying to extol and exemplify in the face of orthodox Christianity the rival current doctrine of the Origin of Species. Thus while, for example, my Aunt Florence read to us verses describing the conduct of Adam and Eve in the Garden of Eden, the ape, our more ancient and sure ancestor, was vulgarly demonstrating, by his almost human outcry, the obvious falsity of so pretentious a family tree. . . . But one morning, when we were on our knees, and while my Aunt Florence was reading, in her humble and meek voice, a prayer for Peace in Our Time, suddenly we heard a scream so loud issuing, it seemed, from some antique world of tragedy, that it made her break off in the middle of the sentence. . . . There was an instant's formidable silence, and then my grandmother's voice broke in firmly, with the words, " Florence, you and Mr. Gramble had better accompany me, and we will see what has happened." Accordingly, they hurried out, while we picked ourselves up and furtively dusted our knees.

What *had* happened was this. When the monkey had thrown out the brick as usual, my Aunt Mary had as usual bent to pick it up for him. In this instant he had swooped down from his swing, and with the deftness and agility of a trained acrobat and pickpocket in one, as well as with the hardened throat of a salamander, he had thrust a simian hand through the bars and snatched from her in a single grab, cap, coiled hair, spectacles, gold chain, gold locket and reticule, and had triumphantly swallowed the lot, relegating this strange miscellany of objects to his pouch. Thus, in a flash, he deprived the poor old lady both of conventional appearance and personal history. It was a final disillusionment concerning — I nearly wrote human nature. . . . Actually, however, the sentimental loss of the locket may not have affected her as much as you might imagine, for her understanding, owing to her great age, was variable : sometimes she remembered, sometimes not. And only a few days before this occurrence, she had shown the miniature of the whiskered head inside it to her younger sister, Blanche, at the same time demanding to be told whose likeness it might represent.

" It's your husband, Mary dearest."

" Nonsense," the old lady replied ; " I never married that man ! Never ! I don't know the face. . . .", and she snapped the locket to, in a fury.

After her loss, she had to go into retirement for a little, the while new hair and a new cap were secured for her. She became, too, more regular in her attendance at family prayers. As for my grandmother, she felt, I apprehend, that Mary had at last learned her lesson. . . . At the same time, it had been a shock ; so she sent for the doctor again, who told her she must rest more often and for a longer time. Mr. Bartlett and Canon Groucher were once more called in to offer her spiritual healing and remained closeted with her for considerable periods. One result, therefore, was that she accompanied us less frequently on the excursions she had planned for the afternoons.

At quarter- or half-past two, when our siesta was over, a message would come to say that " her Ladyship was resting " and would take us out another day. . . . So we would start with Miss King-Church, and roll in the carriage down the deep flower-scented lanes, towards some church — Old Compton, perhaps, with its chapel and its house, where the aged Watts still continued to cover null canvases with a green-grey mist, born of old masters in course of decomposition, and vaguely constituted of beauty and virtue in conjunction —, or in the opposite direction of Albury, with its blue lakes, or else we

would drive along the Pilgrims' Way to visit one of the
churches built of white chalk, with many little crosses, carefully cut, and scooped out at the ends, and glittering white
as though the pilgrims had carved them but yesterday upon
the robust Norman pillars. More than anything, these crosses
carried one back to a legendary period, beyond the Harrison
Ainsworth world of turrets and jesters and fountains, to an
age when great kings spoke noble words and the cross was a
blazing, living reality to be scorched upon the forehead of
the infidel. It seems, indeed, as though the history of his race
lives in the blood of every intelligent small boy, so instinctively
can he grasp — if he is allowed to — the atmosphere and
feeling of past epochs in his own country. . . . At other times,
our outings would be shorter and more business-like. We
would take the road, its every feature so familiar to us, from
Gosden to Guildford, some three miles away. At first, vistas
of common land extended on either side, and then the country
altered, the road passing through narrowing cliffs — in particular there was one precipitous wall, in the crumbling rock
of which sand-martins nested, whirling in and out, and diving
and swooping —, until we approached the broken bastion and
gates of the castle, up above the road, on its hill. In the town
itself, we would leave the carriage near the bridge at the
bottom of the steep hill, and climb slowly up it on foot,
admiring the old red-brick houses that lined the chief street,
and executing various errands for my grandmother, buying
oranges, leaving books and flowers upon the sick, obtaining
special biscuits for the Samoyedes, or going to call for fish
at a shop that seems, as I look back, to have been enjoying
perpetually a miraculous draught of lemon-sole. Then we
would return for tea and, when the house had been shut up,
we would be taken to see my grandmother in the Indian
Room, which lay beyond the Smoking Room at the furthest
extent of the house.

The Indian Room, half private sitting-room and half
drawing-room, — (the official drawing-room was a pretty
room downstairs, with a large bay window) — was by far
the biggest and lightest apartment in the house. By the magic
of her personality, however, my grandmother had insinuated
into the minds of her friends and relations the idea that her
consenting to take the room for her own especial use formed

a typical instance of Christian unselfishness and of living for others. Here, after tea, she would repose on a sofa between curtained windows, as I have described her in the first volume, with a fur rug across her legs, and the Samoyede dogs, one on each side of her, in the manner of the lions on either hand of a Byzantine sovereign. As you entered, a piano, with a pianola attached to it, faced you. . . . It was a fine rectangular room, into the width of which her sofa jutted out at a slight angle, with its back to the four or five large windows ; a room with a lofty ceiling, painted mauve, and walls lined with Indian hangings, scarlet monkeys disporting themselves among the spatulate leaves of palm-trees, upon a white ground. Against them, Burmese figures rippled their sweet hips of sandal and cedar wood, and on the tables and the piano — for nothing must be left naked, except, by some freak of taste and outlook, these posturing oriental images — Indian draperies swept down to the ground, winking their thousand wicked eyes of looking-glass. On the table in the centre, and on the smaller one by my grandmother's side, stood orchids, stove plants with foliage that might have set the pattern for all the flags of the South American republics, and cactuses that seemed to be a surprisingly accurate realisation of the improbable plates in the copies of the *Botanical Magazine* next door (where Mr. Gramble, with all possible parade, was smoking his pipe) ; squat, fleshy creations with patches of iridescent colour and with thick, pulpy, serrated leaves, that gave one the idea that an octopus must have been changed into a plant, as Daphne into her tree. In the evening, by electric light, carefully shaded, and with the fire flickering in the thousand mirror eyes, the room with its white background appeared to glow and glitter. There always seemed to be fine weather, and a full moon then, and one window was often left uncovered, to show it, flowering like a magnolia in its white radiance against the dark and glossy-leaved sky. And my grandmother would lie there, talking to us of my father, "The Dear Invalid", as she called him, or sometimes telling us a ghost story ; of how, for example, she had heard Mrs. Barnardiston, who had died in about 1750, tapping down the passages of her old home at Weston, in high-heeled shoes and with the black cane that she was known always to have carried.

We were alone at present ; only my Aunt Florence was in

attendance. Lady Osborn remained in her own sitting-room, and Mr. Gramble continued in manly seclusion, because Mrs. Frampton-Stanwyck was expected to pay a call, and he refused to meet — or, rather, ostentatiously made excuses for not meeting — this middle-aged Bacchante from the York-shire Wolds, who had somehow or other danced away from her home and brought up near here. Often, accompanied by a nurse as dazzlingly jolly as herself, she would drive over in a dog-cart to see us, and roll her red eyes at us terrifyingly over her untasted tea. But my grandmother was most human in her attitudes of favouritism ; it was almost impossible for those of whom she was fond to do wrong. Thus, because for some reason or other she liked this visitor, she would hear nothing against her, and were anyone, even the beloved Mr. Gramble, to mention the rollicking creature with even a hint of disparagement latent in the sound of his voice, my grand-mother would shake her head grimly and pronounce, in tones that brooked no contradiction,

" Mrs. Frampton-Stanwyck has had a very hard life and the East Wind Inflames Her Eyes."

If my grandmother's explanation were true, then Mrs. Frampton-Stanwyck's nurse must have possessed eyes sensitive too to this particular affliction. . . . But, in reality, it was nothing so harsh as Boreas raging across polar seas that affected them, but the very essence of the sunlit south, " the true, the blushful Hippocrene ", only somehow it was their eyes, and not their mouths, that had become in consequence " purple-stainèd ". Yet they were allowed to come over to Gosden whenever they liked, there perhaps to rout with their deep-throated laughter a whole bevy of pale-eyed curates, in the same fashion that invading satyrs might put to flight a timid band of nymphs.

Mrs. Frampton-Stanwyck ranked to us children as a treat, a strange treat, an unusual treat — but then, many of the treats with which my grandmother provided us were unusual. Thus, from time to time she promised us that if we were good, and got on well with our lessons, she would take us to see and hear a new pianola, worked by electricity, which belonged to a rich brewer who lived near by. . . . And here, again, my grandmother showed her delightful character, richly veined with contradictions, for she used to go to luncheon with him, in spite of her great prejudice against " the liquor trade ", as she called it. There were, she knew, " stories about him ". But, she used to add, " I have seen no sign of IT. . . . Probably IT is only scandal." What precisely IT portended, we never found out — perhaps only more Mrs. Frampton-Stanwyck-trouble, for I heard her say that he offered people his own beer for tea : but I fear that the vagueness of the reference veiled nameless orgies. . . . The pianola was, however, apparently a wonderful machine, the trills and roulades it offered being something that no mere mortal could be expected to produce, but only the elemental force of electricity. . . . It was, therefore, a great disappointment to Edith and myself that this particular treat never came to pass, for, as will be seen in a moment, we were interested in pianolas.

Sometimes, again, she would promise us a glimpse of a human musical prodigy, who lived near by. He was said to be a genius, to be able to play " all Chopin by heart " at the age of sixteen, while his " finger-work ", his mother had confided to my grandmother, was " already the envy of that poor Paderewski ". And he hardly used the pedal *at all*, we were told — as an instance, I suppose, of his scrupulous fairness, for, if you used the pedal, you could do anything : it counted as cheating. This treat, too, then, eluded us. . . . On the other hand, we were often allowed to drive past the walls of the domain of Whitaker Wright, whose recent exploits as an embezzler, and whose taking of poison in the dock, had immensely impressed our young minds. There was not much to see, it was true, but the papers were full of the hidden luxury of his establishment, and the huge expenditure of other people's money that had called it into being. We could just discern — or thought we could — the dappled clouds of deer shadowing, as they passed, wind-swift as clouds, the unrivalled turf, but, though we could catch, too, the silver glint of the lake he had made, we had to construct for ourselves, out of our imagination, the vast, richly furnished billiard-room he was said to have conjured, rather than built, beneath it. . . . Then there were the nursery gardens at Godalming, to which we were permitted to drive from time to time. Here were lines of long narrow hothouses, filled in mid-winter with row after row of Edwardian magnates' buttonholes ; red and crimson carnations that seemed already in their fragrance to hold a hint of the aroma of cedar-wood boxes and cigar-smoke which was to be their ultimate destiny. Other houses were filled with bouquets, in various stages of growth, for the magnates' wives ; malmaisons, rich and deep in their pink shade as the flesh of salmon trout, or pale with a peculiar, glossy and yet powdered paleness. . . . And finally, there were some knobbly old Elizabethan mansions, full of priests' hiding-holes and corners in which Charles I or II had lurked for a night, and where, on our best behaviour, we would be given tea by kind, grey-haired hostesses.

It must not be thought that all our treats were equally one-sided. No ; encouraged by Miss King-Church, Edith and I used, for our part, to think out treats for my grandmother. . . . Suddenly dashing into the Indian Room when she did not expect it, and was suffering a little from her weak heart, we would recite dramatically, and in unison, the whole of " The Absent-minded Beggar " or a large part of " The Revenge ". And occasionally — but this was a very, very great treat — we would sing. . . . Edith, indeed, had started a career of, as it were, healing and singing combined at an early age ; for when she was four, she had broken into my grandmother Londesborough's bedroom, and had begun in a rich if youthful voice the hymn " We plough the fields and scatter " — for even then the idea of the harvest filled her mind with delight. When my grandmother had tried to stop her by appealing to her pity, saying, " Poor Grannie has a very bad headache this morning ", " Then Edith will sing and make it better," the child had replied doggedly, and the old lady had been obliged to submit. . . . As for myself, I had been in no wise behind Edith, though my medium was different. I was an entertainer of a lighter order, content to sing the nigger songs and music-hall songs of the time, with great verve, accompanying myself on the bones. A letter, for example, written by my grandmother Londesborough to Edith, and dated Good Friday, 1899 — when I was six — says : " Aunt Mildred is better but by no means well yet and has to lie on a sofa all day long. Poor Granpapa has had the gout. . . . Give Osbert my love, and say I wish he would come and amuse the poor patients by singing and dancing to them." . . . Of course, this had been some time before, but it will be seen that we were fully equipped in our own opinion to afford this sort of pleasure.

My grandmother Sitwell never openly opposed our ventures of this kind, but congratulated and kissed us. All the same, it was not long before she let our governess know that these treats must not take place too often, because they were over-exciting for her, in her declining state of health, and that they must never occur in the morning. . . . For during that part of the day, she would lie on her sofa in the Indian Room for hours together conducting, as I have said, in her beautifully-formed hand her amazing correspondence. Just as the Indian Room, and its very name, had no doubt been inspired by the most august example at Osborne, so the letters that my grandmother wrote from it, like those of the former Queen-Empress, traversed the world, reached many distant points in the Empire and even influenced others outside it ; there were letters to the Missions in the South Seas and Malay, letters to India, letters to her cousin, the Governor-General of Cape Colony, orders for lilies from Japan, for a kind of china made near Nice, for fruit from South Africa, and endless letters to endless relatives in England and abroad. In addition there was a reply to Sister Adelaide about the Rescue Home at Scarborough, another to one of the girls' mothers — who had written in a most regrettable tone — and letters to the Archdeacon, and clergy and curates of all kinds.

Now, however, after tea, and if there were no visitors to whom she had to attend, we were allowed to interrupt her as much as we liked, so long as we did not recite too often or tease the dogs. She set herself to charm us. Nor, I think, did anyone ever bring more gifts to the art of enchantment. Her voice, her smile, delicate and resigned as that of a Luini — indeed she resembled a painting by him, or sometimes, because of the shape of her mouth and eyes, by Perugino —, her patience, and the sweet dignity of her bearing made her particularly winning if she wished it. . . . At such moments I would forget that she feared I was growing selfish, that she did not really *like* my mother (I could feel this, though she never allowed a trace of it to appear on the surface), and had designs upon the new pocket-knife, with its eight blades, of which I was so proud, but with which she was convinced that I should do someone — probably myself — an injury :

but I would remember it all again on Sunday, when a black fog of piety diffused itself throughout the house, when I was obliged to attend church and when, after church, the tempers became the short, frayed tempers of regular church-goers.

It is of week-days, though, and of evenings that I write. The fire flickers warmly and my grandmother is giving us chocolates, kept specially for us in a box by her side on the table. She tells us to give one also to Thelma, her favourite Samoyede, now growing old, a sleepy bundle of white fur : (the other, beyond the sofa, a one-eyed brigand of a dog, remains in deep disgrace, for he has been out hunting for three days and three nights after the manner of his particular breed, and has only just returned). My Aunt Florence sits quietly in a far corner of the room, at a table on which stands an electric lamp that brings out the bright gold of her unfading hair. She is busy with her water-colours, in an attempt to portray some very feminine-looking sailing-ships, heading as fast as they can for a lighthouse. This sketch seems, looking back, to have shocked no one — but, of course, we were still then in the pre-Freudian epoch.

As a special treat, both for my grandmother and ourselves, Edith and I were allowed to play the pianola for a quarter of an hour at a time, while Miss King-Church, holding her watch in her hand, acted as umpire so as to save disputes. This instrument offered in happy combination the joys of melody and of bicycling — even the roll of music with its thick, oleaginous paper covered with cabbalistic designs of holes and streaks and dashes cut in it, even the tiny screech that the end of it gave as one tightened the roll up before inserting it in the machine, come back to me, as I write, with their old sense of delight. And indeed my performance upon this pianola constituted a great improvement upon my former experiences as an executant musician. . . . These had occurred at Scarborough when I was about five. Edith, who had always loved music, had then decided, on her own initiative and out of the abundant generosity of her soul, to share the joy herself found in it by teaching me, too, to play the piano. Her idea had been, I conceive, that no one should know of the lessons she was giving me until I had obtained a perfect mastery of my means of expression, when I would suddenly blaze out of obscurity to dazzle the world with my accomplishment. It may be, perhaps, that her own qualifications — she was ten — were not then sufficient to furnish me with the entire art. I do not know. But unfortunately the whole house had only too quickly become aware that something was afoot, for even my rendering of the five-finger exercises was so intensely original as to attract, and so loud as to command, universal attention. Added to this, my sobs, my roars, my howls — for I much resented art being thus thrust upon me — formed a painful and resounding accompaniment. As a result, the opinion of the household was unanimous : my lessons must cease, *il faut en finir*.

No. I much preferred the pianola. I listened with pleasure, though with some sense of impatience, while Edith was performing, and, when at last it came to my turn, pedalled away indefatigably, at great speed and clinging, as it were, to the handle-bars. I was fond, too, of using the brakes, for abrupt modulations of tone, from the loudest possible to the softest, were the technical device at which I excelled and wherein I believed the whole secret of my art to consist. And I had found my audience : for though Edith may have disdained the efforts of her rival virtuoso, Sacheverell, who was himself too young to play, listened to us both with a flattering air of respect and, even, of rapture. . . . And in all truth, these hours were memorable to the three of us, for it was therein, and after this fashion, that we first entered the magic world of Tchaikowsky's ballet music, the greatest music of the theatre — as opposed to opera, or to music pure — ever composed, thus that we came to know every note of *Casse-Noisette*, so much of *Swan Lake* and *The Sleeping Princess*.

The loveliness of these works wears no mask or disguise, so that it is singular that the full distinction of it as theatrical music was not comprehended by those who should have appreciated it : it was so pretty, as well as so beautiful, that often it was contemptuously dismissed by those who pride themselves upon the possession of taste. It was so then — and it was so twenty-five years later, when, in a burst of home-sickness for the St. Petersburg of the 'nineties, Diaghilew produced the full version of *The Sleeping Princess*, with parts of the orchestration re-scored by Stravinsky, and with the programme carrying a preface by that great composer, while the décor and costumes constituted the last and most sumptuous of all the productions of Léon Bakst. . . . At the end of the first night — of which I shall have more to say in a later volume — a literary critic, often of discernment, completely disconcerted on this occasion by something to which he was not used, and of which, as it were, the nails were so clean, and the edges so orderly and defined, rushed up to me, and demanded what I thought of it. And when I replied that I considered it the greatest theatrical production I had seen, this good-tempered, intelligent being cried out in a sudden furious anguish, " You are only saying it to *épater* us again." . . . In fact, his response to this production was precisely the same, albeit inverted, as that of the old leader of the Parisian fashionable world, of whom Jean Cocteau tells us, when she was faced with the first performance [1] of Stravinsky's *Le Sacre du Printemps*, with choreography by Nijinsky : " Let us re-enter the auditorium in the Avenue Montaigne, where they wait for the conductor to rap on his music-stand, and for the curtain to go up on one of the noblest events in the annals of art. . . . The audience plays the part assigned to it : it at once rebels. People laugh, hiss, imitate the cries of beasts. The uproar degenerates into a riot. Standing upright in her box, her tiara knocked sideways, the old Countess de Pourtalès brandishes her fan and, scarlet in the face, shouts, ' In sixty years, this is the first time that anyone has dared to make fun of me ! ' . . . The good lady was sincere : she believed it to be a hoax." [2]

Thus Madame de Pourtalès's rage against something new and beautiful which she did not understand, was identical, in the sheep's terror which gave it birth, with that of the English intellectual at something old and beautiful which he had not expected. The audience was as shocked and astonished by this lovely performance of *The Sleeping Princess*, as, let us say, would be a Chinese gourmet, who only ate eggs a century old, at being requested to eat a fresh egg, or a contemporary designer of half-timbered garages in concrete and synthetic wood when confronted for the first time with the architectural system of Blenheim Palace. It had to be withdrawn after the shortest of runs. . . . Yet the music of it alone, one might

[1] This took place in May 1913 at the Théâtre des Champs-Elysées in Paris.
[2] Translated by the present writer from *Le Rappel à l'Ordre* (" Le Coq et l'Arlequin "). (Librairie Stock, Paris, 1926.)

have thought, would have overcome such fashionable resistance to beauty.

It realises histrionic emotion and spectacular effect in a manner that transforms the theatre into the sole genuine fact in a vast world of illusion. Yet, for all the enticing and dulcet prettiness of the airs, they are never merely trivial, never too sweet. Whole series of melodies, one after the other, possess the running loveliness of the names of plants or herbs or flowers :

> . . . eglantine,
> Columbine, celandine,
> Wolfsbane and oxbane,
> Sainfoin and fluellin,
> Wortdragon, snapdragon,
> Martagon, campion,
> Tarragon, rampion,
> Rocambole, pompion,

or still more, the names of Muses and Graces and Nymphs and Nereids that the people of this age retain for the use of the lesser constellations, for though the earth has long lost the old religion, it remains in the heavens enthroned ; such names, I mean, to take them at random, as Ceres, Pallas, Vesta, Hebe, Eunomia, Melpomene, Thalia, Proserpine, Euterpe, Atalanta, Ariadne, Nisa, Calypso, Pandora, Melite, Mnemosyne, Echo, Ausonia, Cybele, Hesperia, Panope, Clyte, Galatea, Eurydice, Antiope and Camilla.

Similarly, these airs are to that identical degree nostalgic and haunted, waking within the hearts of those who listen echoes that lie at a great depth. Nevertheless, they have the very rhythm of life itself, immortalising the everyday feelings of humanity, yet at the same time are strange to us as the music of the ten thousand bells hung on the eaves, successive and aspiring but diminishing in scale, of some Chinese pagoda, its angular outlines ruffled by a wind we have never known, a wind that has risen among orchards of peach-trees and orange-trees embowering the gentle slopes of innermost mountains, and has then swept over the warm illimitable stretches of rice-fields, shining like mirrors, or turning to the shrillest green, vivid as a bird-call, and has lingered round whole towns made of porcelain that float upon water as dragons float upon clouds. But the strangeness has been domesticated, the exotic has been tamed, and builds itself in the middle of the bitterest winter snows, in huge palaces of glass, where the only bells that sound are those of sleighs and of churches crowned with towers that resemble bulbs about to germinate, or of the painted cars that sweep up and down the slopes of Montagnes Russes. The waltzes lie in wait for him who first hears them, and introduce him to a world of peach-skin and of dewy cobweb elegance ; they have not been made, as have Johann Strauss's, for the rather boisterous boots of the Viennese, but for the delicate feet of spectres, whose flesh proves, contradictorily, to be more warm than that of human beings. More essentially still, this music belongs to the thought and atmosphere of children ; it has in it the flashing colours and dissolving patterns of the kaleidoscope, the beauty of flowers seen very close, and their scent, while through the orchestration it is possible to hear the bears marching out of their fairy stories into reality, to hear the wolves and strange beasts as they prowl, and the puppets dangling and jangling upon their wires.

> When we come to that dark house,
> Never sound of wave shall rouse
> The bird that sings within the blood
> Of those who sleep in that deep wood :
> For in that house the shadows now
> Seem cast by some dark unknown bough.
> The gardener plays his old bagpipe
> To make the melons' gold seeds ripe ;
> The music swoons with a sad sound —
> " Keep, my lad, to the good safe ground !
> For once, long since, there was a felon
> With guineas gold as the seeds of a melon.
> And he would sail for a far strand
> To seek a waking, clearer land, —
> A land whose name is only heard
> In the strange singing of a bird." [1]

Even as rendered by the pianola, the sound of the music, though so much of it depended upon orchestration, upon glissandos of harps like descents of angels in a ripple of white wings from the sky, or rolls of drums, sudden and effective as those of the first Turkish armies passing into Europe, was most exquisite and captivating. . . . My grandmother would lie there listening, with her tired smile playing round the corners of her mouth, and my Aunt Florence would flick the

[1] From *The Sleeping Beauty*, by Edith Sitwell.

paper in front of her nervously with a paint-brush ; occasionally the Samoyedes, in their arctic slumber, stirred and grunted
like bears. The flowers seemed richer in their hues, the glow
of the fire to take on an extra brilliance and shimmer and
warmth. . . . Yet in a way this music belonged to Renishaw
more than to this house, for its beauty had a sad and indefinable
shadow to it.

Book Four

The Happiest Time of One's Life

Chapter One
THE HAPPIEST TIME OF ONE'S LIFE

Wᴵᵀʜ an insuperable repugnance I face, in writing about it, the prospect of going to school for a second time. As I am thus obliged to concentrate my mind upon it, the sensation amounts almost to physical nausea, to the feeling of being lost, isolated, of waking up in a strange place and wondering who and where you may be, of being utterly disorientated and confused in the world of the senses, so that what you touch and see is not what your neighbours touch and see, your north is not their north, nor your south their south : a penalty which both damned and blessèd pay in their worlds eternal and equally reprobate of torment or of rapture. So bad, where I was concerned, was the atmosphere of those days, so hopeless and lonely, that it becomes almost impossible for me to write of them without seeking to protect myself by ridiculing them, just as, in the times when men believed in devils and witches, they contrived for their own comfort to mock or prettify, and thus belittle those dark powers. So did Satan decline to a tinselled figure set in a fire made of rags, up-blown on a false wind and lit by a crimson slide, at a pantomime for children, while the covens of witches, with their terrible secret practices, became quaint old figures on broomsticks, fit to be engraved on Christmas cards. In short, so strong is my aversion from contemplating these long months struck by Medusa into stone, that, though I shall attempt to describe those first terms as they appeared to a bewildered boy fresh from home, I shall nevertheless avail myself of every possible escape from school, make the fullest use of every exeat or afternoon off, in the account of it that follows no less than in real life.

How did it shape itself, the morning of that macroscian day which I had dreaded for so long ? . . . I must have been growing more and more uneasy for some weeks, and a letter of mine, written from Gosden and sent to my mother in London a week or ten days before my new life was to begin, reflects this anxiety, shows a wish, for example, to reassure myself with the fact that I had learned the names at least, if not the natures, of some of those who were to be my companions for the next few years, and by repeating that some members of my family knew some members of theirs, to humanise them for myself. This letter, in which the handwriting and spelling are noticeably better than in those penned a few months later from school, runs :

GOSDEN HOUSE, BRAMLEY, GUILDFORD
14 Jan. 1903

DARLING MOTHER,

I hope you enjoyed the Hunt Ball. . . . A woman came to see Grannie yesterday, her boys are at Bloodsworth, their name is Eastwood. I kicked about my football in my football boots yesterday.—Yr loving son, OSBERT.

Curiously, the sensation itself, the approach of the day itself, has faded. . . . I see in my bedroom, for a week or so beforehand, that terrible play-box (how ironical a name !) of white wood, with — painted on it, plainly and immensely in black — as if it were tarred and feathered upon it — those impersonal initials F. O. S. S. I see the preparations, the fussy packing and consequent unpacking ; I hear the worried, excited voices, rather pleased but argumentative, crying, " I can't have forgotten the soap, can I ? The only thing is to see. . . . We shall have to unpack again ", or discussing the various essential items of clothing and impedimenta, figuring in the printed list issued by the authorities for the help of the parents, and classified in the cant terms of the school :

" ' One pair of Black Oxford House Shoes (elastic-sided).' . . . Well, that's plain enough. . . . I'll just pop them in the box before we forget.

" ' One pair best Bowling Trousers.' . . . Now what can they be ? . . . I wish Mr. Wolfe would be more explicit. . . . Perhaps it's these grey ones ?

THE AUTHOR *æt.* 10

THE HOUSE NEXT DOOR (BARLBOROUGH HALL)

" ' One Land-and-Water.' Oh dear, what can that be ?

" ' One strong Umbrella.' . . . That's simple enough.

" ' One pair Association Football Boots (no steel caps).'
. . . That's so that the boys shan't hurt one another."

And so forth. . . . I see, too, the badges of my degradation,
the hideous garb laid out ; and the things intended to compensate one for it in the imagination, the supplies of oranges,
biscuits, Suchard chocolate in slabs, — all, again, purchased
strictly in accordance with rules laid down in the encyclical.
. . . Then I remember nothing more, until the afternoon of
the day itself, when I found myself somehow or other in my
mother's sitting-room in a hotel in London, and an elegant,
perhaps rather cynical friend of hers — a rich young man,
who was a sybarite, and possessed his own hansom-cab, both
horse and vehicle polished from head to foot, and driven by
a personification of every smart hansom-cab driver of the time,
with a hoarse voice, and a red, smiling face, a top-hat, and
a red carnation in his buttonhole, — was pressing a sovereign
into my hand. As he accomplished this conventional act
of tipping a schoolboy, he also, however, gave me a piece of
unconventional advice for which I have always been grateful
to him. " Don't believe what everyone tells you, that school
is the happiest time of your life. Or you'll be miserable. It
isn't. You'll hate every moment of it."

Then follows a lapse, again, until my mother and I were
getting into the train that afternoon. . . . Outside the carriage,
on the platform, in the immense blue fog, lit by gas-jets
like yellow tulips, that piled itself up in vague clouds under
the dingy, scarcely distinguishable glass roof, she recognised the
father of another boy who was also being conducted to the
same place for the first time. This chance meeting was a
comfort to her, for she knew him, and he was a friend of my
uncle, and so in her mind ranked with the elect. But it in
no way soothed my alarm, for to me the man seemed to be
unnaturally jolly, with the jolliness of a hangman on the fatal
morning. I suppose he was only trying to cheer his son up —
but it was painful. It must have been a difficult business,
too, for the parents, because, if they had not talked the whole
time, a laden silence would have prevailed. Between them,
as we jolted from one unknown station to another on that
cold January evening, a conversation arose, which, when not

concerned with the reputed beauties, advantages and comforts of the school to which we were travelling (the headmaster really was a *tremendous* dribbler, the stranger affirmed outright : no one in England could touch him at it), dealt with the almost prehistoric time before I had been born, a remote past when, apparently, my mother and he had often met, and one that teemed with names hitherto unheard. It seemed ridiculous to talk of a time so long ago, and I wished that my mother and I could have been alone. His presence in no way modified the barren look of the country before me, as it did for my mother, and I was almost glad when we arrived.

In the darkness, we only knew which station it was because the masters and school officials were bouncing up and down the stained, damp platforms, barking questions, and asking names. Then followed a drive through wet darkness in a rolling cab. . . . We arrived : a bright maid, in a white apron and a cap shaped like a petrified blancmange, opened the door and ushered us into the drawing-room. . . . I have never seen a room that was so essentially a drawing-room, as though upholding an ideal in a world of barbarism, in the same way that, in Somerset Maugham's story, the Resident in some tropical island always comes down to dinner in evening dress. There was white furniture, I remember, with dainty little silver vases, and bowls of copper and brass, beaten, hammered and generally tormented. These held mammoth chrysanthemums in Liberty shades, bronze, yellow and amber. The fireplace — or is it only my imagination? — had lots of white shelves above it on which to place shaggy china Aberdeen terriers, in default of the real thing, and had heart-shaped openings cut in the overhanging wood-work, here and there. . . . The headmaster's sister, a most charming woman, gave us a kind welcome : but the enormous heads of the chrysanthemums — a flower which is to all other blossoms as a moth to a butterfly, and seems to thrive on winter as carrion on offal — communicated to the air a subtle scent of camphor, comparable to that which would issue out of a cupboard wherein hang the clothes of a man who has been drowned these many years.

I do not know how long we were in the room. I could feel the talk, but no longer hear it, for I knew the moment was drawing near. My mother got up to leave, in order to catch her train back to London. . . . Suddenly she began to cry. I felt this in a thousand different ways. I could not comfort, or attempt to comfort, her in front of the other four new boys — unknown quantities — or in the restraining presence of the headmaster's sister. My mother was the only parent who cried, and I perceived that the rest of them disapproved of it. Indeed I appreciated that, had she possessed the ordinary modicum of common sense, she would not have broken down at all, and I was profoundly grateful to her for not putting herself in such a category. (Indeed, as I came to see later, this deficiency was the great merit, as well as failure, in her character and helped to make poetry possible in her children. For poetry and common sense never walk hand in hand in England ; only in China are they inseparable.) Her sobbing was something that, long after she had left, I could remember. Now the headmaster entered, to say goodbye, and it was plain that he and his sister both despised us for our softness. But, though I suppose there was never technically a bigger " cry-baby " than myself, I courageously, or more probably, obstinately, refused to weep. Dry-eyed, I faced my weeping mother. . . . Now she was at the door, had left. . . . That moment was here, that moment which, in its solemnity and terror, only death can rival. . . . The headmaster's sister turned towards the boys, and said, " Now, dears, I'll take you through into the school ".

She led the way from her comfortable, rather overcrowded room — outpost of civilisation — to a heavy red-baize door that blocked the passage . . . She opened it, and we were in a different world. The air was full of an astounding clamour, as loud with cries and yells and clatter as any madhouse in the eighteenth century. We saw a vista of bare corridors, and of class-rooms with bare floors, reformatory benches with inkstains, inkstands and iron clamps ; it was scented appropriately with the aroma of rusty iron pipes and the sour smell of ink and clothes from the lockers. Boys of various ages were milling round the rooms, shouting, screaming, singing and hitting. A calm fell, as Miss Wolfe was seen.

" Cornwallis," she cried, " act as shepherd for Sitwell."

This injunction sounded comforting in a biblical way. But no sooner had the door clanged behind her than the din started again, and I was surrounded by a mob of small boys, who bore down on me like a cloud of locusts, to devour my self-esteem. This *was* the moment ; the moment that has always, since that time, made me dread arriving in any place strange to me, mess-room or country-house, hotel or lecture-hall, hell, or heaven even. (How was it possible to learn, for example, to identify the faces glaring round me ?) Already the air resounded with heartening shouts of " Here's a new scug ". . . . The word was not familiar to me as yet, but it was plain, from the very sound of it, that its application could not be regarded as complimentary. " What's your name ? " " Your *name*, baby . . . ooo ! Who's a cry-baby ? — not your Christian name." " What's your pater ? " " I bet he's a scug like you are ! " — all this punctuated by hundreds of little kicks and pinches, token payment of what was to come in due course. As for my shepherd, he appeared to be resting from his crook. Indeed, at moments, he took a leading part in the inquisition. . . . As I looked round, and tried to answer — though one was shouted down before it was possible to say a word in reply — the terrible knowledge came to me that I hated school, loathed the boys and — though I could only finally be sure of this the next day — abominated the masters. As I looked at these heads clustered round me, to try to identify them became an obsession. I must know, I felt, the correct labels to them. It was as though I were trying to turn them for myself into individuals, instead of allowing them to remain a nameless, hydra-headed mob. I thought of this problem by day and by night, and even today, if I see some great picture by Hieronymus Bosch or by Grünewald, some canvas crowded with the contorted, anomalous shapes, writhing under their various lusts and evils, escaped from the infernal regions, or some canvas by Fra Angelico, where the devils, conventionally pink and green, are as lovable, as recognisable a part of creation, as are his lions or giraffes, even now, I at once fretfully begin to try to identify the heads of the owners of tongs, pitchforks and pincers.

The fashionable private school, then, where I was sent, and which, in a former chapter, the reader has seen my parents choosing for me, bore the reputation of being a very good school, among the best of the period. The parents felt, I believe, that so long as they had to pay a great deal of money to keep their boys there, it must be a good school.

They spared no expense. . . . There was not within these precincts, so far as I am aware, any case of lice, impetigo or of the other complaints that arise from living in dirty conditions. (I in recent years have myself seen a letter written by the headmaster of one such school, to various parents, detailing with an affectation of gusto, together with a no doubt genuine pedantry, the precise Latin name of the particular louse then roaming the heads of his charges, rather as though the fact that it possessed this nomenclature had bestowed upon it the advantages of a classical education.) Cases of severe illness were comparatively few, because small boys are tough, nor do I recollect, during the terms I was there, a single instance of an inmate dying. Of colds,[1] there was of course a continual and abundant supply — just colds in the winter, " summer " colds in the summer, and " spring " colds, I suppose, in the spring. And infectious diseases in this, as in all similar establishments, occurred with distressing frequency and regularity, formed almost a school tradition. Thus I recall that, thirty years later, when I was talking, one afternoon, of this very school to the former companion of the tree-tops at Scarborough — for one of her sons was there at the time — she exclaimed, " But you can't possibly blame the *school* just because the boys have measles, whooping-cough and scarlet fever the same term ! " — but I do. The conditions to which we were submitted would not for an instant have been tolerated in a State school. (In proof of the fact that conditions were to blame, a few years ago the school was moved to a new house and another neighbourhood, and I am told that since then it has come to deserve the reputation it has so long enjoyed.) The long line of closets, with no open doors, and only flushed once every few hours, were a typical feature of this life so revolting to civilised beings. When we had baths, only once a week, the boys, eight or nine in number, of a dormitory would have to wash their heads and bodies in the same thick, viscous, warm water. As for the minds of the boys, they were scatological, certainly, but free of any knowledge of sex. . . . The good points that they showed, such as their manners, except to other schoolboys, were due to the homes from which they came, rather than the school to which they were sent.

To give the reader an idea of it, this place could be regarded

[1] See Appendix C, p. 302.

as a miniature model prison, essentially middle-class, with all the middle-class snobbery and love of averageness, but lacking the middle-class comforts. The whole system, the meals, the ways of speech and thought were middle-class, and in this manner — for I was used to a different background — strange to me. (Yet how familiar the atmosphere has since become : it returns anew with each war, when all lightness of spirit, all beauty, all exuberance and extravagance, all the super-fluities which have made life worth living, are condemned and taboo.) Toast and marmalade for breakfast, the right of the masters but denied to the boys, was the sum and standard of all joys of the school : its continual sorrow, the heavy middle-class ennui that, at its best, enveloped it, that hopeless fog in which life's suburbs breathe. It presented me with a well-ordered and punctual system of middle-class life — for the beating and bullying were almost as much a part of the order as morning and evening prayers in the dining-room, or attendance at the church near by on Sunday.

In these hideous rooms of brick and timber and pitch-pine, Christianity became what it had been in the first instance, a slave religion, a way of escape for the downtrodden and oppressed — and none the worse, I may add, for that ! — except that now those who were responsible for the wretched-ness of the lives of these victims were no longer pagans but formed part of the hierarchy of a Christian system. The buzzing hymn-tune of the week-day — the accompaniment oᴸ which, by an amateur, seemed to be seeking for notes it could never find upon which to settle —, the strong voices of the masters seeking to guide it, no less than the flashing brass, the surplices and flowers of the Sabbath church, and its stained glass — but stained is a word in no way vivid enough to suggest the Victorian fury of colour in that glass, flayed, it seemed, and decomposing —, all these things, nevertheless, came to have significance again, were an offer of comfort to children lost in the wilderness, and of sanctuary ; ten minutes in morning and evening of a week-day, an hour and a halᴸ on Sunday, foretaste of that heaven only to be found in the sick-room. But though I cried quietly — and I hope unobtru-sively — when one or two particular hymns were sung — identifying myself a little, for example, with St. Andrew, in the verse ;

As of old St. Andrew heard it
  By the Galilean lake,
Turned from home and toil and kindred,
  Leaving all for His dear sake,

I rather enjoyed the services. And this early feeling of
approximation to St. Andrew in sainthood and suffering —
for I clearly persuaded myself that I had heard the call, had
left home of my own accord to go to school — left behind it
an abiding partiality for this saint, in no way shared, so far
as I was concerned, by his fellows. In my mind, I pictured
him, this holy fisherman, as my old friend Owston, bearded,
and clad in tarpaulins and sou'wester. And subsequently, at
Eton, it came as no surprise to me that we enjoyed a whole
holiday every year on his feast : while, much later again, I
used, with feelings of the greatest satisfaction, to observe the
fishermen of Amalfi rewarding their patron saint for a good
catch by attaching a painted tin fish or two to his stone image,
which stood above the fountain in the cool piazza, pressed in
between the torn limestone rocks, with their fragrant oases
of oranges and lemons. No doubt in former days Neptune
had stood in the same place. . . .

To return to school, however, though I grieved furtively
as these words, and certain others, were sung, it was too late
for me to suffer a religious crisis ; that had passed for ever.
Therefore, I was debarred from the enjoyment of imagining
the tortures that in due time — or should I write due eternity?
— would so rightly be inflicted on several, indeed, the majority,
of my small companions. And if the reader has seen how it
was that my belief in a conventional hell — I dare say, quite
wrongly — was dispelled, I must explain, too, that it was the
conception of heaven that I derived from reading the Book
of the Revelation according to St. John — the girdles and
crowns of gold, the glass seas and harps and harmoniums —
which convinced me that this region also would provide no
desirable residence for me — nor for anyone else. The
opulence, the abundance of opal and chrysoprase and jasper
and cedar-wood, offended my taste then, as later did their
recurrence in Oscar Wilde's *Salome*. These slabs of semi-
precious stone were too material in the beauty they offered.
The saints were content, it seemed, to cast pearls to the
starving ; better a crust now. . . . Notwithstanding, I felt

the appeal of Christianity more strongly than ever before. And the works, too, of Charles Dickens, that champion of the oppressed, though I had always loved them since I first began to read, came to have a new splendour, as well as their abiding attraction.

There was not much time, though, for reading Dickens : whereas the hymns belonged to every day. . . . As I heard the rolling, pious voices of the masters, I often wondered how they ventured to join in them. (At least Nero, though a better singer, had never taken part in Christian services.) I hated them — with one exception : the music-master, who happened to be Cecil Sharp,[1] and only visited the school at intervals. But, though I never, until long after I had left the place, realised his distinction, I did, albeit I knew him very little, observe the contrast between him, with his genial, rather red face, his vague air of a hunting-man, and his country-gentle-man's clothes, and the rest of the ushers. I came, indeed, in my own mind to identify him with the hero of the song in which, in preparation for a school concert, he would often endeavour to instruct us : " D'ye ken John Peel with his coat so gay ? " — I thought it was " gay ", but it should be " grey ". The description seemed somehow to fit him. I attributed the difference that I noticed merely to the fact that Sharp's attend-ance was only occasional ; that he was not, like the others, an inmate. . . . How I loathed them ! No doubt unjustly, I saw them, the celebrated dribbler and the rest, as so many uninterested and mentally lazy men, who tired themselves out with physical exercise, to such a degree that they were fit for little else. They would return from the football field, drenched and dripping with green sweat, panting and hollow-eyed, and with an incipient death-rattle in their knotted

---

[1] Cecil James Sharp, the son of a City merchant, was born in London on the 22nd of November 1856 and died there on the 23rd of June 1924. A leading student of English folk-song and dance, he first saw the morris performed at Headington, Oxfordshire, in 1889, and thereafter devoted his life with an extra-ordinary degree of enthusiasm to the attempted renovation and revivifying of these arts. His influence on music was considerable, and all the bumpy country tunes that rollick through English music from 1900 to 1920 are due, in the first place, to Sharp's researches. These were original, as well as extensive, in their scope, and he was particularly successful in collecting English folk-songs from the Appalachian Mountains in America. . . Sharp arranged the incidental music for Granville-Barker's production of *A Midsummer Night's Dream* at the Savoy Theatre in 1914.

throats. Naturally, they were not inclined to exert themselves again until the following afternoon, when they would play once more : even their pipes, in the masters' room, could not bring them solace. A few Latin tags, a knowledge of the more reputable parts of the Bible, an aptitude for footer and cricket — and, of course, fives ; that, they knew, was what got most gentlemen comfortably through life. But while, of course, they liked every boy to be of the same mental height, and with nothing odd, or " weird ", as they would have said, about him, yet they did not actually *want* unusual boys to be beaten to death in the dormitories, for that, too, would have been unconventional, and would interfere with the games : and so to a certain extent they exercised a watchful attitude, at first sight apparently kindly, but really very impersonal, over their charges. Nor, except for the headmaster — and he, only for flagrant offences — did they flog their pupils themselves. . . . Perhaps they were too tired.

As teachers, then, you might judge them, from what I say, to have been uninspired : but you would underrate them. They may not have been on the grand scale, but they possessed magic nevertheless ; they could, with a few words, tear every plume out of British History, and render Latin, from being a dead language, into one that plainly could never have lived. . . . Indeed, a few terms of their tuition exercised a great influence upon at least one of their pupils. Learning ceased to interest me. I could see for myself that the repute in which a boy was held in no manner depended upon it. Even if he did well in school — and I didn't —, it in no way helped his life, either while he was being educated or, apparently, afterwards. We depended, all of us, on the vagaries and idiosyncrasies of the masters. . . . I became too miserable even to try to learn. The result was that my eyes turned outwards, away from books, which were my natural play-ground, towards people. Educated in some other fashion, I should have grown up to be more concerned with historical research, less observant of the horrible and wonderful intri-cacies of human nature. Moreover my state of wretchedness, and the perpetual inquisition, " Where were you when the head beak sent for you ? ", and " Why weren't you kicking about on the football field ? ", obliged me to develop the habit of lying, and thereby forced my powers of invention.

Rudyard Kipling, describing, in his autobiography,[1] a kind of dame's school at which, at a very early age, he lived while his parents were in India, says of the ill-treatment to which he was obliged to submit there, that it made him give attention to the lies he was forced to tell, and that this he presumed to be "the foundation of literary effort". . . . Certainly it was those first months at my first school which produced in me the elements of novelist and story-teller.

The days went on, and I will not say much about them, save to select a few miseries and seek out a few pleasures. But, in order for the reader to gain a correct picture of the scene, and to seize the feeling of it, he must always bear in mind the continuity of the wretchedness, the underlying and enduring stratum of it. Being a boarding-school, this establishment offered a horrible isolation from every warm current of life that had even been lacking in the day-school my father had formerly chosen for me in Scarborough. . . . The days went on : that was the sole comfort to be pressed out of them. . . . Perhaps the end of the week was of a slightly better colour than the beginning, and Sundays had about them a tinge of their own, undeniably more pleasant than that of the others.

To begin with, one got up an hour later in the morning, and the hard-boiled eggs bore upon their shells a date more recent than was usually the case. . . . After breakfast, we lounged about a little, and everybody was in an amiable mood. Indeed, I recollect the hour before church as always being sunny, and invariably associated with flowers, because on that morning we were allowed to wear buttonholes. . . . The late Lord Digby used often to send his son, who was my contemporary, a small box of orchids from Minterne, and I recall the delight of sometimes being given one to wear, for I was already a lover of exotics, and orchids brought with them for me every sort of hothouse enchantment. I liked, whenever an opportunity offered, to walk in those tents of crystal, that exist in their own odorous climate, winter and summer. These fragments, broken off, as it were, from the Spice Islands or from some continent covered with tropical forests, and protected after this fashion with so brittle and glittering a shelter, are always beautiful to me ; albeit never more lovely than after those bitter winter nights, when, in

[1] *Something of Myself.* (Macmillan, 1937.)

the mornings, you find frozen on the panes the shapes of the foliage they shelter, the intricate pattern of leaves of fern and sensitive plant, mysteriously etched by the moisture they exhale. . . . Indeed, this process is still a wonder to me, seeming to offer its own guarantee, however often that may be denied by the folly of men and mocked by wars, hunger and aimless persecution, that life possesses a meaning. Why else should water, freezing as it runs down a sheet of glass, assume these forms of Nature, tracing in misty white the ghosts of many leaves, designs of the Creator ; what laws, as yet unknown, what immense and majestic poetry of life, with deep, internal rhythm, some of it only to be perceived in the central core of this earth, some at the very edge of a universe, ordains and governs such echoes, such paraphrases, such facts as that an empty shell for as long as it shall last seems to have gathered in its opaline cavities the sounds of all the breakers that have passed over it, or that a butterfly's wings should mirror the flowers over which they hover (protective colouring is too dull an answer and places the Creator in battle-dress — at most, it can only be a particle of the whole vast truth), or that a snow-flake, transient reproduction of a crystal, should so delicately present an identical structure ?

I am still grateful, then, to Digby and his father for the magic with which these flowers temporarily touched so dreary an existence. Schoolboys have — or had, when I was young — as their invariable possession and pride, a knife and a magnifying-glass, and when I was given one of these blossoms, I would take the magnifying-glass out of my pocket, or borrow one if I had lost it, and examine each petal of fur or velvet, and the intricate, insect-like centre, and while thus occupied would for a moment forget my surroundings as one does while listening to music. That itself was an inestimable boon, but, further, during the many months that my mother now spent abroad with my father, these tropical, warmly-coloured and dazzling flowers seemed to bring her nearer to me. . . . For example, she left England a few weeks after I first went to school, and letters from her, always difficult to read, written on queer, thin, foreign-looking paper, headed with the engraved likeness of vast hotels, embowered in palm-trees, would arrive for me. Sometimes, as I opened the envelopes, out would drop the stained, ivory rosette of a small cluster of orange-blossom, which still retained its fragrance, in spite of its long and battering journey. No doubt she had put it in the letter under some impulse of affection, or to try to make me understand what the country from which she sent it was like ; but I pictured her — she was staying at Cadenabbia, on Lake Como — surrounded by palms, tuberoses, gardenias and orchids, under an enormous dome of azure sky unflecked by a single cloud. For in my imagination, Italy, — or, indeed, any region covered by that mysterious, alluring term " abroad " — never failed to be tropical in flora and fauna.

All this, though, was a month or two in the future. . . . Sundays, I was saying, were of a pleasanter tint than other days ; they offered protection. In the mornings, you were safe in church — unless, better still, your cold proved too bad for you to go out —, and there was a walk in the afternoon, instead of games, and after tea in the winter months, and after you had written letters home, a master might read aloud a novel by Walter Scott.

I recall walking down a dripping avenue in a large park, the first Sunday, a few days after arriving at school. I see the sky again, the colour of the beech trunks ; I see the varied ground, hilly and covered still with the damp, fawn-coloured patterning of dead bracken ; the lake, by the side of which a few russet-coloured ducks shivered ; I hear again the swirling of leaves under the rain and the tattoo of the heavy drops falling from the branches upon the harder earth beneath their shelter, and I smell once more that bitter, hibernal freshness. How softly, how surely, the rain permeated human consciousness that day, until it seemed as if rain, rather than the word — or, at any rate, the word *rain* — had existed in the beginning. Every now and then a flutter of wind would send the rain down on us with a swifter flurrying rhythm, almost a syncopation, though when we reached the avenue and walked along it, under the trees, a mist prevailed. I was at the very end of the school crocodile, and beside me trudged another new boy ; a very young child, he seemed. The master, about seven vertebrae in front of us, occasionally glanced round and gave him a particular look, as if he would especially have liked to throw him to the wild beasts. Perhaps the weather damped even his energy. But I think my companion liked the weather, for he was homesick, plainly, almost audaciously homesick for some haunted Irish fastness which he had left for the first time only three or four days previously ; homesick with the frankness unabashed of a child who as yet has developed no guile and thinks no ill of his fellows, and his face was wetter than even the rain could make it. . . . Presently he stopped crying and, thrusting his hand into mine, said, " Let us be friends : let us promise ". By the prevailing code, I should, of course, have shouted, "Yah ! Cry-baby ! ", but in fact I was inexpressibly touched, though I scarcely knew how to show it. It was, again, such a friendship as might have sprung up between two early Christians in the arena : but it was not destined to prosper or endure. We were not in the same form, and we slept in different dormitories — though they were next door, and that term I could often hear the sound of his being beaten at night for being a cry-baby.

Nearly every Sunday I walked in that park, and never knew the name of it. Nobody told me, and I never asked. . . . I am not aware whether this may prove to be a common experience of schoolboys, due perhaps to the anonymity of their whole existence, or whether it is some form of specialised stupidity and obstinacy confined to myself, and due to boredom, but, just as during the autumns and winters of 1914 and 1915, when I was at the front, I seldom knew — unless we found ourselves entangled in some battle, or near some place such as Ypres — which part of the line we were occupying, so at school I never mastered the topographical essence of my place of internment. . . . In both instances, I suppose, the surroundings were so laden with bitterness for me that their whereabouts seemed scarcely to matter. . . . I knew, certainly, that the school was in Hertfordshire, near Barnet, forbidden citadel of sweets ; that we were on the edge of a forest called Hadley Wood, in which, very regularly, it seemed, the bodies of murdered women were discovered — but that was all. Beyond these fragments of knowledge, I was ignorant of the locality. Similarly, hell has a climate, but no situation. It lies in the spirit, and not in space.

It was, therefore, with a shock of the utmost surprise that, thirty years later, while passing a few days with Philip Sassoon at Trent, and living in that state of luxury, imbued with the spirit of fun, of which he was the particular master, I recognised the place. . . . What is more, I had paid him many previous visits, and had even stayed there, two decades before, during the last war, when the house had been let, and still remained precisely the same as when, while at school, I used to walk by it every Sunday ; before, that is to say, Philip had started to make a kind of paradise of it, touching it with magic, so that, where formerly had glowered a mid-Victorian mansion of mauve brick, with designs in black brick covering its face, and a roof of mauve slate, turreted and slightly frenchified, now stood an old house of rose-red brick and stone cornering long-settled and stained by time ; before, too, statues and lead sphinxes, smiling from their pedestals, and shepherds fluting under ilex groves, and orangeries and fountains and pyramids, seeming to have been rooted in the bracken for centuries, had made their appearance, and tall old trees, magnolias, and the rarest shrubs that sprung from the ground with something of the same pride with which the swans and multi-coloured water-birds displayed their plumage on the lake below. . . . During that first visit, then, when a zeppelin had startled a house-party by dropping an enormous — or as it seemed at the time, enormous — bomb in the park, I had not identified my whereabouts ; which shows that even bombs were preferable to school. Such had been the intensity of my misery, that it had apparently effected a black-out, mercifully provided an anodyne. . . . And it was only, as I say, after many subsequent visits, when one day my host took me to the wood beyond the lake to show me the great obelisk he had recently bought and removed from Wrest, causing it to be set up here, that, turning round to look at the view, something I saw suddenly coincided with a memory, and looking at the avenue beyond the water, at the edge of which now the most magnificent ducks, striped and barred and chequered, shook their finery, I saw again for the instant the small boy weeping so bitterly by my side in the winter rain. Always hitherto, in my mind's eye I had seen the park with the rain sweeping across it, whereas now, under some kind of spell, a heat-wave seemed ever to prevail within its boundaries, and innumerable flowers swooned in a perpetual hush of summer.

Every Sunday we had walked there in the afternoon, returning in time for tea, and had then to write our letters home — though these were subject to censorship by the school authorities. In a moment I will produce as witnesses two of them that I sent my mother at this time, for in spite of the presence of vigilant masters while they were being written, and in addition to the strict perusal of them which followed, it is possible from reading them to form some idea of the cold, boredom and bleakness of the winter terms. Moreover they afford certain clues to my character, as it was developing, indicate my backwardness in some respects, such as spelling, while they provide, too, evidence of my intense love for my mother, shown by patient remonstrances with her concerning her bad — indeed almost indecipherable — handwriting, and by the way I teased her about her feminine horror of rats and mice and insects, no less than by the more direct pleadings with her to come and see me.

I lived for her visits, and she, with her violent and uncontrolled nature, responded and came to see me, no doubt more often than was good for me ; in the sense that it was difficult for me to " settle down ", as the matron said, or, to put it in another fashion, to acquiesce in my own misery. I was fortunate in being her favourite child, and in thus obtaining much of the love of which my sister was deprived. And though I saw the sufferings of this young creature, it was difficult for me to realise the extent of them ; for I was privileged to the degree that she was penalised. Edith still remained in the schoolroom, and so was seldom as yet allowed to come down to see me. Her personality was too strong, her mind too imaginative, her heart too easily touched, to make her a comfortable companion for the conventional. Besides, my mother saw in her a living embodiment of some past unhappiness of her own. These and other things made her cruel — and she could be cruel. . . . Often my mother would arrive, of course, by a later train than she had named, for she was extremely unpunctual. . . . Trains were the rule, rather than motors, for these were too recent an innovation to be used as yet except by a very few, exceptionally rich, daring or go-ahead. And only one parent invariably drove down from London in her own carriage and pair. This old lady — or she seemed to me then to be old — was the wife of a Scottish chieftain, and never took the train, for she insisted on bringing her parrots with her (I do not know how she travelled from the Highlands to London and back), and the padded and buttoned interior of her barouche was full of their cages ; though sometimes, too, she would set them at liberty, and they would climb about, pecking at buttons, hanging head-downwards from hooks, swinging their gaudily feathered bodies and squabbling and screeching. . . . I looked forward to seeing this old lady arrive : the masters could not possibly approve of this display of so much personality, and, indeed, it was known that when the second master had approached the door, a white-and-yellow cockatoo had balanced on the edge of the window, and shouted very loudly " You bloody cuckoo " at him, and had then roared with laughter. . . . I liked her, I liked her parrots, and I liked her son ; he was quiet and kind and slow and humorous, and, in spite of his breeding, spoke in a delightful Scottish voice, with a run and intonation on his words that were new to me.

If my mother were late, either because she had taken the wrong train, or because the trains were delayed by fog, which seemed always to be present, I had to wait, sometimes an hour or more, in the small room in which the boys met their parents. The matron, with her white cap, tied under the chin, and her sallow complexion that seemed designed to draw attention to her curative systems, her salves and boluses, would look in from time to time, and say, with a certain acerbity coating her native kindness, for she believed in " hardening " the boys — " Fussing again, Sitwell, I suppose. You *are* an old crock ! " And then she would hurry out, because she had to dispense continually the various, but sparse and Spartan, remedies of her eighteenth-century pharmacopoeia : iron, castor oil, licorice, and Gregory powder — and, of course, there was always rhubarb, an immense shadow in the background.

Yet in spite of her remedies, the sick-rooms presented for many one welcome form of escape : they were at least warm and comfortable. I went there frequently for a rest during the terms of which I write. I do not know what was wrong with me ; simply, I think, that when my misery became too great, I developed a sort of miniature nervous breakdown. At any rate, my temperature would go up for a few days. (Later, at Eton, this gift left me, and on one occasion, when I needed a rest, I remember putting the thermometer between the bars of the fire for an instant, while m'dame's back was turned, in order to send the temperature up, and how dis-

ROOFSCAPE, RENISHAW

by John Piper

THE GOTHIC TEMPLE, RENISHAW

concerted and indeed appalled I was to find that the glass melted at once and let the mercury run out. . . . I had suddenly to cultivate an air of utter innocence — and even then the matter required considerable explanation.)

My mother coming to see me seemed to dispel or prevent these attacks. . . . I would wait with the greatest excitement in the small, dark room, and even the matron's abruptness could not depress me for long. I paced up and down, and stopped to listen intently. And sooner or later, I would hear my mother's footsteps — I did not like to open the door and look down the passage, because such a show of feeling inevitably would constitute Bad Form. At last she would come in, bringing the fragrance of tuberoses and sweet geranium, kiss me and take me for a drive. (I think that she felt, as I did, the necessity of getting right out of the place). . . . But even when she came an hour or two late, her arrival did not surprise me, for I knew beforehand when she, or my brother or sister, was coming to see me. Infallibly, invariably and without being informed of it, I became aware the previous day, and even when it appeared most unlikely, that such a visit was impending, and equally I could tell if suddenly it had to be postponed. . . . In after years when my father, who professed to despise all forms of intuition and intuitive knowledge, taxed me with being superstitious — which I denied, though acknowledging that I believed we might at times be granted certain intimations of the future — and I related to him, in order to defend myself, how, when I was at school, I had been able always to tell if anyone to whom I was particularly devoted was coming to see me, he surprised me by admitting that at school he had possessed the same gift, adding " But it dies, as one grows older ".

But now I must quote the letters I mentioned. . . . The reader will notice for himself how in the first, for my mother's comfort, I endeavour to give a favourable account of school life and, generally, to put the best possible face upon it ; though not, I apprehend, in a very convincing or convinced manner.

Feb. 15, 1903

DARLING MOTHER,

Do come and see me son it is rather fun here. It is very pretty round about. Four new boys came here as well as myselfe and the

137

K

Headmaster's Sister has arsked us to tea. I am sorry to say I am at the bottom of the school. I'm afraid Father will be dissapointted about it. Do come and see me son. When you write, do write in a rounder hand.

Did you hear about part of Cony Hatch Assylum being burnt down, it is quite near us and we could see the flames. Yesterday there was a football match, the first Elstre Eleven with colours against our second eleven without colours, and a lecture in the evening called " Some Changes in the Earth's Surface " by Mr. Brown. I suspeckt you will be surprised to see the paper I was givin to send you so creased only I have to do it to get it into the envolop. I have a lot to tell you when you come to see me. I thought you would like the present of a tame rat or mous, so I am going to send you one som time. I think this really the longest letter I have ever written to you.—Yr loving son OSBERT.

The next letter is both more critical and more imperative in its demands for the solace of material comforts :

March 8, 1903

DARLING MOTHER,

Thank you so much for your letter, but I had a little difficulty in reading it. What about the allectric lamp ? If you have not sent it, would you send me the *Sphere* insted of the *Tatler*. Granny Sitwell said something about another hamper, but I hope she wont send me any more figs, as the others were not as good as they might have been and the aples were nearly as good as the figs. Your Chocolate Cake and Barley Shugar are so good. I have just been playing Yard Footer. There was a lecture yesterday by Mr. Stanborough called Moth in Great Britain. . . . I hear it has been raining cats, dogs, cock roaches, spiders, rats, mise (the latter I'm shure you must have liked) at Gosden.—Yr. loving son OSBERT.

P.S. Since I began this letter, the eletrick lamp has come. Dont forget to tell Miss King-Church. What a bother about our having to come back on the 8th instead of the first because of Chicken Pox. Do come and see me before you go away.

Meanwhile my father, in order to help me, was sending from Italy long letters of encouragement, based on wolf-cub standards : " *Feb 3, 1903.* . . . The first lesson of life is always to keep one's temper. In the seven elections I have had at Scarborough, I learnt that a candidate who loses his temper ever so little is throwing all his chances away. In politics self-control is absolutely necessary, and so it is in diplomacy and married life. If you study the husbands and wives you know, you will find the one who keeps his or her temper settles everything. The great Russian diplomatists become more and more courteous when other people are rude to them, and the finest type of British Officer on the days when everything goes wrong is perfectly serene and unruffled. . . ."

I know the letter was written out of kindness, but I am not sure it helped me much. Affection, not advice, was what I needed.

Sunday nights were no different from ordinary nights. Long after the sounds of beating and sobbing and restless whispering had subsided, I used to lie awake, listening to the trains as they hooted and pounded along on the route for Scotland. I knew little geography, and especially, as I have explained, was I ignorant of local geography : moreover, in this unlike many small boys, I understood nothing about the main lines, and believed that this was one of the two that passed near Renishaw, and that from a train thundering along it in the daytime you would catch that glimpse of the long old house, standing, with its garden spread round it like a peacock's tail, among the groups of lofty trees on the top of the hill. From the house at night, I should also hear, I was convinced, the very same clanking of the very same train to which I lay listening now. I tried to pretend that I was back in my room, or opposite in the nursery, in bed there, so that the hooting became pleasant to me — but a boy groaned in his sleep, so that my dream was shattered. Fully awake again, I would change the scene to daylight, and think of the house as it looked in the bird-swift glance of it that the train permitted, and then I would concentrate my mind on some scene in the interior, my mother's bedroom, for instance, in the summer, with the broad, green-painted window-boxes of verbena and heliotrope, the scent floating in at the wide-open windows : but, as usual, there was, in spite of the warmth and sunlight, a huge coal fire in the grate made of Sheffield steel ; the light was reflected, both of sun and fire at a thousand different small points ; in the glittering cut-glass scent-bottles that stood on the dressing-table, with its bellying muslin crinoline, in the silver of the photograph frames, in the mirrors, and in the large pins of the pin-cushion, while the flowers in the vases shone with a feathery lustre of their own. . . . Or I was back in the schoolroom with Edith, and we were listening, open-eyed, to Miss King-Church's reading of Rider Haggard's novels, *She* or *King Solomon's Mines*. . . . What a sense of comradeship it gave to have passed through such adventures together ! . . . A bell was ringing, and I could hear Henry down below giving orders to a subordinate in the pompous voice, so hollow and important, that he reserved for big occasions. . . . I was asleep.

The raw hours of Monday morning, the first days of the week, came with a renewed shock. So did the feeling of dislike, which made itself more intensely felt, for I had early established my unpopularity. I hated games, at times liked to be alone and, beyond these, was no doubt regarded with disfavour on many other counts, but on one especially. . . . Small boys all have their pride, and so, in adverse circumstances, are obliged to build themselves a refuge. My shelter was trivial and flimsy. While other boys unashamedly collected stamps and coins and such things, I openly collected . . . *nibs* ! The discovery of a new kind — and there were many — filled me with rapture. Alas, childish idiosyncrasies of this kind at a school place those afflicted with them at a disadvantage, until they have learnt to hide them. My singular choice of a hobby rendered me, naturally enough, a booby in the eyes of my fellows, and induced even the masters to regard me with contempt. My appearance anywhere at this time was greeted with derisive howls, " Who collects nibs ? . . . Baby ! " All the matter being that I *was* something of a baby, in certain respects over-young for my age : for boys grow at different rates, mentally as physically. . . . And yet, looking back, although it seems a stupid interest to have cherished, I am forced to ask myself what I could have found that would have been more appropriate to my subsequent career ? (Similarly, what could have been more fitting to me than the usual school punishment of being kept in for the whole of the afternoon and made to copy out a hundred or two lines ? It has become my life — I am doing it at this moment.) The child was indeed father of the man. (It is as if we hear the breakers of the sea echoing for ever in the shell's ear again.) Other children collected coins — well, that too was congruous. Many have been intent on amassing them ever since. But already I, by this particular folly of mine, was dedicated to pen and ink : a fact which no one could have inferred, indeed, who at the time regarded my handwriting ; which, yet, from its very vileness may have been a little responsible for my early preoccupation with the technical apparatus of authorship, just as we have seen that later it helped to form my style. . . . To this day, echoes of these, my earliest exploits in the collecting world to which I have ever since belonged, continue occasionally to reach me. And it is not, I recollect, so many years since Siegfried Sassoon described to me how he met in a railway carriage abroad — if I am not mistaken, in Italy, though Switzerland would seem a more probable choice — one of my former masters, who had told him of my youthful weakness and treated it with ridicule. . . . This master was apparently named Mr. Brown and must have been identical with him who lectured, as a letter has just recounted, on " Some Changes in the Earth's Surface ". Well, I hope that, before adding to them, he may be able to read this *apologia*.

The last few days of the term brought with them a sense of longing so intense that each night it seemed incredible that one could continue to live, to breathe until the next morning. Even the examination at the end of the term became dear to one, as being the final obstacle interposed between school and home. Nevertheless, the last day, known as *Pay Day*, was singularly — to a new boy, surprisingly — horrible : more so, perhaps, because the name suggested something pleasant. But it transpired now that all through the term the masters had been keeping the sum of each pupil's trifling offences — untidiness, bad handwriting, answering back, laughing in class, upsetting inkpots, or flicking paper darts about in school hours. On that morning they totted them up inexorably, awarding the evil-doers so many bad marks — known technically, in the prison-jargon they encouraged, as " scug-marks ". These they made you pay off in the afternoon, by keeping you in, and at work ; a more severe punishment, when the prevalent state of excitement and, even, train-fever is taken into consideration, than it sounds at first. *At work*, I have written : but I must modify this statement by substituting the words, *by making you work as far as you were able* — since it was difficult to see out of two black eyes, or to concentrate with a head so confused. Because there was a corollary in the junior world of the system adumbrated above. The morning, while the masters were reckoning the crimes, had been left free for physical torture. Vague and rather menacing references to Pay Day during the previous few weeks by their older school-fellows had yet in no way prepared the new boys for the treat to come : they entertained no idea of what was in the wind, since their elders of every kind had been careful not to tell them. For the bigger boys had all through the term been preparing their own, and much more fanciful, scores. . . . The new boy, in the highest of spirits at the idea of returning home the next morning, his head full of friends, meals, favourite amusements — in fact, fun — would emerge from the buildings to cross the yard. Suddenly four or five bullies would bear down on him. He would find himself being led off into some quiet corner of the playing-ground, at the far edge, as it were, of the whole concentration camp, — to one of the fives courts for choice, since the enveloping configuration of them enabled the masters not to notice what was going on (if they had seen, they would have been obliged to stop it), and served also to muffle the cries. It was impossible to evade the pursuers, because they were in sufficient strength to make all struggle useless. But even at this point, while being dragged along, the poor wretch hardly grasped the full horror and pain in store for him. After a few questions such as " Do you remember cheeking my minor, a fortnight ago last Tuesday week ? ", or " Why did you sneak about that book my major borrowed ? ", and other genial enquiries of the sort, two or three boys would hold the prey while the other two, taking their turns, punched him as hard as they could on the head and face. After what appeared to be an eternity of this treatment, with no hope of an end, he would be released, with a few parting kicks and yells of " Yah ! Cry-baby ! ", and could slink back to the school with two black eyes, and a bleeding nose, and sometimes with a tooth or two missing. The boys older than himself — even the smaller ones, who had (for the ritual was by no means confined to new boys) suffered a similar fate — would openly exult at these injuries which could in no way be disguised. They would dance round, shouting, " Look at the new scug ! That serves him right. Hooray ! " As for the masters, they shared an incapacity, stronger even than usual, to tell black from white, and were resolute in noticing nothing ; though they bore on their smug faces a particular look of satisfaction, as if conscious of having set an example. The adage that " boys will be boys " shone in their dull, complacent eyes.

As for the small victim himself, he knew that the next day he must go back to his home, revealing plainly, by various contusions and discolorations, his unpopularity, the little esteem in which he was held, both by the masters — in spite of their mealy-mouthed assurances that he was " quite a popular little feller " — and by the boys. He was, in fact, left to find what pleasure he could in the reflection that in two or three years' time he too would be able to vent a senseless spite and rage upon those smaller, weaker, and sillier in a childish way, than himself. . . . But in the evening, an organised jollity was to prevail ; there was supper — a highly-coloured supper — at eight, with flowers in vases, and long tables, laden — groaning, though equally conventional, is perhaps an apter word — with cold chicken, boasting the curious Eton-blue tinge to its flesh that school chickens seem ever to possess, and tipsy cake, and jellies shaking in a scarlet ague, as if in personification of all school fevers. There was lemonade to drink and, as though it were champagne, a general atmosphere of Bump Supper, or incipient Hunt Ball, developed. Plainly such exhibitions were hereditary. We suffered, if I remember rightly, all the correct school-concert songs about " Wrap me up in my tarpaulin jacket ", and " Oh ! doodahday ! " ; songs which are no doubt also the vogue in prison and Borstal concerts. We ended by singing " Auld Lang Syne ". To be correct in the rendering of this, we all stood up, hand swinging in hand, to sing. . . . It was touching to watch, I expect. Several masters plainly had tears glistening in their eyes.

The excitement of the next morning, when it seemed as if you would never get your play-box packed in time to catch the train decreed for you, was almost sufficient to induce amnesia. . . . My holidays were spent at Gosden with my grandmother, for my mother had gone abroad to join my father. My grandmother never alluded to my black eyes, for she was a wise old woman who understood the secrets of both pride and humility, but she must have felt that she ought to tell my parents about the matter, and no doubt mentioned it when she wrote to them, for I find a short note, which seems to refer to it, from my mother. Headed Villa D'Este, and dated April 17, 1903, this letter betrays the same lack of conviction about my having " done well " that the reader will have noticed in my own letters to my mother, where the pleasures of school life are concerned.

MY DARLING BOY,
    We have got the report from school. I think you have done very well. Father is going to write to you. We wonder how you annoyed the other boys. You must try and get on with them so as to please father and me. I am sure you will try. Altogether, we are both very pleased.

    I remember little of these, my first holidays. I was, perhaps, a little lonely, for my parents had taken Edith with them, Miss King-Church had left us to marry a former tutor of mine, and to make a home of her own in Rhodesia. She had, before going, told me a lot about Rhodesia, and the depredations committed by white ants for a long time dominated my mind, much as the atrocities inflicted by the other side dominate the minds of the public during a war. Apparently they ate everything, roof and walls and books and pictures, and one had to encase anything one liked in metal. I missed both Edith and Miss King-Church very much. . . . Sacheverell was still only five years of age, and though his affectionate nature made him want to walk with me, he soon grew tired, and had to return to the company of his pet lamb, a creature that carried always a blue bow and a bell, but was so fat and fleecy that it could hardly gambol at all. Occasionally it would skip in a half-hearted way on the lawn, among the daisies and buttercups, or would accompany him in a tour of the grounds, along the paths where periwinkle and blue wood-anemones grew, under the shade of the tall lime-trees, now coming out in their shrillest green leaf. . . . Everyone else, except Sacheverell and his lamb, seemed old, so old. My grandmother was over seventy, my Aunt Mary Osborn had passed eighty now, while Leckly and Wilkinson could scarcely be younger. The coachmen seemed even more ancient, if considerably less sleek, than the horses which drew us along the Surrey lanes, and took us for expeditions. . . . As for myself, I felt in full maturity, grown up, since I went to school. . . . And, indeed, I had altered. How deeply the place had affected my essential self will be seen later, but even superficially I had become different. I no longer read history-books, for owing, as I thought, to the prevailing games snobbishness, I had not been awarded the history prize which should have been mine. I took now no pride — how could one, with two black eyes ? — in my appearance. Or, to be more precise, I was becoming slovenly, except for certain days when I took immense trouble and turned into a youthful dandy. I could find no golden mean. Moreover, these rare festivals only occurred in the holidays ; in the term I was almost professionally untidy. . . . I only mention these small traits because they may provide, I believe, certain clues to character.

Everyone round me seemed so old : yet, when to myself I appeared to miss the society of those of my own approximate age, I reflected philosophically that, so far, I had not much cared for the company of such of them as I had met. I saw the children round me at school as the scheming, bullying, treacher-ous little beasts that they no doubt were — but only at school : and this, alas, I did not know, for no kind friend had told me that any mob, whether composed of dotards, adults or infants, and whether drawn from aristocrats, labourers or clerks, is always detestable and inevitably wrong, however delightful each individual composing it may be by himself. . . . Yet the old were *too* old. Even Mr. Alan Gramble, my grandmother's young friend, seemed to me, with his blue, bulging forget-me-not eyes, and moustache brown and bushy, to be ancient. . . . Yet I liked to be treated as being old myself, and I recollect, when my grandmother asked me to help her choose a governess for Edith in Miss King-Church's place, how much flattered I felt by such a tribute to my years, and to my understanding of human nature. . . . We interviewed together many appli-cants, and in the end our choice fell upon Helen Rootham, then a very young woman of the most vivid character and temperament. With dark hair, and eyes of almost Spanish vehemence, she possessed a passion for truth and justice, together with a love and understanding of the arts, and especi-ally of music, which was of the greatest service to my sister and, indeed, to all three of us. Helen was undoubtedly super-sensitive, apt, even, to be censorious, but she was the first person we had ever met who had an *artist's* respect for the arts, that particular way of regarding them as all-important

— much more important than wars or cataclysms, or even the joys of humanity —, without which it is impossible for a painter, writer or composer to achieve anything. Moreover, at the moment, my sister, whose character was fast developing, found it harder than ever to please my parents : but in Helen Rootham she found a champion, and we all gained a friend. She was a pianist of the most remarkable quality, perhaps the finest woman pianist it has ever been my good fortune to hear. There was no mistaking the fire and magnificence with which she played. And from the moment she came to us, during my next holidays, the music of Chopin and Schumann, Brahms and Debussy, flowered as a constant background to our hours of leisure, and became associated at Renishaw with every expanse of water, every vista seen through green trees. The rooms there were filled with her fine and sensitive interpretation of this music, into which she poured her fervent spirit. . . . How singular, how ironical, that this gifted woman, with her talent for the piano, with, even, the proper physical equipment for that instrument, the right hands, wrists and arms, should subsequently have chosen singing for a career ! For, though she sang with skill and with feeling, she had gone to it too late, and never brought to it the same natural endowment that she possessed for the piano. In this sort of way, in the manner in which she occasionally misunderstood her own gifts, and refused to recognise her own mistakes, and above all, perhaps, in the fact that her sensitiveness led her to be at her worst just at those moments when she should have been at her best, there was much, indeed, to infuriate her friends ; but she never underrated the talents of others, only of herself. All through the years that follow, until her lamented death in the spring of 1938, she will, even when not specifically mentioned, be in the foreground, for she remained the staunch and delightful friend of all three of us. And it must be remembered that by being in our company for so long, she became a recognised authority on our family life, a person whom we could consult about the manner in which my mother or father would act under given circumstances. . . . The best monument to her memory will be found in her excellent translations of Serbian ballads, and in her translation of Rimbaud's *Les Illuminations*, lately set to music by Benjamin Britten ; a fact which, because of her intense love of modern music, and sympathy with it, constitutes a peculiarly appropriate tribute and would have afforded her the greatest gratification. . . .

With her sensitive nature, she must at first have hated being thus plunged into a household strange to her. . . . Indeed she was very nervous, even on the day when my grandmother and I interviewed her. . . . But, at any rate, she stands out clearly from the mist engendered by the old age round me, of which I have complained. . . . Through that miasma, I see, too, very clearly the perpetual prospect of church, presided over by the fanatic and fiery Mr. Bartlett : I would drive there with my grandmother and Aunt Florence, — though, once or twice, my grandmother did not put in an appearance, for Mr. Bartlett had recently announced his intention of marrying again, and I do not think this altogether pleased the old lady. At least, that was what I gathered from Leckly, who told me, I remember, that " your grandmother doesn't hold with a clergyman having more than one wife ". " But has he another ? " I enquired innocently, before I realised that she was referring to his being a widower. . . . As for myself and church, during my holidays, I had relapsed into a healthy heathendom, and no longer was a secret early Christian. I remember that, overcome by the tedium of the service, which even Mr. Bartlett's iron-grey, puritanical eloquence could not redeem for me, I decided temporarily to adopt a fervent high-church attitude, for my relatives disapproved of ritual and Romish practices. Accordingly, I turned right and left whenever an opportunity occurred, and bowed, and crossed myself with fervency and unction. These sudden observances of mine certainly puzzled my grandmother, who yet presumably did not like to oppose new-found religious fervour of any kind, for it might in time develop along lines more congenial to her. . . . And yet, she must have thought to herself, one never could tell : for example, her great-nephew, Reginald Farrer — and no one could have been furnished with a more healthy and pervasive religious atmosphere than his mother had provided for him through all his young life — was said to have become interested in Buddhist practices, and to intend, even, before long, to become himself a Buddhist missionary in England.

The time passed quickly. . . . I recollect poring over

catalogues from Harrods' Stores, in order to try to find new
kinds of knives, bristling with every sort of useless but ferocious-
looking adjunct, so that I could impress my contemporaries
with them when I returned to school. (I think most schoolboys like to show off; at that age they are in that stage of
evolution when possessions mean power.) And no doubt I
looked forward to shouts of " Sheep-face ! Have you seen
Sitwell's new knife ? " . . . As the first holidays swept, at an
increasing tempo, nearer to their end, a tremendous depression
enveloped me. My grandmother must have noticed it, since
she allowed Jane, the housemaid, to conduct me for an evening
to a delightfully rustic and rather slatternly circus, held in
an enormous tent on a neighbouring common. In the darkness outside, you could see animals tethered by the tents, a
few goats that belonged to the villagers perhaps, while the
elephants trumpeted from near by. The arc-lights spluttered
under the dingy white canopy, and Gypsies and clowns lolled
about without much discipline, equivocal, belonging in part
to the audience, in part to the ring. The spangled ladies
pirouetting on the broad backs of their horses had, for all
their sparkle, a soiled vagueness, almost a sadness underlying
it. . . . I enjoyed it, particularly the broad village-fun of the
clowns here ; but I do not think my grandmother would have
liked the jokes, had she heard them. It had been a great
concession on her part to permit me to go to such a place
of amusement. . . . I began, despicably enough, to feel more
religious as the term-time drew nearer, in the same way that
a dying man repents. But the pianola was my chief refuge.
I thundered and squeaked out the waltzes of Tchaikowsky.
And I took more pleasure than ever in the flowers in the
garden, the little azure clusters of the bee-hyacinth, carrying
with it some strange immanent evocation of Greece and Italy,
the large negro-centred blossoms of purple anemone, dusted
as it were with charcoal, the contorted branches of japonica,
with their cups of coral and freckled gold, all these seemed to
have acquired a new beauty.

When I returned, the faces round me had grown the more
threatening because of the rest and refreshment their owners
had enjoyed. Bullying was no longer stale sport, and they
entered with zest upon a further, and longer, period of it.
. . . The very horror of this life rendered the few freakish

escapes from it as enchanting as is a fine day in the English summer. One such spell of freedom occurred soon after I had gone back to school, and once again I welcome the combined force of northern gales and southern breezes that for a single day it brought me. . . . On an evening in May the arch-dribbler sent for me to inform me that my mother and my father — and him I had not seen for over a year — had arrived in London from abroad, and had expressed the wish for me to spend a day with them in London. The school prospectus stated plainly that no exeat was allowed during the term — except, of course, for the Eton and Harrow match. It was most irregular — but in view of the circumstances, he had decided to make an exception in this case, and accordingly my father was sending his servant to fetch me the following morning. . . . The train would leave Barnet at 8.30.

I could hardly sleep for excitement, and at 7.30, while the boys were still getting up, I went downstairs in my best suit — even that fact brought a sense of escape — and there in the drawing-room, amid the fretting decoration and accumulated and detailed furnishing, among the delphiniums, shedding dry blue heads on the parquet floor — chrysanthemums were over for the moment and it was too early, still, for sweet peas —, I found Henry, looking unusually sunburnt, and as congruous in this setting as a whale in a china-shop. . . . We started off at once towards the station, across the golden meadows of the morning. It was gloriously fine. The whole land seemed to be singing, and the sky spilt light upon the ground, so that every small flower seemed to glow with its own illumination, and the crops of buttercups resembled the fields of the stars. . . . Henry was in a good mood, since, in spite of his liking for gaiety and late hours, he loved the early morning. He preceded me for the whole distance by a few yards, as if he were an usher, thereby imparting a certain dignity to the scene. He swung his arms, too, as though taking part in a state procession of some sort, and he was wearing his bowler hat, with its large, impressive black dome. Indeed this headgear possessed a sort of symbolism, constituted, almost, a badge of authority, as do the top-hats worn by the chiefs of certain native tribes. Sometimes I would dart across the intervening space to join him, and examine the familiar, heavy gold watch-chain that, about the

level of my head, swung in two ample loops each side of his
waistcoat buttons, truncating his body ; a chain, again,
which, like that of mayor or cellarer, had something of office
about it. But no, he insisted on walking in front of me, with
his slight nautical roll ; and, by his figure no less than his
gait, it was plain that he had grown no thinner. He must
already have weighed sixteen stone, and was putting on weight,
the result of his enjoyment of Italian fare and the red wine
that accompanied it. . . . Nevertheless, he grumbled continually at the customary Italian diet. I find, for instance, a letter
which gives his views on this and other sensual matters. It
was written by him to Hollingworth, some years later, from
Florence.

You made my mouth water describing the cattle and pigs in
the park. I should just like an English dinner of roast ribs of pork,
sage and onions and a plain boiled suet pudding one gets tired of
all these dishes out here though it is obvious they agree with me
as I weigh 17 stone 10 pounds I am ashamed it must be the
maccaroni. . . . The nuns here are fine strapping young women.
Her Ladyship's maid has gone home to nurse her Mother and a
temporary maid has come, something after Julia's style I am sure
I don't know where all the nice looking ladys maids have gone to
that used to be about some years back.

When we reached the station, we climbed up the steps
and into a first-class compartment, and Henry was soon talking
to me as if I was a grown-up person — or so I thought at the
time, though in after years I realised that there must have
been a good many reservations and taboos. . . . This morning, he told me of his adventures abroad. My father, with
his love of medieval architecture and history, had lately visited
many of the remote towns in the foot of Italy, places such as
Squillace, where Cassiodorus was born, and Lecce, and the
numerous little towns round Bari, rich in buildings of the
romanesque and gothic periods, and with wonderful treasures
and associations — all, alas, now referred to as " marshalling
yards " (Ravenna, I notice in the press as I write, has sunk
to " an important road and rail junction "). These places,
hardly more than villages, in spite of their resounding names,
were, many of them, even then, before the earthquake of 1908
had wrecked Calabria and before armies had fought in the
streets of a wretchedness inconceivable to an Englishman.

Lecce and Bari were, it was true, prosperous in an isolated, old-fashioned way, but the lesser towns were crumbling and vermin-ridden, their inhabitants stricken with disease, and having, in Henry's phrase, " nowt t'eat ". Nevertheless, the people were equally anxious to please and to make money, and were intelligent in a child-like way, though quite innocent of modern knowledge. . . . Country-houses in the extreme south of Italy were exceptionally rare, but my father stayed in one that had been built for King Ferdinand the First and Fourth of the Two Sicilies. His host, a retired colonel, was most anxious to treat an English stranger well, and had determined to serve him an English breakfast, of which he had heard a good deal, and Henry had, in consequence, been obliged to carry up to his master's bedroom every morning at eight a tray on which were placed a bowl of octopus stewed in its own ink, a cup of black coffee, and a glass of the fiery local brandy.

As a rule, neither lodgings nor fare were so luxurious : for the most part they had been obliged to stay in inns that resembled tramps' doss-houses. My father paid little attention to his quarters, if he were interested in the town itself : for, after all, he could make himself uncomfortable in his own way anywhere, and had further devised a whole elaborate system towards that purpose. Wherever he went, he allowed himself, notwithstanding, one luxury, supplementing his meals with an abundant supply of cold chickens " to keep my strength up ". . . . Several of the *trattorie* in which he now found himself possessed no separate sleeping apartments, only dormitories in which men slept eight or ten in a room. But my father had seemed in no way taken aback at such a prospect. Henry would have to make up his bed, arranging the blankets in precisely the accustomed way, so that one or two could be pulled on or off very quickly as the mood took you, then he must sprinkle it lightly with Keating's, and proceed to hang up a mosquito-net by means of the special contrivance my father had invented, — when younger, he had invented many other things ; at Eton, for example, a musical toothbrush which played " Annie Laurie " as you brushed your teeth, and a small revolver for killing wasps. First Henry had to knock a great many nails into the wall, then from them he suspended the back of the net, and, finally, as though plumbing ocean depths, he must throw two cords with lead at the end over the side — out of window, that is —, and this would pull the whole airy contraption taut and into place. . . . Of course, occasionally, a passer-by below would complain that he had been hurt, but one really could not pay attention to that sort of thing. And it was so simple. All that you — or rather Henry — had to do now was to tuck the ends of the net in, all round, and there it was, complete ! If the proprietor objected, and asked who had broken the wall by hammering nails into it, my father would always reply " *Il mio domestico*," and Henry would have to pay up. It constituted a recognised fine, as it were, for clumsy hammering ; and sometimes it was not easy for him to find the money, as my father would only pay his wages once a year — or twice at the most —, and was very difficult over any small necessary advance. But, as my father said, they were not engaged in discussion over money ; it was the mosquitoes that mattered, and Henry should take more care. Very inconsiderate of him to sleep without a net himself. He might be bitten by an anopheles mosquito, contract malaria and remain ill for months, and that would make things most awkward. Indeed, my father entertained a great terror of mosquitoes — and I may say at this point that I have myself seen him drive in the evening for three or four miles along the slopes of a mountain, up a road leading to a small town above, seated in an open cab, the top of which was encased in white netting, so that he should not be molested by the creatures in their flight. Thus canopied, and wearing a grey wide-awake hat and a brown covert-coat, he would eventually arrive in the piazza, peculiarly crowded as it was at this hour, looking as though he were the High Priest in *Aïda*. Only the palm-leaf fans and attendants singing in chorus seemed to be missing.

At the time of which I write, however, the most spectacular feature of the existence of which Henry was telling me was that, wherever my father might be, and of whatever kind the sleeping conditions, the company or the fare, my father always went to his thin-partitioned bedroom or to the dormitory, as the case might be, with its painted tin basin and dusty curtains, in order to change for dinner. And he would appear at 7 P.M. or at 6.30 — for the hours of his day moved earlier and earlier as he grew older — in the dingy dining-room with its fly-blown appointments, its soiled cellars of yellowing salt, its bunches of fennel roots in bowls, its gimcrack chairs and humming clouds of insects, and there astonish the solitary malarial waiter and the one or two other guests by the splendour of his evening dress, the gleaming stiff front of his shirt, the white, shining cuffs and collar, white tie, white waistcoat and black swallow-tailed coat. Indeed his arrival, thus attired, would cause a stir outside the room as well as inside, would rouse the spectators from their jaundiced apathy. Dark faces would be pressed against the bleary window-panes to watch *L' Inglese Pazzo* eat and drink, a new interest would show in them, combined with an utter lack both of envy and surprise. There had been invasions led by Norman barons before in this part of the world, and people were therefore used to such ways. Certainly this tall, fair man, with the Kaiser-like moustache of the period, with his high-bridged nose, carefully carved nostrils and air of remoteness, which the homely, yet far-fetched, comedies wherein he unwittingly involved himself and those with him, never impaired, belonged to this type, and resembled the gothic effigies reclining on the tombs in the neighbouring churches that he had come hither to see. He was much nearer to them in type and blood than were the swarthy, tattered grandsons of brigands and punchinellos who lived here, squatting in the almost African dust.

In some of the villages, Henry told me, my father had acquired a reputation for healing. It had begun thus. So remote were these places in those days, so cut off, that it was often impossible to reach a doctor, and therefore, in one village a consumptive priest, seeing a stranger, had decided to consult him about his health. My father had brought, as always, a lot of medicines with him (he habitually kept these wrongly labelled, owing to his suspicion that the hotel servants helped themselves to them, and this sometimes made the finding of the correct remedies rather confusing). He had realised at once, however, that fresh air was what the poor patient needed, but that if he was merely told to sleep with his windows open, he would pay no attention, the advice being too simple to be impressive. Instead, therefore, very cleverly reverting apparently to the methods of the medieval pharmacopoeia, my father had given him some harmless medicine, which nevertheless carried the magic of physic with it, and had told him to take it at bedtime every night for several months, emphasising that, when it was taken, the window must be wide open and must not be shut until the following morning, otherwise the medicine could not cure him ; the evil vapours had to find their way out. By this means, the priest had been induced to undergo a fresh-air cure : and it had proved so efficacious, that when my father and Henry had returned to the same little town the following year, crowds gathered to ask The Englishman to prescribe for them.

All this Henry described to me in the train, going to London. . . . His Italian adventures were to culminate later, as I hope before long to show the reader, in an unexpected, indeed a unique way ; but I remember also another singular incident of which I believe he told me on this journey, though it may be that I am making an error, and that it really belongs to a period a year or two subsequent. . . . My father had been settled all the winter, on and off, at Naples, at Bertolini's, then the most luxurious establishment of its kind, riding with mast and pennons above the city, as though it were a white ship dedicated to the protection of the rich, an ark, stranded by some volcanic freak upon a hill-top. It was against his principles to stay here for long, since it was most expensive, but he liked the view and thus remitted himself the comfort he enjoyed, on esthetic grounds, and because, also, it was a good centre from which to carry out his raids on southern Italy, where the prevailing low standard of life which he was obliged to adopt there — even though he succeeded in raising it a little with the aid of cold chickens, mosquito-nets and the various paraphernalia of his system — no doubt salved his conscience. Be that as it may, when they returned from these expeditions, lasting a week or two, my father always went straight back to this hotel, and to the same rooms. . . . The winter passed, and in the month of April, the height of the Neapolitan season, when the management of the hotel were often hard pressed to know where to put the visitors, he had set out, accompanied as usual by Henry, to visit Puglie. Returning, after the usual period of absence, to Naples, they arrived late one night and drove straight to the hotel. Henry, far from realising how crowded the hotel had become in the interval, did not even trouble to make

enquiries at the desk, but, taking it for granted that everything was as usual, told the porters to carry the heavy luggage
up in the lift and leave it outside the door of 143, the room
my father had occupied all the winter. Himself had then
climbed the stairs and, when he had reached the correct
landing, had walked along the passage, to find the trunks
already waiting for him outside the door. He opened it,
without turning on the light, and — for he was very strong,
and knew the exact position of every piece of furniture in the
room — took up my father's heavy, old-fashioned leather
portmanteau and threw it on the bed. . . . Immediately the
air was filled with loud groans of pain and terror ; then light
flooded the room, and two trained nurses dashed in from
doors each side. . . . The victim was Hall Caine, who had
come to Naples a few days previously, suffering from a nervous
breakdown.

The sudden shock of this assault may, I am afraid, have
somewhat retarded his recovery. The one-time earnest young
friend and embryo Boswell of Dante Gabriel Rossetti was now
a man at the height of world-wide fame, though not yet
knighted, a figure in each continent, his novels being translated into every language, including, it was said, Bantu and
pidgin. Nor were his books more widely known to the public
than his own personal appearance. His dome-like brow, the
look of which convinced others as well as himself that he
resembled Shakespeare, his hair, flowing down on each side
of it, his gleaming eyes, black cloak and large black hat, were
familiar to all those millions who read his books and to further
millions who did not. Even if one entertained no particular
admiration for his work, to see him by chance in the street
on his way, perhaps, to his publishers, was an event.[1] But,

---

[1] Often as a very young man, before the opening of the 1914–1918 conflict,
I would pass Sir Hall Caine in the street, and always found a certain pleasure
in it, equivalent to that, it may be, of identifying a rare bird. He was usually
on his way to his publishers, who then were in the neighbourhood of St. Martin's
Lane. . . . I remember one of the partners in the firm, a man now dead, talking
to me about him, and stressing how impressive he was as a personality, and how
misunderstood as a writer. Money, in spite of the vast sums he made, my acquaintance averred, always came second with him. Only that very morning, for
instance, the great man had called at the office. One of his books had happened
to be lying on the publisher's table. The author had taken it up, with a certain
diffidence, and then, opening it, his eye had lighted on a passage so effective,
and so full of moral grandeur, that he had begun to read it aloud in his fine
voice, rolling and resonant. The paragraph ended with some such words as

in addition, he was immensely esteemed by the foreign intelligentsia, for translation into European languages apparently changed his books into what he believed them to be. And if we consider the repute in which various living authors are held, it provides an applicable footnote to such a valuation if we recall that when Gorky visited London a year or two before the First World War, and a party was given so that the eminent visitor might meet all the more distinguished figures of the contemporary literary scene — such persons, let us say, as Hardy, Conrad, Shaw, Moore, Gosse, Wells and Bennett —, he entered the room, glared in vain at the welcoming but disconcerted faces of the great, and demanded loudly, " Where is Hall Caine ? "

It will be seen, therefore, that the treatment to which Henry had subjected the popular novelist was, most emphatically, not of the sort to which he was accustomed : yet it cannot altogether have poisoned his recollections of the visit, for seven or eight years later, I discovered, in one of the public rooms of the same hotel, a brochure ; of the sort that when you want to write a letter in a hotel abroad, you always find in a drawer of a writing-table, and take out, under the impression that it is note-paper. This example consisted of a list of testimonials to the comfort and beauty of the establishment, written by various celebrities ; and the first and most important, composed by Sir Hall Caine, began with these alliterative words of an almost Dracula-like suggestion, " Clinging breathless to the balcony of Bertolini's Palace Hotel ". . . . How vividly they enabled you to picture it, the black cloak, the hat, the eyes, the final vespertine swoop !

When Henry related the incident of the groans, he laughed in heartless fashion, his huge body rolling from side to side. He talked, loud above the sound of the train, all the way to London, and by treating me thus, as someone whose good opinion he wanted and whom he liked to amuse, he restored, in the same manner that we have seen Miss Lloyd had mended previously, my self-esteem. I began to feel again a human being, instead of a helot. He told me, I remember, that my father was " quite himself again ", though he would not

" So, ladies, though your fate may be different, be not hard upon a fallen sister ". As he finished, he was quiet for a moment, then commented, " Beautiful, beautiful," and added, as an afterthought, " and money in every line of it ! "

admit it. Nevertheless, he still suffered from relapses and, as it happened, that very morning, when I arrived in London, he proved to be too ill to see me, except for a few minutes. I found him lying listlessly in a darkened room, with a look of such extreme dejection that it saddened me for the day. . . . I spent the rest of it with my mother and Edith, and was taken to drink chocolate at Charbonnel & Walker's in Bond Street, then the chief place where children of the richer sort were conducted for a treat. And, indeed, the chocolate was memorable. . . . I did not see Edith much alone, but enough to gather that my father really was better, and also that, while abroad, she had been obliged to submit to more intensive nagging and bullying than ever before. But, though she was unaware of it, help was already on the way, for Helen Rootham, most faithful friend and champion, was due to appear in a few days' time. And she was the first grown-up person to seize the quality — though even then, perhaps, not at first the gifts — of this young girl, with her face of brooding and luminous melancholy, with her lank, gold-green hair, and her features, of so distinctive a kind, but which her character, though developing so fast, had not yet fully carved out of the soft matrix of childhood.

Henry accompanied me back to school in the evening — but I recall nothing of the journey. The light had gone out of the day. Fortunately, as soon as I arrived, it was time to go to bed. . . . But I slept very badly that summer, and the trains, with their puffing and hooting, filled me more than ever with nostalgia. . . . I lay awake, listening to them, and to the croaking of the frogs, a sound new to me. Even then I loved that music, ragged and of the mud, muddy, yet so boastful and personal that, much more easily than in bird-song, one could detect individual voices, bragging of their amours. Sometimes, too, a bird sang from a tree outside, for me a foreign delight, since my country experience — except in the early spring, when no nightingales have yet arrived from Africa — was north of the Trent ; that true dividing-line, separating peoples and habits, Danes from Saxons, and also fixing a boundary to the circulation, northward and southward, of newspapers. As I have said, even the frogs croaked less vehemently, hardly at all beyond that river ; their intonations being as much fainter than the music of those which I was now hearing, as was this chant than that of the bassoon-voiced frogs of Tuscany, with whose music I was to become so familiar in future summer nights. But even this cracked and earthy singing tinged the nights for me with a certain charm that the rest of the twenty-four hours lacked. At least, during these hours, one's thoughts were one's own. And so I would lie there in the darkness and listen until I fell into some trance-like condition between waking and sleeping ; a condition which, when it comes on me today, terrifies me no less than when it occurred the first time, which I so well remember, during that summer term.

As one drew near to sleep, faces would float close to the eyes, very close. Usually they came in the guise of familiar heads, of people one loved, but, hardly had they materialised thus in the mind's inner eye, when a change would set in, they would be lit by frantic lights and jets of fire, and would become subject to the most surprising and tragic distortions. At other times, they would be the faces of strangers, equally realistic — where, one would wonder, could one have seen them, for surely it was impossible thus to create character and appearance. . . . Then, the same process would take its course. Some power, not so much of caricature — which unless carried to its ultimate limits, has about it always something of a worldly level — as of the most intensely grotesque and pungent stylisation, deep and sombre, terrifying in the force of its despair, was at work, either in the subconscious mind, which controls within it all the hordes of heaven and hell, or, who could tell, perhaps in the vast undefined, and even illimitable, distances outside it, for certainly it was odd that something that one created oneself could so frighten its creator. It seemed, this power, to be able to bend to it all forms, all shapes, whether accustomed or unfamiliar, with such mastery that even the great exponents of the modern theatre could achieve no more startling effects. In front of the eyes flowered these faces, immense now, flaring, illumined by the sacred or diabolic flames in which, after the habit of the salamander, they had their whole existence. They appeared to possess a life of their own and could refuse to be dismissed. The effort to rid oneself of them was almost too great to be borne. . . . What was the meaning of it, what did it offer ? Can it have been thus that, sometimes, the grotesque heads, with their frenzied wickedness or in their splendid rage, appeared to the Italian masters who drew them ; were, perhaps, Goya's gnarled and tormented faces, that misery had turned into the roots of trees, as their bodies had been transformed into stumps, of similar origin ? And, again, occasionally these heads would become corrupt and earthbound as the bloated masks of Gillray or Rowlandson. . . . I told no one of this nocturnal grappling with monsters, but I dreaded them none the less.

What else can I tell you of school ? . . . For one thing, I was privileged to see at work in this section of a primitive and savage community, — resembling one of those layers of earth extracted from an ants' nest, and placed in a flat box made of glass ; objects that remained so popular with schoolboys of the period, though they had been created to teach something —, the birth and development of a myth. Due, perhaps, to the intense boredom of the life round them, which even those boys who pretended to like it must have secretly abhorred, these myths — in that, perhaps, akin to the atrocity stories that come into being to enliven and envenom apathetic hearts and to lessen the appalling monotony of war details, or to the ghost stories that have arisen to relieve the tedium of country-house existence in England, or the scandal that floats up like incense from the vicarages of seaside towns — are invariably of a kind to frighten those who tell or listen to them, and thus add a spice to dull lives. Herd — or heap — instinct gives force to these reports, so that they grow with a life of their own. . . . So it may have been then, that curious stories began to circulate, and to be accepted by the boys, tales of attempts to kidnap a school-fellow (who remained, no doubt, himself in ignorance of these rumours), of men on ladders, faces at windows, footsteps in the darkness. Even the masters heard these legends, and seemed inclined to pay attention to them, perhaps because they, too, were so intensely bored. In any case, they soon found that, with the best will in the world, it was impossible to discover any foundation for these mysteries. . . . Personally, I enjoyed them, allowed myself to be pleasantly frightened : though I was not then aware that I was being privileged to watch, too, something of great anthropological interest, that same process from which sprang with such grace, such rough spontaneity, the nymphs and naiads, the satyrs and centaurs of Greece.

On summer Sunday afternoons, I, and my two friends Marcus Pelham and Clive, would, after tea, walk round the large pool whence at night rose the song of the frogs, discussing these terrors, agreeable because they were not believed except on the surface. . . . There were also other topics, more of this world. . . . Clive — who, alas, died of wounds in 1916, — possessed a sense of humour together with a certain spirit of audacity. . . . And I recall how we talked of the trouble in which, as the result of a joke, he had recently found himself. In all schools of this sort, the Navy League used to indulge in propaganda : lectures used to be given, and each term the boys received printed forms, with a request that they should enter against one enquiry the sum of money they wished to give the institution. In a fit of high spirits, Clive had written " two million pounds " against his name, and had sent it off : a form of exaggeration not appreciated either by Navy League or by schoolmasters. . . .

There is but little more to relate. The grand fête of the school year took place in the summer : the exeat, which I have before mentioned, for the Eton and Harrow match. . . . This break was no doubt intended to impart an Etonian bias to the boys at an early age, for this school was essentially preparatory for Eton. Great excitement prevailed for three weeks or so beforehand, especially among those who, like myself on this first occasion, had nowhere to go. (My parents would not leave Scarborough and come to London for the match.) I find the following particularly ill-spelt letter on the subject from myself to my mother :

DARLING MOTHER,

The Whinney-Finckes [1] cannot have me to stay after all. *Where* shall I go for the Eaton and Harrow ? I must see it.

Thanks for the Water-Pistol. It is very useful.—Yr loving son OSBERT.

I would really have preferred to go home, but it was recognised by boys and parents alike, that this, albeit officially permitted, in order to placate those pariah-fathers who could not easily afford such treats for their children, entailed an inevitable loss of caste. But in the end I went to stay with some cousins, and so was able to attend the festival. One

---

[1] My rendering of the well-known name Wynne Finch.

had to sit there, clad in Eton suit and top-hat, for hours, watching the cricket or pretending to do so. . . . For the rest, I observed with interest the smug-faced crowds, the happy families, that promenaded in the intervals, keeping in clumps, across the ground. As they walked through the glowing, spangled air of summer, it was their clothes rather than their faces which held the attention : the waisted gowns, the high lace collars, the frills, the richness and weight, and yet lightness of these full July clothes, the feather boas, ethereal as dusting-brushes, the hats, plumed as though they were bright fowls about to take wing, or flowered, as if they were full summer baskets from a rectory garden. Even now we were not, except for a few round the Court, in full Edwardian swing. Paris was still a long way for these bright-coloured crowds to go. In the summer months, London yet resembled in the daytime a transcendent garden-party, for these clothes I have attempted to describe were made of fabrics especially manufactured for the English market, as we, in our turn, produced cottons for the Congo ; they were covered with splendid blossoms which no other country knew, crawling over every inch. In spite of Edwardian sophistication, a sort of unsophisticated elegance, debonair but cloudy, was the mark of these county families, now up in London for the week. Indeed all classes still exhibited — albeit absolutely unaware of it — a national costume, from the fresh and dowdy grace of these clothes, which filled Sloane Street and Eaton Square, and the whole neighbourhood, down to the charwomen, in life true to their image in the comic papers, who, in their black mantles and bonnets, could still be seen hurrying everywhere of an early summer morning : as for the men, they wore frock-coats, grey or black, and grey or even white top-hats. . . . But within two or three years, Paris had supplanted the native fashions for the women, at any rate, of the richer classes. . . . Yes, I liked watching the crowds, and enjoyed the intervals, the meals, better than the game itself. No longer was I worthy, alas, to play against Rhodes or Hirst. Even the Londesborough family connection with cricket — my uncle, like his father before him, was President of the M.C.C., and sat in a box, with a band playing to him —, even W.G.'s sponsorship of my name at birth for that august body, even such glories, availed me nothing. I was hopeless at cricket and hated watching it. . . . On the other hand, the ices and the cider — especially the cider — during the intervals were a great pleasure to me ; and I now suspect, looking back, that the slight sense of exhilaration without reason which I then experienced may have been due to an initial encounter with alcohol.

Soon after this break came the first summer holidays, and we spent that lovely, long spell of hot weather at Renishaw. Freedom would have been complete, except that I found myself provided with a tutor, who followed me everywhere, and prevented Sacheverell and myself from ever going out alone. Though my faithful friend and companion was so young, this did not prevent us from indulging in the most violent quarrels, such as only brothers can engage in : but the strength of our rage, the fury with which we combined, when occasionally the tutor would try to intervene, must have seemed remarkable to strangers. Beyond that, I could not help feeling that it was unfair that I should be plagued with lessons in the holidays, too. I wanted to go for a drive in the pony-cart round the woods, to walk with my mother in the gardens, to listen to Edith playing the piano, to fish, to catch butterflies with Maynard Hollingworth, to eat fruit in the orchards — and here I was, doing sums again, or hitting a ball with a bat. I complained : but my father countered by pointing out how woefully bad I was at my work (he was afraid, he added, that I must be taking after my mother's family), and how shameful a lack of interest I displayed in games. Within doors, puff-ball had now succeeded ping-pong as the recreation of master minds — but even for that I showed no aptitude. And I must try to walk faster. To walk fast was an indication of a mind that worked rapidly. That, too, was the reason why he ate so quickly — it had nothing to do, in his case, with greed. Sheer mental activity. And, who could tell, if I quickened my pace, perhaps my mind might become quicker too ; like the minds of my two cousins, the Arthington boys. Look how well they did at cricket — and at work too. Excellent essays they wrote already. They would go far, probably become famous writers as well as governor-generals. One ought to be able to play a good game of anything. Then there was riding ; I held the crop the wrong way — like that — quite wrong. And books. I seemed to read Stevenson and Dickens, whereas I ought to be getting ready to tackle Darwin's *Origin of Species*. Logic, too, was an interesting subject. If one must read novels, why not Walter Scott? An excellent picture of the period (charmin' feller, Ivanhoe). And I ought to learn to sing. (Nothing made a man so popular as singing after dinner.) How could I wonder that he had felt himself obliged to find a tutor for me? He was sure he only wished it had not been necessary; it was a very grave expense. Even with a tutor, he doubted whether I should ever attain the level reached by other boys.

The real advantage of engaging a tutor consisted, of course, in the fact that his employment by parents of a certain fortune enabled them to continue to evade the responsibilities of parenthood, during the holidays as well as during term. . . . But from the point of view of the children, it was a detestable arrangement. Somehow or other, no walk was ever so nice, no game ever so enjoyable, in the company of a tutor, whereas things you disliked became to a similar degree more hateful (thus I loathed riding more than ever, now that when I bumped along the drives in the woods, I was accompanied by one of these spoil-sports). Nevertheless, a tutor attended us during every holidays, except for the Christmas vacation, which we spent regularly for several years at Blankney; where, as will be seen in the next chapter, there were enough resident and visiting spoil-sports to regiment a whole pack of children.

The only tutor, then, whom I liked, was, naturally, at the same time the only tutor whose example was dubious. A celebrated gambler, a spendthrift, a ne'er-do-well, who had given a great deal of trouble to his family as well as to himself, Mr. Ragglesedge had been strongly recommended to my father by an agency as " a man of the world as well as scholar, and a thoroughly good influence on others ". Though, I suppose, from the angle of dress and manner, in the phrase of the day, " a bit of a bounder ", he was certainly a most amusing companion, and, in addition, was kindly and amiable, understanding human nature to a far greater degree than any of the other tutors who came to us. Always he tried to mitigate the attitude of paternal fault-finding that prevailed, and indeed, with the development of my character — not necessarily on the lines for which my father was confidently planning—, increased.

. . . But this, again, was later, for Mr. Ragglesedge returned to us at fairly frequent intervals over several years, and remained a staunch friend to Sacheverell and myself. Eventually, when we were too old for tutors — and after he and a friend had made a most enterprising attempt to sell my father a motor-car, of which incident I hope to have more to say subsequently —, he went, with the warmest recommendations from my father, to some extremely devout cousins in Scotland. Their whole lives were passed in prayer-meetings and low-church good works : but even there, with his easy, friendly temper and adaptability, he created the best possible impression, until one day, when the family was engaged in the most earnest session of sweet, silent prayer in the dining-room, Mr. Ragglesedge, who was supposed to be leaving tracts on old women in the village, and who did not realise that the prayers on this occasion were to be mute, was heard, very distinctly, speaking on the telephone just outside the dining-room. And it was plain, even to those on their knees within, that he was sending a telegram connected with racing to a bookmaker in Glasgow. After that, alas, he was dismissed, and we, too, were no longer allowed to see him.

With the exception of Mr. Ragglesedge, therefore, I spent during the holidays a considerable amount of time in sneaking away from my tutors. It was easier to evade them at Renishaw than at Scarborough, and I liked to escape with Betts, the gardener, Henry, or Hollingworth. . . . Sometimes, for example, Maynard Hollingworth would obtain my father's permission to drive me over to Whiston or Brampton-en-le-Morthen — villages about ten miles away, where my family had held land for many centuries —, so that I could make the acquaintance of the farmers there. . . . Here we were in Yorkshire and, though so near in space, in actual miles, to reach these remote districts would occupy a whole day. Indeed my father, when he went round them, always stayed in an inn in Rotherham, first warning the proprietors with the same laconic telegram, which ran invariably " Ship Hotel Rotherham Chicken Apple Tart Dogcart Sitwell ".

Hollingworth and I would start about nine in the morning, and after going to see a few tenants, would have luncheon, about quarter to two, with one of the chief farmers. . . . Everything in this region, the farms, flowers, buildings, food, no less than the people and their manner of talking, was of a different kind to any in our immediate neighbourhood, and so, the day's outing offered a complete change. Brampton-en-le-Morthen resembled no village in Derbyshire. It consisted of a single L-shaped street of substantial stone houses, some bearing escutcheons over the doorways. Though situate in the middle of highly industrialised country, the majority of these buildings dated back to the years just preceding the Civil Wars, and the difficulties of reaching the place kept it singularly unspoiled. It was curious, too, that a small rustic community should reside in such handsome houses ; squires' houses, one would have said, yet they stood above a high pavement in the street, or hung above it with an over-sailing storey, carried on great beams. (The finest of these old mansions, incidentally, bore the coat of arms of the family of Bradshaw the regicide.) But everything was on an unusual scale here, even the barns seemed stone temples, so proud were they in fabric and proportion, so lofty their huge doors. . . . Or again, take the isolated farms that appeared to be part of the hills on which they were pitched, slopes that swept down to streams below with the particular beauty of the Yorkshire countryside, not with the almost physical beauty of line that one notices in Derbyshire; but having a distant, sad, pure beauty that breathes the air of perpetual childhood. These hills had all the freshness of air that was possible, in spite of the vast furnaces and mines only a few miles away ; they were brown from the sun, and huge bushes of wild rose grew on them, and in fullest summer, knots of harebells frail and luminous in their nodding blue. These last, as well as the wild roses, though of a different kind, grew near Renishaw, but the wild daffodils which in the spring lined certain hedges here, could not be found in our neighbourhood. And, just as these Yorkshire farms seemed larger than those, so near them, in Derbyshire, and richer, the hill country more open, so did the clouds piled above these hills seem more robust, more castellated and turreted, more icy and steely in their structure. Leagues of snow, fathoms of snow, towered there always, even in spring and summer, waiting for the winter to set them free upon the land. But autumn here was the most beautiful, no less than the most typical season, for, in this like all northern regions, — and essentially it belonged to the north —, it was a country of berries more than of flowers.

As for the farms themselves, they were clean with a northern or Dutch cleanliness ; they looked as if every morning they rose anew out of a flood, but a flood of soap-suds. The wide, painted panelling, and the floors, either of stone, magnificent in their whiteness, or of bare boards, all were shining yet mellow, even the kitchen table was beautiful in its graining from the continual washing ; the glass-eyed pike, fixing you — from a case with curved transparent front that might have been composed of limpid, slowly-flowing water — with the bright, immovable gaze of a paralytic, and a superb white pheasant that occupied another case, seemed larger, finer and more clean than in life. In the parlour one or two chairs, in a rustic Chippendale, and made of elm more often than mahogany, would be ranged stiffly round the walls, and inevitably a grandfather-clock would give life to the room, with a wheezy ticking and striking. Here and there brass would gleam, in a hinge or handle of the late seventeenth century, or in some object on the high mantel, with its bold projection, and pewter would show its dull, complacent gloss. In the most comfortable chair, an old-fashioned armchair, covered with a chintz, would be a piebald tangle of cats and kittens. . . . And inside the room, the old people — for the young would all be working — talked to me of my grand-parents, whom they had known better than they knew my father and mother. . . . As for the dinner, is there any better food than that of a Yorkshire farm, the roast chicken and bread sauce, cooked in a way of which the farmer's wife of no other county has the secret, the butter, the cheese and apple tart, the pears, with the very fragrance of the north in them ?

Sometimes, again, Sacheverell and I would spend a whole morning in the pantry ; where Henry now reigned. Stephen Pare, fixing his large, melancholy, nearly sightless eyes upon a silver bowl, which he held up to the light, so as to catch its glint, would be polishing it and acting as chorus for the great man. He did not talk much, but would chuckle quietly, as he drew Henry out, prompting him and leading him on, but when a footman entered, they would both look solemn and disapproving. From where Henry stood, near the window, with his name incised on the pane, he could see everything that was going on outside. The St. Bernard, in his large kennel, would gaze back at him with an equal stubbornness, and sometimes a workman or farmer would call a greeting to him through the open window. Pare said to him — for Henry, though now promoted to be butler, still called my father in the morning —

" And how is Sir George today, Henry ? I haven't seen him."

" Well, when I called him this morning at five o'clock, 'e was laughing fit to kill 'imself. He was, really, Master Osbert. He laughed and laughed — never seen 'im so jolly. He 'as all sorts of good jokes up there by 'imself. Only 'e doesn't let on to us."

At this moment, my father's resonant, rather thin voice could be heard echoing down the stone passages :

" Henry, have you seen Master Osbert ? "

" No, Sir George . . . I thought I heard him just now. He'll be at work, I expect."

Or he would be heard asking for the agent or the clerk in the office, or answering in pained, patient tones, " Yes. Wha-a-at is it ? ", or demanding that more workmen should be sent to help with the erection of the two statues he had bought in Italy, of Neptune and Diana.[1] . . . He was, indeed, beginning to be himself again, and the garden was cobwebbed with ropes and full of pulleys.

He had gone now, to the library, or to one of the seven rooms in the house which he used for writing, covering chairs and floors and tables with a thin layer of business letters and notes of antiquarian interest. " You see, with my system, I can put my hand on anything I want. . . . Let me see ; where have I put it ? . . . Just for the moment, I can't find it." But perhaps the housemaids, who had strict orders never to touch the papers or attempt to tidy them, had been dusting, for almost immediately a bell rang. . . . As Henry remarked, it was difficult to talk with any enjoyment when the bells never stopped ringing. You couldn't settle down to a subject. " Sometimes ", he added, " I wonder what would happen, if ever they had to do anything for themselves. There's Major

---

[1] By Antonio Calegari (1698–1777) of Brescia, a friend of Gian Battista Tiepolo, who was said to have sketched the design of these statues for him in the first place.

Viburne, ringing again for those primrose-coloured boots of
his. He wore them at Balaclava, and the socks go with them.
Not a bit worn-out. Only been to the wash once or twice ;
that's what wears things out — that, and putting them on and
taking them off. . . . There's Miss Vasalt's bell. It always
rings like that. ' Would you mind bringing me a biscuit and
a glass of port, Henry ? ' or ' Aren't there any peaches yet ?
. . . How late they are ! ' The doctor's frightened about her
health this year, she says, and's given her a diet. 'E told 'er
it's dangerous for her to have anything but peaches and a
glass of champagne between meals — every hour, she ought to
have it. No wonder she's hungry, poor lady, and not a penny
to bless herself with. . . . O Jericho ! That's Her Ladyship's
bell — and hell to pay, by the sound of it. I'd be happier
if I was a nigger slave ! " . . . When he came back — for
he thought it best to answer that bell himself — I remember
he told me about one of the gardeners, John Thurtle, who,
like Ernest de Taeye after him, lost all his hair as the result
of touching some plant. I do not know whether it was the
erecting of Neptune or Diana in the garden, or the fact that
he had lately visited Matlock, about twelve miles away, and
watched bowler hats being turned to stone by the process of
being thrown down a well, that gave him the idea, but he
suddenly said : " Have you seen John Thurtle, Master Osbert ?
Lost every 'air on 'is 'ead, and even his eyebrows and eyelashes.
Not one left. . . . My word, 'e looks peculiar ! Something
like an Ancient Greek." Then, after a pause, he added,
reflectively : " I wonder Sir George doesn't 'ave 'im petrified
and turned into a garden statue."

Or he might talk to me about the tutors, relating to me,
for example, certain of Mr. Ragglesedge's adventures. . . .
As a sportsman, our tutor naturally looked forward to the
Doncaster Meeting in early September as one of the turning-
points of his year. On this first occasion, he attended the
opening day of the races, and in the evening had telegraphed to
my mother, " Doing very well staying till tomorrow Ragglesedge ". Then passed several days with no sign of life, no word
from him. . . . My mother, who sympathised with any form
of extravagance, managed somehow to gloss over his absence
to my father. . . . On Saturday, the truant returned in the
evening with a crestfallen though by no means apologetic

air. Indeed he attempted to brazen it out, maintaining that he had still paid his expenses. But Henry told me that a postcard had arrived, on which was written in large, clear letters, " If you can't bloody well pay me the fiver you borrowed, you might at least send me the price of the blasted railway fare ".

Alas, I could wait there no longer, since the tutor of the particular time came to claim me. . . . But he of the first holidays was the most displeasing of all, and naturally and inevitably, since my father was his employer, adopted the same point of view on every single score. My mother, though, often took my part, and it is because of the sequel to one such occasion that I recall this tutor so vividly — for I remember something he said, an outburst which he should never have made to me. . . . We were out together walking, at a pace, by my father's instructions, with which I could hardly keep up. I had almost to run beside this man in spectacles, and he did not speak, but looked in front of him. No doubt my mother, in defending me, had spoken woundingly to him, for when she was annoyed she showed no mercy in what she said. So we raced along, he and I, through the curiously oppressive and lowering afternoon, in absolute silence, until we entered the drive known as the Chesterfield Approach, a sombre plantation, full of old dying box-trees and other moribund shrubs in enormous clumps. Then it was as if some evil wind of prophecy hovered over him, remaining poised there in the air for a moment, while all the leaves suddenly whirled back and retreated under this invisible fluttering of sable wings, and he turned and spoke to me.

" You can think what you like," he said, " but one day your mother will do something of which you will be bitterly ashamed."

At these words, a feeling of misery, so acute that I remember it still, overwhelmed me. The air seemed cold and dank, with the darkness of the shadow I have mentioned, and familiar heads were distorted as in that dream or trance that lay between waking and sleeping.

Chapter Two
RETREATS UPON AN IDEAL

Though in the next chapter I shall have to revert for a few pages to my early school-days, in order to sum up their effect, in mind and body, upon at least one boy, here we will leave the scene of them for a while. First, however, I must produce a letter, written in my third term, because it gives, despite cacography, indications of character, in others no less than in myself, and serves as a kind of preface for the chapter that follows. . . . Victor, to whom it makes reference, was, I must explain, my cousin, exact contemporary and, at that time, chief foe.

Nov. 4, 1903

DARLING MOTHER,

I hope you are quite well. Do let me know your adres in Naples. The aples have arrived. Thank you so much.

I am better but wish I had no teeth. They are aching as hard as they can go.

If there is any chance of our going to Londesborough or Blankney for Christmas, do find out first if Victor will be there, becaus I should not enjoy it if he was. I am also afraid I shall be shy there, and that they will make a fuss if I do not taulk all day like when I was at Blankney last Christmas. Please write to me *at once* when you get my letter. I do miss you.—Yr loving son OSBERT.

P.S. Please let me know about Blankney.

Blankney stood, a dead weight in the snow, pressing it down with a solidity pronounced even for an English country-house. For us it loomed large at the end of each year, and the roads of every passing month led nearer to it, an immense stone building, of regular appearance, echoing in rhythm the empty syllables of its name. The colour of lead outside, its interior was always brilliantly lit, its hospitable fires blazing, flickering like lions within the cages of its huge grates, so that it seemed to exist solely as a cave of ice, a magnificent igloo in the surrounding white and mauve negation. What was the purpose of these spacious, comfortable tents of snow, that appeared all the more luxurious because of being pitched in so desolate and empty a whiteness, and that were full of a continual stir ? . . . Ease, not beauty, was their aim ; for beauty impeaches comfort, disturbing the repose of the body with questions of the spirit and, worse still, pitting the skeleton against its encasing flesh. . . . So there were few fine pictures in the large rooms, leading one into the other, only perhaps one, the Lawrence of Elizabeth Denison, Marchioness Conyngham, founder of the family. There were pleasant portraits, such as that by Sir Francis Grant of Lord Albert Conyngham, her son, surrounded by a few pieces from the celebrated and superb collection he had formed, now, except for jewels and plate, all dispersed. Here and there, ivory mirrors and other sumptuous objects, given by King George IV to Lady Conyngham, and bearing on them the Royal Arms, survived ; but for the most part the rooms contained little to look at. The Saloon, chief sitting-room, was long and rather high, full of chairs and sofas, piled with cushions (the aim of which was plain, to get you to sit down and prevent you from getting up and so to waste your time), with tables with many newspapers lying folded on them, and the weekly journals, and green-baize card-tables, set ready for you to play. The light-coloured, polished floor had white fur rugs, warm enough and yet suggesting the pelts of the arctic animals that must prowl outside : but to counterbalance such an impression, there were tall palm-trees, and banks of malmaisons and carnations and poinsettias, a favourite flower of the time, a starfish cut out of red flannel, and the standard lamps glowed softly under shades of flounced and pleated silk that mimicked the evening dresses of the period. There were writing-tables, too, and silver vases, square silver frames, with crowns in silver poised above them, containing the photographs of foreign potentates, posing in their full panoply of flesh as Death's Head Hussars, or with flowing white cloaks and firemen's helmets, their wives, placid, with folded hands —, silver inkstands and lapis paper-weights, and near the fireplace, two screens, cut out of flat wood, and jocularly painted, a hundred or so years before, to represent peasants in costume. On one wall hung a large portrait by a fashionable artist, of my aunt balancing her second son in an easy position near or on her shoulder. There were many silver cigarette-boxes, ash-trays and boxes of matches of every size from giant to dwarf. Certainly the rooms had a supreme air of modish luxury, and no quality so soon comes to belong to the past — for the skeleton outlives its flesh. . . . What more do I recall : the broad, white passages — out of which led the bedrooms —, so thickly carpeted, and the white arches, on one side of the corridors, looking down on hall and staircase ? What else ? The warmth, the fumy, feathery scent of logs and wood ash, and a lingering odour, perhaps of rosewater, or some perfume of that epoch, a fragrance, too, of Turkish cigarettes. . . . And for a moment, I see the women, their narrow waists and full skirts, and the hair piled up, with a sweep, on their heads, or surrounding it in a circle. Above all, I hear the sound of music.

Sometimes a string band would be playing in the Saloon — Pink or Blue Hussars insinuating whole Hungarian charms of waltzes, gay as goldfinches — but more often the tunes would be ground out by innumerable mechanical organs. There seemed to be one or two in every passage. You turned a handle, and these vast machines, tall as cupboards — objects which, since they have been superseded by gramophone and radio, would today constitute museum pieces — were set in motion, displaying beneath their plate-glass fronts whole revolving, clashing trophies of musical instruments, violins that shuddered beneath their own playing, frantic drums, tambourines that rattled themselves as at a séance, and trumpets that sounded their own call to battle. I scarcely recollect the tunes they played, overtures by Rossini and Verdi, and — of this I am sure — some of the music of Johann Strauss's *Fledermaus*. The warm golden air of these rooms trembled perpetually to martial or amorous strains, yet they are not in memory more characteristic of the place than are the sounds of the family voices, variations, that is to say, of the same voice. For this house was the meeting-ground of all the generations surviving of my mother's family, and these tones were the particular seal and link of it, containing, as they did, a special quality of their own, lazy and luxuriant, sun-ripened as fruit upon old walls. They seemed left over from other centuries, even those of the youngest, and former ways of speech still persisted among the older members of the family, tricks of phrase that might have seemed an affectation ; but then, my relatives on this side did not read much, and so these ways were traditional. All learning came to them by word of mouth. And, at the same time that I hear again these voices, and the music, I hear, too, something scarcely less typical, the quarrelsome, rasping voices of packs of pet dogs, demanding to be taken out into the cold air, their bodies surrounding the feet of the women of the house, as they walked, with a moving, yapping rug of fur, just as in frescoes clouds are posed for the feet of goddesses. And as, at last, these creatures emerge into the open air, they bark yet more loudly, jumping up, lifting their ill-proportioned trunks to the level of their mistresses's knees.

How far this passion for dogs, shared by men and women alike, was a family trait, or merely indicative of class or period, I am not aware, but on occasion, and particularly in my grandparents' time, it reached to the strangest level of fantasy, to a height of distorted exaggeration. Thus, an old friend, writing to me lately, gives an instance of what I am trying to indicate, in an account of a visit he paid to my grandfather and grandmother at Londesborough in the 'nineties : " I remember ", he says, " arriving at the station one dark winter's evening. When I entered the park, I was surprised to find it brilliantly illuminated, lamps being hung all up the fine old trees. I wondered if there could be taking place that night a county ball, of which I had not been warned. After the festive air prevailing, it was, though, something of a shock when I reached the house, to find all the family, more or less, in tears, and I could not imagine what could have happened and what could explain all these various contra-dictory phenomena. It was, therefore, a relief to learn finally the cause ; a pet dog, who had escaped and gone off hunting in the morning, had not yet returned. The lamps had been lit to show him his way home." . . . A similar devotion still inspired the owners of these dogs we have noticed, their barking attending the coming-in or going-out of any member of the family, like the fanfares of heralds.

The music came out of the door, as it was opened, in a loud gust, stronger than the barking of dogs, and the intense cold for a moment refined it, gave it increased clearness, until its reverberations muffled themselves in the snow. . . . The house, the church, the stables, the kennels formed a dark and solid nucleus, a colony in this flat landscape that did not exist : the village was somewhere near, yet out of reach as the equator — perhaps it was interred under the snow. For an hour at midday the cold yellow daylight poured down, else always it was mauve against the electric light. Snowflakes scurried past on the east wind, that lived so conveniently close, in the sea, just beyond the edge of the negation ; of which all one knew was that somewhere in it, about eleven miles away, stood the ancient city of Lincoln. This town shone, indeed, in my imagination, as a kind of Paris, a *Ville Lumière*, beckoning across the plain. But until it was reached, there was nothing, neither hills, nor mounds, nor mountains, nor trees — nothing except stretches of flat whiteness for hounds to run over, or occasional gates or barriers of twigs for red-coated, red-faced men to set their horses at.

Nearer, in the park, and in what must have been the meadows beyond — but until a few years ago I never saw Blankney at another season, so could form no idea of the country buried under this enveloping white shroud — were many enormous pits, containing whole armies of Danish invaders. . . . Of this my father informed me, for, to tell the truth, he found himself, had he permitted the existence of such a word, bored, in a house where all the interests were of a sporting nature, and, in consequence, called his bluff. Moreover, it was made worse for him by the fact that the remainder of the guests enjoyed themselves to the same extent as he was miserable. Pure self-indulgence. But he could always find solace, he was thankful to say, in thinking over historical associations — so long as they were of the correct period. And here he was fortunate, for the great slaughter, of which these pits were — if only you could see them — the abiding sign, had taken place between A.D. 700 and 800, and nothing much had occurred in this district since then to spoil the idea of it. Therefore, he could always take refuge with the Danish dead, always cause his blood to tingle, by telling me how these huge excavations, filled with bodies of warriors, killed by the retreating Saxons some eleven hundred years before, had been dug out, and how they had been covered first with the branches of trees, on which the earth was then shovelled — that accounted for the mounds. The very thought of it, in the American phrase, made him " feel good ". With gusto he described the brave invaders, their bronze helmets and primitive axes, until for the first time I visualised that Wagnerian world of firemen armoured in bronze, with flowing moustaches, and long hair, led by bearded, resonant-voiced kings, pot-bellied, who pledged their cave-loves in blood drunk from the skulls of their enemies. It was not, I found, a world which I much liked : but my father, I recollect, used to declare that if only the members of my mother's family were more intelligent, they would spend their whole time in digging up the bones, instead of in hunting, shooting and going to circuses. . . . He would also tell me — this, I think, in order to make himself feel more at home in a house given over to relatives by marriage — that Blankney had been " held " in the twelfth century by the Deincourts, a Norman family of whom, through the Reresbys, we were the representatives, entitled to quarter their arms. (The Londesborough escutcheon he considered, he owned, as shameful, a " horrid eighteenth-century coat, *all* wrong in heraldry ".)

In fact, my father shone at these family gatherings with a lonely and peculiar lustre, since he was the only man of intellectual pursuits who appeared in the small court centring round my aunt and uncle. (On the other hand, my uncle admittedly knew more about music than my father could ever begin to comprehend.) But, in general, I realise, now that I have read *The Chronicles of Clavijo*, that most of the other male guests of his age would have probably felt more at home at the court of Tamerlane the Tartar than in the contemporary world, and would have formed the most appropriate leaders for a new Golden Horde. They were scarcely at ease out of the saddle, and tended to fall asleep if they entered a house and sat down for a moment, except at meals. They were all tall : for height was an ideal in this circle ; everyone, especially the women, despised the undersized as elsewhere the talented look down on the half-witted — and it may be that this natural response was not so stupid as it would seem, since, for example, big men are more sure of themselves, less disposed to want to force their wills upon those with whom they live. Further, with an exception or two, they were good-looking, with the gloss and ease — and the generous outlook within narrow limits that accompanies these particular qualities — of those whom the world has always treated well. But, though in their fashion they were most kind, yet if during the daytime a spare moment not already occupied with slaughter occurred, it, too, must necessarily be devoted at once to killing : otherwise they would consider they had wasted their time. No small creature on four feet, no feathered thing with wings, as it ran over the snow, was safe ; neither the fox — but that was a lengthy business and very ritualistic —, nor hare, shrieking its soul out like a human being, nor pheasants, designed so splendidly for a brief autumn, nor partridges, more discreetly clothed than those who shoot them, nor the dank, long-beaked birds of the marshes, snipe and woodcock, nor the ducks, with their hints of water in white and blues and greens, their bright feathers that might, when wet, so well be scales — none of these could hope for much mercy : while as for rabbits, they were collected by the attendants, put in sacks, and emptied out of them at a moment when there was no other killing to be had, so that tweed-clad hordes of men, and the women, many of whom accompanied them, could set their dogs on these confused, bolting creatures, and knock them on the head with sticks. . . . Should these amusements fail, ratting could always be improvised through cellars or in lofts. (Only the mouse, alas, was too small, unsporting little beast !) . . . Yet if the leaders of the Horde appeared to be consumed by some divine fury against the fowls of the air, and the soft, furry beings of the wild creation, perhaps in their own minds they compensated for it by their fantastic devotion to horses, their insane passion for dogs ; the horses constituting, as it were, the gods, the dogs the angels or patron saints.

The men of the Golden Horde were almost as kind to children as to horses and dogs — though, naturally, they regarded them with less reverence —, but to any male of the species who did not run true to type, they could show an equal cruelty in many directions. For example, this was a generation that had been much addicted to practical jokes (in proof of this, I recollect a contemporary of my parents saying to me that in the 'nineties it was impossible for anyone to get into bed in a country-house without having his toes bitten by a live lobster). Here the custom survived, and the chosen butt, recurrent every year, was a middle-aged, quarter-witted cousin, comfortably below the level of the stupidest fellow guest. He talked as though his mouth were full of sugar-plums, with a voice pleasant enough in sound, yet carrying the family voice beyond the characteristic to the pitch of anomaly and caricature, as, let us say, Charles II of Spain carried the Habsburg chin ; moreover, he was wont, when in the grip of trivial misfortune, to bellow like a calf, accompanying the ludicrous inflections of his voice with angry but similarly absurd gesticulations. . . . My uncle and aunt could not omit to invite him every year, for he would have resented such neglect ; they would have liked to protect him, and in fact did so whenever possible — but it was difficult, for, ever since they were boys together, these men had played upon him the same tricks. Plainly, however, he bore no rancour, for he would sob without restraint if he heard of illness or accident falling to the lot of any single one of his tormentors. This sad, ramshackle, loose-limbed zany nevertheless possessed a pride of his own, and much resented it if any injudicious attempt to tease him were made by those who had not grown up with him, and whom, therefore, he considered not to be entitled to the privilege. Such presumption he quelled with an unforeseeable but compelling dignity.

The repertory of tricks played upon him every Christmas by the elect was simple enough ; consisting of booby-traps of every kind, pails and sponges full of water balanced above doors or just behind them, fake telegrams sent and delivered, messages concocted, apple-pie beds, hens tethered under the bed and lobsters let loose in it. Most of the fun was physical. At dinner, while he was enjoying the food, the flowers, the flow of champagne, his face would be seen to be assuming gradually a curious shade, as though he were in the grip of some secret dolour — and so he was, the explanation being that as usual, each year, a mustard plaster had been sewn into the seat of his evening trousers. Though, as will be seen, the children of the Golden Horde inherited a taste for practical jokes, and, albeit that it was, I regret to say, funny, this was not my sort of fun. The artist, like the idiot or clown, sits on the edge of the world, and a push may send him over it ; there, I felt in my bones, but for the grace of God, went Osbert Sitwell. Edith, as the most sensitive person there, naturally hated the entertainment ; nor, either, did my father much care for it ; he too felt sorry for this poor buffoon, and, I think, secretly preferred his company and conversation to those of many others present. . . . " An interesting survival," he used to explain to me, " the type of medieval court fool." . . . No doubt such buffoons had existed, too, at the court of Tamerlane.

Almost everyone, except those instanced above, seemed to enjoy each item of the business, each surprise prepared, however staled by custom. This was true in particular of the poor relations, the fun brigade, the members of which sought to avoid similar fates by joining in, and being the merriest of the merry. . . . No doubt they sometimes felt depressed at night, when they retired to their rooms, wondering what would happen to them if the knowledge themselves possessed, that they were not in reality in the least amusing, but that it was merely a tribal convention, became, by means of some sudden and divine illumination, a generally recognised truth. They must banish such thoughts, or the façade would crack. If was no use being morbid. Fun, such fun.

The figureheads of the family were always on the move, going away for a night, and returning the next day. Only the old — the very old, they then seemed — remained at rest, — and, of course, the fun contingent, for this was its Christmas station, and the members of it could not afford to rush backwards and forwards. They must wait at least until after Twelfth Night, before starting on the rounds again (" Isn't it all such fun ? "). Meanwhile, they must contrive to get on as well, one with another, as they could and treat the place as a kind of sorting-house for information, agreeing to exchange individual items of the fun-material they had collected. (" Did Gertrude mention to you, darling, what Geraldine said to Campbell-Bannerman at the Opening of Parliament ? " " No, do tell, do tell. . . . And then I'll tell you about Muriel and the German Emperor.") In this way, and by the necessity of their continual laughter, they imparted a subtle, bitter, pervading flavour, as of caraway seed, to the entire background. Particularly did they help to make luncheon — a meal at which the young were present and scanned closely for minute faults of conduct — something of an ordeal.

Further, it was not possible here to find Henry, as at home, and relieve one's feelings by talking to him about Miss Vasalt and her colleagues. His every moment was occupied, but

more in amusement than in duty, for he too was a guest. He
would be engaged in taking a lady's-maid out for a walk in
the snow, in talking, singing, dancing — he was one of those
elephantine men who are born to dance beautifully. The
visiting servants lived in style, and were always addressed,
ceremoniously, it was said, by the names of their master and
mistress. Thus, Henry was translated into " Sir George ".
It would be no use my trying to grumble to the servants of the
house, rank on rank ; they were too impersonal and well-
trained to talk. . . . Only my uncle's former valet, Midwinter,
a man of great charm, who knew everyone and could supply
sufficient tact to furnish out a Foreign Office, who had something of Tweedledum in his composition, both in physique
and character, something of an ambassador, something of the
Italian Comedy, and a touch, perhaps, of Figaro, possessed
individuality — only he, and Fat James, an enormous footman
with powdered hair, who was apt to fall asleep while handing
round the dishes.

What made luncheon particularly trying was this : it was
the Edwardian mode of the moment for a large party to break
up for this meal, and re-crystallise at little round tables for
four or six, rather than sit at one long table as at dinner :
(" It makes it so much less formal," people said ; " and more
fun," echoed the brigade, " more fun "). And so it was far
from easy for a child to know where he should sit or be sure
whether he was wanted. As in all houses of this kind, the
food, however delicious, carefully thought-out and elaborate,
must nevertheless be bolted, the plates swept from the table,
as course replaced course, with the greatest speed : this constituted the reaction against the lengthy Victorian meals,
which the ruling generation was always deriding, referring to
them as " those awful Lord-Mayor's-Banquets ". But to the
greedy the meals of the day must have proved a banquet of
Tantalus ; and I have often thought that, with this same
set of people, the growing popularity of restaurants was due
to the fact that in those places they were not chivied over their
meals. Yet it was themselves who had been responsible for
introducing undue celerity as the English standard of service ;
which goes to prove that those who lead a mode, do not
always enjoy conforming to it. . . . The time, then, given
to luncheon was short. Soon those who feasted must be at

their killing again : it got dark so early — or, indeed, was hardly ever light —, and so those of the ruling generation wanted for these few minutes to engage in its own talk, to discuss the current or probable divorces of the time, which must not be mentioned in front of the children — nor, as for that, in front of the old, who were wont to look down their formidable noses at the mention of the word : whereas the Edwardians, though they did not smile on those who had been through the divorce court, fawned on those whose conduct should have entailed the process, according to former standards.

As for the old, though they would try to be amiable to the young, by now crossness had settled in their bones. The women seemed always to live on for ten years or more after their husbands, and dowagerdom possessed its own very real attributes. Moreover, they made their age felt through the medium of many devices. It was not, after all, merely that they *looked* old ; on the contrary, they gloried in their age and the various apparatus of it, and indulged in a wealth of white wigs and fringes, sticks, ebony canes and Bath-chairs, while, as for strokes, these were *de rigueur* from sixty onwards. In fact, it was a generation which, unlike the next one, did not know how to grow young gracefully. . . . Thus, my grandmother Londesborough was seldom now to be seen out of a Bath-chair, though she was still able to exercise her charm on us without effort, and equally to deliver the most portentous snubs when she wished it. . . . Nevertheless, her world had changed — for though she had been train-bearer to Princess Mary of Cambridge, afterwards Duchess of Teck, at Queen Alexandra's wedding to King Edward, and had stayed at Windsor for the ceremony, which took place in St. George's Chapel there, and though, too, she and my grandfather had always belonged to the pleasure-loving, yet she was never Edwardian in the sense that her son and daughter-in-law were. She possessed a stricter outlook, a more severe sense of duty, and all the rather naïve, unsophisticated courage of the Victorians, as well as sharing their genuine belief in the conventions.

In general, each Christmas the representatives of the older generation were the same, invariably numbering in their company my grandmother, her brother-in-law and sister, Lord and Lady Ormathwaite, and Sir Nigel and Lady Emily

Kingscote. Lord Ormathwaite was even then over eighty — he lived to be ninety-three. Both he and his wife were of a deeply religious nature (it was very noticeable how much more devout were the old than their sons and daughters), and one of the favourite amusements of the children, I remember, was to hide in the broad passage outside the bedroom of this old couple, and listen to the vehement recitation of their lengthy and extremely personal prayers. Another frequent Christmas visitor, until her death in 1903, was Adza Lady Westmorland, who belonged to the same epoch, being the mother of my aunt, and a sister to the 8th Duchess of Beaufort and Lady Emily Kingscote. She was a godchild of Queen Adelaide, as was her nephew the Duke of Beaufort.[1] Adza Lady Westmorland, indeed, came of a family much devoted to Queen Adelaide, since she was the daughter of that Lord Howe — the 1st Earl Howe — whose singular conduct at the Royal Pavilion at Brighton, when King William IV was living there, had roused the malicious interest of Charles Greville. Lord Howe, a handsome young man " with a delightful wife ", hovered dotingly round Queen Adelaide whenever she was in the room, remained gazing at her with eyes full of love and admiration, and behaved altogether, the diarist relates, as though " a boy in love with this frightful spotted majesty ". . . . Adza Lady Westmorland, as I remember her, was a very old lady in a Bath-chair, who wore a black dress and a large, shady black hat. But she still retained her wonderfully exquisite manners and her great charm, for both of which she had been celebrated. In her time, she had been responsible for several small social innovations for women, such as wearing tweeds and smoking cigarettes.

As for the young, they were for the most part the same as those we saw a few years before at Scarborough : my cousins, Raincliffe — Frank —, and Hugo and Irene Denison, Veronica and Christopher Codrington, Enid Fane and her brother, Burghersh — who was my particular friend and companion at that time, in the same way that Victor was my enemy elect —, Marigold Forbes, and other young relatives.

[1] Henry Adelbert Wellington FitzRoy, 9th Duke of Beaufort (b. 1847), was named Adelbert after Queen Adelaide, and Wellington after the Iron Duke, his godfather and his father's great-uncle. He died in 1920. The last surviving godchild of the Duke of Wellington was His late Royal Highness the Duke of Connaught, who, born in 1850, died in 1942.

Entertainments were provided for them — and, as we shall see in a moment, by them — with regularity. Presents were plentiful. . . . I do not know how much the old or the young enjoyed the parties — scarcely as much as the members of the ruling generation, I should say ; to the old, certainly, these Christmas festivities brought a feeling of sadness, of deposition. . . . Among the children, I am sure that the child who felt least happy, an alien among her nearest grown-up relations, was my sister. Acutely sensitive, and with her imagination perhaps almost unduly developed by the neglect and sadness of her childhood since she was five, she could find no comfort under these tents. She loved music, it was true — indeed, where music is, there, always, is her home —, but the music of this house meant little to her, and the formal conversation between children and grown-ups, even if they were trying to be kind, frightened and bored her ; while she did not care for the machinery of the life here ; the continual killings seemed to her to be cruel, even insane. She ought to have asked to go out with the guns, even if she herself did not shoot ; she might at least have *attended* a meet. And, if anything, my father's inclination to nag at her on the one hand, my mother's, to fall into ungovernable, singularly terrifying rages with her, on the other, because of her non-conformity, seemed stronger when there were people, as here, to feed the fires of their discontent, and other children to set a standard by which to measure her attainments. " Dearest, you *ought* to *make* her like killing rabbits," one could hear the fun brigade urging on my mother. But while my father was angry with his daughter for failing to comply with another standard — his own —, for not having a du-Maurier profile, a liking for " lawn-tennis ", or being able to sing or play the zither after dinner (it did not affect him that his wife's relations would have been very angry if she had attempted to play the zither at them), he was also disappointed on another score. She seemed far less interested than I was — or even Sacheverell who was only six or seven — in his stories about the Black Death (a subject he had been " reading up " in the British Museum), and she seemed to have no natural feeling for John Stuart Mill's *Principles of Political Economy*. . . . The Victorians, I think, appreciated Edith more than did the Edwardians. . . . But Irene was the particular focus for grown-up attention and affection, not because she was the only daughter of the house, but because the delicate loveliness of her appearance, with her fine skin and huge, dark-blue eyes, and a certain kind serenity, unusual in a child of her age, made everyone want to spoil her. But it was in vain — she remained absolutely unspoilt, gentle, amiable, full of kindly feeling towards the whole world.

Another permanent feature of these festivals, held, as it were, for the re-creation of the family spirit, was the number of governesses present : French and German governesses, governesses old and young — for governesses —, outdoor governesses and indoor governesses, governesses militant and governesses civil ; the cause of this seasonal plethora being that my uncle and aunt, hospitable equally by nature and tradition, invited hither for Christmas those who had instructed their own youth. . . . None of these old ladies of assorted nationality ever went home to their own countries to live ; they preferred to exist in subsidised, rather angry retirement in the suburbs ; where, out of the faded splendour of their anecdotes, they peered unseeingly at their neighbours, as fish in glass cases look at you from their background of dried grasses. But these visits revivified both them and to a certain extent their anecdotes, and this brief spell now constituted the annual event to which, more even than to their three weeks by the sea, they most looked forward. It afforded them an admirable opportunity for criticising the work of their successors, as well as to renew past friendships and, still more, to rekindle ancient feuds. For it, they prepared their richest wigs and most royal fringes, polished their beads, shook out, free of dust and camphor, their most splendid, but always discreet, dresses. Here, too, the oldest generation of French and German governesses fought again the well-remembered battles of Metz and Sedan. And the fact that none of their former pupils could speak any of the languages in which these ancients had been hired to instruct them (the members of the ruling generation were patently less cultivated than their parents), plainly by no whit lessened self-esteem.

The marshal of the French armies was a most irascible and dauntless old woman, known as Dicky,[1] who had been

---

[1] See " Mademoiselle Richarde " (*The Collected Poems of Edith Sitwell* — Duckworth).

governess to my aunt, and to her cousin, the Duchess of Sermoneta. She was curiously insect-like, resembling several species at the same time. Diminutive, neat-waisted, fussy and fiery as a wasp — and at night she emphasised this similarity by often wearing an appropriately barred evening dress of black and yellow — she was also wooden-coloured and timber-dry as the nameless creatures that live inside a nut, while at other times she had something about her of the strict, industrious ant. Her wig was the most precise, the most accurately poised, of the whole house, her waist the most pronounced. Almost everyone was frightened of her. *Taisez-vous* and *Tenez-vous droits* fell continually with an arid but an authoritative clatter from her thin, wooden lips and, in her easier moments of talk and reminiscence, she took us back to that mythical past, remote as Troy or Caerleon in their Golden Age, when our grandmothers had been young girls. Yet she remained practical, of the present day, liked to command and take a part in everything.

Usually — to the rage of the servants, who hated them, and counted the consequent extra trouble to their score — they feasted upstairs ; whence often their voices could be heard rising in shrill dispute. They descended to the dining-room, however, for special occasions ; when, too, the children were allowed to sit up late. On such evenings, except for Dicky — resolute against compromise — the guest governesses were determined to quell their successors by a show of suavity and a mood of high reminiscence, more than by open warfare. . . . But what they chiefly enjoyed, more even than Christmas night or that of the New Year, was the French play, and the rehearsals for it.

This annual stage event took place on Twelfth Night, the parts being filled entirely by the children in the house between the ages of five and fifteen, and owed its existence to some vague idea of my aunt's. She associated it, I believe, with Christmas, presumably from some memory of her own childhood. At any rate, she was wont to say, " The children had better give another play this year. . . . It does so much good ", though she never defined the nature of this benefit, or to whom it accrued. The audience was chiefly drawn from among the villagers, whose attending the performance each year constituted a kind of *corvée*. I do not know what they

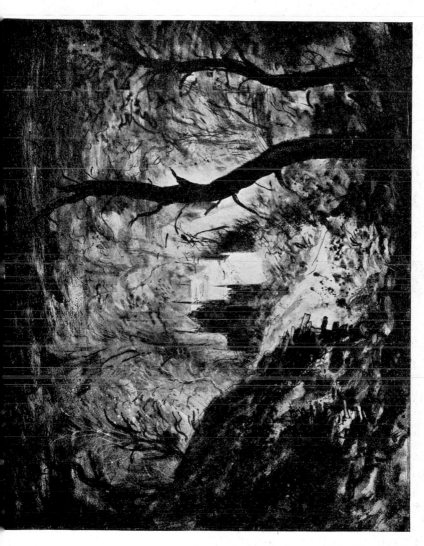

THE ARCH IN THE RAVINE, RENISHAW
by John Piper

THE KENNEL COTTAGES IN THE PARK, RENISHAW

can have made of it, for we were almost as deficient in French as our parents, and these labourers and farmers could hardly understand English, let alone French, and talked in the broadest of splay-tongued Lincolnshire. It does not do to dwell on their sufferings. Indeed, except for my aunt, for the mothers of the children, who peered in at the rehearsals from time to time, commenting that we " looked neat ", and for the superannuated governesses, who, I have said, immensely enjoyed the play and the preparations for it, because these made them feel useful again, and that it would be impossible for their host and hostess to get on without their help ; except for these, then, everyone, I apprehend, hated these performances. . . . As for the youthful actors and actresses, they were beside themselves, even at the prospect of them.

The plays required a good deal of stage-management, even to produce the effect that was produced, of ineffable boredom, on the part of every child on the stage and adult in the audience. . . . Where the pieces were found, for what company or theatre they can have been composed, it is impossible to imagine. The action always took place either during a *jacquerie*, in the glade of a forest, or in a room at Versailles or the Tuileries during the French Revolution, and the stage was erected at the end of the dining-room, just beneath an enormous electric organ, appropriate incidental music being thus easily provided. The boys were usually pre-revolutionary French peasants, with silk breeches, velvet coats and red silk stockings, and the girls, too, often played the role of peasants, wearing powdered hair, pannier skirts of sprigged silk, while they carried high Pompadour sticks, with bunches of ribbons attached to the top, in one hand, and baskets of artificial flowers in the other, after the presumed fashion of peasants in that idyllic time. Or sometimes, again, they were the well-known women of the French eighteenth century. The costumes, as will be seen from the foregoing description, were fairly elaborate, and all the maids in the house undertook to help with making and fitting them, though the chief dresses always came from London, and inevitably, in the Christmas rush, arrived too late to be tried on. This caused every year a great commotion, and display of temperament, especially on the part of the retired governesses, but even without this recurrent trouble the dress-rehearsals proved an ordeal. The maids, kneeling, with mouths full of pins, would every now and then remove one of them, in order to indicate where the clothing should be tighter or looser, and, in doing this, would be sure to jab an impatient child in some peculiarly tender portion of the flesh. Moreover, the governesses, who found in the rehearsal a perfect medium for exercising their powers of interference and correction, would try to help the maids, who, on their side, remained insistent on their rights and determined not to be put upon.

On the occasion of which I am writing, the piece was one of those concerned with the French Court. . . . I forget who played Louis XVI, but my cousin Irene acted the part of Marie Antoinette, while Edith impersonated Madame de Lamballe. Dicky of course was in supreme command, and under her the other French governesses coached the children in the correct pronunciation of their language — a matter in which the audience of Lincolnshire peasants would be quick to detect any mistake —, nor were the German governesses at all averse from giving their views, albeit every year they got trounced for their trouble. Though the days before we had started had been peculiarly embattled, even for the season of peace and goodwill, during which children always quarrel with that special ferocity, born of digestive chaos, which they reserve for it, and indeed several of the small boys — including Victor and myself — had come to blows, the rehearsals themselves were passing with less than the usual friction. Even Dicky, highly critical by temperament though she was, seemed well content ; the children appeared to know their parts, and had not answered back much when rebuked. . . . So far, so good : yet surely it must have occurred to some who watched, that this calm was unnatural ? . . . For example, usually Raincliffe and Burghersh — both of whom were about the same age as myself — complained a good deal at being kept in one room, in this state of waiting, learning how to say these wretched French words, but this year it was obvious that they were perfectly satisfied. But there were things about it more difficult to understand. They showed a new fastidiousness about their places on the stage ; Burghersh always got too near the front, and Raincliffe would not come forward far enough. When not actually rehearsing — and they had only small parts, being for that short span again transformed into French peasants — they spent a long time every day engaged in perfecting some mechanical invention. It was difficult to make out exactly what it could be, for the youthful inventors — to me they presented more the appearance of conspirators — were oddly uncommunicative. You would have expected them to boast. But no, they remained intent, silent, preoccupied. The apparatus looked simple enough, its principal features consisting of a button, a reel, a lot of winding gear, and a fish-hook. The line, it seemed to me — and I watched them attentively, and not without a certain jealousy, had to be wound very patiently round the button for a minute or two at a time. Raincliffe was absolutely immersed in this task, while Burghersh attended to the other side of the business, throwing the hook, again and again, as if for practice. Every one of their elders was plainly rather pleased that the two boys had at last found something with which to occupy themselves. Even the censorious Dicky remarked how much they had improved in manners since the previous year. . . . But they would not reveal their secret, however often we other children pressed them to tell us. No, they said, it was to be a surprise : we should know on the night — and so we did.

The dining-room was crowded with guests staying in the house, with neighbours, and with people from the village. Indubitably, more of an air of expectancy than usual prevailed, as if we were in for a treat of some sort. . . . The curtain went up. The French Revolution was in full swing upon the stage, but the first scene passed off without incident. Wearing her black and yellow dress, Dicky, as prompter, was sitting in lonely splendour a few yards away, enjoying the glow of the footlights, which she shared. In the interval she received the congratulations of her old pupils. Then she gave a signal, and the curtain rose again. This time, an interminable dialogue developed, in rather halting French, between Marie Antoinette and the Princesse de Lamballe. After about twenty minutes of it, there were shouts behind, and a gang of French peasants broke in, among whom were Raincliffe and Burghersh. Burghersh dashed to the very front of the stage and threw something over ; Raincliffe remained at the back, and wound with a furious concentration at his reel and button. Everyone must have wondered what they were doing. . . . After an instant, Dicky's wig was seen to rise off her head, revealing a bare poll, and sail with slow dignity towards the stage. . . . Amid the tumultuous applause of the actors and actresses and, it must be said, of the simpler members of the audience and of some of the servants, the curtain was rung down. For a moment, the old lady plainly did not realise what had happened, then clasping her pilgarlic with her hands, she rushed for the exit. . . . Until two or three days had passed, neither Dicky nor the two so successful young inventors were seen — not, indeed, until somehow or other my uncle had been able to repair Dicky's sense of self-importance, and to restore to Raincliffe and to Burghersh a sense of sin.

In a way, I was sorry usually when these plays were over. The rehearsals enabled me to stay indoors during the hollow hours of the morning, when all the sporting men and women went shooting or hunting, and only the actors, their coaches, and the old remained behind. . . . One dreaded going out. The country on the other side of the long sheets of glass, some of which caught the light of the fire and so interposed a false glow, as of sunrise or sunset, between us and the snow, looked colder, much colder, than that round Renishaw even at this same season. It was impossible to tell the shape of it, what lay under the various blurring masses and deposits of white ; white mounds, white tufts, white slabs, white undulations, the roads being only recognisable by dirty brown streaks in the snow. White roofs, white trees, these alone were to be identified, and the light spilled over these spaces as though it were lime from a bucket, splashing them with a terrible reality, as if the harsh gods of the north were determined to force man to comprehend the cold, by emptying down on him for the brief midday hour this immensity of steely, or sometimes of yellow light, reflected from the unattainable snow palaces in the great sky. . . . Yet it appeared even more bitter, perhaps, in the long, lilac hour of dusk, when, alone, colour came to it, and every wide stretch of snow, every height of cloud, built up into such a demented architectonic mass of torn towers and crags, took up this tone of violet, cruel and sterile. Then, particularly, the bones of the Norsemen under their feather quilts must have felt at home.

If on week-days the stage erected in the dining-room offered a refuge from Nature as she showed herself outside, on Sunday such escape was never possible, because no snow-drift, however deep, was vast enough to prevent one from having to walk across — or, rather, above — the lawn to church. A path was swept, and, holding our prayer-books, we proceeded through this snow lane ; for the weather was not allowed ever to spoil the sombre magnificence of our elders, no longer clad in the usual tweeds of the morning, but decked in the semi-sacred splendour that belonged to the late Victorian and the Edwardian Sabbath. . . . The grooms and estate workers we passed were also dressed with care and a sort of smothering respectability. They wore, beneath their bowler hats, and protruding bangs of hair upon their foreheads, a look of ox-eyed and almost aggressive unwatchfulness, and they walked with a special, slow, Sunday gait. As we entered the church and sat down, there would be a little whispering among the congregation, and the governesses were particularly observant, to see how we children were behaving. Nudging or smiling was barred. My uncle took his watch out of his pocket, and placed it on the ledge of the pew, with his prayer-book, for he carefully timed the sermon, which he would not permit to last for more than ten minutes. But the whole service was short, and it was the half-hour which came after it that I really dreaded, since it had to be passed in the stables, under the almost professional eye of sporting relatives. They noticed with disapproval the repulsion I felt from these creatures to whom I was obliged to offer a carrot and pieces of sugar, and how I shrank from their slobbering over my outstretched hand.

We attended stables, as we attended church, in our best clothes, thereby no doubt showing the degree of respect due to horses, no less than to the deity : but afterwards, before luncheon we changed into ordinary clothes. Though children object strongly to changing and especially to washing their hands, yet on these occasions, how hard, and with what delight, I used to scrub them, seeking to rid them of the horses' slaver. . . . Nevertheless, we could not shed Sunday with our clothes ; it remained an awkward, bad-tempered day. There was the sense of relief that church was over, and meals, it is true, were more delicious than ever, and tended to be longer than on week-days. But what damped the spirits of sportsmen and sportswomen alike, what rankled, was that convention forbade the killing of animals on this day. It was waste, sheer waste.

Even my uncle seemed vaguely disturbed by the circum-ambience of Sunday. He would be more than ordinarily restless, suddenly get up from luncheon, without any explanation, and begin to play the organ. But that again was nothing very unusual, for often he would go straight up there in his pink coat, still stiff and tired from hunting all day, and play for hours, as I have related in my first volume. One could read his naturally restless disposition from his hands, long hands, in keeping with his large frame, beautifully shaped, but always moving : he wore, which was unusual, two rings, a wedding ring, and another, set with turquoises, and he would move them uneasily up and down his finger when bored or worried. He had a peculiarly charming voice, deep and rather floury, but often he would sit silently, fidgeting with his rings, until someone said something to amuse him, and his delightful laugh would sound out again. . . . I think his duties as a landlord, though he carried them off with a certain air, must have bored him profoundly. I am sure he hated the great entertainments that were given here and at Londesborough, and in London, while, on the other hand, he welcomed the excuse they offered him for working into them the occasion for a small orchestra or the importation of a circus. He needed the continual stimulus of the outside world to rouse him from his curious apathy, under which, although he was easily pleased and amused, smouldered, as with all his family, a temper of the utmost violence. I do not think he much enjoyed going to church, yet, judging by occasional outbursts, he appeared to be on terms of closer intimacy with the Almighty than anyone I have met : for, in addition to the often imaginative nature of his swearing, which I have already mentioned, it would, on the other hand, sometimes consist of the most direct invocations, such as, on the golf-course ; " Oh God, you know I hate missing the ball ; why did you let me do it ? ", or, in the dining-room, " Oh God, why do you always give me a wing of pheasant with a shot in it, so that I can break my tooth ? "

My aunt was certainly very different in temperament : tall and imposing, she had at this time the fairness and pallor of a northern goddess, she saw the world through a veil of vagueness, which, although her interests were more usual, removed her from the category of the ordinary. It struck one as singular that even with the aid of competent secretaries, grooms-of-the-chamber and the like, she should have been able to pay such minute attention to the physical welfare of her guests, so that, to take a single small example, a large jug of rain-water and a smaller one, filled with rose-water, were placed in each bedroom, and to organise, too, with such triumph the parties she gave in London. Perhaps it was an inherited ability, for her grandfather, the 11th Lord Westmorland — the cele-brated patron of music[1] and founder of the Royal Academy of Music —, and his wife had been famous for their hospitality, in London, Vienna and Berlin. As my aunt grew older, so the splendour of her entertainments mounted, together with her vagueness, which was yet curiously mingled with an almost soldierly directness. And this combination of qualities some-times led to amusing results. Thus while on a visit to Berlin in 1912 or 1913, she asked the Kaiser, straight out, whether the great German military and naval preparations then in progress were being made in order that he might attack England. She must, I think, have been the only person to ask so plain a question, and he was considerably taken aback by it. On her return, she told me about the ensuing talk, as if it had been the most natural thing in the world. The Emperor had, from the start, denied any hostile intention, so my aunt had proceeded relentlessly :

[1] John Fane (1784–1859), Lord Burghersh, succeeded his father as 11th Earl of Westmorland in 1841. After a distinguished career as a soldier, he became Minister in Berlin from 1841 to 1851, and Ambassador in Vienna from 1851 to 1855. Himself the author of many operas, cantatas, masses, hymns, madrigals and airs, he was a great friend of Rossini's, whom he helped financially. When the news of Lord Westmorland's death reached Berlin, the principal military bands massed together, and played Beethoven's funeral march, one of the dead man's favourite works, in his honour. He married Lady Priscilla Wellesley-Pole (1793–1879), daughter of the 3rd Earl of Mornington. As Lady Burghersh, she was a well-known artist, and the engraving of her portrait of her grandmother, the Countess of Mornington, surrounded by busts of that lady's other famous son and his two celebrated brothers, appeared in reproduction in the first volume of this book.

Lady Burghersh was the favourite niece and frequent companion of her uncle, the Iron Duke, who was also very fond of her younger son, Julian. Lady Desborough, Julian Fane's daughter, relates, in her *Eyes of Youth* (privately printed, University Press, Cambridge), how when he was a very little boy, someone enquired if he knew the Duke of Wellington, and the child indignantly replied, " Do I know him? Why, he is my near relation, and I am his most particular friend."

" Then what do you want all the armies for, sir, and this enormous new navy ? It's quite unnecessary."

" Because it interests me to manœuvre such large quantities of men," the Kaiser had replied, after a little hesitation.

This unusual talk took place some ten years later than the time of which I am writing. Though the Kaiser had very recently championed the cause of the Boers in the war, this was — or seemed — an age of peace, never to be broken in Europe, and the idea that he and his country would dare to fight Great Britain remained as yet incredible, outside the bounds of possibility. . . . Looking back at those days, with their formality and ritual, there are several features of them that arouse amazement : the quantity of creatures killed every day, for instance, and the comfort in which the sportsmen went to the massacre. They fed, even when out shooting, as though preparing their strength for armed combat against a mortal foe. Another matter for wonder was, of course, the continual changing of clothes that I have mentioned ; the guests always changed before tea, as well as before dinner. And though, as I have said, the children objected — I remember particularly an agonised outburst of Sacheverell's, when he was five or six, " I hate these parties ! Nothing but changing my clothes and washing my hands ! " —, the women no doubt took pleasure in it. There were always present here at Christmas certain famous beauties of the day — and the beauties of the Edwardian reign undeniably looked their best displayed in evening dress, by artificial light. They needed and enjoyed every inch of finery, every aid to allurement.

Little knots of maids and clumps of housemaids — phantoms who, in the next generation, were to inherit the earth — would be grouped together, like so many Cinderellas, under the arches above the staircase, to watch the party go down to dinner, noting, with envious feminine acuity, the silks and velvets, the huge puffed sleeves, the wreaths, the flowers, the jewels, the furs, the fans, the fringes and puffs. Many of these women, descending the stairs, already bought their clothes in Paris. The great fashions of the time, the moment when once again they became consciously fantastic, would not arrive for another few years, for we are yet in the first years of the reign. These dresses, for all the richness of their material, still possessed on the surface a kind of tasteless and disfigured naturalism, allied to musical-comedy standards, to the pink-and-white paper trees that do service for fruit-trees in the spring, and to the bumpy tunes : (we are approaching the apotheosis of musical comedy in *The Merry Widow*). The favourite colours were mauve and violet and rose. As for the figures to show off these dresses, the fashions of the day aimed at particular but not general slimness. The thin woman, like the ugly woman, hardly aspired to be a *femme fatale* until Léon Bakst had introduced her as paragon into Western Europe. The waist, alone, had to be slim, the body must iut out in front and behind. The stay-maker, rather than the costume-designer, appeared to be fashion dictator of that time, and, though the waist had not to be as minute as formerly, a good deal of constrictive torture, comparable to that caused in the contemporary Chinese Empire by fashionable binding of feet, still existed. As for the rest, every adjunct must be conventional and costly ; the dresses must be cut very low, while on the contrary the white kid gloves without which at dinner the women would have deemed themselves naked, and which could only be worn once, must reach as high as possible above the elbow. The mode was not yet fully modish, but all these women except the governesses, when present, and the members of the fun brigade, bore about them, nevertheless, the air of the latest mode of the minute ; an atmosphere that had been banished from the English *femme du monde* for over seventy years ; a period during which it had been confined to women of a different sort, on the smartness of whose appearance had depended their livelihood. Not since the florid days of King George IV had fashion been similarly triumphant.

It seemed as though this world, new born, would last for ever. One thing alone in this panorama might have suggested — though only then to those prescient to an almost prophetic degree — its coming disintegration. (Not, perhaps, that many of these people would have taken the threat very seriously, had they been able to foresee it, for the political doctrine of the Edwardian generation, as well as its altruism, was expressed very aptly in their favourite apophthegm — " Never mind ! It will last our time ".) One object alone might have given them a vision of a civilisation falling to chaos, and of the cities they loved, laid waste : the motor which sometimes tinnily vibrated and steamed in the frost outside the door ; for this was the first appearance of the internal combustion engine which was to destroy them. A few of the older generation, it is true, fought the very idea of their ultimate destroyer, but this was because of the novelty of the conveyance, not because of any instinct for their own protection : and perhaps, too, because their sons and daughters took to these machines as if born to them — which, in fact, they were. 1903 is the year of which I am speaking, and it was a very early date to own a motor-car. But even ten years later, when motors were established and had everywhere ousted horses, and, further, in spite of her dearly loved son's infatuation for them, I find my grand-mother writing in a letter to me : " I think motors such dangerous, horrid, odious things and always feel ill for days after I have been in one. Your dear grandfather would have hated them."

This last reflection was, of course, to her mind, conclusive evidence of their worthlessness, though I am sure she was incorrect in her assumption, for my grandfather loved speed. But most of her generation felt in that way, and the news, therefore, that my mother and I were going for a drive, had to be kept from my grandmother as carefully as from my father, so many years her junior. As for her contemporaries in the house-party, they could not help hoping, I conjec-ture, that one afternoon, this rare machine, puffing outside, would fail to return, and the audacious passengers with it. Further, it must be admitted that the accidents in which the motors of those days were continually involved, occurred as frequently, and often proved as fatal, as the bicycle acci-dents of ten years before or the aircraft accidents of ten years later.

This primitive motor vehicle of which I am speaking, belonged, I suppose, to some species of wagonette, now extin-guished in obedience to the laws of evolutional survival. Then it was still uncertain what shapes the motor would assume for its purpose of speed on land ; it could not have been foretold any more than millions of years ago the image of fish or bird or animal could have been deduced from the nature of a mollusc. This particular motor-car had inherited its features from horse-drawn carriages ; a black, oblong creation with the seats facing each other sideways, with a top that opened and shut — I was going to say at will, but, at any rate, under pressure, for it had first to be fought, and then knocked out and strapped down, as if it were a dangerous lunatic. This arduous combat was entered into on our behalf by François, the driver ; a Frenchman who, wearing a dark coat and a black cap — for chauffeur's hats had not yet been invented —, sat at the wheel, in order to control his luxurious and frisky machine. Just as the French tongue was acknowledged to be the language of diplomacy, since it offered the fullest scope for entering into the crafty devices and subterfuges that were necessarily the chief part of any diplomatic business, so too, French, it was recognised, would constitute the medium between driver and motor, could it talk — in short, English for horses, French for motors. No Englishman could be found tricky enough to manage such a novel and temperamental contraption ; a prejudice that is now history, crystallised in the English language by the word *chauffeur*.

Often I would accompany my mother and Sybil Westmorland when they went for a drive. Usually they would go just as far as Lincoln, in order, as they said, " to get the air " ; but these excursions at that date were also in essence romantic, similar to the night drives of King Ludwig of Bavaria, and an instance, too, of that passion for speed without purpose which members of their and the ensuing generation — including, I may say, myself as a motor-addict — were to develop to so intense a pitch that they could not be happy except at sixty miles an hour, or over : a passion which perhaps had begun in the attempt to escape from themselves ; if only they could go far and fast enough, how different they thought the world would be ! . . . We were supposed to start at about half-past three. But, in spite of my eagerness to be off, we would be sure to be late, and, by the time the preliminary bustling with fur rugs and struggling with hoods was finished, the lilac dusk had already begun to wrap the world round. . . . Before you could believe it, we were out of the park, with its plantations that were filling with shadows, upon the high road, and the primrose glimmer of lighted windows of cottages, sagging under their weight of snow, was already diminishing at the most improbable rate in the darkness gathering behind us. It was hardly credible, we would say to one another every now and then, in order to bring it home to ourselves, that such a journey could be accomplished in a mere half an hour. Already the towers of Lincoln Cathedral, clustered upon its hill, showed dimly, tangled with cobweb mists. We approached them with the same sense of venture and modernity with which today the air-minded descend on Africa or America. . . . Lady Westmorland and my mother would sit near the door : they were clad in caps and furs and capes and mufflers and many veils and thick fur gloves as though equipped for arctic exploration ; which, as a matter of fact, the look of the landscape as we whizzed — or comparatively whizzed — through it, over the crackling knife-blades of the frost, did make our jaunt a little resemble.

This is no guise, however, in which to introduce to the reader Sybil Westmorland, a famous beauty of the time ; because, for her to look her best, with a certain enamelled perfection, as of an Edwardian Bacchante, in the way of animated creation as fine an achievement as were the jewelled, expensive examples of Fabergé's craft in the inorganic, she needed, not only the attributes of her own individuality, myrtle leaves, cigarettes, scents, jade cigarette-holders, but also the full apparatus of a beauty. And as a rule, indeed, this was provided in abundance. But even more than her looks, based on superbly right proportions of features, and of ear to neck, and neck and head to body, was the *allure* which emanated from her, the aura of a famous beauty. It would be impossible, either, to recall her, without thinking of her voice, the deep intonations of it and of her laughter, that distinguish even today the members of her family. She was connected with my relations in several ways : for example, she was first cousin to Cecil Sitwell, whom I have mentioned earlier, and sister-in-law to my Aunt Londesborough. She was, moreover, a great friend of my mother's. But to children she seemed rather aloof, though never unkind to them. She was devoted to Burghersh and kind to me, and I often went to her house in London in Mount Street, and can still see the prosperous Edwardian sun streaming in at the dining-room windows at luncheon-time. Outside an electric landaulette would be waiting to take her for a drive. Though perhaps in her greatest beauty in the few years before the King came to the throne, yet her span was really the brief Edwardian decade, and her death was a symbol of its close.

At Blankney, I watched the Edwardian Age ripen. After 1905 or 1906, we stopped going there for Christmas and, though often the guest of my aunt and uncle elsewhere — for my aunt, despite her vagueness, possessed a very strong sense of family and tried to be kind to all her husband's and her own young relatives —, it so happened that I never saw it again until one summer's day, over thirty years later, when my cousin Hugo was to be married. This was in fact the first time that I had seen the country taken, as it were, out of cold storage. Then only was I able to form an idea of the configuration, of woods and meadows glowing now in a splendour of light, contained in that vast radiance held between sea and sky. Yet even now, this light, and the sky, filled the whole field of vision, seeming to be of so much more importance than the land, a flat country which might have been formed that very day out of light, as, across the sea, Holland had once been engineered out of the water. I found a place altogether strange to me. I had never before, even, seen the local landmarks, such as the immense column that rose on a slight eminence a few miles away, bearing on its top an effigy of King George III. (This pillar had been erected by a loyal subject, with the old, mad king to preside over it, as a lighthouse to guide travellers at night over the flat and lonely heath below.) Even the roads, I now discovered to lead in directions I had never suspected. All these things had been hidden by the snow, which at last had melted to reveal the surroundings, in the same way that the passage of time, flowing behind us, had revealed in the interval the trend of events, the fall of empires, the rise in their place of atrocious tyrannies. Now one could see the ground itself, but not the people it hid : my uncle and aunt were dead, Raincliffe, their eldest son, was dead : all the old were dead long ago : even the laughter of the fun brigade was silent. The kind of life itself which had been led here was rare today ; Russia, Austria, Germany, in all three of which it had flourished, were empty of it. To live in that way would seem lonely, now. Looking back at it was like regarding some previous existence of which we had once been part. . . . The house was just as it had been, though some of the rooms had grown smaller, while the various objects that a generation before had been responsible for evoking such an impression of luxury, now meant nothing, had attained a period air that made them almost seem to belong to a museum. Even the large portrait of my aunt and her son — the bridegroom of the day —, a picture which had formerly seemed so intensely of the present, had retreated into a vanished past.

That was the last time I saw Blankney — except once more, in a dream, a singular incident which I will relate. And since it concerned my cousin Hugo, whose marriage I had attended that summer afternoon some two years before, I must first explain that though we had always been friendly when we met, of recent years I had not seen much of him, for I was often abroad, while all his interests, hunting and racing, were of a different kind from mine and tended to keep him in the country. . . . It occurred in the early spring of 1937, when I was living in a villa near Vevey, on the Lake of Geneva. One night I was very restless, waking up at about two, and finding myself unable to get to sleep again for hours. . . . Eventually, about 6.30 in the morning, I fell into a long, troubling and involved dream, which yet did not pertain to the realm of nightmare. In it, I was in the Saloon at Blankney again, and Hugo, the owner of it, was talking to me very urgently. His words were simple enough, but laden with a weight of presage, and of sad and menacing feeling, and I knew that in his last sentence he was conveying to me something of importance. He said, " *There will be a party here at Blankney in ten days' time. All the relations are coming. They arrive by special train in the morning, and leave by special train in the afternoon.*" . . . Then I woke up ; to find I was being called by my servant. He handed me *The Times* of the previous day — it always arrived in Vevey twenty-four hours after it had come out in London. I sat up, still unreasonably distressed, opened the paper — and the first heading that caught my eye as I did so was " Serious Illness of Lord Londesborough ". . . . It was impossible to misapprehend so clear a portent, although in my dream seen in reverse : but I still hoped that I might be wrong, because I knew that all the members of Hugo's family had hitherto been buried at Londesborough, and this detail, so incorrect, seemed to falsify my reading of it. Howbeit, I was still so much oppressed by the feeling of the dream, that I told two friends, who were staying with me at the time, of it and of the sequel in the paper. . . . For a while it appeared that Hugo was better, but a week later he died, and three days after that was buried at Blankney.

Contrasted with this world I have attempted to describe were the holidays spent each spring during my father's absence abroad, with two cousins of his, two maiden ladies of middle age. No powdered footmen or groom-of-the-chambers, no grim housekeeper or still-room maids served in their small house, standing in a garden behind stone walls, in an Oxfordshire village, of which even the walls were thatched. The whole scene, the elaborate late-gothic church — large as a cathedral and with a spire too lofty even for so important a building as that —, round which the little village, built of golden stone, its every house thatched and having mullion windows, congregated with a curious perfection on the slopes each side of a small stream, appeared to be set, not as at Blankney in some eternal snowdrift of the senses, but in a perpetual springtide that belonged, because of the light and the perspective, because of the way the golden walls and buildings, with their roofs of thatch, looked against the landscape, and in spite of the fact that the country possessed hills, to the Dutch seventeenth-century masters or to the Flemish painters of an earlier time. The light had a golden edge to it, defined, yet ragged and hazy as the petals of giant sunflowers. And they, indeed, would have seemed the flowers most appropriate to beauty of this order, but my brother and I always arrived there in the season of primrose, daffodil and tulip. Then, the garden running down to the stream developed a special pre-Raphaelite charm that only belongs to small gardens in England, and, beyond that, to those situated by the side of water ; each blossom, though the flowers grew in drifts, seemed separately illumined, prospering in its own nimbus of life-giving spring sunshine. Every bird showed the arc or its flight, every feather, in blue or green or russet, startled you with the soft purity of its colour, every branch, every twig, every leaf now unfolding in lily and silver and pale rose, retained still its own entity, its individual value, had not yet entered into the full symphony of green. It was the instant of spring equivalent to that at a concert before the conductor takes his place, when every musician in an orchestra for a moment or two practises his own instrument.

Sacheverell and I would arrive in the evening, when the sun was staring in at the windows of the house; one cousin would be sitting on a painted bench against the wall, the cramped branches and coral-pink clustered cups of a japonica forming a background for her, while cousin Flora, the elder, would be carrying a trowel, or weeding, moving among the clusters of polyanthus, the complacent, fat faces of the double daisies, pink or red, or the anemones and narcissus which starred the grass, or she might be examining the apple-trees, their trunks white-coated with lime, that lifted foamy crests into the blue and humming air.

Cousin Flora was sober in attire, religious, serious-minded in outlook, though not intellectual, with a great belief in the benefits to the community of Sunday Schools and Physical Culture (it was due to her that my brother and I attended a gymnasium here), and a weakness for seed-cake : my younger cousin, Frederica, gay in mind and body, was given to mauve and blue as colours, liked to wear lace, ribbons and pieces of jewellery, was frivolous and proud of it. She used to tell me that immediately after she was born, her nurse had been obliged to give her a bath in brandy — or Eau-de-Vie, as she called it — to set her circulation going, and who knows but that this may not have been responsible for her genial temperament? My cousin Flora presided over the outdoor activities with one exception : the hunter belonged to cousin Frederica, who went out with the hounds regularly. Moreover, she attended local point-to-points and race-meetings (of which her sister disapproved, preferring her married sisters' prayer-meetings), and even occasionally, and with a sense of daring, indulged in a mild flutter — or so I gathered, one day, when, returning, she looked at me in a meaning way, and remarked, " Nothing venture, nothing gain". The farm and garden were cousin Flora's realm, but, if she arranged which cockerel was to be decapitated, and when the asparagus was ready to be picked, it was yet cousin Frederica who most enjoyed eating them, for she took an enterprising interest in food, and, after the manner of Pope's young nobleman, had

> Tried all hors d'œuvre, all liqueurs defined,
> Judicious drank, and greatly daring, dined.

Indeed I think she would sometimes have liked her elder

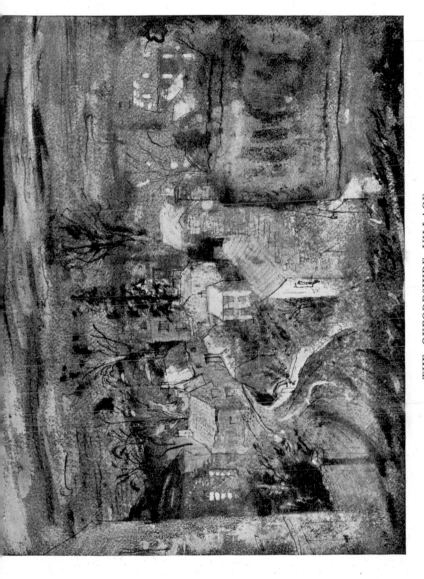

THE OXFORDSHIRE VILLAGE

by John Piper

THE ROOF ON THE HILL, RENISHAW

sister to have shown more interest in the cooking of the products for which she was responsible, and I remember her remarking to me once that the manner in which Flora, when she returned home after an absence of a month or two, entered the house, went straight to her special cupboard, and then, if she could not find the relic for which she was looking, straightway demanded " Where is my seed-cake ? ", was strongly reminiscent of the three bears in the fairy story of that name.

Again, my cousin Flora liked the company of clergymen or of relatives — which often came to the same thing —, while Frederica preferred the sporting, though she liked them to be a little godly too. Every Sunday, we would issue forth, down the hill, across the bridge, and up towards the church, Flora in very sable garb and carrying with determination a black prayer-book, Frederica, prim yet debonair, in an azure flutter of finery, crowned with a feathered hat. Even her prayer-book seemed more gay than that of others, more gleaming with purple and gold. Once in the pew, she would sit back, and only pretend to kneel for prayer, whereas Flora would kneel rigidly, taking protestant pleasure in her pain. During the sermon Frederica would allow her gaze to flit with a certain air of amused interest round the faces of the congregation. She would notice who was there and who was absent and comment on it afterwards. Her limpid, wide-open, bright-blue eyes, with their habitually quizzical expression, would rest, rather longer than on the other pews, upon one, usually empty, for she was especially worried that a neighbouring rich sportsman — he was said to have five thousand a year — so seldom attended his place of worship. . . . He was a bachelor. . . . There were stories. . . . It all seemed such a pity, such *waste*. A charming man to talk to. . . . But in any case Flora disapproved of him. Her eye remained fixed, with an almost death-like beadiness of concentration, of grappling with sacred subjects, upon the occupant of the pulpit. . . . Similarly, in the house, cousin Flora liked every window to be open, whatever the weather, while cousin Frederica liked them all to be shut, and if possible would order the fire to be lit. " I'm a chilly soul, I'm afraid," she used to say, warming her hands at it.

Notwithstanding the dissimilarity of their appearances and

the divergence of their views, they undoubtedly possessed various characteristics in common. Thus, without looking to see, it was often difficult to tell which of the two was talking, for they both spoke with the same clear voice, inexorably certain of its rights and used to evoking in others, in response to it, an attitude of deference. The syllables were spaced and stressed and used with an architect's sense of proportion, yet this music, with its assured unfolding, held its surprises; for instance, a sudden downward inflection, that resembled the swoop of a toboggan or switchback. It was a family voice — though very different from that of my mother's relations that we have heard so recently — and, like the many books to be noticed in the library, linked up with the Peninsular War. It belonged to the tradition of the sweet and imperturbable Bishop's wife, whom no one, not even a naked, fuzzy savage, could startle, anger or abash. It was a voice relentless in the prosecution of a conversational object and in its conviction of being in the right. Nothing, one was aware from the first moment of hearing it, would ever put it off key. . . . It was impossible not to wonder how the two voices would sound and behave, if a quarrel were to break out between the ladies. . . . But, in fact, they got on well together, in spite of their differing so often in the opinions they put forward. In the past, however, certain disputes had taken place occasionally, so that each sister had pasted somewhere on every article of furniture belonging to her — whether it were an oak chair, a table, a bronze, a chased-silver photograph-frame, or merely a Japanese vase full of last year's pampas-grass — a label, which bore on it in clear, black, decisive letters, admitting of no question, the name FLORA or FREDERICA. Thus, if either of them decided of a sudden to quit, she could accomplish it immediately, departing with her own belongings and without the possibility of further discord.

These were still the days — for my two cousins carried the late-Victorian reign with them wherever they went, and died, as they had lived, in it —, when every unmarried woman must " have a hobby ", something that would distinguish her attractively from others, so that, for example, when, in conversation, someone asked " Do you know Molly Mohacksfield ? ", another would be sure to interject " Do you mean the striking-looking Miss Mohacksfield, who does the poker-work ? " — or more often "who goes in for poker-work?". Well, it was typical of my cousins that Miss Flora "went in" for "artistic leather-work", embossing Renaissance tulips in fretted shallow relief upon pig-skin wallets, and even upon unoffending blotters, while Miss Frederica made "*bon-bons*", as she termed them, or "*fondants*". These comfits, bright as faded flowers, tasted of lavender-water and violet cachous; for her liking for good food somehow stopped short of her own confections. (The end to which most of them came, together with her sister's *terre-à-terre* fantasies in pig-skin, was a church bazaar, at which they were always much in demand, bringing in a good deal of money, for usually they would first of all constitute a prize in a lottery or raffle, while the winner could always be depended on to put them up again immediately for auction.) Further — and this was more audacious — she made liqueurs, which beguiled without intoxicating the consumer.

The consumers were few, for my two cousins lived in no blaze of entertainment. But though there were few servants, I made many more friends here than at Blankney. The cook — Mrs. Otley, if I remember rightly — and the groom-odd-man, these soon became my dear and indulgent friends: — he, Emerson, in a few years' time retired and became the village carrier, loitering in his cart down the network of country lanes all through the long summer days, and the brief hours, glittering under the rain's lances, of the winter, only making a rare, resplendent and cockaded emergence on occasion to drive my cousins for some important outing, thereby perhaps dislocating temporarily the goods traffic of the village. I became acquainted, too, with many of the shopkeepers, with their bow-windows full of boot-laces, ribbons, buttons on cards, and bull's-eye peppermints in jars. Looking back, the villagers here seem to me to have resembled French peasants more than the ordinary rustic English; they even possessed the same long, small, narrow noses and thin-lipped, sullen smile, and, in addition, that particular carriage of the head, poised midway between stiff-neck and goitre, which is yet a spiritual more than a physical attribute, associated with the desire for independence and a resolve to get the best of a bargain; an aspect to which Modigliani, alone of portraitists, has done justice.

The house, though of comparatively few rooms, offered

that luxury only to be obtained in old houses, plenty of waste space. The broad landings zigzagged unnecessarily, and turned in on themselves. I had as bedroom an attic, with beams at cross-purposes ; but the sort of a bedroom a boy likes. And there, in spite of my tutor, I used to retire for long periods, sitting among the vases of flowers which I had gathered, and read Dickens. The house contained few books that I wanted to read ; they were mostly collected volumes of early nineteenth-century sermons, the novels of Mary Cholmondeley, a relative, or interminable two-volume works about the Peninsular War. (My cousin Frederica, who liked to read fiction, always obtained her novels in Banbury, choosing them on the advice of a gay young assistant ; " I hope it is not too *risqué* ? ", she would ask with a certain smiling hesitation, as of one tempted.) In consequence, I saved up my money to buy cheap editions in Banbury, always at the same time buying — which shows the lessening of sales-resistance effected by tradition — an indigestible, but undeniably original, Banbury cake. The tutor would accompany me on these jaunts, but somehow he never appeared so objectionable or offensive as at home, melting into the background, as it were, in the same way as the prayers. For I suppose there *were* as many prayers here as at Gosden, and almost as many clergymen, stretching, frieze-like, between lych-gate and garden entrance.

The stars, too, in our conversation were the identical ecclesiastical luminaries, the brightness of whose shining here was compensated for by their dimness elsewhere. One, I recall, a connection of ours, was always referred to as " The Chancellor ", and so, since he never materialised in the flesh, ever remained in the imagination for me, clothed in black robes and a mortar-board, a bottle-nosed, lack-lustre survival from the eighteenth century. A brighter star, here as elsewhere, was Randall Davidson, then the Bishop of Winchester. And Canon Groucher blazed here too, until his final eclipse, with the same leonine strength as at Gosden. There were, however, more modern touches. The two ladies talked much of Reginald Farrer, their nephew, now at Oxford, and of his friends. If, on the other hand, I happened to mention any of my nearer relations on my mother's side, a perceptible hush would fall, and my two cousins would catch each other's eye, bead answering twinkle, for my mother had often been disagreeable to them, and in any case her relatives belonged to the wicked world of pleasure. And though the idea of this frivolous existence may at times have captivated Frederica, it must be remembered that she was merely the most pleasure-loving member of a serious-minded family, and that her own proclivities towards pleasure were controlled, like the exercise of nuns in a cloister. . . . They never overtly expressed their disapproval, though; nor, in return, did I ever disclose my secret views on curates.

Of the two cousins, I preferred the lively Frederica. And so, though fond as well of Flora, neither Sacheverell nor I could repress our laughter when, on one occasion having come to the gymnasium, where a sergeant with a waxed moustache, beer-coloured face and a painfully indrawn belly was instruct-ing us, she suddenly, while we were going through our paces, protested loudly, " You're not doing the parallel bars cor-rectly; this is the way to do it ! ", and, taking an earnest running leap at a similar apparatus next to ours, landed with an unforgettable wallop on the floor beyond. . . . Neverthe-less, we are grateful to her for her kindness, and for her example in most things — only a little less than to my cousin Frederica who gave me a piece of advice by which I profited more than by any other I ever received. . . . As a child, I tended to be unduly suspicious of people's motives and, indeed, to ques-tion their honesty. I think I considered myself clever and grown-up for adopting such an attitude. . . . Thus, when on one occasion I went up to London with Frederica, I lost a shilling-piece, and telling her about it, remarked, " I wonder if it was stolen." To my surprise, instead of applauding me for my interesting theory and offering sympathy, she replied, " Well, if it has been taken, you had better try to forget about it, or even persuade yourself that it hasn't been stolen at all, or, when you grow up, you'll ruin your life with your ridiculous suspicions, as I see your father doing. He always thinks everyone is trying to rob him, and it poisons his whole existence without preventing his being robbed. Indeed, in some ways, I believe it *makes* people rob him. . . . Besides, nobody steals a shilling. It is much more likely to be due to your own carelessness and untidiness."

We did not resent such outspokenness, and liked being with them. Moreover, the simplicity of the routine here, the weeding and gardening and cutting of flowers, the actual processes of the house, the sacrifice of a fowl or two before a favoured guest was coming to stay, possessed its own scale of interest, which enabled one to banish trying or extraneous matters without bother or even effort, and, further, taught one certain valuable facts. Hitherto, for example, roast chicken had been hypocritically disassociated in my mind from the bird I saw scratching the ground in a run : but here the connection became plain, emphatic, yet, somehow or other, was debrutalised through common sense. It was taken as a matter of course, and Mrs. Otley would discuss with me beforehand the prospects of the victim turning out to be a " good fat bird ". Similarly, the dappled litter of black-and-tan Berkshire pigs surrounding their mother, as the petals of a flower surround its golden centre, became the raw material for pork and bacon. Such lessons helped, too, to develop political sense, so that one became suspicious, later, when it was explained that we only needed great armaments in order to preserve peace, and had taken our various colonial possessions merely so that we might help the natives.

In such respects, in that it was small enough to bring you up short against life — or death —, this place offered the strongest possible contrast to Renishaw or Blankney, as in all others. Even the flowers that grew here were different from those round my home. By the hedges and banks of this country — a country that flowed with a small but regular rhythm, and was not, as in Derbyshire, a mountainous land, in which every hill inclines to be a minor mountain rather than an enlarged mound, not possessed of the tragic spirit as was the landscape in which we had been nurtured, full of broken chasms and sudden gulfs —, by these quiet unobtrusive features were spread whole carpets of violets, mauve, lilac or white, and scented beyond any garden variety. And I was taken, too, to see a meadow where fritillaries, mottled as snakes, speckled as guinea-fowls, bowed their heads. . . . Sometimes, again, we would be provided with treats suitable to the spring weather, a morning bicycle-ride with the tutor round the neighbouring villages, where the butter-coloured sunshine dappled little hills and lofty spires, or a day at Warwick, or at Stratford-on-Avon, where we inspected Anne Hathaway's house, and passing over a bridge, saw Miss Marie Corelli —

Hall Caine's opposite number — reclining in her gondola.
But my cousin Flora disapproved of her books, in spite of their
strongly moral tone, and said she considered a gondola out of
keeping with the Avon, an error of taste. It was bad enough
to find one of those horrid, snorting new motor-cars in Shakespeare's birthplace : what would he have said ?

Once, too, we drove over to Weston, to see my grandmother Sitwell's old home, often mentioned in these pages.[1]
It was situated so far from a station that we were obliged to
make the whole expedition in the carriage, covering a distance
of some fifteen miles or so each way, down country lanes
that seemed to lead nowhere except to banks of blossom,
each journey occupying several hours. My Aunt Puss,[2] to
whom the estate belonged, still lived in Scarborough, and in
consequence the house was shut up. Ever since Sir John
Blencowe had bought it for his daughter it had remained
in the family, always descending on the distaff side, and
usually acting as a dower-house, connected with a larger
demesne. In consequence, it presented a picture new to me,
of a house that had been for two centuries the home of women
— young girls, maiden ladies, widows, old women, but seldom
of men. It was still full of ineffaceable shadows of the past.
My aunt's long absence, therefore, made little difference to it,
for the place seemed then as if it could never appear unlived-in,
though my aunt was away, any more than it would ever
appear lived-in, however many people should come to reside
here. Even the approach, which led out of a hamlet lost in
remote and placid country, just sloping enough to bar each
distant perspective, making every view a miniature world, so
that the house, standing above grey garden walls, covered
with lichen, and retaining their gothic coping, looked across
a tangle of laurels in the wildest, most delightful disorder at
the façade of Armada House, a golden Elizabethan manor built
in the year of the great Spanish disaster, and thus existed in a
vista of its own, closed to space and time ; even the gates, even
the ancient trees, so tall and rugged as to be out of proportion
with the landscape, seemed cobwebbed with time as was the
Palace of the Sleeping Beauty.

The doors of the stables, I remember, were open as we

---

[1] See *Left Hand, Right Hand!* vol. i, pp. 35, 40-44.
[2] *Ibid.*, vol. i, pp. 168-9.

drew up, and I ran to look inside : the sole vehicle it contained was an antique carriage, the interior of it padded in cobalt blue, super-buttoned, and with door-handles of silver and ivory. It must, I suppose, have belonged to the 1840 period, and the fat horses that once drew it had been dead half a century and more, though the stalls still smelt of them. The house, with its *bibelots*, toys and clothes, all carefully preserved by this air, so peculiarly clean and pure, though laden with odours of the past, was as feminine as Renishaw, with its breast-plates, old guns, stags' heads and rusty stirrups with lanterns attached to them, was masculine. Children's games of two centuries before were lying on the dustless tables, even the pack of playing-cards went back to a time before the French Revolution ; upstairs, in a lacquer chest, were the unworn suits of a young dandy who had died, at the age of nineteen, just when Mozart was at the height of his genius (let us always assign events to a period after this fashion, rather than connect them with the enormous, senseless catastrophes ever and again precipitated upon us by our own and European politicians) ; and I found on a shelf over the door in the lumber-room a flint-and-tinder box, still waiting there for the visitor to strike a spark.

I enjoyed staying with my cousins, then, the everyday existence, no less than these treats. I entered into the life with zest. The whole place appealed to me with an unusual strength. My two cousins knew it, but they never comprehended the chief reason for this attachment — it was here that I fell in love at first sight for the first time ; a thing which has happened to me on many occasions since.

What is it, what can it be, some chemical affinity or magnetic force that is responsible for the *first-sight* kind of love ? That you see someone for a moment, and the next the whole world is changed, so that you wonder what can have happened. It is as though you had hitherto been colour-blind, and now, by looking for a moment at the face of a stranger, had been made whole and given the entire world of vision. . . . I suppose all children feel strong attractions and, indeed, have tentative love-affairs, but do they suffer from these shock-tactics in the same way ? . . . I do not know. This was my initial experience of them, at any rate, and that which surprises me most in recalling it is that I was not more surprised.

For what, that one knew, could it mean? Just because I had suddenly seen, had almost run into, a small girl of about my own age, who had been standing by the stream, talking — and in broad Oxfordshire, at that — to a group of rather dirty, small village boys, just because I had, in that instant, observed the sunlight shape her head and ruddy neck, and had seen the flushed, rather dark face glowing through the shadow cast on it by her wide-brimmed hat, and had then, for a second, gazed involuntarily into her brown and doe-soft eyes, which seemed to contain a warm and passionate melancholy that was unusual ; why, then, when I was, as a matter of fact, as yet inclined to be a little homesick for Renishaw and the company of my own family, should this single glimpse of a stranger raise life to a level I had never hitherto known, and why should the memory of it remain with me now, albeit I have long forgotten the child's name, to persist, no doubt, until the hour of my dying? What could it have led to? — for physical paths were still barred to us, and I seem to have been singularly, obtusely incurious. I knew nothing of how human beings came into the world ; of those great mysteries tied to the sun and moon and stars, of those minute, individual vibrations of the whole tremendous rhythm of the universe, complying with laws beyond it, before the very nature of which we are at a loss ; of these manifestations of the vast and incomprehensible, known, so unimaginatively, as " the facts of life ", I still remained in utter and resolute ignorance. As yet the time had not even arrived, when, before school, I used to be sent for by the headmaster, or be taken out for a walk during the holidays by a tutor, or some other official representative of my father — he tended to avoid the discussion of such matters with me —, appointed to enlighten me. Even then I could not understand, just *could not* take the information in. At the end of these long interviews, I remained as obstinately innocent as at the beginning. The matter had to be explained to me over and over again, until pastors and masters had exhausted upon me the whole scholastic euphemism of the language of flowers, and were at last driven to abandon their ingenious use of symbolism, and, by now themselves wearied and shocked, to get down to brass tacks and call a spade a spade. So, this passion, the nature of which I was so far from grasping, this biological urge without reason which I was experiencing, must, I suppose, have been experimental, a way devised for the young to test and learn. At any rate, under this influence the whole of life became suffused with the light of the sun — and this at the very moment when, since I could not understand it, or what it was about, I skipped in the novels I was reading every page devoted to a love-affair ! My feelings may appear — and may have appeared then — absurd, but they were intense, the sensation was physical, certainly, the effect curiously spiritual and uplifting, bringing out — for it must have been innate — a new and most acute consciousness of being part of the world, of union with the animal creation, of kinship with trees and birds.

Moreover, just as a peacock drums and dances in the courtship season, so I behaved in the classic manner lovers know. That is to say, I got in the way. I loitered, with a slightly shamefaced air, in those spots where my sweetheart was likely to appear. I made her, and myself, look ridiculous — or might have done so. If I did not find her where I expected, I wandered everywhere through the village, seeking her. I succeeded in identifying the house in which she lived — her mother kept a rustic odds-and-ends shop — and thereafter was continually passing it, and, if I could possess myself of the courage, entering to buy something I did not want, in order to be, even for the brief interval of such a transaction, near someone connected with this marvellous being. I provided myself with excuses of every kind to play by the border of the stream at all hours, because she usually waited there, by the side, under the stone bridge, for a little every day, while she talked to her friends. I began at this time, too, to pay considerable attention to my clothes, often sporting a flower in my buttonhole. To my cousins, who must have been astonished at so sudden a departure from the slovenly appearance I had acquired at school, I pretended that my smartness and my unnaturally clean hands were part of a genuine tidiness campaign. . . . In fact, I was out to make an impression.

The little girl must, indisputably, have asked herself what this tall, fair-haired, long-faced boy was doing, always near her, always crossing her path, staring at her with such a fixed gaze, with so longing and perhaps startled a look, as though he had been translated ; why, in short, did he never speak, but just gape — for I do not remember that we ever spoke, except to say good-morning and goodbye? I believe she guessed my secret, for she seemed to respond with a sort of coquettish solemnity. She continued to go down to the bridge nearly every day. . . . Sometimes I would cross it and join her for an instant or, much more often, merely stand, a little way off, above, by the parapet, and, still staring at her, remain there. She would pretend not to notice or, at any rate, not too much — for she would, or so it seemed to me, give me occasionally in return a dark, lingering glance, in which a smile dissolved like Cleopatra's pearl in wine. I can only hope that my admiration may have in some way or other been a source of pleasure to her, in the same fashion that the kindness towards me, which I assumed from her behaviour, affected me, affording so exquisite an uplifting of the senses. . . . Had she been shy, run away, or made village fun of me, my self-possession might have been shattered beyond repair. As it was, I had not to think of *how* to see her. I knew the locale. But the amount of time I wasted, mooning down by the stream, even at hours when she was not likely to be there, in case she came and I should miss her, eventually impressed itself upon the minds of my two cousins, or perhaps of my tutor, though I do not think they knew what to make of it. And so my younger cousin, the gay Frederica, said to me one day :

" What were you doing down by the bridge today ? You're always there now."

This direct attack took me by surprise, and I must certainly have blushed, as I answered weakly and with a certain lack of candour, " I was looking in the water, to see if I could see a fish."

" I suppose we shall have you fishing for tadpoles next — I believe all boys do —, and then poor Emily will have additional work drying and cleaning all your clothes," she said, in a somewhat acid tone. . . . Little did she know what heights and depths of romantic feeling she thus brushed aside.

One small episode, a ridiculous episode, I now recall as being mixed up with this early love-affair, though it sprang in the first place from my childish nocturnal nervousness, to which allusion has already been made. . . . I slept upstairs in the attic, and though in the daytime I loved it, there were hours, especially before falling asleep, when it seemed very far-off, high-up and lonely. I used to read until as late an hour as I could without being found out, and, no doubt, alarmed myself a great deal more with Dickens's exciting plots, devoured at the tremendous speed at which I now read everything. Often it seemed that such dark happenings as the murder of Mr. Montague Tigg in a wood had taken place instead in my very room, or as though the fettered stranger from the marshes, in *Great Expectations*, was looking in at the small window in the roof, clanking his chains as he drew himself up. . . . Anyhow, one night I was so terrified that I crept softly downstairs to near the door of the drawing-room. It was after dinner, my tutor had successfully gulped down one of my cousin Frederica's liqueurs, derived, it seemed, in conjunction from oranges that had left their country for their country's good and from the hot heart of caraway seeds, burning the throat with a sugary but abiding fire, and the ladies and he were sitting there talking. The light in the passage outside had been extinguished, and only the flat, golden chinks between the door and the jamb showed where the drawing-room lay. . . . The reader may begin, from what I have related concerning an occurrence of the same sort at Scarborough, to conclude that I was an eavesdropper : but herein he will be wrong. It was not so. Some nameless fear, in which the aspect of my room, the shadows of the beams and the dark corners that, in flickering candlelight, extended it until a Piranesi-like sense of fantasy and doom possessed it, had suddenly overwhelmed me ; the light from the door proved a solace, so I waited there, and could not help hearing the conversation.

My cousin Flora was talking, in her clear, slow, deliberate voice, in which every syllable had its correct value.

" Of course, Osbert *is* quite an intelligent boy," she was saying, " but in some ways he seems very backward for a boy of his age. . . . What a pity that HE NEVER DOES ANYTHING USEFUL ! "

This judgement, and the sounds of acquiescence in it that now reached my ears, smote me to the heart, and I slunk away to bed with something worse to think about than nocturnal terrors. . . . So *that* was what they thought of me ! . . . The words haunted my conscience. I had not known my cousins very well hitherto, but had quickly become attached to them and, in return, had hoped to create a good impression. Alas, now it became clear to me how unsuccessful I had been, because I was aware that they held the terrible, newly-imported American doctrine that everyone ought to do something : (hence leather-work and liqueurs). . . . Moreover, what they said was *true* : I felt it, acknowledged it. Worse still, it proved that I was *not worthy* of my love down by the stream. . . . I was determined to correct as soon as possible the so grave defect in my character that had been thus revealed to me, no less in order to recapture my self-esteem than to obliterate the unfavourable opinion it had caused others to form of me. . . . But what could I do ? What could I do ? . . . For a time I decided on escape to Klondyke, the retreat to which fellows like myself (but they seemed usually to be *younger* sons) appeared in the end always to consign themselves, to show of what stuff they were made. I had recently been reading some romance pitched in that rough scene, and it had greatly pleased me : but, in addition, one continually in those days heard whispers of it, for scarcely a county family in England but had some cousin there, a black sheep of a fighting disposition, living in a shack, with nothing to read but the Bible given him by his mother, and with his garden edged off with rows of broken whisky bottles. I pictured myself, brave but forlorn, wearing a pair of huge caribou-skin trousers, with the butt of a revolver peering out of a hip-pocket, a dirty shirt, with two pockets in front, and a wide-awake hat, digging, sifting, sorting, and then proudly sending an enormous nugget home to cousin Flora. Alas ! on reflection, and after looking at a map, the journey to this arctic Eldorado seemed both long and difficult. . . . What then remained that I could do that would be *useful* ; some task nearer home, at which I could work unobserved, until suddenly I chose to reveal the results of my labour in all its splendour ? To what could I turn my hand ? . . . And now some beaver-instinct came to my rescue — or perhaps I had been reading again, this time about the great engineering feat in progress at Assouan, and the benefit British rule brought to Egypt by flooding the temples — I could build a dam !

Fortune seemed to smile on my plans. For two entire days my tutor went away " to visit my people ", as he phrased it, and for the whole of that time I was able to give my undivided energy and attention to the great public work to which I had determined to devote myself. Accordingly I set to, in a fever of love and wounded vanity, labouring with an immense zeal, and suffering little danger of interference. Stones, bricks, beams, tins, old boxes, old sacks, a pair of boots, even, everything I could lay my hands on, went to the completion of my self-imposed task — or job, as I preferred to call it, for that sounded more workmanlike. Nor was it as messy a performance as one might have presumed, for there had been a prolonged spell of fine weather hitherto ; spring weather which offered unclouded skies, wherein the birds bounced and sang with unsurpassed blitheness. The stream had dwindled almost to nothing, and the ground was so dry that my clothes luckily afforded no clue to the nature of my present occupation. . . . Everything appeared, then, to be going well — and, indeed, I must have builded better than I knew, for when, on the third morning, the weather broke with a sudden, inconjecturable fury, my dam held up the water so competently that it formed a miniature pool, until finally, after an hour or two, it burst with appalling results. The bottom of my cousins' garden, of which they were so proud, was devastated ; this was its most sheltered spot, and so the flood swept away all the latest and most precious and delicate shrubs, on which they had lavished care and money, all the new blue primroses and dwarf daffodils and new rose-bushes, and the fine Italian terra-cotta pots of which my father had made them a present, and which had only just been moved into the open air — (they placed so great value on them that they were kept indoors, away from danger of frost, all the autumn and winter). Even the rustic wooden bridge, lately constructed, was now in irremediable ruin. Nothing remained but mud and broken sticks. . . . Worst of all, the children who played by the stream, my sweetheart among them, incurred the blame, for my cousins recognised immediately, by the nature of the damage, the extreme force of the water, and the fact that it had held up for a full hour after the storm had finished, that there had been foul play.

" Those wretched children," I heard Frederica say, " must have crept in under the bridge when we were out, and worked at it for days ! "

To save others, I must own up. . . . I asked to speak to my cousin Flora.

" I'm afraid the flood was my fault," I said.

" *Your* fault," she enquired incredulously. " What do you mean ? "

" I'm afraid I built a dam."

" But what ever induced you to attempt such a thing ? "

" I was trying TO DO SOMETHING USEFUL," I replied.

She received the confession kindly, though she looked rather cross, and added :

" Now we know what you were always doing down by the stream. . . . We couldn't make it out."

So, in these petty terms, my great love and my great labour were both dismissed under a complete misapprehension.[1]

---

[1] The incident of the dam had altogether faded from my memory, until revived, a year or two ago, by reading of the exploits in America of a beaver who had found himself in rather similar trouble. Though averse as a rule from including nature jottings in the pages of my autobiography, I cannot in this instance refrain from recording the gist of what I read. . . . The beaver had been captured, and for some reason the hunter took the beast with him to his small flat, high up in a New York skyscraper, before proceeding the next day to his country retreat. . . . His wife received the unexpected visitor kindly, and it was decided that the best place for the animal to pass the night was in the drawing-room. Accordingly they placed a wooden box, lined with straw, in the apartment, so that he could curl up in it, and locked the door. . . . When they entered the next morning, they found nothing else in the room, except the beaver and a dam. The creature had apparently knocked over a small table with a vase of flowers upon it, and the consequent finding of water on the floor had brought his dam-building instinct into play. He had carefully sawn up all the eighteenth-century chairs and tables, by which his host and hostess set such store, and had, with the portions and with the aid of cushions and books, constructed a remarkably perfect example of a dam.

Chapter Three
A BRIEF ESCAPE INTO THE EARLY
MORNING

AFTER my first term at school, I settled down —
as it seemed for life — in a dunces' class, under a dunce master.
Before long, I had reached a state of dunder-headed despair,
out of the depths of which I could not rise. I could, for
instance, pass no examination, since, in order for me to do
my best, or even tolerably well, at anything, I had then —
as I have today — to be congratulated very warmly and at
frequent intervals upon my performance. I knew that I
could do better, but the conditions governing such a hypo-
thetical improvement did not exist. . . . It was a cruel predicament, because I could find no way of escape ; being
comparable in that respect to the religious crisis in which I
had earlier found myself involved, and wherefrom the reader
has seen my father deliver me. For over a year I dwelt in so
dark a valley, lived in so deep an abyss of spiritual misery,
that the physical collapse ensuing at the end of it should have
offered no matter for wonder to parents or masters. Illness,
however, did eventually come to my aid. It freed me.

During my second summer term, a mysterious and novel
epidemic, said to be of pleurisy, broke out, and introduced
a certain element of variety into the usual curriculum of
school diseases appropriate to the season : colds, influenzas,
pink-eye, chickenpox, measles (German and Empire), scarla-
tina, scarlet fever, whooping-cough — or " whoopers ", as it
was familiarly known — mumps, boils, blains and ringworm.
Since cases continued to occur, we did not again reassemble
after the customary exeat for the Eton and Harrow match.
My mother decided to take me to Scarborough, where, as
our arrival was unexpected, I for once found no regular tutor
in ambush for me. Major Viburne had, therefore, hurriedly
to mobilise himself and his faculties, and come, every morning,
a military figure, in his thin, primrose-coloured leather boots

THE ESPLANADE, SCARBOROUGH
by John Piper

WOOD END

through the sunshine that lay in pools upon the asphalt paths, black and white like spotted dogs in reverse, that were such a feature of the town, to Wood End, some mile and a half away, so that he could teach me once again the rudiments of those things that I had forgotten at school. It would be true, I think, to state that both he and I possessed a genius for making my lessons dull. For myself, I had completely lost interest in work — and never found it again until I stumbled into my profession. I repelled with alternate attacks of fury and baffling dullness every attempt to instil knowledge into me. I made it plain that I knew nothing, and was determined at all costs to defend my sacred ignorance. In consequence, I became almost as unpopular at home as at school. . . . Edith, accompanied by her new governess, had just gone to live for some months in Paris, in order to perfect her French, and my chief companion was Sacheverell. To everyone else — even to my mother, who did not pretend to any respect for learning — my conduct during the fourteen days or so that followed must have brought a sense of frustration.

The hours of liberty that I spent at this time possess, as I look back at them, a singular atmosphere, surcharged, perhaps because of my approaching illness, with feelings and impressions. In the East Riding, hot weather is rare enough, but now, for the short space, the whole town sweltered, though its green summer seas appeared so cool. A curious heat, veiled but glowing, brooded over the northern streets, flicked into life again at morning and evening, or at the change of tides, by a breath, brief and salty, of cold air. In spite of the mist, which compelled short perspectives, the parti-coloured shirts, with their pellucid yet aqueous tints that looked as if seen through clear, deep water, and the peaked caps of the jockeys, astride the ponies that drew the carts, quivered and shone as they rode by. Soon these light and rapid vehicles were to vanish from this scene, their only home, to which they lent so unique a charm, obscured by the dark clouds of the petrol fumes generated by the conquering motor-car. Already a little of the splendour had departed. No longer, for example, was there to be seen that familiar turn-out, with yellow wheels and silver fittings. This equipage had been formed by a once notorious, but now forgotten figure of the late-Victorian world, Benzon — the Jubilee Juggins or Plunger, as he was known to the crowds on the great race days, and in the pages of the daily and sporting papers of the time. The jockey who drove this cart, which used to have its stand near the Royal Hotel, wore the racing colours of the owner, that extravagant and vulgar fantastic who had lavished his fortune on the turf. Nevertheless, many of these vehicles, effective and jaunty, still remained, to compete in varnish and watery sparkle with the more exuberant painting and gilding, on a white, involved ground, of the hokey-pokey carts which flashed in the tarnished sunlight down on the foreshore. From there, and from the old town beyond, was wafted the smell of fish, floating above like a banner to proclaim its trade. The cobbles of the slums that ran down the astonishingly steep hill from the Castle to the harbour were always slimy with scales. The houses of this quarter, in Dumple Street for example, had seen better days, presented façades of red brick that, though tattered and shabby, were pleasantly designed, set behind eighteenth-century railings and iron-work ; but at the back of them lay reeking courts, foul and desolate, only to be reached through alleys dark and long, where every shadow seemed to possess an equivocal significance, as well as a different substance from shadow elsewhere.

In the combined degradation and vigour of its life, Dumple Street still appertained in very essence to the days of Hogarth, rather than to our own, just as the shopping thoroughfares on the hill opposite belonged to the world of the 'seventies and 'eighties, to the pretty, fluent canvases of Tissot, and the great paintings of Seurat. In those dapper streets across the bay, it seemed to me that every shop was now offering fruit for sale, and its drooping fragrance, slightly tainted, permeated the air ; there were pyramids of apricots, rare in ordinary years, with their red skins toughened by the sun and wind of the Yorkshire Wolds, where they ripened on grey stone walls, there were freckled, rather damp strawberries, and raspberries, the scarlet juice from which stained the stiff white paper under them, and mounds of plums and greengages, spilt, bursting and in disarray. Once out of these busy streets, full of the quacking of everyday life, of busy tongues, prodding, grasping fingers and the clink of scales and weights and measures, a limpid stillness prevailed in the misty light, and sounds from far away reached one as distinctly as the odours ;

the barrel-organs assumed a more southern tone than usual as they creaked out their rattling tunes from *Florodora* or *San Toy* — tunes that seemed to have been composed to be tinkled on the bells of bicycles and to be whistled by those who rode them —, while down below on the beach, in their ruffs and sugar-loaf caps, the white-clad pierrots who had by now wrested each sandy pitch from their defeated rivals, the nigger minstrels, could be heard singing their fatuous songs, and laughing at their own jokes against the immense background of the sea, today quiet and controlled, but, because of that, none the less overwhelming : so that their voices, lifted against it, sounded as if their owners were trying to scratch their names upon the granite of the Great Pyramid.

The vapid melodies and cracked piano strove, too, it seemed, to cover up the cries of the old woman who sold fish — but they could not compete. It was as though her voice belonged to the sea, was part of its roaring might, just as her wares lived in it. She pushed along a huge tray on wheels, piled up with the pearly light-flecked riches of the ocean, semi-transparent or opaque and armoured ; plaice and sole, and whiting and haddock and cod, but especially whiting and cod. The whiting had already become, as it were, conventional, each one forming an opalescent circle, with its tail through its mouth, but a large, dark-bellied crab still battled its plated legs against the air, and the flat bodies of the other fish, their skins white and cream and fawn and beige and grey, often dotted, too, with a sprinkling of red spots or finished, seem-ingly, with patent leather, glistened damply in the sun. And all the feeling of these, her wares, was in her voice. It is singular how melancholy, how harsh and piercing, is the cry of fish in every country, every tongue, as if those who sell it derived their tonal inspiration from cats, acknowledged to be the species transcendent in its love of fish, but in Scarborough there were exceptions to the rule, and this voice, though so astonishing in its volume, was pleasant. Moreover the owner of it possessed a rival here, a man by name Bland, an itinerant vendor of shell-fish. He might, in other circumstances, and had he been trained, have made a singer : certainly his grand cry, in a tenor voice, loud and vibrant, of *Cockles and mussels, alive, a-live O ! Fine cockles ! Cockles all a-live*, was impressive in itself, and despite the burden of its words, had about it a quality almost of emotion, but even then it could not contend with the mighty contralto of the woman's voice in sheer carrying power, — indeed in that respect I have known only one throat to equal it, that of Achmet, a Turkish overseer, who superintended the loading of cargoes on ships visiting Adalia, and seemed to make the whole coast of Asia Minor, as far as Troy, where Stentor himself had served as herald, to resound under the starry stillness of that night. Yet, in my mind's ear, above his guttural bellow, I still hear the old woman's cry, *Fresh whiting, fine whiting! Fresh codfish, fine codfish!* as I have heard it often on the Esplanade, issuing from some street near the harbour more than a mile away, or as it has reached me in the very heart of the house itself. For on many occasions I have been present in the morning when my mother in her bedroom — and though all the windows were shut — would notice this tremendous cry, and mention it to the hairdresser, who had come to arrange her hair.

The combined scent of methylated spirits and hot irons perfumed the whole room, absorbing even the strong fragrance of an enormous bunch of tuberoses in a green glass vase, on the long dressing-table. My mother sat at it, in a dressing-gown of blue Chinese brocade, and in the large mirror in front of her she could see reflected the busy form and fingers of Mr. Follis, with his grey moustache, cut and curled, and his elegantly disposed hair, now waning at the temples. She watched him, as, gossiping all the time, he removed the curling-tongs, which lay on a grill above a blue-green flame that rose from his small oblong metal box, and then, after deftly twirling one side of them in the air for a little with the skill of an artist, brought them slowly toward his cheek, to test if they were yet of the right temperature. My mother knew Mrs Hick, the owner of the voice, but Mr. Follis went on telling us about her ; she lived in Castlegate, and for over forty years she had risen every morning so as to be at the pier by five, buying her fish and skinning it there — such of it as was to be skinned —, and then delivering it in the fashionable quarters of the town, in golden crescent and stuccoed terrace, whether prospering in the pleasant morning light of summer, or baffling the winds in the grey crepuscular winter's dawn, by seven o'clock. For the rest of the day, she pushed her barrow and cried fish. No one, Mr. Follis assever-

ated, was more to be relied upon for the quality of her wares,
a real eye for fish, and all the visitors to Scarborough liked to
have a word with her. . . . Very different from the other old
woman — the one who died the day the Boer War broke out
— (thank heavens it was over. What a *horrible* war : one
had thought it would last for ever ! How was it possible to
imagine such savages ? Mr. Follis added that if he told us
some of the atrocities which he knew to be true, we shouldn't
be able to eat or sleep . . .), Mr. Follis reminded my mother,
as he proceeded to twine a lock of her hair round his little
finger, and, after extracting this, to insert in its place for a
moment, with a very swift professional movement, the tongs
now heated to the precise temperature required. . . . I, too,
remembered her, an old woman who, after the manner of
fishwives, wore a shawl over her head, while from the folds
peered a pair of curiously bright brown eyes, and protruded a
nose that was yet spatulate at the end. Her home had been
in Dumple Street, and she had been so devoted an adherent
of my father's that she always got drunk on election nights
— for joy, if he won ; for sorrow, if he lost. Her voice had
never been as strong as that of Mrs. Hick, nor had it been so
continuous, omnipresent and invariable. There had been
gaps at other times besides on polling days, for her emergence
into the fresh, if fishy, air would alternate with short periods
of repose, a fortnight or so, awarded to her by magistrates
for having been fighting drunk, or, as Mr. Follis phrased it,
" for acting outrageous while under the influence ". . . . Mr.
Follis was still talking, still curling, and Mrs. Hick must, from
the sound of her voice, have been drawing nearer.

I opened a window, and put my head out. Over the dark
leaves, silver-lined and thus possessing a curious sparkle to
them, of an ilex shone a shrouded but blue expanse of sea.
It was very hot ; and the voice seemed near at hand. One
seemed, too, to detect the odour of fish ; which, indeed, in
many parts of the borough, even though the herring harvest
was a full month and more ahead, routed the fragrance of
the fruit I have attempted to describe. . . . But I did not
often go into the town this summer. I suppose I felt too ill
to stray far in the heat, and Sacheverell and I used for the
most part to play inside the grounds of Wood End. The
garden stretched in terraces down a hillside. (My father

had not yet set about it, for he had only been given the house by his mother a short time before, but in another year or two he was to make it wither like the barren fig-tree ; for this small area of lawn and terrace was destined to be by no means numbered among his successes, and one high retaining-wall alone, the very linchpin of the whole garden, and built at great cost, collapsed no less than seven times.) Its most characteristic features were the rugged old elms at its boundaries, an ilex or two, their thick, sombre but glittering leaves projecting over the terraces, and offering the best possible shelter from the sun, and, at its western edge, in a far corner, built in the identical style as the house, and of the same stone, a square, four-storeyed tower. Everything about this lofty erection with its stone balconies and outside staircase and colonnaded cupola, level with the sunny green mounds of the tree-tops, was rusty, forlorn and derelict. The windows, smeared and dusty, and the locked doors creaked in a dark breeze that only blew within, and for no reason. On a platform in the deep shadow at the base of this tower, under the cawing of innumerable rooks — descended, as I have said, from an improvident but philoprogenitive couple brought hither from Renishaw in an injudicious moment by my grandmother — stood a most peculiar dwarf statue, that now I can see resembled the portrait sculptures of Benin and the Congo. Representing with a degree of stiff realism a three-foot-high Duke of Wellington, in a top-hat, frock-coat and tight trousers, this image added to the mysterious atmosphere of the place, for it was impossible to conceive what the great hero was doing here, or from what height had been degraded to this green seclusion.

Through the misty panes of the bottom storey of the tower one could perceive nothing of the interior except the blowing, silken banners, tattered and grey, of the spiders' old triumphs, but, if one climbed the narrow stone steps to the first floor, one could distinguish the shapes of a number of large jars, and of ovens, that inevitably recalled Ali-Baba and the Forty Thieves, whose adventure I had lately followed in a pantomime, or the experiments of medieval alchemists : in fact, a perfect playground for small boys. . . . We forced the door. The room appeared to have been deserted for a hundred years. But the apparatus, though it seemed to serve no purpose in the modern world, had actually been installed by my grandmother some thirty years before, in order that Miss Lloyd might bake there the china she made, and taught my grandmother and aunt, and later my mother, to paint.[1] These objects, when thus embellished, used to be sold at bazaars, either in support of the Conservative Party, or in maintenance of a Home for Fallen Women which my grandmother had founded. . . . So that the tower had once, and not so long before, possessed a purpose : but now the trees, the glossy-winged, cawing birds, and the heat which glazed the whole scene, all combined to make it look haunted and romantic. Inside the room, it was cold, even made one shiver. . . . I felt listless and very hot.

After a fortnight at home, it was discovered suddenly that I had developed a high temperature, and had evidently become afflicted with the same illness responsible for the early disbanding of my school. . . . Now the whole tenor of life changed ; everything was done for me, every desire, if its execution was conformable to my state of health, granted almost before I had expressed it. I lay in bed for nearly three months, in a large room cut off from the rest of the house. No longer did I suffer here at night from feelings of terror, for three nurses attended me, and one of them had to sit up all the time in the room with me. Nevertheless, the nights and days were distorted, and tinged equally with dreams, so that

---

[1] One or two of these pots, usually bearing an incised white pattern of chrysanthemums on a pale, Scarborough sea-blue, still linger in a lumber-room or two at Renishaw. Such painting was an elegant accomplishment of the time. Lady Desborough, in her *Eyes of Youth*, tells us how as a girl she was taught to paint china by Miss Garnett, the sister of Richard Garnett (Keeper of Printed Books in the British Museum 1890–1899, and author of, among other volumes, *The Twilight of the Gods*) : "briar roses", she writes, "and well-worn French mottoes being the favourite decoration ". Miss Garnett, in late middle-age and old age, resided in Scarborough, and had, before going to Lady Desborough, been governess to my father and his sister, Florence. Lady Desborough describes her, in 1880, as " very tall and very plain ", and says that she " wore her hair in long ringlets (a quite out-moded fashion) and dressed in most brilliant colours. . . . She was indeed a very strange sight, but her inward qualities triumphed over all that, and I — or somebody — soon persuaded her to pin up her hair, and to wear more sober tints. . . ." She must have remained faithful to them, for when I remember her, some twenty years later, she was always dressed in grey that matched her hair and resembled a hippopotamus decked out as an elephant ; a tall, large-boned, rather heavy old woman, who always came to luncheon with us on Christmas Day, if we spent that festival in Scarborough. Her ugliness by then was so striking, indeed terrifying, that it triumphed over the term, and became raised to the level of a Chinese grotesque.

now they were difficult to disentangle. Certainly, however, this short period was the most important of my whole childhood, because it gave me that which is granted to so few children : time — apparently endless time — in which to think and still more to feel. In my mind the whole perspective of this illness and the months to follow is immensely magnified, no doubt because of its moment to me. Nor am I the only person by any means to have found a physical crisis of this kind helpful to development. For example, I once asked Sir Edwin Lutyens, who was one of thirteen children, whether any other member of his family shared his genius or had found a similar direction for their gifts. He replied, " No. . . . Any talent I may have was due to a long illness as a boy, which afforded me time to think, and to subsequent ill-health, because I was not allowed to play games, and so had to teach myself, for my enjoyment, to use my eyes instead of my feet. My brothers hadn't the same advantage."

Similarly, I owe an immense debt to those few months of exterior struggle and growing interior calm and reconciliation : and though I endured a great deal of pain and restlessness, I found peace to an extent of which I had never before been conscious. Yet I inhabited no pleasant or comfortable world, though at any rate it was one in which the imagination could flourish without hindrance, was, on the contrary, helped and forced on. . . . During the day, if I were not asleep and the room were not darkened, I lay watching through the broad windows the flights of charcoal-winged rooks flapping their way over the tree-tops into the sky, where, in a splendour of golden light, existed those cloud-continents that one so seldom for long examines, for, in health, the eyes prefer a world that is on their own level. But now I looked at them until, when I turned my glance back to the objects in the room, I could see little of these ; I gazed at the shifting and melting castles, the fulgent towers and palaces, shapes that in their turn revealed processions from times past, antique and plumy triumphs of arches and spears and helmets and cars drawn by wild-maned horses, or, with a sudden change of scale, dissolved into superhuman torsos, their golden muscles rippling in the wind, or into the likeness of gods and furies, all these being brought to life by the flickering and hispid sun. I visited countries and kingdoms I was never to see again, equatorial vistas of sand, and snow landscapes with an organisation of their own, more wild in architecture than the forms to which even limestone can lend itself, floating alpine heights built up in a golden flame that was like a lion's steadfast glare, vast cities washed by huge seas, that undulated in answer to the moon's call, through a mist of prismatic spume — metropolises of a thousand spires, a thousand belfries from which, very occasionally, I caught the sound of the solemn but brassy peals rung for immense victories I could not fathom, and then, my eyes dazzling with rainbows, I was forced for a moment to shut them, and so was asleep again.

During these many weeks I saw no one but my mother and the nurses, for Edith, as I have said, was abroad, and my father, with his neurotic dread of germs — perhaps a consequence of the long illness from which at last he was beginning to recover —, refused even to approach the door. Sacheverell, too, was forbidden to venture near the room, though he often surreptitiously made attempts to visit me. On the other hand, my mother came in to see me continually. Moreover, I made a new friend in the devoted chief nurse who looked after me, and this friendship, following on a period when I had acquired nothing but enemies, inspired me with a fresh confidence. In every direction, it was felt that the only thing to do was to let me have my own way : I could, for example, be induced to eat nothing I did not like, and every day I was brought either claret, burgundy, champagne or port, in the hope that I might drink them and that they would restore my strength — but no, though I tried them all, I disliked them and the blurred sense that they induced of all being well with the world for no particular reason. Indeed doctors then supplicated me with as much vehemence to partake of these wines, as, since I have been afflicted with gout, they adjure me, in equally old-fashioned style, to lay off them. . . . But though such spoiling of an invalid may prove the best possible method of healing, yet better still than any treat or gift was the news that my father — albeit with the intention of sending me to another school later when my state of health permitted it — had decided to take me away from the care of the Arch-Dribbler.

I had been just ten when first sent to that fashionable

place of internment for the sons of the rich. I had gone there, a tall, well-made boy, with a strong temper, high spirits, and, although of nervous temperament, possessed of a naturally sociable disposition, while, if in one or two respects backward for my years, nevertheless, as I find an old friend of my mother's complaining to her in a letter, I was "somewhat serious " for my age. Thus, though my spelling and hand-writing were bad, still, I read Greek, Roman and French history, in addition to English, and certainly knew more of all four of them than I do to-day. I hated games. . . . To sum up, in return for the large fees received, the school restored to my parents a different boy, unrecognisable, with no pride in his appearance, no ability to concentrate, with health impaired for many years, if not for life, secretive, with no love of books and an impartial hatred for both work and games, with few qualities left and none acquired, save a love of solitude and a cynical disbelief, firmly established, in any sense of fair play or prevailing standard of humane conduct. . . . I wonder what the headmaster made of it in his own mind. I suppose he was a nice man,[1] personally kind, but I saw so little of him that I can hardly judge of this for myself. Others seemed to like him. On the subject of my leaving his flock, he wrote a letter to my mother which contained the sentence, " I am sorry for Osbert, as he will lose all his friends, and it is not very nice having to start all over again ". But indeed it was ! I lost my enemies as well as my friends.[2]

---

[1] As I was writing these words, I stopped and opened the newspaper at an obituary column devoted to him. It was headed " A Great Centre-Forward ", and moreover, specifically mentioned the accomplishment of his to which I have more than once alluded. I reproduce a sentence or two, merely in order to emphasise the sense of proportion that always inspires us where games are concerned.

" Mr. Wolfe, who was considered by many to be the greatest centre-forward of all time at Association football, died yesterday at his home . . . at the age of 71. . . . With his wonderful sense of balance, he could dribble past the best defenders, and his passing was so accurate that many inside forwards . . . were indebted to him for many goals. Wolfe, though he was a maker of goals rather than a scorer of them, invariably shot low and with surprising power. . . . Wolfe, modest and unassuming, seldom watched big football matches after his retirement, but he was always ready to help those interested in the game. . . ."

[2] I will say no more of this school, and as little as may be possible of any other. . . . But for those who like to see the fun that can be distilled from any system or situation, if the courage requisite to contemplate it can be found, I place at the end of this volume — as Appendix D, on p. 303 — a long passage extracted from one of my novels. Even therein, though the characters are created through the imagination, it is a general sublimating of experiences

Convalescence was slow and trying, and the local doctors were in some doubt as to the nature of my illness, but they agreed in advising my family to take me to spend the winter in a milder climate. After long correspondence, and making enquiries of friends, a suitable villa was eventually found in San Remo. On the way there, we passed a night or two in London, and I was taken to see a young doctor, who a year or two previously had pulled my uncle through a serious illness, and was at this time beginning to come into fame. . . . Dr. Dawson [1] was — and is — a remarkable man. Nearer akin in type, even physically, to the artist than to the ordinary physician, he combines unusual powers of diagnosis and psychological understanding with an immense capacity for hard work. He comprehends immediately, when he sees a patient, the effect upon him of the other temperaments round him, and the questions he puts often startle the person interrogated by their acuteness and insight into conditions of which he can know nothing, except by processes of inference and deduction. Further, he shows a remarkable ability to instil confidence in the minds of those who come to consult him ; if he tells them they will soon be better, they are persuaded that it is truth. He must himself possess a great strength of constitution —, as, indeed, his frame and general appearance, tall and distinguished, suggest —, for he has been continually at work for several decades. When I first saw him, he had the calls, both of a Teaching Hospital — where he lectured nurses and students, as well as working in the wards — and of Consulting

acquired and, in addition, of what I have heard from friends of other places in later days.   In no way does it set out to be a literal *transcription* of life. . . . But I must nevertheless ask those of my readers who find those pages at all entertaining, to recollect how many months and years of suffering and boredom withal have been compressed within that narrow span.

[1] Later, the Right Honble. the Viscount Dawson of Penn, G.C.V.O., K.C.B., K.C.M.G. My uncle played a certain part in furthering his career. . . . Both King Edward VII and the Prince of Wales — subsequently King George V — were coming to stay at Londesborough for a shoot, and my uncle decided that a doctor ought to be present in the house. His own medical attendant was away, and in consequence he decided to ask Dr. Dawson, of whose skill and talent he had formed a very high opinion, to take his place. . . . Though Dawson had been presented on a previous occasion, this visit gave him the first opportunity of a long talk with the King. One night, a cousin staying in the house, was taken ill at dinner. King Edward later sent for Dawson to ask what was the matter, and they remained in conversation for a long time. The King was struck by his ability, and a year or two later he was appointed Physician Extraordinary, it being thought that a younger doctor should now be added to the Staff.

Practice ; so that he was obliged to give his consultations, either early in the morning, before going to the hospital — and not infrequently he visited the London Hospital twice a day —, or after leaving it at five or six in the evening. Yet his immense energy enabled him neither to show, nor to feel, any sign of overstrain. He was never in a hurry. He used to go round to his consultations in a hansom — generally in one of three particular cabs, with the drivers of which he had become friends ; they liked the job ; for while Dawson was in consultation in the house, the horse could rest outside, sometimes for two or three hours. . . . On the occasion of which I write I believe that he certainly saved my life, for I was still very ill, and he both cured me and removed my sense of being an invalid. He asked endless questions, no doubt summed up my character, and then, instead of advising treatment of a medicinal kind, merely recommended that, when I reached Italy, I should learn to fence — with my left hand —, to walk every day up one of the surrounding hills, and as often as possible to ride into the mountains and spend the whole day there.[1]

San Remo is no more romantic than Margate, but it is, in landscape and people, Italian. And the very first morning that I woke on Italian soil, I realised that Italy was my second country, the complement and perfect contrast to my own. As I looked out of the window of my room, I knew that this was how I had always hoped the world would appear. There are painters who allege that the light in France or Holland — or even in England — is more beautiful, or at any rate better for painting : but this was the light I needed and in which I thrived. Here there was no necessity to struggle for breath with an encompassing and enveloping fog : here, on the contrary, was serene and aromatic air, scented on the mountains with herbs and in the valleys by orange-blossom, here was not the occasional, savage, polar light of the north, to which I was used, but light that was hyaline and yet varied, and such — I came to know later — as had given birth to the most perfect works of art in Western Europe. . . . Light ! Light was everywhere again, spattering ceilings, walls and floors, even through the narrow slats of the green Venetian shutters, which were kept closed throughout the middle of

[1] This account of Lord Dawson was written a year before his death, so deeply regretted by innumerable friends and patients.

the day, light from the sky and light from the sea again —
but how different a sea from that of Scarborough —, trembling,
moving, affording an infinite richness of texture to every plain,
dull surface. The whole landscape was made alive by light,
even when deserted : though, when inhabited, the human
being held to it so different a proportion from that comfortable importance which he maintains in relation to every part
of our islands. Light vivified everything, there was no need
for defiant colours. Since every stone glittered as though it
were of gold, and every patch of lichen, even, swam in almond-
husk green or rose, the vegetation here was darker, more grey
than green, so as to afford contrast to the flowering skies and
to the Mediterranean, with its tessellations of wine-colour and
azure and copper, holding its hints of gold, and of a green
more intense than that which clothed the land. And, as if
the life-giving, creative light, besides calling out this entire
range of colour, this wide vision of form, penetrated, too, to
the heart of every human being, purifying it, I discovered
the simple and unspoiled nature of the people of Italy, who
laugh and cry and sing — or sang in those days — so easily.
Moreover, though this town seemed comparatively new, something told me that existence here, especially among the fishermen and peasants, was immemorially old.

Forty years ago, the towns of the Riviera, both French and
Italian, still possessed character. Even the railway stations
of this coast — so different from those in England, each of
which in any season, lined with encaustic tiles echoing the
melancholy hooting of the trains and the coughing of porters
and clergymen, forms an advanced-post for the winter's fogs
— were inviting, painted in light tones, festooned in the silliest,
most light-hearted manner with pink roses and sky-blue con-
volvulus ; guards and railwaymen sang and shouted cheerfully.
As for San Remo, it was then a comfortable international
settlement of square villas and oblong hotels, in cream and
white and pink, set among tufted palms, with gardens of
exhibition tangerine-trees, and of flowers like cockscombs,
ragged and highly-coloured, resembling mad foliage rather
than blossoms ; all this being placed in a landscape devoted
to growing the pink and mauve carnations, brittle, dry and
rather scentless, of the Riviera, so that whole square miles
had to be draped with sacking every afternoon to protect

them against the coming of night. Above these arid parterres, divided by small trenches filled with water, stood the groves of olive, running up the hills on little loose-stoned terraces, while above the hills rose the mountains, clothed with forests, and crowned with bare rocks or snowy peaks. . . . The various enclaves in the town, Russian, Austrian, Polish and English, possessed their own places of worship, and there was a church with onion-like bulbs, painted blue, in which the Queen of Italy's Montenegrin relations were buried. The shops were luxurious, many of them, and organised for foreigners, but the life of the town, and even of the villas, was Italian, though, as night released or gathered to itself this landscape, for those lingering moments, time and place were lost, and sea and landscape sunk once more into the Homeric world out of which they had come ; a world which I comprehended instinctively, though I had read only so far feeble tales for children that had been gathered from the *Odyssey* by some pedagogue.

I took to everything under this sky and by this sea, the food, the fresh sardines, cut open and fried, the sour bread, the acrid black coffee, the flame-coloured persimmons ; I admired the umbrageous garden of our villa, with flowers, few but strange, with orchids — can I have imagined it ? — growing upon the branches, stout and mossy, of the trees, and the house itself, unluxurious, with a prim Scottish interior, here exotic and suggesting in equal proportions porridge and prayer-books, and with mosquito-nets, a secure but diaphanous shelter, on which in the morning the sun played as it does on clouds ; I enjoyed the shopping, the walks, the rides on mules, the drives — and now, as if to complete life's perfection, Edith arrived from Paris to join us for a little. Though it was only six months since I had last seen her, I found my sister a changed person. Tall for her age, she already wore her hair up, the lank, green-gold locks puffed and frizzed now in the mode of the time, and she was encased, too, by my parents' orders, in clothes that, though no doubt designed to suit the young girl of the period, were most inappropriate to her gothic appearance. Still more, though, did I notice an alteration in her way of looking at things, for her absence from home — and, as a result, the discontinuance of the perpetual nagging to which for years she had been obliged to submit

— had lifted the whole range of her spirits. She knew, now, that she would be going away again before long, and the result was to make her much more amenable, because hopeful. In the peace that she now obtained for the first time, no longer fearing every moment that she would be found fault with, able to attend concerts and go to galleries with her governess, and come back home without having to face scenes, all her interests had blossomed in the short interval that had elapsed, and music and poetry burned in her blood like fire. She had become the most exhilarating and inspiring as well as understanding of companions. And, in spite of her disfiguring, though expensive, clothes, the brown plumage, physically as well as mentally, of the cygnet had gone, and the swan's green-white ruffling surge of feathers had come to replace it. . . .

I enjoyed everything ; to my surprise, I even enjoyed the fencing lessons. My instructor in this art was a Garibaldian veteran, a very broad-shouldered Piedmontese dwarf, the somewhat goitrous product of mountains and victim of iodine deficiency. An enormous, grey, Vittorio-Emanuele-II moustache swept down towards his swelling neck, and up again, and his beaver-brown eyes were set in a face, puzzled by nature, but of intent ferocious. In reality, he was the gentlest, most kind of men. . . . Alas, his name escapes me now, after forty years, though I remember that he would, whenever an opportunity offered, produce a visiting-card which had several things written on it in different kinds of printing, all of them grey in tone : *Colonnello in Reposo* was the chief item on it, beneath his name, and the fact that he was *dei Nobili*. . . . The hall wherein his pupils practised had little windows, placed very high up, and on the walls hung many framed diplomas, in which heavy-browed females, draped classically in yellow and a sour green, made formal presentation of a sword embowered in laurel, the name of the Colonel being entered on a scroll beneath, in a large, sloping, impersonal hand, the ink having now faded, as though by some process of protective colouring, to the same tone as the clothing of the figures, or as the enormous eagles with spread wings which hovered above their heads. Then there were, too, a large photograph of Garibaldi, hirsute and heroic, his square face crowned with a round high cap, and a picture of the old king, affording his army a lead by the determined, but rather affected, ruthlessness of his look ; as well as several crossed foils, with bits of cork at the end of their thin blades, and a dusty branch or two of bay. There was also a bottle of *grappa* in a cupboard.

I manifested, I fear, no aptitude for fencing, but at any rate I was encouraged to use my left hand (one of the reasons of my crabbed handwriting being that, whereas it came natural to me to employ my left hand, I was made to call my right hand into service instead). The old man was very kind and amiable, and would tell me long stories about his exploits. I understood no single word of them, but greatly enjoyed the vivacity, the run and intonation of his voice, and the accompanying gestures, as they were related. I liked, too, the rhythm of the lesson, the " *Uno-gabble-gabble-due-gabble-gabble-tre, e finito !* ", and was sorry when each lesson drew to its close. . . . Coming out of this cool, dark hall, one was dazzled and blinded, as though issuing out of a cave. . . . After a rest, I would be taken for a walk round the harbour, still filled with sailing vessels (how different were these brigantines and schooners, painted in their bright, Mediterranean colours, from the cobles, battered by gigantic seas, of Scarborough, as different as red mullet from herring !). Or we would go to look at the old town, with its houses painted, either in plain, bright colours, or architecturally, in the Genoese fashion, in grisaille, and churches with minaret-like towers. I admired prodigiously the interiors of the churches, the pillared vistas, smoky with incense, the paper flowers and silver hearts and coroneted virgins, though my tutor characterised the whole effect as " tawdry ". He was among the more innocuous, if boring, of my holiday companions, one of a large family, all the rest of whom were female, so that he was always referring to them, I remember, as " the gurls at home ". Sacheverell, more fortunate, was now taught by a French nursery governess, a woman of great charm and simplicity, and was soon speaking in very fluent French, marked by a strong Marseillaise or Provençal twang.

Every day was fine, and often we would set out at an early hour in the morning for our expeditions into the hills. The particular person, whoever he might be, to make these decisions, — sometimes my mother, sometimes the owner of a neighbouring villa who would invite us to join the children of the house for the day — would suddenly announce the previous

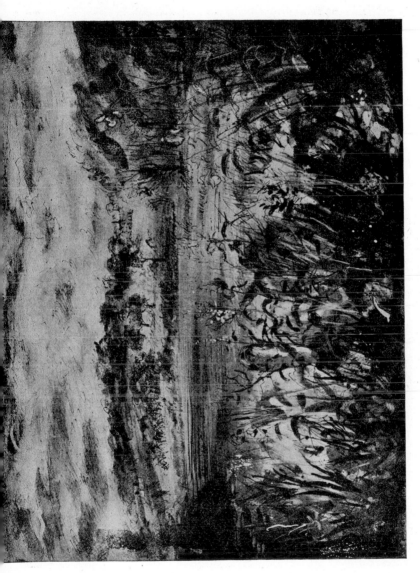

THE LAKE IN SUMMER, RENISHAW

by John Piper

evening that tomorrow would be a holiday. We would be
ready to start at eight, and soon after that we would begin
to climb the steep, cobbled tracks, the mules straining and
striking sparks as they went, mounting higher, past cascades
where, in damp, spray-blown crevices, grew tufts of maidenhair fern, hitherto only known to me as one of the prides
of English florists' shops. The beasts would be continually
exhorted by their attendants, smelling strongly of garlic, who
walked silently in rope-shoes beside them and told them what
to do. After twenty minutes or so, we would reach the level
of the olive groves, here so fine, though the trees, esthetically,
resemble the fruit they bear, in that they are surely an acquired
taste. The leaves are more beautiful, perhaps, in the patterns
they make against the sky, and in the hues they call out of
it, than in themselves. Yet is there no sense of peace comparable to that which steals on you, after a time, if you lie
under an olive-tree and look up through its grey and open
foliage. . . . On we would go, until it seemed as if we had
been out whole days instead of hours, the mountain air filling
the lungs, inducing a kind of intoxication of well-being. . . .
And now we were ascending the sides of the mountains themselves, and could see the flashing tents of the Alps beyond,
with clouds floating from them as their pennons. Finally we
would reach one or another of the deserted villages that are
to be found on the higher slopes here ; villages left empty
after an earthquake some forty years before. We would
unpack luncheon and eat it in the gardens of a roofless house,
under the shade of orange-trees — which were still well-kept,
smooth-trunked and glossy-leaved, being tended by peasants
from a village far below, the fruit hanging like so many miniature constellations in the dark-green night of their foliage. . . .
In charge of us, usually, would be my tutor, or occasionally
— and with what rapture all the children welcomed the change !
— Henry. Our companions were, as a rule, three families
of English children, and two young Poles, brothers, with whom
Sacheverell and I had soon made friends. Their father had
been banished by the Tsar for his outspoken patriotism, and
the sons inherited the paternal temperament. The quickness
of their minds, and their sudden rages, which generally arose
from wounded pride, made them different from other children
I had met, and I admired equally their lavishness — they

were always giving away toys and chocolates — and the fire and ease with which they took affront.

As well as these rides, there were other excursions, drives in cabs, drawn by two horses wearing fly-switches and straw hats, *à la bergère*. The hoarse-voiced, extortionate cabmen who drove them, and wore on their heads fantastic short top-hats of patent leather, or bowlers occasionally of the same material, were hired by the hour, and so were determined to proceed at but a snail's pace between the parched fields in which grew the ranks of Riviera carnations we have already noticed ; dry flowers, yet of a considerable gaiety of appearance, and possessing about them, in spite of their lack of fragrance, a sort of freshness that was agreeable. . . . Better, more vividly than all else I recall my first visit to Monte Carlo. Motoring there — and that in itself still constituted an adventure — to have luncheon with my Aunt Londesborough, we arrived safely, only to discover that my mother, by nature unpunctual, had on this occasion overlooked the difference in time that existed between France and Italy, and thus had added an hour to our fast. In the unusual predicament, so far as she was concerned, of having an hour to spare, she spent the time in walking us round this citadel of naughty pleasure, as it then was, showing us its elaborate gardens and *tapis-vert*, in which every blade of grass ranked as elsewhere would a flower, and had to be watered separately, whereas each flower was common as a blade of grass, albeit carefully brushed every morning and sheltered every night. Even the leaves of the palm-trees appeared to be clipped like poodles, and numbered, the flower-beds to be creations as artificial as the large hats of the women seated by them, listening to the music of *Sole Mio* being played by a band in a café near by. . . . After this agonisingly hungry interval, we were taken to luncheon at Ciro's, a Pompadour-1890 glasshouse built on a terrace. Our fellow guests were that prop of the Edwardian system, the late Lord Farquhar, who seemed, in his grey suit and panama, to be almost more of a man-of-the-world than it was possible for anyone to be, and Princess Alexis Dolgorouki, an English heiress who had married a Russian prince. I remember her the more distinctly of the two strangers, because she had six fingers on each hand, and, although before we arrived my mother had warned us children to pretend not to see anything unusual in this dispensation, at that age it nevertheless required an effort to keep the eyes averted in a manner that would appear perfectly natural. . . . It is odd how certain things remain for so long in the memory, and I recollect hearing at luncheon that day that one must never mention the Casino by name to the Prince of Monaco : he did not recognise its existence, although deriving an enormous revenue from it. And, when he, in his palace in Monaco on the rock opposite, had to allude to it, he always did so by saying, with a vague nod in its direction, " *En face là*."

After luncheon we walked across to the Casino, and, children not being allowed into the Rooms, we gained admittance instead into the theatre — that enchanting, square, ballroom-like theatre by Garnier — and it was there, while my mother and aunt were gambling near by, that I consciously made acquaintance with the music of Wagner, for the orchestra played the Overture to the *Meistersinger*. But music did not count here — only gambling mattered. And, though we had set foot on the sacred ground, and entered, as it were, into the very narthex, yet the vaulted halls of the Casino, haloed by legend, always retained for me thereafter the fascination of a forbidden place. Ever since that first visit, I have felt a weakness for Monaco, and for Monte Carlo, a place as unusual in its way as Venice, a pleasure-city built of plaster, its houses disposed along rocky ledges, sun-heated, its boulevards lined with oleanders, rose and crimson, and with the primrose hail of mimosas, instead of with plane-trees. I have applauded the appropriate sense of the destiny which made the state a sovereign principality, with an army of a few men, clad in old-fashioned white uniform and white patent-leather topis, and, it seemed, always asleep in their sugar-stick sentry-boxes outside the old Italian palace of the potentate ; which decreed that it should possses a vast marine museum and aquarium, wherein the rare and splendid fish could goggle and mouth back, as though gazing in a mirror, at the gamblers and croupiers, now temporarily off duty and come to examine them ; and ordained, too, that on the cliffs beyond the town should be laid out an exotic garden, where an arid wealth of prickly green squids and tentacular, torpedo-shaped vegetation should grow from a narrow sward of cement. As for the Casino, the heart of this principality, and in aspect as representative of its purpose as the most functional of the buildings of the 1930's, the stories I was told about it that day, so long ago, in order to frighten me — tales of wild gamblers who shot themselves, and corpses carried out in pianos — only succeeded in crowning it for me with a special aura of romance.

Meanwhile, as we children were listening to the Wagnerian strains — plain and noisy herald of two wars, and, in all probability, of a third still to come — my mother was playing roulette. Gambling, whether she won or lost — and she seldom won —, constituted a tremendous pleasure to her. . . . In illustration of this trait, I like to recall an incident that occurred one October, some twenty years later in Italy. My father had taken my brother and myself for an expedition along the coast towards Salerno, while my mother stayed on in Naples, where we were to rejoin her. On returning, after absence of a week or ten days, Sacheverell and I went straight up to my mother's room. It was nearly midday, but she had not risen yet, and her coverlet, with the sun shining on it, was littered with small sheets of printed paper; a drift, in fact, of lottery tickets. As we entered, she handed out to each of us bundle after bundle, saying, " Here, darling! Here's a present! " . . . The explanation of this scene was that, while we had been away, her Income Tax rebate, a sum of about seventy pounds, had arrived, and she had at once cashed the cheque and invested the whole of the proceeds in five-lire lottery tickets : the lira was then in the neighbourhood of two hundred to the pound, so she had been able to obtain some two thousand eight hundred tickets. Of course none of them brought her in anything, and sometimes I wondered whether, even if she had drawn a winning number, she would ever have found out about it, for she was excessively vague as to the outcome, what rules governed the draw, where it took place and how the results were announced. . . . Over such matters my father would get very angry, yet — and I must give this anecdote as a pendant — he too went in for speculations of other kinds. Thus, the summer following the visit to Naples, while staying with him at a hotel in Dieppe, I went in to say good-morning, — for I knew only too well that he was an early riser — at eight o'clock. To my surprise, he was still in bed, lying back : his coverlet, under the green north light from a window looking on the sea, was similarly snowed-over with half-sheets of paper, on each of which was written a note of a line or two in his small, rather scratchy hand. . . . I glanced at one ; on it was written " Time *is* Space. G. R. S."

" What *have* you been doing ? " I enquired.

" Just tackling Einstein," he replied. " I find the brain is at its freshest in the early morning."

On the characteristic afternoon, spent in Monte Carlo, that I have been describing, my mother had *won* : almost the only occasion it ever happened. . . . And consequently that same evening, while we dined, the garden of the Villa Teresa resounded with the songs, and trembled at the heavy antics, of two rival troupes of self-styled Neapolitan Singers, for whom she had sent hurriedly on her return, in order to celebrate her triumph over the tables. Through the French windows we could see them, dressed in appropriate costume, the men in red stocking-caps, blue breeches and white shirts, the women in square white head-cloths, wide red skirts, with tightly-waisted white blouses, standing in groups or dashing into action. . They filled the night, illumined by lanterns which shone beneath the glazed leaves of the palm-trees, with snapping of fingers, and cries of " FUNICULÌ, FUNICULÀ ! ", with *salterellos* and *tarantellas*. . . . My father was pained and worried, for he wondered how much the whole thing would cost : no such fears oppressed my mother. For once she had been able to obtain some money without asking him for it.

The life at San Remo must have been healthy and Dawson's advice good, for I got well very rapidly, though I still suffered from insomnia. On the night I have mentioned, I had been allowed to dine downstairs, but, as a rule, Henry would bring me my dinner to my room, and sometimes, as a treat, Edith would be allowed to share it there with me, and we would talk for hours. But usually by nightfall I was so tired that I would go to bed directly after dinner, and, though I tried to read for a while, would be so sleepy that I had to turn off my light and, the moment I did so, would fall into a deep slumber — only to wake up at two o'clock, with no possibility of getting to sleep again. Once more I would read, but this time with success and for a long period, — though my parents, of course, did not know this — and it was now that my habit of reading at night started. I read everything I could find, though mostly these books consisted of exciting stories — in the Tauchnitz edition, — of treasure, long buried and mysteriously discovered, or of inventors who by chance had stumbled on a process by which they could turn all things to gold. (In the spirit of the epoch, these poor scientists were immensely admired for their achievements, instead of being pitied, as was Midas.) Often I would still be reading at dawn, and would go to the window to watch the sunrise and look far across the Mediterranean, to where it was said that at this hour, as at sunset, one could distinguish the outline of Corsica, some seventy miles away. I never descried it myself, though sometimes I thought I caught sight — only for an instant; then I lost it again — of lands more distant and more fabled. I waited there, at the window, watching the tender cool green light, the colour of the very young leaves of orange-trees, first band the horizon just above the water, and then the whole wide sky gradually catch fire as the sun tipped itself above the cliffs. On occasion, though, the sky was so cloudless at this moment that it afforded no material, no tinder as it were, for the sun to kindle, there would only be, above the sea, the luminous, successive rings of green and scarlet and gold, and over them a vast dome, still full of night and with one star lingering. On other mornings there would be streamers, banners and pennons of pink and scarlet against a vibrant and amazing blue, but nothing foggy or smoky, as in the north of England, where only thick clouds and fumes can create colour in the sky. Here, a fine sunrise signified a fine day to come, whereas at home if you saw a single cloud take to itself glory at this hour, old adages rushed in to oppress the mind with their burden of gloom : " Red in the morning, shepherd's warning." Here the sun could paint the whole sky red, without a shepherd having to turn a hair for it — and what was more, there really were shepherds in this country !

When full daylight came, I would fall asleep. And this routine can have done me no harm, for my mother and father never noticed that I looked tired ; nor did I feel it. A kind of ecstasy kept me awake at the window, because at that age every child is immortal, and I could see in front of me an infinity of days, each one of which held the chance, even if it failed, of being as beautiful, as full of every kind of joy, as that which was dawning. Here I saw suggested, on these vast canvases of earth and air and sea, the sketch of another world that at points fitted into the one before me ; a world hitherto hidden from me, and to which I felt I belonged — the world of the Mediterranean.   Never again would it be possible to undergo the sort of hopeless misery that I have described.   Henceforth one would at least be aware that other things could — and did — exist ; there would always be the knowledge that there were mountains and jungles, olive groves and roofless temples where the writ of the English Sunday and of the Municipal Council did not run.   After catching this single glimpse, though only from its perimeter, of such a world, after experiencing during these months the intensity of light, and observing the multiformity of man, it would be difficult ever again to feel so dull, so utterly cast down as in the past year at school.

Only once have I been back to San Remo, and I found it then but a trivial and fussy shelter for the sick and elderly. The whole landscape had disappeared behind glass.   Vast winter-gardens had attached themselves like limpets to the sides of the hotels, and the carnations had discarded their former protection of sacking for glasshouses.   From the ledges on the rock, everywhere these great stretches of glass flashed in the sun.   It seemed now such a town as councils dream on, a " sun parlour ", full of trams, railways, buses and municipal bands.   Gone were the cascades, gone the maidenhair.   A concrete border edged every former paradise.   But in my imagination it still lives with a vividness and beauty which perhaps it never possessed.   Moreover, in the course of the intervening years, it had become imbued with the colours and sounds of the other Italian towns which I had been able to see while still very young.   And for this great pleasure and stimulus to mind and spirit, my father was responsible.   We children accompanied him regularly to Italy or joined him there, even when it may have been inconvenient for him, and though it must have been expensive.   Moreover, in spite of his prevailing parsimony, veined as it was with the strangest and most contrary extravagance (albeit this he would never acknowledge even to himself), he continually encouraged us in sightseeing and never grudged the money he gave us for visiting churches, picture galleries or palaces.

First in time came Florence, most austere of Italian cities,

teaching the beauties of form more than of colour, showing
often in its architecture a rugged, leonine beauty that alter-
nates with that of the lily, and contrasts strongly with the
surrounding mellifluous country, full of the song of nightingales
and pink-winged Tuscan cherubs, flying up into the fragrant
darkness that lies under the branches of cypress and stone-
pine. The great golden fortresses of the town, the Strozzi and
Riccardi palaces, unfold into the later buildings, as shaggy
buds open into the most delicate and perfect blossoms. And
even in the later centuries, such a building as the Palazzo Pitti
— the sort of residence a sea-god would have erected for
himself, so that you could almost perceive the weed still clinging to the huge rusticated boulders of the retaining walls,
from which it seems the ocean has only just receded — teaches
you to look under the surface for supreme beauty, and points
the way, as do few other ancient buildings except the Escorial,
to a kind of beauty — today still hardly called out of the
future — that it will be the pride of the modern world to
plan and construct. Though in these days of my boyhood
I would go every day to the Uffizi or Pitti, or to examine
the innocent heavens and hells created by Fra Angelico in
the Convent of San Marco, it is curious to look back and
comprehend how little one absorbed consciously at that age,
how much unconsciously. The early Florentine memories
that come back to me are less of pictures — except for those
of Botticelli, so singular in their apparent easy naturalism and
in their actual extreme sophistication, with the naked toes of
the figures dancing up from the flowering earth, and necks
protruding like those of tortoises from their flower-spangled
muslins, that they are not easy to forget — than of casual
impressions that have remained : the granite shaft, for example,
that once helped to support the roof of the Baths of Caracalla,
in shade as far up as its capital, coming then into sunlight,
so that the porphyry figure of Justice, with her bronze scales,
showed with the colour of a Judas-tree in flower against the
Italian sky, or, again, the pillared, delicately vaulted, open-
air Flower Market, as it looked of a Thursday, the chief
market-day, when it teemed with the accumulated riches of
the Florentine spring, flowers simple and flowers rich, thick,
rustic double daisies, tulips, with very pointed petals streaked
in pink and white, sheaves of tuberoses and lilies, scarlet

anemones, roses, dewy as if the rain had touched them, huge pots of azalea, and wistaria, mauve or white, that seemed, in the way they grew, to carry their native oriental countries with them, and branches of blossoming trees resembling small white clouds that had floated under the arches ; or the Lung' Arno in the sun, or finally — and who that has seen this can fail to recollect the first time he saw it ? —a pair of milk-white bullocks, their horns garlanded with leaves of vermilion leather, pulling a creaking cart up the long slanting hillside roads, between two lines of thin-spired Tuscan cypresses.

Never, though, did I feel in Florence that same contentment tinged with wonder that always came to me in Venice — because, no doubt, my mind tends to be fleshly, or at any rate, sensuous ; I prefer painting to sculpture, velvet to sack-cloth, jewels to bones, the canvases of Rubens to the agonised mystics and saints, spread-eagled on dark panels, of Spain. And there exists no city in the world which, even today, though admittedly it can look dingier than Seven Dials or more garish than Blackpool, offers the same allurement and appeal. It is not only the stars of the place, world-renowned palaces and churches, neither St. Mark's and its unique Piazza, nor the Grand Canal, nor the columns of St. George and of the Winged Lion, nor the paintings of Titian and Tintoretto and Veronese and their peers, that constitute its peculiar attraction, but every mouldering patch of paint on every wall, and every vine-leaf. These have a value of their own that they would lack elsewhere, while the green seaweed that makes the steps of the forlorn palaces so slippery, no less than the crest of every little wave, the striped posts that stand in clumps in the canals, the nondescript boats no less than the gondolas, all these things, details of no importance, mount up in the mind to paint for it the only civilisation that has arisen out of the sea. . . . And I suppose, too, that in those peaceful times of which I write, Venice itself *was* different, a little different : the lagoons which flower every day anew in shallow, startling fields of blue and green, then washed this city as they did in the days of Bellini and Carpaccio, and as they do today, the sea still flapped against the steps of the palaces (how clearly, as I write, I hear that sound, sweeter to me than music !), and the small, green-black crabs still scuttled away, just above the water-line, as you got out of the gondola, steadying yourself by holding on to the great bronze ring attached to the palace wall ; the cries in the streets and upon the canals were the same, just the same ; the barges laden with vegetables and flowers pulled in to the same mooring-grounds, the pitches of the street vendors were as they are today : no, the change is more impalpable than that. For example, the military music which sounded so often from the Piazza signified nothing, one thought, contained then no brag or menace. It was merely that Venetians liked loud music, doubled by stone walls and quadrupled by stone floors, and here were granted the perfection of it. (It was under the arcade, opposite Florian's, that Wagner used to sit, drinking coffee, and listening to the band — then an Austrian one — playing his own music, until, so he tells us in his reminiscences, he became better acquainted with it than by any other means.) The food that people of all classes ate in a thousand restaurants and *trattorie* was not adulterated ; the governments of Europe did not yet consider it their duty to poison and starve the people they ruled in order to provide instruments of death and torture for their neighbours. An air of long-maintained peace and of traditional pleasure animated the scene and was never, even when the curtains of the rain were drawn round the city, absent from it. . . . An air prevailed of laughing good-nature, of friendship, which we shall never know again, now that the calamitous folly of politicians the world over has obliged Italy to offend us, and us to strike back at Italy, so that Europe will always be haunted by the image that lay ever at the back of the eyes of Orestes, who slew his mother.

Nor, even to look at, was the Piazza the same, for the Campanile had temporarily withdrawn itself from the scene in a cloud of dust, and the proportion of the buildings was, in consequence, different. St. Mark's, for example, had become more imposing, less of a toy. The Piazza itself appeared to be twice as large, and, as the music sounded out, as the waiters in their aprons came to the openings and lounged there to listen, the arches seemed grander, more majestic. . . . The brassy trills and thunderstorms of Rossini were surely a pure Italian delight, but in the yearning, domineering themes of Wagner, perhaps, after all, each note turned to a spiked helmet, a multitude of helmets darkening the mind's horizon. . . . And then there was another concert, too, which comes

back to me now, absurd in itself yet bearing a burden of
premonition. . . . A large yacht lay at anchor, between San
Giorgio Maggiore and the Piazzetta, and the municipal band
serenaded it from an enormous lantern-hung barge. . . . I
have in front of me, as I write, the programme, with a most
decorative blue border and an inset of the Lion of St. Mark
on the cover.

*Programma del Concerto da eseguirsi dalla Banda Cittadina di Venezia, a
bordo della gallegiante in Bacino San Marco, in onore delle L.L.M.M.
l' Imperatore e l' Imperatrice di Germania, la sera del 14 Aprile dalle
ore 20.30 alle 22.30*

1. { (a) Inno Germanico — Haendel.
   { (b) Inno *Sang an Aegir.*[1]
2. Sinfonia *I Vespri Siciliani.*
3. *L' Oro del Reno.* Entrata degli Dei nel Walhalla — Wagner.
4. *Gioconda* — Danza delle Ore e Finale III — Ponchielli.
5. *I Maestri Cantori* — Wagner.
6. Rapsodia Ungherese — List.

Il Maestro, CARMELO PREITE

This programme, so perfectly poised in its juxtaposition
of Handel, the Kaiser and Wagner, began an hour late, and
went on for a very long time. . . . At last, however, well
after midnight, it wound up and, when the various anthems
appropriate to the occasion had been played with patriotic
tedium and solemnity, a figure in naval uniform, with rather
a proud moustache and a certain air of bravado — which in
fact its owner had been forced to adopt in order to hide his
acute consciousness of possessing a withered left arm — was
seen saluting on the deck of the yacht. . . . The crowd roared
at him its appreciation of a Composer-Emperor — perhaps the
first since its other favourite, Nero.

At this same time there was a singular, and now to my
mind more interesting, if less august, visitor in Venice,
Frederick Rolfe, self-styled Baron Corvo. . . . Not that in
any sense I consider this curious and unhappy man to have
been a good writer, but, as a human being, he was most
assuredly not banal ; a morbid interest attaches to him and
to his life, and, in his book *The Desire and Pursuit of Happiness
as a Whole*, undoubtedly he achieves a new balance between
fact and fiction. In spite of extreme affectation of style, in

[1] Composed by the Kaiser.

spite of omnipresent pretence, in spite of the clumsy and often fatuous words he invents, the opening of the book, wherein the earthquake rocks the waters, makes you feel the dark immensity of the scene, while the later portions of it, dealing with Venice in the years of which I am speaking, and from the pages of which still arises the image of a wraith torn by hunger and its dreams, and ravaged by passions that continually escape from its control, cannot but impress the reader. . . . Even had I seen Rolfe in those days, I should not have known who he was, for I never heard of him until 1919, when Gabriel Atkin, a great and early admirer of his, lent me one of his novels. . . . It might easily have happened, though, that we did hear of him, or even see him, as I will relate.

My brother fell ill at Danieli's, and was confined to his room for a fortnight. This, though in itself a hard blow for a boy of eleven, was made worse by the prevailing darkness, for my father had taken especial trouble to obtain, both for Sacheverell and myself, rooms that were lit only by the original *bifora*, or small, delicately-arched gothic window, split in half and supported by a marble column. It was a favourite theory of his, and doubtless soundly based in esthetics, that a view looked amazingly different from what it would otherwise look, and infinitely more beautiful, if framed by a window of unusual shape. Certainly the gondolas and sailing-ships of Venice, the mysterious, shadowy canals, or the wide stretch of blue-green water, marbled by its foam, on which floated so lightly the stone raft carrying San Giorgio Maggiore, must be seen through a Venetian-Gothic window. (All the same, he would explain — another theory —, Venetian Gothic was not true Gothic.) It did not matter about Edith, she could have an ordinary bedroom — in which, incidentally, she could see —, but he had been determined that Sacheverell and I should, each of us, enjoy this typical experience, which ought, in his favourite phrase, " to prove splendid training ". But the necessary modern additions of glass and blinds and curtains made the single small aperture insufficient. Poor Sacheverell, thus immured, used to gaze longingly out of window at the steamers starting for Dalmatia — for already he was familiar with the marvels of that country, since guide-books constituted his favourite reading, and was eager to begin his travels. . . . His only other distraction was the

visits of the English doctor, then resident in Venice.[1] Dr.
van Someren was a charming, kind being, possessing — if
such a contradiction can be allowed — a sort of cheerful, as
it might be bustling, melancholy. The most distinctive outward feature he presented, however, was the sandals he wore
invariably — an article of dress then even rarer than they
became subsequently. It can be imagined with what fascination my small brother contemplated the novel glimpse he thus
obtained of the doctor's toes ; which, indeed, only divided
his interest with the notebook that Dr. van Someren carried,
for it held a carbon copying paper, the first he had seen, and
that also constituted a new toy. . . . Well, at this very moment,
had we only known it, or had ever heard his name, Corvo
was staying with Dr. and Mrs. van Someren. They had out
of kindness taken into their flat this wretched, penniless ex-priest
who was again approaching the point where he would once
more have nothing to eat, and nowhere to sleep, unless it
were the shelter offered by the tumbledown, green-stained
doorway of some damp, neglected palace. Alas, Corvo was
already preparing for the doctor's hand, and that of his wife,
the particular rabid bite, by the scar of which it was always
possible to recognise those who had fed him. . . .

A genius, — perhaps under-rated today, — inhabited often
at this time a small palace, painted the colour of bullock's
blood, on the Grand Canal : d' Annunzio. But I never saw
him here (probably he had gone to France), though he had
been pointed out to me one day in Florence, on the steps of
the Club in Via Tornabuoni, a small figure, wearing no hat,
but very carefully dressed, and with several elaborate rings
on his hands. He stood on the top step, partly in shadow,
watching the people passing by, and talking nonchalantly to
a friend, and as he did so, he fingered continually these rings,
so that a stone flashed in one of them. . . . But I hope to
have more to say of him later, and must now pass on to
mention a being of a different kind, more legendary than
Corvo, more royal than the Kaiser, who was also at this
period still living in Venice. . . . I cannot do better than
reproduce a passage describing him there, as he emerged from
his home on the Grand Canal, written by my brother.

[1] Dr. van Someren, who suffered from melancholia, aggravated by his experiences of the 1914-18 war, subsequently committed suicide in Venice.

The floating ease of an afternoon spent in a gondola was enlivened, of a sudden, by much noise and stir coming from the water-gate of a near-by palace, the Palazzo Loredan. The iron gates were thrown open, a wooden gangway was put down, and an immensely tall old man with a square white beard, dressed, if I remember right, in black, but wearing, certainly, an enormous black sombrero, came down the steps, and leaning on the arm of a little black page, crossed the plank into a waiting gondola. The negro page followed him, and stood in the bows of the boat, while six gondoliers in magnificent liveries lifted their painted oars in stripes of red and yellow, and in an instant the gondola slid out from the shadows into the sunlight and was gone. To our enquiries we were told that this was the Pretender to the Throne of Spain. It was, in fact, the embarkation of Don Carlos.[1]

To others, again, there were, flitting through Venice, people more interesting than either the Kaiser or Corvo or Don Carlos. My brother and I were allowed comparative freedom, but my sister had to remain all day cloistered in the dark splendour of the hotel — which only came to life by electric light —, because Edna May, who had recently been starring in London in the title-role of *The Belle of New York*, was staying there, and so, if Edith went out for a moment, she might thereby lose a musical treat of the first order : you never knew, great artists were temperamental, and the whim might suddenly take Miss May to step into the lounge and sing. Imagine missing that, imagine *wanting* to go out ! And the child was supposed to be musical. . . . And then an incident of another sort comes to mind. . . . Henry fell ill, seriously ill. My father sent word, through my mother's maid who was nursing the robust invalid, to ask if there was anything he wanted ; the answer came back, " Nothing — except to be buried with feet in the direction of Whitby ". . . . The difficulty of such an act of correct orientation even then occupied my mind. A compass would be necessary, and elaborate calculations.

Above all, it was the amazing variety of Italy, the beauties of every kind and every age, compressed into so narrow and ideal a space, that caused a traveller almost to hold his breath. Take Venice, Florence, Ravenna, Rimini alone ; these were as different from each other in their feeling, in the influences they had received, and in the development of their spirit and

[1] From *A Background for Domenico Scarlatti*. (Faber & Faber.)

the monuments that were the concrete expression of it, as were Pekin and Paris, Ispahan and Mexico City, though under all four Italian cities flows the common current of warm Italian blood, acting upon a foundation of antique culture. . . . There were the smaller towns, too, to which my father took me : Vicenza, with its vistas, its great moulder-ing boulders of stucco, through which the brick showed, its clouds of statues above the roof-lines of the palaces, its air of majestic and derelict calm, a theatre set that has achieved immortality, with, as the very heart of it, out of which the whole town grew, Palladio's own Teatro Olimpico, the most perfect theatre ever built. Here I will not discuss in detail the innumerable wonders of a hundred cities, but there were certain things seen perhaps only for an instant, in these places of such threadbare beauty and elegance, which indelibly impressed a young mind, and to which, when distressed or distracted, my thoughts would revert, finding in them a sort of refuge ; seen through a door left open for an instant, a carved well-head, with a vine in front of it, coming into leaf, and a pillared loggia as background, or a vista — at Vicenza again — of a double row of statues, stiff deities with a kind of rustic formality about them, lining a road leading up to a temple on an artificial mound, the whole conception being yet arranged with such art that, seen through the tall arch-way of the palace, the short avenue stretched for miles, and the slight eminence became almost a mountain ; or the first sight of the huge golden view which washes the foot of the hill whereon stands Bergamo. . . . These impressions, frag-mentary, remembered as though seen in a dream, often meant more to me than my recollection of famous monuments, or than the memories of vast cities, such things as I have already described. Suddenly encountered, swiftly passed, these unpre-meditated glimpses pulled at the heart in the same way as does a great line of Shakespeare's, familiar, yet read in its context for the first time, revealing the whole permeating life and vision of an epoch. Here, in these quiet places, it was possible to find an antidote to the vulgarity and growing brutality of the modern world. . . . Yet today these cities have been threatened in a manner that none but the present most bestial age would have allowed, an age which, even in its most reactionary aspects, is democratic. One man, one bomb — or rather, one foreigner, one bomb — is the answer in every country to one man, one vote. But I care more for art than votes, and the best age for me is that which produces the finest flowers of the spirit. To me, Athens, based on a system of slave labour, will always be of more interest than a Free and Democratic Liberia.

I mention at some length the effect, and lingering influence, of Italy on my brother, my sister and myself, because it provides a clue to the work which later we set ourselves — or which set itself for us — and have since striven, however imperfectly, to accomplish. By this path we came to the classical tradition, through the visual arts, rather than through Greek or Latin. In a sense, as artists, we thus belong to Italy, to the past of Italy, hardly less than to England, to that old and famous combination of Italian influence and English blood. We breathed in, without being wholly conscious of it, the space and proportion of Italy which for centuries gave grace to Western Europe and even to the Marches. We learnt our lessons in a school that teaches by example and feeling rather than by precept ; we came to be able to tell good things from bad, to use our own judgement and not believe anything about the arts that we were merely told. So, though it is with what came to be known as the Modern Movement that our names will be associated, it was partly due to this same upbringing that we were able to perceive genius where it existed in unfamiliar guises, to understand at once — to take three things at random — the force and the fire of a Stravinsky, to see the constructive truth of Modigliani's peasants and the new element that had entered into the theatre with Monsieur Diaghilew's Russian Ballet. The several modern manifestations which we have championed in England, when they needed it, thus owe, through us, something to the past of Italy.

These many trips with my father to which I have alluded were often in themselves delightful expeditions. Though perhaps a little frightened of him, of his strong will and often obstinate misunderstanding of motives, I cherished at that time, nevertheless, an immense admiration for his acuteness and knowledge, and for the originality of his mind and character. Indeed, I believed that his every opinion on every subject must be the correct opinion. I enjoyed his more abstract conversation about works of art, history or politics, and I liked to persuade him to tell me of his boyhood, and of his relatives and what they did and said, for I loved to hear details about people, even about those I did not know. I began, however, appreciating as I did the unusual qualities of my father's mind, to be continually surprised at the streaks of conventionality that I found in it, especially about people — it was there that I first noticed how, when you did not expect it, he would suddenly accept current values, especially where human beings were concerned. . . . Moreover, he induced in those round him a sense of strain, and possessed a gift, which increased with the years, of lengthening the hours, so that nine o'clock — by the last stroke of which on these occasions he would like to be in bed — often seemed, until you had counted its tolling, to be midnight. It interested me, nevertheless, to observe the System at work, to watch Henry rigging up the mosquito-net in the manner I have described earlier, and to examine for myself the infinite details that had to be studied and which, as a matter of fact, so often went wrong.

One such visit with my father — to Viterbo — I remember with particular distinctness : it occurred a little later in time, when I was in that limbo between leaving school and having a profession thrust upon me. My father took me there, chiefly to see one of the four gardens — that of the Villa Lante — of which he had written recently, in the pages of what is perhaps his best book,[1] and nearly every day we motored there, and spent the day, so that he could study at his leisure the lay-out and the principles which had produced it. . . . But let me here give an extract, typical in its merits and faults, from his description of this garden. The passage that follows, written between thirty and forty years ago, has not yet quite attained a period interest, but has, still, the air of draggled finery that always attends the dresses of a period of a similar distance from ourselves. (And, in parenthesis, we may notice the passing of time has damaged two words occurring in it, one, " loveliness ", with its persistent echo in Hollywood, the other " wizardry ", now tainted by slang.)

The Duke of Lante's garden is of another character, a place not of grandeur or tragedy but of enchanting loveliness, a paradise

---

[1] *On the Making of Gardens*, by Sir George Sitwell. (John Murray, 1909.)

of gleaming water, gay flowers and golden light. The long, straight, dusty road from Viterbo leads at length by a bridge across a deep ravine to a gap in the town walls of Bagnaia, 'twixt Gothic castle and Baroco church, then turning at a right angle in the piazza one sees in front the great Renaissance gateway which opens into the garden. But it is better, if permission may be obtained, to enter the park, and striking upward by green lawns and ilex groves to follow from its source the tiny streamlet upon which pool, cascade, and water-temple are threaded like pearls upon a string. Dropping from a ferny grotto between two pillared *loggias*, this rivulet rises again in an elaborate fountain surrounded by mossy benches set in the alcoves of a low box hedge. Four giant plane-trees lift a canopy against the sun, and tall stone columns rising from a balustraded wall warn off the intruding woodland. Thence, running underground, it emerges unexpectedly in the centre of a broad flight of steps between the claws of a gigantic crab — Cardinal Gambara's cognisance — and races down a long scalloped trough, rippling and writhing like a huge snake over the carved shells which bar its passage. From this it drops over the edge of a small basin between two colossal river-gods into a pool below. The fall to the next level gives us a half-recessed *temple d'eau*, with innumerable jets and runlets pouring from basin to basin ; and here, flanked by stately plane-trees and by the two pavilions which make up the casino, is a grass-plot commanding the loveliest view of the garden. Before us lies a square enclosure jutting out into the vale below, with high green hedges, sweet *broderies* of box bordered by flowers, and in the midst a broad water-garden leading by balustraded crossways to an island fountain which rises like a mount to four great figures of sombre-tinted stone. Water gushes from the points of the star which the naked athletes uplift, from the mouths of the lions by their side, from the masks on the balustrade, from the tiny galleys in which vagrant cupids are afloat upon the pools. It is a colour harmony of cool refreshing green and brighter flowers, of darkest bronze, blue pools and golden light. Much there is of mystery in the garden, of subtle magic, of strange, elusive charm which must be felt but cannot wholly be understood. Much, no doubt, depends upon the setting, upon the ancient ilexes and wild mountain flank, the mighty hedge of green at the further end with its great pillared gateway and the dark walls and orange-lichened roofs of the houses and tower irregularly grouped behind it ; upon the quiet background, the opal hues of green, violet and grey in the softly modelled plain, and shadowy outlines of the distant hills. But the soul of the garden is in the blue pools which, by some strange wizardry of the artist, to stair and terrace and window throw back the undimmed azure of the Italian sky.

I remember Viterbo, though, not so much because of the many peaceful hours spent in that garden, or in the ilex wood above it, in which wild boars still roamed, nor for the many special features of the town itself, the numerous gothic fountains that it contains, built in a style peculiar to this small city, nor for the exterior staircases of stone — another architectural feature of the place — in the courtyards of the palaces, nor for the especially delicate façade of the Palazzo Populo, as because of the odd way in which Henry behaved during our stay there. . . . We lived in a hotel of singular atmosphere. Most solidly built of stone — and far too grandiose for Viterbo, by no means a tourist centre —, though utterly without comfort, it was in its way a rather beautiful building ; too beautiful, indeed, for its purpose, though it had been erected as a hotel some fifty years previously, and not converted into one. Every room, every passage, was nobly proportioned, while the details of arches and pillars and vaulting showed still in their construction a trace of the great tradition. Why the hotel continued to stay open, why the proprietor did not go bankrupt, remains a mystery : for few people entered its doors for a meal, and we were the only residents. And here, for the first and only occasion in my life, I found Henry nervous, glancing round corners as if he feared to meet a ghost, starting if you called his name or met him suddenly. At the time I could not understand this extraordinary change in his demeanour ; all the more difficult to comprehend, because, the very moment we left the station at Viterbo, he reverted to his normal appearance, ways and conduct. . . . Many years later I heard the explanation, and in the course of the next chapter shall give it.

These cities and towns, then, and not the dull routine of my second school, nor the listless days at Eton that followed, appear, looked back on, to have represented the *real* part of my life. Of the second school my parents chose for me, I have no complaint to make, in spite of its inevitable lack of interest. I must emphasise, too, that though boys were more frequently beaten than at my former school, the headmaster was thoroughly kind and conscientious, albeit perhaps latterly too much of an invalid to exercise a proper control over masters or boys. He took a genuine personal interest in his pupils, and when later I was submitted to pressure and, further, even to considerable bullying, at home, about a choice of a career, he was the only person of the elder generation to protest at the way in which I was being treated, and to assert a belief in my capacity and intelligence.

I will say little more of my second school, but content myself with relating an incident that occurred during the summer holidays after I had first gone there, when I was twelve years of age ; because this presents to me certain typical and bewildering features, and emphasises the importance, however difficult it may prove, of a parent trying to be consistent in word and conduct. . . . I must first explain that my father's health was much restored, and that he again fully dominated every scene. Many of the themes he used were the old favourites, dating back to the days before his illness. He was still as much concerned as formerly with the various errors into which people fell in modern life, by not heeding the example of their ancestors. What a mistake it was, for instance, that we no longer, all of us, got up at five — or even four —, as they did in the medieval romances ! (The reader may recall the introduction of this theme in the beginning of Volume I.) Think of the improvement in the general health that would result, for at that time in the morning there was " a tang in the air " which could be found at no other moment, and toned up the whole system, as well as adding immensely to the enjoyment of life. But today, the ordinary person preferred to lie wallowing in bed ! He called it disgusting, to throw away in that manner the best and most beautiful part of the day.

All this he said during the second day of the holidays, and on the third morning I woke up at half-past four. It was early August, and the air was warm, though a northern freshness lay under it. . . . I went to the window, which looked out onto the south front from the third storey. It was a high enough level, indeed, to make the window seem that of a tower, and the whole world beneath, deceptively near, lay bathed in a golden hush. No bird sang, nothing sounded except a stir and bustling in the great holly-bush that extended its rounded top towards me, far under my window. The garden looked in perfection, as though created like this, and still untrodden by gardeners, unspoilt by tutors. The lawns, smooth and green, yet having a faint pattern or nap to them, the fountains and pools, the hedges of yew, the abrupt fall of the land, and the watery expanse of the lake beyond, with their woods, and to me well-known tracery of fields, now covered with the burnished glow of the harvest, and, in places, with their clothing of light mists, the hills, rising almost to be mountains, these, all of these, plainly invited one to come out. It was light again, they proclaimed, and the irrecoverable summer. The light swept low under every branch, filtered through the green leaves of the boughs nearer the ground, lay in pools upon the open spaces and, like some gigantic gold bird, left a trailing feather even in the alleys under the dark trees. Everything combined to call me out into a world of unknown enchantment, where no one would interfere or get in the way, a world full of the order man maintains, and yet not subject to his fussy commandments. . . . Liberty itself came with the dawn.

Of course I must go out. I would please my father — that was one thing — and, in addition — and this I had not expected the day before, when he had been urging it, I found that I *wanted* to go out. . . . Hurriedly I dressed and crept downstairs. The light lay in unexpected places, so that every room looked different from what I had ever seen it ; the light caught the crimson thread in the tapestry, the silver face of the clock, or lay along the blue and pink spaces of an Aubusson carpet, and imparted to the whole house a strange air of gaiety that in no way depended on humankind. I walked very quickly to the garden door, which I had known so well when it had been my height : (it looked very small now). The scent of stocks and tobacco plant was less strong than in the evening, but there was a dewy freshness that brought out the very heart of rose and clove carnation. I stole up the green slope, and then down the avenue so that I should not be seen — but that must have been due to habit, I reflected, for my father would be delighted, and so no one could object. I stopped under the shade of an old lime, its leaves rather sticky at this season, and turned to look at the long, machicolated front of the house, with its deep breaks and shadows. I saw that the blinds were down in all the bedrooms except mine, and I noticed with surprise that my father's room was closely muffled, and did not even have a crack of window open so that he could derive benefit from the healthy morning air. . . . He must have forgotten.

With what strength that walk abides in my memory ! I ran down the steep hill, my legs carried down it, so sharply did it fall, by my own impetus, so that I could not have stopped if I had wished. . . . Sometimes in the garden and park one would be frightened, for no reason except the impression, perhaps, of age, of being watched by past generations, or of the woods being tenanted by unseen beings, and, since those days, I have wondered, again, whether it might not be in part due to some emanation from the lost Roman road, that once ran between the two settlements of Chesterfield and Rotherham, and must pass very near, through the park, or in the Wilderness : but now, this morning, there was nothing to be felt but a peculiar exhilaration (I saw what my father meant — that *tang*), and a sense of prevailing and blessed beneficence. Moreover, my bones told me that on such a morning as this one could walk for ever. . . . As I went on, the particular, shining, sparkling quality of the light began to explain itself, for the grass round the lake was long and drenched with dew, more utterly soaked in water than rain could ever make it. As I moved my feet through it, the drops tumbled off the blades into the interstices in the front of my shoes. Here and there a trail of mist rose from the mirror-flat surface of the lake, in which banks of willow were reflected, and the poplars shivered again with their never-failing ague. . . . How strange and exquisite the world looked ! Great, drowsy dragon-flies, in gold and green, and smaller ones, that flew always in twos and threes and matched the blue of the sky, winged their way over the reeds. The cylinder-heads of the bulrushes were turning to sepia, the loosestrife showed its magenta spires in clumps, and the air was scented with the wild mint that, with its humble mauve flower, grew so thickly at the water's edge. The cascade, which my father had recently caused to be erected on the shore, just beyond the island, seemed to have caught a rainbow in its spray, and I stopped again for a moment to examine it. . . . To my surprise, I was beginning to feel rather tired. I looked at my gunmetal watch — appropriate gift to boys of my generation : it seemed very early still, only half-past five. Another two and a half hours before breakfast ! (I was beginning to feel extremely hungry : but my father had said

that getting up early gave one an appetite.) I walked on.
There was nowhere to sit. Even the fallen tree-trunks were
very wet and — I touched one — cold. . . . By this time the
edge of my very jacket was sopping with dew from the high
grass and reeds, and breeches, stockings and shoes looked as
if I had been bathing in them. The further I went, the
wetter I got. I was at the far end of the lake, a long way from
home. And how tired one became, in spite of that previous
exhilaration !

When I reached the house, it was still so early that no
housemaid could be heard stirring. I was too much exhausted
to walk any more, so I sat down in the hall, on the uncomfortable Charles I oak sofa bearing rustic high relief on its back
of Abraham preparing to sacrifice his son Isaac, and began to
read a book that was lying on the table. I did not concentrate on it much ; my thoughts wandered : how pleased
my father would be when I told him what I had done ! . . .
I suppose I must have fallen asleep and have only woken up
when Henry found me, to tell me that breakfast was ready.
He looked at my shoes and stockings — breeches and coat
were dry by now — in a surprised way and asked me what
on earth I had been doing.

" You'll cop it, Master Osbert, when the Great White
Chief sees you," he added.

His remark made no impression on me at the time. I
raced in to breakfast — my father was not down yet — and
helped myself to some scrambled eggs and bacon. . . . I felt
refreshed now. . . . The sun poured in at the windows,
fluttered on the roof of the apse at the end of the room, and
splashed the green coat of the boy — about my own age —
in the Copley picture, showing very clearly, too, the playing-
cards that he held up in one hand. The fragrance of coffee
perfumed the air, as the swinging brass machine, with its
steamy glass dome, gurgled and sent out of its spout a jet of
vapour. . . . Now my father entered, in a grey suit, looking
aloof and preoccupied though good-humoured. At first he
did not notice me ; as he bent down to help himself to a dish,
I observed that the hair was beginning to grow a little thin
on the top of his head. . . . I still said nothing, enjoying the
feeling of the surprise he would have when he saw me, first
down to breakfast. . . . Now he turned round. . . .

" Good morning, Osbert," he said carelessly ; " down early for once."

It had fallen flat ; so I decided to tell him now what I had been doing. . . . But as I proceeded, the change in his demeanour startled me. The appearance of good-humour dropped from him.

" You had no right to get up at such an hour without letting anyone know," he pronounced. " It's most dangerous — and disrespectful, too. *I* should never have dreamt of doing such a thing myself at your age, without consulting my mother — or at least the tutor. We shall have you ill again. . . . Go up immediately, and change your shoes and stockings. They're wet through ! "

A fortnight later I fell ill, it was feared with a return of whatever illness it may have been that had attacked me the previous summer. I developed a high temperature, and was in bed for ten days. And during the short period of con- valescence that followed, I was left in no doubt as to the cause of my illness. That idiotic walk in the early morning ! Most inconsiderate and ill-advised. Even my mother expostulated with me about it, and in her anxiety arranged for various people — Helen Rootham, Major Viburne, Miss Vasalt, Henry, — to drop into my room, casually, to see how I was, and then lecture me about it. . . . Finally, when I returned to school, my father wrote to the headmaster to explain that owing to disobedience and lack of discipline, I had made myself ill. . . . It was most puzzling ; but I had the memory of green banks, rushes, dragon-flies and shining water to console me.

I LIKED Eton, except in the following respects : for work and games, for boys and masters. . . . Preparation for going there used to be elaborate in the extreme. The school was — and at the moment still is — in mourning for the death of King George III. Yet even grief sincere as that which inspired this obligatory mute's outfit was made to serve the purposes of local trade, because we are a nation of shop-keepers, and schoolboys are for their part as conventional as other savages in their outlook ; the correct top-hats, black coats, white ties, and shoes could only be obtained at mono-polist establishments in the High Street. Thus I first saw the place, when, accompanied by Henry, I went there from Renishaw, in the golden and hazy days of a first week in September, in order to try on my suits — for which the cloth had been chosen by my parents and the rather amateur measurements sent off to the tailors some weeks before —, to look at my shoes, and fit the top-hat, let it be softened with an iron, or have a wad of paper inserted between the end of the silk lining and the leather flap. I remember the day so well, can almost breathe its air, for I had never been in this part of England before, had never before seen Windsor, the castle floating like a legendary gothic city upon its hill, or like a fragment from the Arthurian Cycle, yet so solid and robust for all its air of fable. The very material of its walls, the so varied texture, was new to me, and made me, many years later, appreciate the description of it sent me in a letter by a very witty woman : " the castle, on its hill, looked like a collection of pebbles and flints of all ages and sizes ". . . . Henry and I, I recollect, had luncheon that day in an Italian restaurant opposite the base of the Curfew Tower, and not far from the river — near enough for the aqueous light to throw a Venetian quivering upon the ceiling, and to illumine the enormous jars of lemonade which stood in the dusty window, surrounded by dry, crackling, lemon branches, no doubt supplied to the proprietor by his relatives in Naples or Sicily. Streams of holiday-makers, men with brown faces and without coats — then a very daring innovation —, and with, as part of their equipment, girls leaning on their arms, came from the direction of the river, and stopped to buy fruit at the many barrows, wheeled along by hawkers, who shouted their wares in broadest cockney. The fruit they sold imparted to the scene an air of Jordaens-like opulence; there were melons, and yellow-fleshed peaches, with their Gypsy skins, and bunches of grapes. I examined them greedily, as I crossed the bridge after luncheon, and walked on, down the street, to Eton.

In the summer holidays only a skeleton garrison of gowns and mortar-boards held the scholastic citadel, most of the masters being engaged during the month of August in those usual Alpine exploits of theirs which seem so often to culminate in tragedy. . . . It was extraordinary how delightful, easy, cheerful the school looked, without masters, matrons or pupils. Nevertheless, I dreaded going there. . . . The day came nearer — steadily, inexorably nearer. Nothing, except death, could prevent its approach ; nothing could cheer one up ; so I thought. . . . But my father contrived to delight me with one of the unexpected twists in his character ; he provided me with ample pocket-money, and at the same time complaisantly presented me with a small, thin and extremely useful crib to Horace's *Odes*. This little book, a faithful friend to me for several years, had the Latin printed on one side, and a competent literal translation into English on the other side. Moreover, it was of just the right size, and easy to handle in class without fear of detection. In giving it to me, my father explained that he was not satisfied with the way Latin was taught at Eton ; it was far better to read the English first, and know the rough meaning of what you were going to translate. . . . In any case, he added, to use a crib only showed a determination to get on. And of his own contemporaries, the one who had shown most skill and persistence in cribbing had since achieved by far the most distinguished career, George Nathaniel Curzon, of Kedleston.

To my amazement, I enjoyed the first month at Eton, because of the comparative liberty the system offered, the novelty of being allowed to buy what you wanted, books, sweets, fruit : in consequence I remember the first few weeks with some distinctness. As gradually I came more and more to dislike the place, I recollect events, such as they were, less easily. . . . There were the feasts, going to breakfast on a Sunday with one of the masters, Stone or Vaughan. " Toddy " Vaughan, as he was called, had been a housemaster for several decades, and to me the fact that he had been abroad with my father, as his tutor, so many years before I was born made him seem infinitely old. But, though he must have been a good age, he still possessed all the narrow enthusiasm and stunted interest of a schoolboy ; the perfect equipment for a master. . . . There were the tea-parties. And I remember one glimpse of another world. My tea, like that of most other boys, used to be sent in from Little Brown's,[1] eggs or sausages, or roast chicken — or something of that sort. The shop was small, old-fashioned and charming ; but one day, when I was there, a door opened, and I saw through it a vista of about twenty hags armed with pokers, toasting-forks and long rusty knives, their forms lit by the fires they tended, their draggled, unkempt grey hair and toothless, sweating, scarlet faces, seen dimly through the ascending, fragrant steam. The sound of a universal sizzling supplied music for them. . . . The sight haunted me. No wonder we were not allowed to see through that door, for an utter lack of cleanliness prevailed. Moreover, it seemed wrong that those who ministered so faithfully to our comfort should be exposed to such conditions. . . . Mostly, though, I recall absurd and isolated incidents.

One such episode occurred during the first half-holiday of my first term, about two days after I had arrived. *Absence* is a ceremony which takes place at two o'clock on every afternoon that is not to be devoted to work. A master mounts some steps and calls out from a roll held in his hand the names of all the boys who should be present, and they answer him, so that he can be sure that they have not sneaked away. Well, my first *Absence* was in full progress, when, suddenly intoxicated by the possession of a pea-shooter — a weapon that had by some chance never hitherto come my way —, I fired in a friendly manner at a new acquaintance whom I saw at the other side of the crowd of boys, but, missing my aim,

---

[1] Little Brown's no longer exists. Its place was taken by a shop run by the school, and this shop occupies another site.

instead accidentally hit the officiating master on the neck. The wounded beak, as he was called in the cant term of the school, roared with surprise and anger —, and the boys, some hundreds of them, roared with him. As the noise subsided a little, he suddenly demanded " Did *you* do that ? ", and the powerful squint from which the poor man suffered induced me to suppose that he was addressing someone else rather than myself. Had I realised that he was putting the question to me, I might, perhaps, have lied : as it was, I owned up to my crime. Though on this occasion I escaped with a light punishment, the master naturally concluded from my bold behaviour that I was an unusually unruly and obstreperous boy. In consequence he pursued me throughout my career with a special watchfulness, inspired either by a desire for revenge or, perhaps, by a genuine belief that I was a dangerous malefactor.

In reality of a quiet temperament and a law-abiding disposition, I felt myself quite unfitted for the brief span of fame, and even of esteem, that this startling adventure brought me. Alas, I quickly recovered my unpopularity and retained it until the end of my time at Eton. Indeed, I was astonished and disillusioned only a few days later by an occurrence which brought home to me the fickleness of my school-fellows. Still comparatively fresh from my triumphant exploit with the pea-shooter, I found myself obliged to play football one afternoon. Accordingly, I changed and went down to the field, only to discover that my playmates had already assembled and were " kicking about " before the game began. As soon as they saw me, however, guided by some instinct of mass animosity, they bore down from every direction, aiming their footballs at me as hard as they could kick. . . . Nevertheless, while remaining, as I say, unpopular, I soon — no doubt owing to physical causes — gained a considerable vitality, which enabled me to take things as they came and to a certain degree to remain cheerful. Moreover, I could on occasion, if I wished, amuse my friends as well as discomfit my enemies.

Another incident connected with the ceremony of *Absence* comes back to me from about the same time. The Lower School by custom assembled for it in Cannon Yard, an enclosure with, on one side, a hideous red-brick portion of a cloister, on the other, iron railings, and, in the centre, the eponymous relic of the Crimea. . . . There had gone to Eton the same day as myself a young Scottish chieftain — it is remarkable how much character the young of that stock appear to maintain in spite of the prevalent tendency towards uniformity —, a wild, rather unsociable, though jolly boy, who liked to roam by himself. If, however, a row of any kind broke out, he would, although one so seldom met him otherwise, materialise in an amazingly short time, and, throwing himself into the thick of it, become the very centre of the storm. . . . On this occasion of which I am writing, he seemed to have been out of trouble for some days. . . . But suddenly, during *Absence* on a Saturday afternoon, when a good many ox-eyed parents were listlessly wandering about outside the railings, there was a vast explosion from the Cannon, accompanied by a long, spluttering, popping fizzle, an apocalyptic rushing of flame, wind and soot, and a discharge of such miscellaneous objects as unwanted buttons of all sorts, and old boots and toothbrushes. Stars and whorls of fire seared the air : hats were blown from heads in every direction, and even the mortar-board of the officiating master — by some mischance the same whom a few weeks before I had laid low with my pea-shooter — was lifted from his head and dashed to the ground. And for some minutes the air remained dark, as after a volcanic eruption, with falling lumps of hard, apparently cindery matter and pieces of charred paper. Through the railings, the blackened, hatless faces of parents gazed in wondering dismay. . . . The Scot had contrived it, to enliven a dull mid-term. Having hoarded a great many fireworks which he had bought just before Guy Fawkes Day. Catherine-wheels, rockets, squibs, Roman candles and many other joys once common on that now forgotten festival, he had then acquired some black-powder, a compound of charcoal and saltpetre, in those days to be obtained at shops, it being used for smoking-out wasps' nests, and, having collected anything else that he thought might come in handy, had set himself, with the aid only of his native ingenuity and application, to prepare for us this pleasant surprise. But none of us could ever understand how he had been able to put in as much work on the job as plainly he must have done, without it being detected. He owned up to his crime in a most imperturbable manner, as if proud — as well he might be ! — of what he had achieved. . . . Many years later it came as no surprise to hear that his career in the army, during the 1914–1918 war, had been most distinguished, and his men would follow him wherever he led, and that his ingenuity and gallant conduct had earned him many awards and mentions in despatches.

Again, a most singular episode took place in Lower Chapel during one of my first few terms. . . . The service had been of a tedium unexampled in my experience. The hymn-tunes bumped about, and cringed and whined and followed one like dogs. Finally, towards the end of a hymn there stepped into the pulpit one of those very ancient clergymen who whistle through their teeth in the style of an old-fashioned comedian — Fred Potts, for example —, but, of course, involuntarily. The type, though in this instance admittedly decrepit, was that which at the time the authorities at Eton seemed specially to favour for visiting parsons, the 1906 model, as it were. There had lately been several in succession (they would have found that hard to say, it was the sibilants that trapped the old gentlemen). The sermon proved to be an endless maze of allegory of a rather weak-kneed kind : really, it was hard to bear with equanimity. . . . After about twenty-five minutes of it, the boy who sat next me, a mild and amiable lad in the same duffers' class as myself, took out of his trouser pocket a box of those now extinct matches called fuzees, and flung it down with great force and a gesture of defiance into the middle of the aisle, where it broke and burst into blue-green flames, full of hissing, glowing, incandescent heads, as the fuzees caught fire in batches, and gave off their typical, rather pleasant, incense-like fragrance. . . . Apart from their sizzle utter silence prevailed. Not a boy stirred. The old clergyman himself had stopped whistling — probably surprise produced that perverse effect on him, making him refrain from, as it causes others to indulge in, this music. It was a dramatic, almost dream-like moment. . . . After some minutes, the flaming box was removed by a verger with the aid of a long pair of tongs which, by some means or other, he had procured. He walked out, down the aisle, slowly carrying it at arm's length in front of him. Now the preacher was led from the pulpit, and into it, in his place, strode furiously the Lower Master, splendid in robes. Pointing a trembling finger at the culprit (who was by this time, I think, himself beginning to feel a little alarmed at what he had done), he launched an anathema at him. I remember the very words with which he began : " *You* have disgraced yourself as a Christian, a Gentleman and an Etonian ! "

After this exordium, he went on in very definite terms to prophesy that my neighbour would come to no good end, but would in adult life pay bitterly for his crime. . . . And now follows the curious sequel to the story : the rhetorical inspiration of the Lower Master proved to be correct. This boy, who surely had so little harm in his composition, being, to the contrary, of a kind and reliable nature, was, some fifteen or so years later, sentenced to a term of imprisonment in connection with telegrams despatched to bookmakers, after, it was alleged, he had received from another person by telephone the result of the race on which he was making his bet.

Such ludicrous incidents as I have described are apt to remain in the memory longer than more serious occurrences, for they contain the essence of the public school in England, in its absurdity, its lack of any bias towards learning ; and because they could not have happened as one grew older. But, of course, there were other sides to my life at Eton. Though, as I have said, so far from being popular, yet I had succeeded in acquiring various friends. And two principal friendships chiefly enlivened my days here : one with Peter Lycett Green, now the well-known collector of pictures, the other with William King, of the British Museum, and most of the pleasurable hours I spent at Eton were passed in their company. These two, by their attitude of a nonconformity similar to my own, helped to remove the feeling that it was stupid to read at all, or talk, instead of playing games, and we carried on a continual skirmish, and from time to time engaged in pitched battle, with the Philistines. Peter, who went to Eton the same half as myself, was wonderfully gay, kind and resourceful, in spite of his boredom with school life, and interested himself with fervour in all manifestations outside the constricting walls of Eton — pictures, theatres, opera, music. The most loyal of friends, his advice was particularly sound, and before taking any step, it was well to consult him. . . . In the holidays we would exchange visits. . . . I insert here a letter from Henry, addressed to me when I was staying with Peter at his grandfather's home in Norfolk. (Henry had accompanied me as far as Sheffield station.) I give it because it offers an objective sketch of myself, and helps to demonstrate how all schoolboys resemble one another, the members of the minority who hate school life and the army of those who like — or pretend to like — it.

OH TALL AND MERCIFUL MR. OSBERT,

I hope you have not erred nor strayed from your way like a lost lamb Nor has followed the devices and desires of your own heart (where chocolate and fruit is concerned) nor offended against the laws of the Railway Co. nor has done those things which you ought not to have done or left undone those things you ought to have done but hope you arrived at Snettisham in peace and I trust your stay at Ken Hill will be joyful and when you depart that place you may safely come to your home and eternal joy and lemonade.

Trusting you are in the pink of condition, Sir George is A1.— Yours obediently, HENRY MOAT.

William King was younger, an intellectual by nature, detached, precise, determined, but bringing to everything an exhilarating dash of the fantastic and absurd. Like Peter, he possessed naturally good taste, as well as considerable powers of application, and his looks reflected his keen and precocious intelligence. Peter and William, though both younger than myself, achieved more distinction than ever I did at Eton, and were much higher in the school. But there were, of course, other boys who had come here the same half and were in the same division as myself with whom I liked to talk. And indeed I much appreciated, even then, any evidence of character. Cranborne, for instance, took the same form as myself when he arrived, and I liked to watch his unruffled and distinctive Cecilian concentration. Nothing that occurred, however startling, disturbed him, even if it made him smile in a charming, rather rueful way. But he was soon wafted into another, higher form more worthy of his ability.

Titchfield,[1] by disposition as indolent as myself, was also for several terms in the same form ; but his beautiful manners, humour and good-nature, served to make the long hours a little less disagreeable. There was Oliver Lyttelton, too, with his unusual blend of burly energy and brains and fun, and the

---

[1] Now 7th Duke of Portland.

welcome break-away that he showed from the ascetic Lyttelton type, as represented at Eton by his uncle, the headmaster. . . . I must also mention the presence in the background of Philip Heseltine, who became better known in later years under the alias of Peter Warlock. I knew him for some twenty to thirty years, and must have met him scores of times in Venice and London and Paris. I even saw him, as I tell later, on the day of his death, but though he was my exact contemporary, we were never friends, and I never cared for his songs, which seemed to me, musically speaking, to have come straight out of Wardour Street. He may have had a great knowledge of early music — of that I could not judge —, but certainly his knowledge in other directions in which he was said to be learned was often nugatory. I remember, in Venice, his telling me how painting did not interest him, but only mosaics ; it then transpired that he had just come from Sicily, but was unaware of the presence in that island of the great mosaic churches of Monreale, Cefalù and the Capella Palatina. . . .

There were other, older boys, whom one knew only in that peculiar relationship of fag to master. And I enjoyed being fag to Philip Sassoon, very grown-up for his age, at times exuberant, at others melancholy and preoccupied, but always unlike anyone else — as he remained, I am thankful to say, all his life —, and extremely considerate and kind in all his dealings.

Looking back, I find it excessively hard to picture *how* I spent my time ; the avoidance of playing games whenever possible, or of watching them being played, is at best — and it could be exciting — but a negative occupation. I took no interest in my work and had lost any ability to concentrate that I had ever possessed. Occasionally, at the end of the term, we would be told to take a story from the Bible and turn it into blank verse. That was the only thing — apart, perhaps, from an occasion when I won the prize for a holiday task without reading the book whereon the examination was based — at which I showed any aptitude. I belonged to no society, debating or literary, and no one ever suggested that I should join such a body — if it existed. . . . I did not, except for my first term, reside in the same house as Peter, but we saw a great deal of each other. In the summer we established ourselves as wet-bobs of a meagre and uncompetitive kind, and spent pleasant spare hours in the afternoons, on the river, or in bathing, or wandering round Windsor, buying books or prints or eating ices or strawberries. (Usually after the first few days I had exhausted my pocket-money, and always ended the half with a heavy and unauthorised debt of four or five pounds to tradesmen and dealers.) In the winter, too, the river provided my principal, though brief, pleasure. . . . The reader can imagine for himself with what eagerness I looked forward to the moment when the kindly Thames should overflow its banks again, thereby putting an end for a short span to the incessant playing of games. Further, water imparted to the look of the place, no less than to the life it sheltered, an agreeable sense of alteration, of change from the routine of every day. . . . Usually, if I remember aright, the floods, which seemed then to recur regularly and without fail each year, would show their first sign of arrival about the 10th or 12th of December. At every break from school, I would run to the meadow's edge to watch with joy the encroaching sheets of water. Partly I welcomed them because of their direct usefulness to me, partly because of the suggestion that they brought of canals and of lagoons and, still more, because of the Dutch light thus created, directing at all objects that dared to impose themselves between the immense, shining, neutral spaces of sky and what had hitherto been earth a minute and scrupulous attention that omitted no detail, thus doubly focussed, of rough bark upon a tree or pitted brick in the construction of a house. . . . Alas, these transient and shimmering meres, which brought to all things such an enhancement of their quality, seldom existed for more than four or five days. With a sorrow equal to my previous joy, with a sense, too, of life going flat again, I saw these calm and gentle waters begin to recede, until they had gone, leaving behind them only a thin layer of mud, and a lingering faint scent, enduring for a day or two, of moss and weed. . . . During the rest of the winter term I did nothing but lounge or slouch in the approved manner, or read in my room.

My tutor — Tatham — was consistently kind, noticed that I liked books, and used to discuss with me for a few minutes in the evening what I had read. He was an unusual man : in appearance he resembled a hot-tempered, good-natured

walrus, shambling and roughly clad, but he possessed a strong
sense of religion and decorum, and was capable of real generosity and fire. Shy, and in consequence rather difficult to
know — indeed his nature was obscured by this shyness —,
his individuality was marked, and he manifested all kinds of
little likes and dislikes, though these were yet less personal
than general. Especially — albeit in appearance and opinion
so dissimilar to the great Lord Chesterfield, who had nevertheless shared this same prejudice — he hated loud laughter
and, if he heard a raucous shout of it at any time, would
snap out in his rather thick voice his favourite phrase in this
connection, " I won't have any boy in my house laugh like
a cat ". . . . He would read aloud to us — which I believe
was unusual at Eton — in pupil-room, and sometimes on
Sunday mornings or evenings, after chapel, would give us
the simple allegories in the form of stories which he wrote
himself. Of course, compared with other authors he was in
a privileged position, resembling the Emperor Nero in being
placed above the criticism of his audience : nor, I apprehend,
should I today much enjoy those brief, homely tales in a
Churchwarden English, born of an early surfeit of Bunyan,
were I to be given again the opportunity to hear them ; but
at the time they much impressed me. . . . It seemed wonderful to be able to write. . . . Further, his literary taste, in
spite of its strongly prevailing Church of England standard
— for his outlook resembled that of a cleric, though he had
never taken Holy Orders —, was of great help to me. He
liked chiefly, as I did, to read novels, and his library contained
all the best nineteenth-century works of fiction.

If my tutor was helpful about books, my fellow students —
if such a term can be applied to them — proved the reverse.
They liked particularly to burst into my room and throw
the books out of window. . . . Eventually I fixed a strong
wedge under the door, attached to a cord, long enough for
me to be able, while remaining seated at my desk — or " burry "
as it was called —, to pull this obstacle away. So I would
sit reading, and then, when I heard the crowd hurl itself on
my door, ramming at it each time with greater force, I would
whisk the wedge away, and hide it in my pocket, while my
enemies tumbled into the room, some falling on their heads,
others unable to stop their rush until they hit the table by

the window. Finding me thus seated peacefully at my desk, they would be so breathless and taken aback that they would feel it best to pretend it had been a joke, and retreat, unless, as on one or two occasions, they began attributing their misfortunes to some fifth-column activity, and broke into fierce fighting among themselves. But this trick, alas, could not be worked indefinitely. . . . Tatham, however, used to allow me to go to his library and choose books, and in that refuge I spent many grateful half-hours, secure from interference. I would take volumes out from the shelves, examine them to see if I should like them, put them back, take them out again to read a little more.

As for what I read, Peter and I were a little priggish in our tastes in this matter, and each kept a carefully annotated list of the books we read, with the dates of reading them. We were competitive, bidding against each other, as it were, in the highbrow market. We both of us liked works with a reputation. For example, I read nearly all Shakespeare's plays at one draught, in the space of ten days — an exploit about which I was teased by my family, but which, all the same, possessed certain advantages for a boy of my age over other methods of becoming acquainted with these masterpieces ; so might a barbarian have profited, had he taken himself to Rome for ten days, and there filled his head with its wonders, no less wonderful for being only partially understood. The jumbled impressions intoxicated me, and left behind a sediment, a deposit on the mind. . . . Apart from Webster, I read few other Elizabethan dramatists, and little poetry at that time except Shelley and Pope. I had with me in my room, I recollect, a miniature edition of *The Rape of the Lock*, with illustrations by Beardsley, which already was one of my oldest possessions, for my father had given it to me when I was seven. But for the most part I read novels, Smollett, Fielding, Richardson, Fanny Burney, Jane Austen, the Brontës, Meredith, Hardy, Wells, and plays by Wilde and Shaw — of whom I was a great admirer. I also read Ruskin and Pater, and, oddly, Gissing, and I notice on my list, also, Arthur Morrison's *Mean Streets*.

I read, in fact, without purpose, as cattle browse. But my father, when on occasion asked what books I liked, used to give that little downward, waving flutter of the right hand, descending from almost shoulder-level to elbow, that was one of his favourite gestures, and reply, " *Osbert* reads for style ; *I* read for information."

This statement constituted both rebuke and in itself excuse. While protecting me from the charge of absolute frivolity, it at the same time pointed the way to me, by insinuating that I preferred to read novels, instead of grappling, day and night, as I should, with *The Origin of Species* and sprightly primers of Political Economy. It was true that he rated beauty, as he saw it, above all other things — but it was his, and he made it. His sons should improve their minds. Ruskin he commended, but Meredith, who was liable to write in a nasty, sneering way about rich baronets, incurred the full measure of his condemnation. Moreover, the formula I have quoted above was, in addition, another way of regretting that I concerned myself so much with human beings, their behaviour and the things they say, that they interested me more than they did him, and that, in fact, I was dependent on them. In that direction, he had learned, lay unhappiness, if not disaster. . . . At times, notwithstanding, he must have believed that I read for content as well as for amusement and outward glitter, for I remember what happened when he opened the bill addressed to me from a bookshop. It was for *Tom Jones*. Supposing that I had been attracted to that novel by the impropriety of its subject — of which, when I ordered it, I knew nothing — he made a tremendous rumpus which lasted for many days. . . . To me, the taste which ruled the books I gave as presents seems stranger than that which governed the books I read : for I find a letter from my grandmother Sitwell, addressed to me while I was at Eton, which begins—

MY DEAREST OSBERT,

I thought it so very kind of you to send me that book [1] about ants and wasps. I read it with the very greatest interest : but I have *done* with the black ants ! They are horrors, carrying off live insects and murdering them. . . .

Time was going on. The ninety-nine years of peace had nearly run its term, though no one yet appreciated the fact. The *Entente Cordiale*, that Juggernaut fitted with every modern

---

[1] Was it *Ants, Bees and Wasps*, by Lord Avebury?

convenience, and destined to crush the bodies of two generations of Englishmen and one of Frenchmen, and to annihilate
for a time the spirit of the most enlightened nation in the
world, had started on its career through streets decorated
with flags and gaping faces. . . . One can only judge of a
policy by its results — but even at the time of its being brought
to birth, there must have been doubts as to its wisdom. And
Sickert told me, many years after, of how, at the time of the
inception of the *Entente Cordiale*, he and the Spanish caricaturist, Sancha, stood in a crowded boulevard, to celebrate
the new understanding between the two countries, as the
President of France and the King of England drove by in
state. The whole city seemed to resound with cheers, but, as
the carriage passed them, the Spaniard turned to Sickert and
said in his ear, "Did you see the Furies riding behind them?"

King Edward VII, to whom the public assigned much of
the credit for the foreign policy recently inaugurated —
though, in fact, it belonged to the Kaiser, and to the politicians
of the two countries — was continually moving from Paris
to London, from Homburg to Biarritz : and he lived much
in public, more than any previous English monarch. Thus
it was easy to see the King, and I often saw him as he drove
to Windsor, and, too, heard him speak when he came to
open the School Library — a memorial for Etonians who had
been killed in the Boer War. King Edward's voice possessed
a very individual and husky warmth, together with that particular rolling of the *r*'s that distinguished his generation of
the Royal Family. There was, as he spoke in public, a
geniality in its sound, as of one who found in life the utmost
enjoyment, and, in spite of a rather prominent and severely
attentive blue eye, and a certain appearance of fatigue, the
chief impression was one of good-humour — an asset of which,
according to Lytton Strachey, the King well knew how to
make use. . . . In example of this trait, he told me the
following story, which had been recounted to him, when he
was at work on his *Queen Victoria*, by one of the courtiers who
had been present at the occasion to which it relates.

In June 1904, two months after the inauguration of the
Entente Cordiale, King Edward had been obliged, none too
willingly, to pay a visit to Kiel, and, in particular, to attend
a banquet offered him on board the imperial yacht, *Hohen-*

zollern, by the Kaiser, and graced by the presence, amongst other royal personages, of the Crown Prince and of Prince Henry of Prussia. It could not, under any circumstances, be a pleasant visit for an English monarch and head of the Royal Navy, for the Kaiser had made it very plain to the world at whom the widening of the Canal and the construction of a great German fleet was aimed. . . . When, dressed as an English admiral, the Kaiser rose to propose, in the course of a long speech, his august uncle's health, the English courtiers felt intensely anxious, for they knew that their royal master, though he was growing old and tired, could still be angry, and they dreaded what he might say in return of the Kaiser, who had lately been in one of his most extravagant moods, if that monarch should flaunt his tactlessness too openly and provoke him. But the Emperor's speech transcended their worst fears. With a swashbuckling air, he began : " It affords me high satisfaction to offer Your Royal and Imperial Majesty a welcome on board a ship-of-war. . . . Your Majesty has been greeted by the thunder of the guns of the German Fleet, delighted to see its Honorary Admiral. The Fleet is the youngest in point of creation amongst the navies of the world, and is an expression of the renewal in strength of the sea-power of the German Empire. . . ." In this fashion he continued. . . . The courtiers felt that they had good reason to tremble as King Edward, dressed in the uniform of a German admiral, stood up to respond. But he presented an appearance of being supremely unruffled. Speaking very deliberately and in excellent German, an air of the kindest patronage lay under his words ; some such words as these : " In expressing my most sincere thanks to Your Imperial and Royal Majesty for the extremely kind words which Your Majesty has employed in drinking to my health, I am happy to have this early opportunity of giving expression to my high appreciation of a splendid reception. . . . I am especially glad that it was possible for me to pay Your Majesty a visit at a time of year when I am ordinarily occupied at home. The interest, however, which for many years I have taken in [slight pause] *yachting* . . . exercised too great an attraction to allow me to miss the opportunity of convincing myself how successful Your Majesty has been in inducing so many to become interested in this sport in Germany. . . ." The King proceeded scarcely to mention fleets, armies or high policy, but instead allowed his audience to glimpse the prim green lawns and the clinking tea-cups of Cowes, and British and German sailors engaged in pacific and friendly competition with toy ships. The Kaiser fidgeted and looked fierce, but King Edward spoke as if he enjoyed making the speech — no doubt he did —, and the audience loved it. It proved to be, said Strachey, the perfect reply, as if inspired, to fanfaronade, and in itself formed a complete justification of constitutional monarchy.

In November 1907, the Kaiser paid a state visit to this country, and King Edward brought his nephew to Eton, where they visited the school buildings. On this occasion the Kaiser obtained for us a week's extra holiday — the only debt, I think, that Etonians of my generation ever owed him. Even on this, the interest charged amounted to usury, for seven years later he took away from us by the sum of his actions at least four years of our lives, and in many instances the whole period that remained. . . . Another royal visitor to Eton at about this time was King Carlos of Portugal, his large figure swathed in a white cloak. King Edward drove through the town of Eton with him, and was alleged subsequently to have sent a message to the school authorities, " Cheering is forbidden neither in England nor in Portugal. . . ." But, though the boys may have been undemonstrative, in any case Eton used on such occasions to present a gay and, indeed, enchanting exterior. Throughout my sojourn there I always appreciated the unrivalled atmosphere of *festa* and gala that it could develop for such events or for the great local holidays, such as the Fourth of June or St. Andrew's Day. The customs of the place certainly lent themselves to the perfect celebration of holidays — more easily, I apprehend, than to habits of work. Every building seemed to blossom. And to me it was a pleasure to find that my birthday coincided with a whole holiday, falling, as it does, on Founder's Day, the day on which King Henry VI was born.

Sacheverell meanwhile had gone to the same school [1] as I had left to come to Eton. And perhaps I should break off here

---

[1] He went there towards the end of September 1907 ; a date which, by chance and for another reason, is easy for him, and for every boy of his epoch, to remember ; because on the precise morning of the day in question motor taxicabs first made their appearance on the streets of London.

to explain that during the whole of our long and far from distinguished careers at school, although we were at the same places of education, we were never there together, so that neither of us saw the other humiliated or unhappy, or in the lowest spirits — no doubt an important element in our relationship, and in the estimate each formed of the other—, though we described our adventures and said frankly, in frequent letters, how much we hated our places of internment. . . . Sacheverell had now grown into a sturdy small boy, tall for his years and resembling in appearance a lion cub, with his broad face, green eyes and tawny hair, or perhaps King Henry VIII as he may have looked as a child. With an intelligence already highly developed, he set himself, out of school, with an energy and intensity that were remarkable, to amass knowledge — but, of course, the sort of knowledge *he* wanted to amass. My father, in his own defence, was continually having to protest " Not so many questions, please ". Our visits to Italy emphasised the natural trend of his young mind. He used to write me long letters, and I print here a letter I received from him when he was ten and I was fifteen. It is noticeable how well he spells — in this being very different from myself, at his age.

GRAND HOTEL BRUN, BOLOGNA
MAY 14, 1908

DARLING OSBERT,

How are you ? Father came back today at 5.30 and we go to Venice on Saturday. Our address is Hotel Danieli. I will send you post-cards of Venice. We leave here at 6.40 and arrive at 3.40 in the afternoon. Bologna is lovely, nearly all the streets being arcades, with red plaster walls. The Aqueduct is very interesting. On Wednesday we went in the morning to the *Museo Civico*, it contains Egyptian mummies, Roman tombs, vases and implements, Stone Age remains, Umbrian Vases, Turkish and Italian armour, Music of the fifteenth century, an old library, some fifteenth century majolica, and some things from America used by the Aztecs, in all about 140,000 objects. (It also included a collection of old coins, from shells down to 1380, also a room with relics of the French Revolution and the Garibaldi war.) We were shown round by an old man who had had his leg cut off by a cannon-ball and his hand run through by a lance (there was a picture of him in the Museum, he was one of the first to join Garibaldi). Next day we went to the Picture Gallery, and this afternoon to the Cemetery, in which were 460,000 bodies, it is on the top of an Etruscan and Umbrian Cemetery. I like Bologna very much. Today we went to San Stefano, seven churches in one, in imitation of the Holy Sepulchre. It is built on the site of a Pagan Temple. All the pillars are still there.

On Thursday we went to San Michele in Bosco, an old monastery, most of which was turned into a hospital in 1865. The part we saw was wonderful. There is a picture in the Cemetery which looks like sculpture but is a picture.

There was an odd drunken man in the hotel this afternoon, he began lecturing everybody and at last as a peace offering gave a boy his pencil and a sheet of paper after having asked him questions and having written the answers in his notebook.

Major Viburne wrote to Mother that a Miss Gamworth, who lives in Ilkley, married a young man some years ago. Last week he went to the bank, drew out £100 (belonging to his wife), and ran away, leaving behind a letter, saying he had left for ever with someone he adored through the odiousness of his wife. She at once went away, too, taking with her her heaviest coat, a hairbrush, £10 — all that she possessed — and a riding-crop. But she could not find them.

Last night we had for dinner, soup, chicken and vanilla and chocolate ice. I am writing this at 5.45. I am in bed because I stay up so late tomorrow night.

Now I must finish. Am sending you two post-cards.—With very best love, ever your loving brother, SACHIE.

I may remark in passing that Sacheverell showed at a very early age, as well as great feeling for history, innate taste ; a fact to which, as well as to his already developed sense of compassion, a rug in this house to this day bears witness. This object, unusual in design and bold in colour, he commissioned at the age of seven from an old negro whom he found in the workhouse at Scarborough.

Now the Edwardian Carnival was at its height, but my immediate family took little part in it. Every spring, we would go abroad, and my father and mother now would usually pay a second visit to Italy in the autumn. My father never went elsewhere, neither to Spain, nor Portugal, nor Holland, nor Morocco, nor to any of the other countries that, it might have been supposed, would interest him, except France — that is to say, Paris, as a stopping-place *en route* for Italy —, and Germany. Russia he had visited as a young man, to attend the Coronation of the Tsar Alexander III, but he seldom spoke of his travels there, except to commend the double-gauge railway. It was Italy that appealed to him and he kept to the track he had made for himself.

In the world outside, the era of the Stock Exchange was in full swing. The institution now set every standard. Musical Comedy filled the theatres devoted to it, and this was its peak, the Age of *The Merry Widow*. This play, first produced at Daly's on 8th June 1907, ran for over two years, during which time its music, by Franz Lehar, served as background to every meal in a restaurant, every dance and every garden-party that was given. . . . I remember being taken to see this piece during an exeat from Eton in the autumn of 1907 : we sat in the stage-box, and so I was able to watch the expressions of the members of the audience, reproducing in their own fashion the sentiment and humour that came to them from the stage.

> I'm going to Maxim's
> Where fun and frolic gleams ;
> The girls all laugh and greet me ;
> They will not trick or cheat me

reflected the current ennui with the responsibilities of life to perfection ; how marvellous, many of those seated in the theatre felt, to be able to say that, and to cast away your cares in this manner. And as, later, the banal, but in a way charming, waltz sounded out, and Miss Lily Elsie came down the stairs to her prince, and as the glare from the stage fell on those in the front rows of the stalls, on the stiff white shirts, flashing studs, white waistcoats and self-indulgent faces, brown or white, on the noses, hooked or snub, and gleaming, pouchy eyes, of these members of the Cosmopolitan Bourgeoisie, I can recall contemplating them and wondering whether it were possible that in the future such entertainments or such an audience would — or could — be considered as being typical of their epoch, or providing a clue to it, in the same way that we looked back, past our fathers, to *La Vie Parisienne* or *Die Fledermaus*. I decided, then, that to adopt such a view would be to overrate both entertainment and spectators — but I was wrong. It held a suitably designed mirror to the age, to the preference for restaurant to palace, for comfort to beauty, and to the idealisation of Mammon. Mammon underlay the smudgy softness and superficial prettiness of the whole performance, as the skull supports the lineaments of even the youngest and freshest face. . . . Nor was it only to the stockbroker that *The Merry Widow* appealed. So popular was it, that at its farewell performance, at the end of July 1909, the theatre was besieged all day, the earliest arrival taking his stand at half-past five in the morning. . . . But even then the piece had not finished its career. It was revived frequently, and eventually entangled itself with history by becoming Hitler's favourite entertainment : curious that he who so hated the Stock Exchange, and saw himself as ordained to destroy it, should thus share its tastes.

Apart from a visit about once a year to one of the trivial but popular musical comedies of the day, my father seldom patronised the theatre. Even at that, he preferred the native brand to the Austrian. His real dislike of music helped him, it may be, to enjoy these entertainments, and I think the experience of being able, indeed of finding himself obliged, to laugh at the same jokes as the rest of the audience allowed him to feel to a certain, even agreeable degree, fashioned of the same clay. . . . Besides, in medieval times — and they were drawing nearer to him every year — even the Castellan had enjoyed watching jesters and fools. And afterwards there had been round-dances in the great hall. . . . Such a pity to let that sort of thing die out. . . . For the rest he disapproved of the theatre, and especially of the intellectual drama. . . . As a child, therefore, I had seldom been allowed to go to the play ; but now, during " long leave " every half, I would usually accompany my mother or uncle. Often they would take me to see the Follies, a celebrated company of the time, the chief organiser of which was the great Pélissier, an enormous figure of comedy ; though his gift, perhaps, was more for pure fun, without implication, than for the satire and irony at which his devotees considered him adept. There was little distortion — the essence of satire — in his art ; only a naturalistic exaggeration, as though one looked through a magnifying-glass.

In addition, at the end of my holidays, when I was passing through London on my way to Eton, my parents would usually detail Henry to take me to a theatre, and this we would not seldom interpret as meaning a music-hall, a form of entertainment of which we were both very fond. . . . Often he would conduct me to the Alhambra, then still the most typical and, in its own atmospheric way, the most beautiful of London theatres, untouched since the 'sixties, when it had been built. The honeycomb ceilings and stalactites were painted in blue and red, and there was, too, a great deal of dark gilding, though obscured by the clouds of cigar and cigarette smoke that hung under the wide, flat dome. In the background as we entered, I caught a glimpse of the pro- menade, where women in hats the size of bicycle-wheels, piled up with ostrich feathers, their faces powdered and painted in the various shades of mauve, pink, salmon and cyclamen that had contemporaneously been introduced in the new varieties of sweet-pea — a flower which must remain as typical of the age of *The Merry Widow* as does the camellia of the age of crinolines and muslins, — trailed the trains of their dresses along the carpets in a haze of cheap, strong scent, tobacco smoke and dust. To me, these unknown but formal priestesses of primitive unrecognised rites and urgencies seemed less enticing than portentous, frightening and of an immense age. We quickly gained our seats, and there, from compara- tive darkness, watched the figures on the stage, consumed by and consuming the light of a world that by the help of a label — a gesture, a mannerism, a lisp, a laugh — they would create. Here, for example, I first saw the minute, irresistibly grotesque figure of Little Tich, surely a dancer of genius, as he stamped magically, with a dynamic power of comedy, upon the boards ; his huge boots, half the size of himself, being shaped like skis. His whole stunted body seemed the expres- sion of his dance, rather than the dance an expression of his body : as surely as the lion was created for its leap, so Little Tich had been moulded, the spectator felt, for this purpose alone, for rousing laughter out of a crowd, in the same way that a bellows fans flame out of smouldering logs.

Here, too, I first saw a ballet : in those days still billed as " The Italian Ballet ", *Italian* being used to indicate the identical sort of transcendent excellence that came to be signi- fied later by the use of *Russian* in the same connection. A ballet then always occupied the final forty or fifty minutes of such a formal variety programme as still survived at the Alhambra or Empire, a lingering tradition from an earlier period. Built upon a long, humourless and involved plot, it was executed by surprisingly large women and old men ; the representatives of both sexes, indeed, seeming left over from some other era. They used a peculiarly stilted and yet coherent technique of foot. gesture and expression ; to these three means, their art, such as it was, had been confined. They aimed at no use of the body, except for heaving, panting, and showing emotion, and at little expression by the limbs. The chief male dancers were heavily moustached, a conventional stroking of these long appendages being a favourite gesture, to show either self-satisfaction or a sudden determination, according to the manner in which it was done. The principal ballerina, if I remember rightly, was titled the Great Leonora . . . was it Leonora ? . . . but I recall her appearance, a large, dark, flashing woman, who seemed always to be balanced on the knife-like edge of toes surprisingly small for the support of such a frame, or to be indulging in imperious, whirlwind gestures or foot-stamping. The whole thing was staged in a flat and jejune manner, alternating with outbursts of a pantomime-like splendour. . . . One could not fail to be amazed at the lack of reality displayed, and I formed a great distaste for the ballet, little foreseeing the new art at that very moment being shaped in Russia out of the amorphous mass of time by the genius of Diaghilew, or that I, together with those others of my generation interested in the arts, or gifted for them, should find more pleasure in it than in any other form of theatrical entertainment. . . . But, after all, who could predict the soaring of a phoenix, only just re-born — and from what dusty ashes ! —, who could deduce from this banal staging before me, from this less than mediocre dancing in front of me, or from these insipid strains which now tinkled in my ears, the genius of *L'Oiseau de Feu*, with its encroaching bands of ogres and harpies, or the high tragedy of *Petrouchka*, the sweeping lines of the music summing up the world of fire to come, who could divine in the overstrained bodies and overloaded emotions of this pedantic and puerile survival, the leap of Nijinsky into his momentary glare of world fame, the doomed grace and alluring beauty of Karsavina, Lopokova's humour born of limbs as well as mind, the fantastic, inspired satire of Massine, or foretell in the antics of this *corps de ballet*, quarter-trained over forty years, the vital significance of movement in *Les Noces* or *Tricorne* . . . ? Yet this ballet before us was own cousin to those I was to see, sharing the same high descent.

The romantic age, it seemed, the romantic gloss, had vanished, both in life itself and in my surroundings. . . . Something had gone wrong, and farce, public and private, was sweeping the boards clear for tragedy — or at any rate for disaster. The shadow was inspissating, becoming homicidal in the world at large, and material and squalid at home. . . . Relations drifted in and out of Renishaw, but it seemed emptier than in the years when I was a very small boy, the guests fewer and fewer (they were to increase again before the coming of the First World War). Partly this was due to my father's fear that they might " disturb his literary work ", partly to his growing dread of any expenses incurred save in building or altering, partly to the fact that he had at last decided that he rather disliked some of my mother's friends, and, looking round, seemed now to have none of his own. . . . Odd ! . . . Perhaps, he consoled himself, it was really better so. Friends often exercised a frivolous influence. . . . And it was more interesting to see strangers — you acquired more information from them —, or to show a little kindness to those who needed it. (Really, he must ask the editor of the *Scarborough Post* to stay !) Every now and then, though, he liked to indulge in a burst of entertaining, and then the question arose, whom to entertain ?

One such occasion, the biggest of its kind, is possibly worth describing. When my sister was nineteen, my father resolved that she ought to have a coming-out party. It was the correct thing to do, and though he disapproved of conventional ways as a rule, for some reason the idea appealed to him. . . . But again, *whom* to ask and what for ? . . . Well, my mother could invite one or two of her relations to help her, he decided ; and the party must be for the Doncaster Races. . . . Into this last decision certainly entered an element of ancestor-worship, together with his individual brand of extravagance mingled with economy ; because he possessed the silver badge which had belonged to his great-grandfather, one of the founders of the meeting, and which, worn in the buttonhole, would still obtain for him a free admission. Hitherto he had never worn it. . . . And in any case he was determined to try the effect of one last sortie from his ivory tower, not yet completed.

Preparations — the Doncaster Races, I may remind any non-sporting reader who may happen to see this book, take place in September, usually in the second week — were of the widest scope and occupied many months. The following letter was written by the sub-agent to his friend the agent in June of the previous year :

I have an enormous list of work to be done for Sir G. Yesterday he went round and showed me what painting and papering is to be done, and I had a warm time this morning from 7 to 1, with 3 men, transforming the Ball-Room into a sitting-room. I have to design a French-window for it, to open on the lawn.

Lady Ida's room. Paint and paper ; a ceiling paper with a " faint, quiet pattern " to be put on. Patterns to be sent Sir G. at Scarborough.

Repair cornice.

Sir G.'s room. Re-cover green-baize door.

Duke's Dressing-Room. Paint and Paper. A paper with " *small* quiet pattern to suit pictures ".

Tapestry-Room. Paper and paint. Paper with " pattern in low tones " to suit tapestry.

Red Room. Paper, paint and plaster end.

Small Drawing-Room. Repair, paint and line ceiling. " Bring out old gold tone."

General. Get mirror for *Hall-Chamber* fireplace 1'–9 inches high, similar to mirror in Duke's Room.

Hang 2 pictures in *Ball-Room.* Clean and Varnish.

Repaint windows in *Ball-Room.*

Take down all curtains and put up again in month's time.

Ditto stair-carpets.

Have *Drawing-Room* curtains dyed dark red.

Make design for French Window in *Ball-Room.*

Paint seat outside garden-door.

Get sconces for small mirrors from abroad.

Lay water on to 3 new marble fountains.[1]

---

[1] The fountains had arrived on 22nd March of that year. The following letter from the sub-agent to the agent conveys the facts and the atmosphere :

DEAR SIR,

The 3 marble fountains arrived today. We have them all unloaded on the lawn, ready for putting in their places tomorrow. They are not so ponderous as Sir G. leads one to believe, the heaviest portion (the basin) weighing 2 tons, 6 men can handle them easily enough with the aid of rollers and planks. We are to put one in front of *Drawing-Room* and *Ball-Room* windows, but it was made to go with its back to a wall, so will not look right in proposed position. I hope Sir G. will not want us to move them to new positions often, as it will be a full day's work for 6 men to take one of them down and put it up again. . . .

TAPESTRY, THE BALL-ROOM, RENISHAW

Africa (one of a set of the Four Continents, *designed by Urbin Leyniers and executed by Louis de Vos*)

OLIVER'S MOUNT, SCARBOROUGH
by John Piper

Fix sun-dial.

Re-arrange terracotta vases. Take some away.

Syringe poison into all the worm-holes in the furniture.

I will send you a complete list soon.

I am on the look-out for a fresh job when Sir G. returns in July !

Three weeks later, he adds a postscript to another letter to the same correspondent : " Sir G. continues to write daily ".

It will be noticed that the arrangements he was making did not include the addition of another bathroom. Here we may remark, as a singular footnote to the period, but a thing in no way unusual at this date, even for so large a house, that Renishaw still possessed only one. And, in this connection, I remember Lutyens complaining to me some years later, that even when he planned for rich clients new and most luxurious houses, he found the greatest difficulty in persuading them to allow a bathroom to each bedroom. . . . In other directions, continually the pace increased. By the end of August the following year, nearly everyone on the estate, and in the house, had been driven frantic. Chefs arrived. Enormous parcels were delivered every day from London. New linen was bought. All the silver plate, some of it unused for many years, was got out of the bank. Extra footmen appeared, and Major Viburne was called in to manage the whole thing as if it were an officers' mess. The running of special trains to Doncaster and back was arranged with the railway company, to convey to the Races those who did not want to go by motor. Motors were hired. A Blue Hungarian Band was engaged for ten days. . . . And for a full month beforehand I used to see my father, sitting later than usual at breakfast, with eight or ten small glass jam-pots — Bar-le-Duc — in front of him, labelled in French, red-currant, white-currant, scarlet strawberry, white strawberry, gooseberry and so on. When I enquired what he was doing, he would reply, as one manfully executing a duty, " Just trying out the jams for the Doncaster party," for he believed in personal supervision. Like a soldier, he stuck to it, in spite of the strain on the liver : but after a few weeks, one could see it was beginning to tell on him. . . . Excitement mounted. And when the great day came, and every bedroom was prepared, and the thirty or so people arrived, we were amazed at the total of their combined ages. The whole point of the party had been that it was for my sister. But every single one of the guests, with the exception of my cousin Veronica and one or two others, was well stricken in years, while several had kicked over the matrimonial traces. The only young man present was a nice American, who had been faithfully retrieved for the occasion by a cousin of ours, and who was frankly puzzled at finding himself in this gallery of antiques. Altogether the party was scarcely suitable and revealed the lengthening gap between reality and things as my parents were beginning to see them.

It was a party, I suppose, none the less — but it seemed curiously impersonal in composition and aim. Nobody knew anyone else in the house — unless it were so intimately that to ask them to meet should have been deemed a work of supererogation —, and nobody particularly wanted to know anyone else. In addition, my father detested racing, and Edith loathed it. My mother, alone, enjoyed the pointless stir and activity of it — and, of course, the opportunities it afforded for betting. The meals were long and good. (The Bar-le-Duc jams, then a novelty in England, were consumed with relish.) The Blue Hungarian Hussars, who put up at the Sitwell Arms in the village, may have puzzled and perturbed the habituals of the inn, colliers and agricultural labourers, by their sallow appearance, raven locks and Magyar swagger. (They carried up to the house each day suitcases, containing their frogged sling-jackets and cherry-coloured breeches, and local opinion, until it became informed, inclined to the view that they were Indians or Armenians peddling carpets — the type of foreigner with which the neighbourhood was best acquainted.) But within doors they were in constant demand, whenever racing was not in progress, playing under the gilded Tudor Rose of the Little Parlour, next the Dining-Room, during every meal except breakfast, and were in continual discourse after dinner in the ball-room. Every restaurant in Europe must have been ransacked to find the repertory. " The music makes things go," said my father, " and prevents people from feeling they *have* to make conversation." (Better still, it prevented him from hearing it.) Only "The Blue Danube", a piece of which the band was fond, was here rather frowned on, being taken by some of the guests, I fear, as a reflection upon their ages. They pretended never to have heard it before. " What a delightful old-fashioned thing ! " they used to exclaim.

" What is it ? . . . But let's have something we know, ' The
Merry Widow ', or one of those delightful tunes from the
Gaiety ! " . . . Trains and motors ran in their ordained
grooves ; the garden looked its best, swooning under a special
weight of flowers. It was usually only visited in the morning, when clematis and rose and honeysuckle and holly-
hock glowed in the butter-coloured golden haze, born of sun
and morning mist — or was it from a ground frost, it was
difficult to tell which, for even after hours of hot sun, the
grass still remained wet, and the rose-heads full of moisture —,
or in the late afternoon, an hour at which the whole summer
seemed to return in epitome, so that it was impossible to
believe that we stood on the very brink of autumn in this high
country, and the scent of the flowers, out-prest by the warmth,
seemed to linger in the air with an unwonted persistence, while
the fruit, ripening on the dark red-brick walls, appeared to
shine in its own radiance and heat. The house, too, seemed
to be in commotion at both ends of the day. In the morning,
the housemaids and footmen struggled upstairs with old-
fashioned tin baths, resembling Egyptian coffins, and hip-baths
like gigantic snail-shells, and enormous cans of steaming-hot
water, to the rooms respectively of female and male guests.
Then there was a hiatus in activity at midday, when the
party had left for Doncaster. Henry would enjoy a siesta : the
chef would drink a bottle of wine. The gardener would come
round to see to the flowers in the house. Finally, hammering
would sound out again from the kitchen. . . . The party
would return : baths would be carried up once more. . . .
And soon there would be the procession down to dinner, down
the oak staircase, across the flagged hall, through the Little
Parlour. " Racing makes one very rheumatic ", the guests
would say to one another when their knees creaked as they
descended the stairs, — for it could have nothing to do with
their ages.

. . . Yes, I think the party must have been adjudged a
success. . . . If any doubt lay at the back of my parents'
minds on this matter, the blame was allotted to Edith. "Très
difficile," my father would say, for he reserved his rather
restricted knowledge of French for the crystallisation of such
domestic problems. He complained that she did not play
tennis — " lawn-tennis ", as he still called it —, while my mother

regretted her addiction to books. She had not " been out " long, and already she had created a bad impression elsewhere, while staying with relations, as well as having excessively startled the late Lord Chaplin, by enquiring of him, during an evening when she was placed next to him at dinner, whether he preferred Bach to Mozart. She had been hastily withdrawn from circulation and sent home. It would never do. . . . Still, one could try one's best. . . . The party was nearly over.

Only Major Viburne was, as major-domo, patently a failure. Owing to what must have been high blood-pressure, still further inflamed, no doubt, by his ferocious military opinions, or, perhaps, merely as a result of endeavouring to help my father by " trying out the jams ", he began again to have fits of giddiness. Especially when he was showing visitors from neighbouring houses round the gardens would these attacks descend to overwhelm him, and, suddenly grasping for safety a thick post — shaped like the ragged staff held by the bear in public-house signs, — up which grew climbing roses, he would spin wildly round it, unable to tell which way he was going and leading those to whom he was acting as guide in circles, much to their surprise.

" There's the Major playing ' Here we go round the Mulberry Bush ' again in the garden ! " Henry would remark. " He's too old for that sort of game now, if he'd only realise it. . . . The guests don't like it."

And my mother, as if he had done it on purpose, would complain that it made her feel giddy even to look at him.

Sacheverell and I, and our tutor Mr. Ragglesedge who might have enjoyed the race-meetings, were not permitted to attend them, nor the meals in the Dining-Room. My brother and I feasted on scraps in our attic. . . . It seemed rather lonely, not being allowed to join in. Never being able to realise when I am not wanted, I decided one evening to bicycle through the park and meet my father — who was that day motoring back from the races — at the gates. I was wearing a best new blue suit, appropriate to the occasion. Free-wheeling blithely downhill, through a grove of trees, I paid no attention to where I was going, caught the back of the heel of a cow, which was mouching across the drive, with my front wheel and, flying with an unexpected elegance and agility over the handle-bars just as my father was entering the park, landed, with torn trousers, grazed knees and a black eye, a few yards ahead of him. It was a silly thing to have done. . . . I sensed as much in the atmosphere. I had let the side down. Further, I had ruined, unnecessarily, a new suit — a fact of which, ever and again, I was reminded during the remaining weeks of the holidays.

Gradually the music faded, the musicians, clothed soberly in black, returned to London, the guests left — many of them were never to see such a party again —, Major Viburne's dizziness began to pass off, the head chef went back to London with a large cheque and a scalded hand, the train service relapsed to the normal and the motors stopped breaking down and raced home. My father abandoned the life of the time as he saw it, and sped back to the gothic centuries. In addition to his never-ending studies of medieval life, he was at work on his book *On the Making of Gardens*, and continued entering notes on many and diverse subjects. I find the following jotting, under the heading " Venus ", dated September of the same year : " The author of the book on classical statuary which I have been reading, does not allow for the great interest attaching to ideal types of womanhood. The Venus of Syracuse is really very beautiful. Of course, the proper place for a Venus is in a private or a public bath."

As for Venus, whether in private or public bath, she was certainly more in evidence in England than she had been for a hundred years. The goddess seemed more openly to be occupying men's thoughts. For the first time for many decades, clothes had become highly stylised again, with an elegance verging on absurdity. At Ascot, and on the lawns of garden-parties, it was to be noticed that women had at last begun to shed once more the multitude of their garments, had left behind the veilings and feather boas in which we saw them wrapped at Lord's, and were now clad, skin-deep, in tight silks, were sheathed in satin, or wore slit skirts and silver anklets. For the world took its note from Musical Comedy rather than from the immense tragedies that were being prepared in the wings to replace it, and the production of *Les Merveilleuses* at Daly's in November 1906 had introduced, or at any rate popularised, Directoire dresses. The hats were gigantic now, and covered with ostrich feathers. The colours were those of young grass and leaves, the chequerings of

branches against a grey sky, or rose-pink and azure-blue —
they had about them a peculiar ephemerality, a butterfly-like
character that was the essence of modishness. Paris had again
asserted her leadership, and marched behind the smiling mask
of the *Entente Cordiale*, to take London captive, yet London
was now becoming, in her place, the pleasure centre of the
world.

Motor-cars had at last become common for private owners.
. . . It must have been in the summer holidays of 1907 that
Mr. Ragglesedge, sanguine by temperament and I suppose in
need of money, decided to repair his situation by selling to
my father a motor-car, and, towards the accomplishment of
this project, improvised an audacious farce. He did not
take my brother or me into his confidence. . . . First of all,
he told my father that a friend of his, the son of a multi-
millionaire, was motoring down from Scotland, and was very
anxious to see Renishaw. He had heard such a lot about it.
Might he stay the night ? . . . My father gave his consent,
and a few days later, with the accompaniment of a great
deal of honking of horns and of brass flashing in the sun, the
young millionaire materialised at the door in his open motor
of the period. For the heir to so vast a fortune, his wardrobe
was singularly modest, consisting, Henry told me, of the brown
suit, with knickerbockers, and over-elaborate stockings and
garter-tabs, in which he stood up, a borrowed dinner-suit —
for his name was Scrutton, and inside the coat was written
W. T. Jenkins —, one alternate collar and a toothbrush : but
for this comparative poverty he compensated by the grandeur
of his talk. We got to know, almost, the precise measurements
of his father's grouse moor. The young plutocrat was, in
fact, the earliest example I ever saw of a motor tout, complete
in every detail. . . . My father remained blind to the obvious
fraudulence of these pretensions — the only person who did.
The rest of us enjoyed the farce as it unfolded itself — besides,
we hoped he would buy a motor. Mr. Ragglesedge played
cleverly on my father's competitive sense by relating how our
Scottish cousins, — those whose prayer-meetings were soon to
prove so disastrous to him — had bought a machine by no
means as fine as this. For it now transpired that not only
was our new friend willing to oblige my father by selling this
motor — he had tired of it, he grew tired of possessions so

easily, they meant so little to him, and he often disposed of things that had cost him thousands just for a few pounds — for eighteen hundred, but, should the price prove more than my father felt inclined to pay, there were other, cheaper, motors in his garage, three or four of them, of which he would like to rid himself. After the manner of the Athenian in days gone by, his soul ever craved new ideals. . . . The visit lengthened, for my father — we perceived — entertained no intention of buying a motor. . . . Nine days passed ; (and the alternate collars would not, we could see, be able to do service for much longer). Yet Mr. Ragglesedge and Mr. Scrutton both felt, somehow, that they were very near, that it was growing hot, and that one more day, just one more day, might settle the deal. . . . Finally, after wasting nearly a fortnight of the tout's time, my father — who had to go up to London on business — announced that he would test the motor by going up to London in it. . . . Accordingly, full of excitement, Scrutton drove him there, and Mr. Ragglesedge accompanied the party, in order to praise the motor whenever an opportunity served, and, as it were, to talk out any breakdowns that might occur. The journey occupied nine hours, but my father had saved the amount of the train fare. On arrival, he complained that motoring " tired " his back, and that he had decided in consequence never to buy a motor. . . . Poor Mr. Ragglesedge's rage, and that of his friend, knew no bounds. More or less, they came into the open about it. Dear Mr. Ragglesedge went back to our Scottish cousins, and the tragedy I have mentioned occurred shortly after. We never saw him again, or Mr. Scrutton.

The reader might expect our knowledge of this person to end there ; but no, our family sleuth, aged eleven, was on the track, and I find the following perspicacious and informative letter addressed to me and dated from his school, on 31st March 1908 :

Darling Osbert,
How are you ? There are three new boys here, one of whom lives near Maidenhead, where Scrutton lives. Scrutton has about 800 a year and is in the motor-trade. He very often has a man to stay with him (most probably Ragglesedge) who has a very bad reputation for being in debt, borrowing money and never paying it back. He is the son of a diamond-merchant, and a nephew of

Ragglesedge, the ecclesiastical outfitters, so Ragglesedge is also a cousin of Scrutton, whose mother is aged about seventy-five and has 1200 a year of her own, her husband was a fur-seller and a money-lender, being a Jew. He made his fortune, but went bankrupt and is still living at the age of 87, he is undischarged. Scrutton is his stepson, his original father being a cousin of his step one. He also was a money-lender and lost 150,000 pounds by a bank breaking and died in 1903 at the age of 79 or 80 : but he was not undischarged. Scrutton is about 40 or 38 but looks younger. Ragglesedge was in the army but was thrown out for debt in 1901.

Thought this would interest you.—With love from your very loving brother, S.

Other dramas were on the verge of being produced. . . . We must now take a step forward in time to that visit to Viterbo which I mentioned in the last chapter, and watch Henry's behaviour. Because, in spite of the new nervousness to be observed in him, this is the moment of his apotheosis, and after it, though his companionship and wit never failed, I fear his glory began a little to decline, becoming legendary more than active. The reader will recall that I wondered why this courageous and in some directions unimaginative man should have succumbed to a sense of fear that made him hurry through the narrow streets of the old city, and flicker his eyes at every corner, and in every turning of every passage. What could be the matter with him ? . . . I *should* have guessed, I ought to have given fantasy the fullest rein : but herein I failed, though the clue was to my hand. . . . A few years later, in 1913, Henry left us. Then followed his longest separation from my family, and not until he returned, in 1919, did he reveal to me the essence of the mystery. . . . And, indeed, I found the matter interesting, when he told me of it, for this was the only time that his private life nearly, so nearly, impinged on public affairs.

At the moment of which I write, the Italian Government had decided at last to make — or try to make — an end of the various secret societies within its territory. In particular, swooping down on the headquarters of the most famous, the Camorra, it had seized any papers it could find, and had subsequently arrested many persons suspected of belonging to it. Thirty of them were now standing their trial for the murder of a fellow member and his wife some five years before at Torre del Greco, a suburb of Naples. What is more, they were on trial at Viterbo. This town had been chosen, one may suppose, because it was a small hill town, with the innocence of the mountains inspiring its population, whereas in the great cities, in Rome and more especially in Naples, where the Camorra had its fount and home, there would have been too many people either sympathetic to its cause or else in its clutches for the authorities to be able to guarantee the safety of those presiding over the court or engaged in the prosecution. So dangerous were the prisoners considered, so dangerous, doubtless, were they, that the dock, though guarded, was thought to be an insufficient barrier for the protection of the others present, more especially of the witnesses — whom, indeed, it had been far from easy to persuade to give evidence at all —, and, accordingly, the accused were confined, as if they were a howling pack of wild beasts, within an iron cage, erected in the court, while the informer, who played a big part in the trial, occupied a cage of his own. . . . Of all this I was aware ; I knew that in a cage, in the court, in Viterbo, where at that very moment we were staying, thirty ferocious members of the Camorra were undergoing trial on a mortal score — what I did not know was that Henry Moat, as a fellow member of the society, the only Englishman to belong, might have been arrested at any moment, might even, though guiltless of murder, have been deemed, as a member, an accomplice of the crime, and be made to share the communal cage. . . . No wonder, then, that he slunk — if a whale can be said to slink — down every street in terror of being recognised by a *confrère* or denounced by an enemy ; if he were seen and identified by other members, disguised but still at large, who were certain to be posted in the town as counter-spies, he would have run a terrible risk, because they would have inevitably concluded that, since he was here without having entered into communication with them, he had turned King's Evidence. Who could imagine the vengeance that would fall on him, perhaps immediately, perhaps when the trial was finished and the Camorra had been given time to recover and reconstitute itself ? . . . The worst punishments of all, he knew, were reserved for those suspected of being traitors. . . . Why, he remembered, only a year or two back, when a Sicilian farmer, who had betrayed the similar society to which he belonged, the Mafia — island rival to the Camorra —, had been cut in pieces, and these morsels had been found decorating the top of the wall bounding his land on the outskirts of Palermo. . . . The hotel in which we were staying, with its empty, dingy vistas and echoing, sinister halls, must have seemed to him the perfect setting for a drama of terror and conscience. " It seemed almost like spite on Sir George's part taking me there," he said to me afterwards.[1]

Here — although this book cannot, as I would like, engage itself with the history of Italian secret societies — a word must be said about the Camorra. Its great days, when it had been able to exert considerable influence upon the ruling of the country of its origin, had been before the fall of the Neapolitan Bourbon dynasty, from the 'forties to the 'sixties of the last century. Then it was better for a foreigner to leave the realm at once, had he by chance offended someone whom, whether beggar, shopkeeper or prince, he suspected to be a member of that powerful body. Essentially democratic, it had always drawn, and still drew, members from every rank of society ; nobles, burgesses, waiters, fishermen, pimps, gendarmes, brothel-keepers, all belonged to it. (At Viterbo, among those on trial in the cage, was, I regret to say, a priest.) Branches existed throughout the mainland of the Two Sicilies. It must be emphasised, moreover, that, superficially, the Camorra possessed an agreeable side, engaging in social and philanthropic activities as well as, in the opposite direction, in kidnapping, torture and murder. . . . But let me give an illustration of the pride of this secret body, combined with a good instance of the considerateness it could show and of the effective manner in which it was organised.

My old acquaintance, the Prince of Nocera — a Neapolitan aristocrat of mixed Greek and Spanish descent, who, with his rather long face, hollow cheeks, refined but bony features and white, pointed beard and moustache, and with his delicate, nervous, well-shaped hands, presented exactly the model for a portrait by El Greco — told me the following story of a personal experience. . . . The Princess, lady-of-the-bedchamber to the beautiful Queen Margherita, wife of King Umberto, was expecting her first confinement, and she and her husband were living at one of their castles somewhere in the wild and

---

[1] For an account of the trial, see Appendix E, p. 306.

mountainous country south of Naples. Things were not going
well with the Princess, and the Prince was worried, for it was
the middle of the winter and snow lay on the higher levels
of the hills. Roads were almost impassable. . . . Suddenly,
a few days before the child was expected, the Princess was
gripped with the most urgent longing for some mountain
strawberries. . . . In vain he tried to find some for her,
telegraphing to friends in Naples — but how was it possible
to find them in this weather and at this season ? . . . In
despair, for he imagined gratification of her wish as essential
to her health, he invited the head of the local Camorra to
come and see him, and explained to this man the situation.
By the same evening, a large basket of the ripest, the most
delicious mountain strawberries had reached the Princess.
When the Prince called at the headquarters of the Society
in the neighbouring town, lost in the hills, in order to thank
his benefactor for this feat of magic, as it seemed, he expressed
his eagerness to pay for the fruit and the trouble involved
in obtaining it. But the chief indignantly rejected his offer.
Such things, he said, could not be accomplished for money ;
the Camorra existed only in order to help people !

As for Henry joining the Society, it had all happened so
simply. . . . He had often met a Neapolitan courier in the
service of that old Herr Krupp [1] who was head of the notorious
German armament firm and owned a villa in Capri. All
one winter, Henry and this courier had encountered and
re-encountered each other in all kinds of surroundings, in
small hotels, in quiet little places like Amalfi and Ravello,
in the better-known hotels in Naples and Sorrento, and in
cafés, music-halls and night-haunts. One evening the courier
remarked to him, as if in allusion to a club of some kind ;

" I often wonder you don't join the Camorra. . . . It's
very convenient. . . . I could propose you for election. . . .
It would save you tons of money. . . . You'd get in free
everywhere — they're only too glad to see you and give you
a welcome."

With his Yorkshire sense of thrift, the suggestion had
appealed to Henry, and in due course he had been triumphantly

---

[1] Krupp died about this time, and was said to have committed suicide at
the command of the German Emperor, in order to avoid being implicated in a
scandal in Capri.

elected a member of the venerable and celebrated Neapolitan institution. (All previous foreign candidates had been blackballed.)

"After all," he said, " Sir George was much safer, with me being a member — but it wouldn't 'ave done to tell him so. 'E wouldn't 'ave understood. . . . Better to say nowt."

Thus, when my father had gone to bed, Henry used to set forth for a night of amusement. A single glance at his membership card procured his admittance anywhere without charge. And his brother clubmen proved the jolliest possible set of good fellows — everyone in the fishermen's quarter of Whitby would have approved of them, he told me, and there they applied no easy criterion — real, downright good sorts. . . . Often he would be out all night, and would only return to the hotel, with a rather unsteady footstep, in time to have a cold bath and call my father. Then, when his master left the hotel, at about nine, to visit the gothic tombs in the churches, to go, for example, by train to Capua in order to examine the foundations of the Emperor Frederick II's palace there, or to take notes on the pilgrims' road, and whether any inns remained from that epoch, Henry, in his turn, would take his rest, enjoying a long and comfortable siesta behind closed Venetian shutters, through which penetrated a soft light and the sleepy hum of insects in the garden.

Looked back on, his career as Camorrista appeared very gay, but almost innocent — and now here he was, in danger of immediate arrest by the police ! . . . Even at home, he would hardly feel secure : there was the danger of extradition. . . . And the stories the Italian Press published ! They shocked him. Such lurid and exaggerated tales might easily do harm and " put all sorts of ideas into Sir George's head ". . . . Meanwhile it was best to avoid, as far as possible, going out into the town, or even walking along the corridors of the hotel. You could never be sure. . . . But Viterbo, he confessed, was a dull little hole at the best of times, not like Naples. It wasn't very amusing, having to sit in his cold bedroom, with a cement floor just like a . . . well, just like a cell in a prison.

" And you wouldn't believe the number of times Sir George sent me out into the town ; you'd have thought he know'd something and did it on purpose. . . . One moment it would be 'Henry, just go out and get me a freshly baked roll for breakfast,' or 'Go and buy me some fruit,' or 'Go out and get me the latest edition of the paper. I want to read about the Camorra trial.' That was the worst of all, the crowds round the men selling the papers. I was fear't to death."

How much I had missed from never being aware of all this at the time! How many pleasant hours it would have given me thinking over it, when I had returned to Eton. Henry was a member of the Camorra — whereas I never even got into Pop! . . . To my delight " the happiest time of my life " was nearing its end, and when, eventually, my tutor became involved in an Alpine accident, and was killed, I persuaded my father to allow me to leave. As will transpire in the next volume, in doing this I committed a tactical error, but it seemed at the time a great step forward towards liberty. The next half I returned to Eton for the ritual of being given my leaving-book — the inevitable Gray's Poems. In presenting it to me, the headmaster, Dr. Lyttelton, mentioned his disappointment and surprise at finding that I was not to take Holy Orders — but his surprise can have been as nothing to mine when I heard him make the remark.

To its credit, one can say, I believe, that the Eton system does little to alter a boy's character ; it either develops it, if ordinary, or else, if unusual, drives it in on itself. It exercises in no wise so formative an influence as does a private school. But, albeit that Eton had little effect on my character, I yet believe that my career there — I left in 1909 — and the example of my friends, produced some effect on the life at Eton, by making the average boy more tolerant, so that the intelligent Etonian of ten years later reaped a certain benefit, was given an easier time, and was not so much victimised by games.

There were many problems that puzzled me while I was there. One of them was this : as I regarded some of the bearers of names made famous by statesmen, generals, diplomats and governors, I asked myself how it was possible that these boys could be the sons, grandsons or heirs of generations of men of attainments, often of intellect, at any rate of strong character, possessing in the highest degree powers of decision, qualities singularly lacking in their descendants before me. I wondered if something had gone wrong with the stock and, contemplating them, looked to a future wherein they might be called upon to rule, or at any rate to exercise influence — a position for which they were assuredly not equipped mentally — with (though, it may be, as things have turned out, not with enough) dismay. . . . So much did this question worry me, that on one occasion when my father came down to see me, I asked him whether, in his time at Eton, his contemporaries had seemed equally lacking in interest, capacity and intellect. . . . After, I must say, some considerable reflection, as if he were rather in doubt about the matter himself, he said, yes, but it was, he thought, only an apparent deterioration, in no way actual. Eton taught you, he pronounced, to be a leader, to command. (But was it, I could not help wondering, a good thing to be *taught* to lead, if you had not mental qualities to support such an attitude?) If any increased weakness was really to be remarked, he added, with the curiously practical, almost Chinese application of his ingenious mind, this might be due to a fact he had noticed, that the small children of the rich now had all their food cut up for them, long after they should have been cutting it up for themselves ; a process which constituted one of the principal means of self-education for the very young. . . . Perhaps this may, indeed, afford a clue to the cause of degeneracy in certain instances ; as, for example, to that of the Spanish Habsburgs in the seventeenth century ; perhaps too much had been done for them as children. So simple does it sound that it may be true : and if true, it is at least a fault that offers the advantage of being easy to cure.

How priggish my doubts, and with what cruelty did fate resolve them ! For when these boys round me grew up, I was, indeed, to form a different opinion of them, and to come to understand that in part it was only that I opposed my own different but as lively intolerance to that of my fellow Etonians. I possessed a liking for things of the intellect, a passion for the arts, which already I placed above everything. . . . All through my school life, from that first day I have described, the same faces had haunted me — those faces that for so long I found difficult to memorise and to which the reader has watched me vainly endeavouring to attach a name. Having gone to two private schools, I had the disadvantage when I arrived at Eton of being greeted by two sets of familiar faces instead of by one alone. They continued to arrive in strictest order of seniority. They accompanied me, at the stated intervals, from class to class, and from game to game. I had observed them as small boys and big boys ; I met them now as youths : some of them ordained by the hierarchical system, that then still prevailed, for great positions in the State — positions whereto, notwithstanding, the majority of them never attained, for they were killed in the 1914–1918 conflict, fighting with the vigour and debonair courage of their ancestors. I had seen them in the past as the treacherous and vindictive mob that, collectively, they formed. In consequence it came to me with all the force of a shock to find later, as I shall tell, what brave, generous, loyal and often lovable companions these young boors, dullards and bullies, with whom, on and off, I had been interned for so long, and with whom after that I had lost touch so willingly, but for so brief a while, only for the two years that followed my leaving Eton, had become in that space ; a magic interval of metamorphosis wrought by the functioning of minute glands, a wonder of Nature that caused the mob to break up, and then integrate into individuals again (the same process that attends the change from war to peace), a phenomenon comparable at the stage I seek to indicate with that which converts a squirming handful of furry grubs into so many brave butterflies, roaming their whole world of the garden, flitting where they will from flower to flower, in spite of the immense and unpredictable dangers that menace them from all sides.

APPENDIX A

THE VERELSTS

THE history of the Verelsts presents a microcosm of an English county family in the making ; though it must be admitted that it is unusual to find one boasting so many talented progenitors. Nevertheless, it has the strain of exoticism so often present, but always unexpected. . . . Simon Verelst or Van der Elst, whom Horace Walpole describes as " a real ornament of Charles's reign ", was born at The Hague in 1644. He became a flower painter, being very well known already in his own country before he settled in London in 1669. In that year Pepys, going to see another Dutch painter who lived in St. James's Market, was by mistake directed to the rooms of Verelst, or " Evereest " as he calls him. The young artist showed him a flower-pot of his painting, and the diarist grew enthusiastic about it, characterising it as " the finest thing I ever saw in my life ", and adding that the drops of dew hung on the leaves " so I was forced again and again to put my finger to it, to feel whether my eyes were deceived or not . . . it is worth going twenty miles to see it ". Flower painting such as this, executed with a minute exactness, appealed to the taste of the day, and his art soon became the fashion. The Duke of Buckingham acted as his chief patron, but having, in the words of Walpole, " too much wit to be only beneficent ", made sport of the artist's excessive vanity by continually urging him to paint portraits. Verelst, deeming no achievement to be beyond his capacity, at last accepted this challenge and painted the Duke himself, but placed him in such a riotous thicket of fruit and sunflowers that King Charles II, to whom the new portrait was shown, took it for a flower piece. The novelty of the treatment, however, and the precision of the likeness, when once perceived, soon triumphed over ridicule, and these portraits became so much in demand that Sir Peter Lely lost half his clients and was obliged to retire to Kew. Simon Verelst, however, became in time so intoxicated with his own talents and his own success that he went off his head. He declared himself to be " the God of Flowers ", and, when not permitted to have the three-hour interview with King Charles II which he demanded, he vaunted publicly, " He is King of England, I am King of Painting ; why cannot we converse familiarly ? " He was confined as a lunatic for a time, but in the end recovered his senses, though never the full extent of his gifts. He lived to be an old man and died in Suffolk Street, London, in about 1721.

Pictures by him figured in all the great contemporary English collections.

Simon's brother, Harmen Verelst, practised his art in Vienna, until the siege of that capital by the Turks and the success of his brother in England brought him to London in 1683. He painted, in the phrase of Walpole, "history, fruit and flowers", and died in London about 1700. A son, Cornelius, also became a well-known painter, and died in London in 1734 : but Harmen's daughter, Maria, who resided in the house of her uncle, Simon, was even more celebrated, being famous for her beauty and her accomplishments, no less than for her painting, which resembled in style that of her uncle, with whom she worked. She spoke many languages, and it is related that in a London theatre she once sat next to six Germans of high rank, who expressed with hyperbole in their own language their admiration for her air and her looks : whereupon she observed to them in German that "such extra-vagant praise . . . conveyed no real compliment". One of them now repeated his former utterance, this time in Latin ; to him she replied in the same language he used that it was unjust to deprive her sex of "the knowledge of the tongue which was the vehicle of true learning and taste". . . . The party of Germans then enquired who she might be, and upon being informed, each of them at once commissioned from her a portrait of himself on the most generous terms.

Cornelius left behind him a son, William — who probably painted the portrait of Henry Sacheverell which began this dis-cursion — and who painted a renowned portrait of Tobias Smollett. . . . But now the family suddenly breaks fresh ground, for William's nephew, Harry, the grandson of Cornelius, entered the service of the East India Company and rose to the position of Governor of Bengal. . . . In 1770 he returned to England with an ample fortune, and settled down in the neighbourhood of Renishaw, at Aston Hall, a house he bought from Lord Holderness, and which continued until a few years ago in the possession of his descendants.

APPENDIX B

FATHER TO SON

HOTEL STRAUSS (Geo Ott, Direktor), Nürnberg
1 May 1901

My DARLING OSBERT,

Purpose of this letter is to descript Nuremberg and its environs, and here-with I include an exemplar of Woerl's traveller-book, as it may be useful to you when you are grown up and able to under-take more extended route-journeyings on your own account. This city is rich in art-treasures of all kinds, and affords many interesting perspectives : the old houses with their beautiful jutwindows embellished with gable statues of saints impart a very romantic aspect to the streets and do attract frequently the visit of travellers. Especially St. Lorenzo's Church in consequence of the consistent execution of its style, produces a great impression, and if after knocking at any of the doors it is not opened, the attendant can be found at the jutroom on the other side of the street. Nuremberg was once a great centre of trade, being a half-way house by which that of Venice and the East was carried to the free cities of Northern Germany, and it has still a lively commerce in railway construction carriage works, black lead pencil manufactories, not to omit the long celebrated gingerbread trade. The discovery of new ocean passages adversely influenced its prosperity, but not to the extent as it was affected by the general ruin induced by the war of the reformation, latter obtaining a footing in the year 1525. Woerl has a note that watches were first invented here and were called Nuremberg eggs, and states that " partakers of old watches and time-measurers of all centuries will be find its " by the Speckhart collection. No doubt Miss King-Church will be able to tell you what he means.

And now to descend to less classical and more colloquial English, Nuremberg next after Venice is my favourite city and is certainly the most picturesque place I have ever seen. This is due chiefly to the high-pitched red-tiled roofs and the air of immemorial antiquity which pervades the whole town. In England all the roofs are flat and mean, and English architects complain that tiles are very expensive to maintain. But when they are laid at the proper slope, no roof covering lasts longer, and people here who have covered their roofs with slate have had to return again to tiles. The roofs are used to store firewood and dry linen and are divided sometimes into three

298

or four stories, and in each there is an overhanging window by which firewood can be drawn up in a bucket to the top of the house by a pulley and bucket, that being easier than to carry it upstairs.

The land round the city was once all a forest of firs, in which wolves abounded. Long ago one of the peasants a few miles away had to carry his tribute of corn to the Burgrave of Nuremberg on a fixed day, and as he had heard the wolves howling near his house on the previous night he told his wife on no account to open the doors till he returned. But when he arrived at the Castle a great feast was being held, and the Burgrave could not see him until he had waited for two hours or more. His wife, as the time for his return drew on, heard the wolves crying and quarrelling near by, and thought they must be attacking her husband, so she took a hatchet and went out to help him. So when the poor peasant returned, he found nothing but the bones of his wife and children picked clean by the wolves, and he put them in his basket and rode back to the Castle. The attendants admitted him again, as he said he was bringing more tribute, and he uncovered the basket before the Burgrave, saying " Now see what you have done ". I hope you will remember this story, and be a good man of business when you are grown up and not keep other people waiting, for those who are not find in the long run that creditors are more ravenous than wolves.

The Emperor Henry III built a castle here about the year 1040, of which two towers are still standing, and at the same time the great castle well was dug by the prisoners in the dungeons. It is more than three hundred feet deep, and near the water level are underground passages, one going to the Rathhaus or Town Hall, and the other to a secret sallyport two miles away in the forest. The forest used to be haunted by robber-knights who captured the rich merchants and held them to ransom. One of these robber-knights, Ekkelein von Gailingen, was taken prisoner late in the 14th century and confined in the Castle dungeon. When he was brought out to be executed, he asked as a last favour to be allowed to mount his war horse for the last time, and after galloping it round the castle yard he set it straight at the moat and actually landed safe on the other side. One of the horse's forelegs was broken, but its rider knew the byepaths in the forest so well that he escaped.

I have been to see many of the old houses here which once belonged (some of them still belong) to patrician families. Inside are fine courtyards with balustrades pierced with gothic traceries, fountains and fine stone staircases. That of the Tucher family was built in 1533 and still remains precisely as it was when built, the decorations, tapestries and furniture being all preserved. It is quite marvellous how everything has been preserved at Nuremberg. In St. Lorenzo church is a lamp given by the Tucher family in 1327 and kept burning ever since. In the Tedzel chapel which I visited today there are painted wood escutcheons commemorating the death of every head of that house since 1397, and ending with one of 1730 which is turned upside down to show that this was the last male heir of the family, which is now extinct. The house of Albert Dürer the great painter and engraver is still to be seen as also that of Hans Sachs the cobbler poet, and that of Adam Kraft the sculptor in stone.

On Saturday I went over with a guide to see Rothenburg, a little medieval town in this neighbourhood which stands on the top of the hill with its old circle of walls and red roofed towers unbroken, and not a single house in it, as far I could judge, built in the last two hundred years. The Rathhaus, built late in the 14th century, has a dungeon under it, in which Burgomaster Toppler was confined about the time I have just mentioned. His wealth made him enemies ; and they falsely accused him of gambling away the town of Rothenburg to the Burggraf of Nuremberg. He was imprisoned in an underground cell without light or air ; his friends made a tunnel to reach him — the exit can still be seen closed with tiles and mortar, but when they forced their way through, he had already died of thirst and starvation. In the Rathhaus we were also shown the glass drinking cup which was instrumental in saving the town from destruction in the 30 years war. It has the date 1613 on it and painted figures of the Emperor and the seven electors round the bowl, and would hold about two bottles and a half of wine. In 1631, Tilly the Catholic general captured the town, which indeed was not strong enough to make much of a defence, and riding to the Rathhaus he had the Burgomaster and the three principal councillors brought before him, asked them why they had dared to resist, and sent for the executioner to behead them. At that moment the Burgomaster's daughter came in with this flagon of wine, and Tilly after drinking from it said to his four prisoners, " Now if one of you four can drink this cup dry without drawing breath, he shall save your lives and the whole town, but if he fails I will set fire to the four corners of it and give it over to pillage as I threatened." The Burgomaster made the attempt and succeeded, but he used to say afterwards that when he had drunk he saw not one but twelve towns being burnt and destroyed. Rothenburg is a wonderful lesson how one ought to build houses or castles, and how picturesque effect is to be gained by the honest use of good materials in the rough without any elaborate ornament. The roughly chiselled stone and solid oak shaped with the axe, and coarse red tiles, are far more beautiful than any finely finished work could be. Now I must conclude as we are leaving for Venice.—With best love to E. and Sachie, Ever your loving father, GEORGE R. SITWELL.

I have bought an old picture in one of the curiosity shops for £40. It is dated 1480, and is painted by some painter of the Wohlgemuth school. W. was Albert Dürer's master.

APPENDIX C

THE HISTORY OF THE COLD

Iᴛ seems possible that the cold is an English invention; (and if, as some say, Napoleon's defeat at Waterloo was due to it, it has been racially useful). At any rate in the eighteenth century foreigners seem to have been much struck with this feature of English life. . . . Thus Mozart's father, while he and his family were staying in London, writes on 23rd August 1764, from Chelsea, to his friend Lorenz Hagenauer at Salzburg, in the following terms : "Mᴏɴsɪᴇᴜʀ, Do not be frightened ! But prepare your heart to hear one of the saddest events. Perhaps you will have already noticed my condition from my handwriting. Almighty God has visited me with a sudden and severe illness. . . ." [1]

A week or so later, to the same correspondent, Leopold Mozart adds : " . . . I now state that every day, although my progress is slow, I am feeling a little better. . . . So that you may know, however, how my illness started, I must tell you that in England there is a kind of native complaint, which is called a ' cold '. That is why you hardly ever see people wearing summer clothes. They all wear cloth garments. This so-called ' *cold* ' in the case of people who are not constitutionally sound, becomes so dangerous that in many cases it develops into a ' *consumption* ' as they call it here ; but I call it ' *febrem lentam* ' ; and the wisest course for such people to adopt is to leave England and cross the sea ; and many instances can be found of people recovering their health on leaving this country. . . ." [2]

[1] *The Letters of Mozart and His Family*, translated by Emily Anderson, vol. i, p. 72. (Macmillan, 1938.)
[2] *Ibid.*, vol. i, pp. 73-4.

APPENDIX D

PATERS' MATCH

THE pages that follow consist of extracts taken from a chapter entitled " Paters' Match ", out of one of my novels, *Those Were the Days* (Macmillan, 1938). In the book itself, a little before the words I quote, is a sentence asking the reader to note, for the sake of period-accuracy — for the school described is supposed to exist in the 1930's —, that mastoid and sinus are new school tortures, introduced into the preparatory school curriculum since my day.

" Miss Prentiss-Pendergrass had just left the Conservatory and was walking towards the drawing-room. Concolorous, she was dressed in a gala gown of beige lace, which matched exactly her eyes and complexion, and the effect was completed by a large beige hat, with a beige ostrich feather running round the brim, under which showed a small, curly beige fringe. ' She's such a pleasant-looking little woman, with her nice smile,' the parents used to say, in order to damp unpleasant doubts, ' not pretty exactly, perhaps, but such a *nice* way of showing her teeth, when she laughs.' (Behind her back, the boys called her ' Tusker '.) She sported a small moonstone pendant that seemed a solidified soapsud, and a small moonstone, on a small gold chain, tinkled from each ear. Diminutive moonstones and giant chrysanthemums were her signature-tune, her speciality, almost, you might say, what she lived for. . . .

" She proceeded to the dining-hall, to see for herself that everything was in order ; a large panelled room, with a beamed ceiling, and monastic tables, on which, to-day, stood various silver cups, deformed and squat ; each one the reward of a different unnatural agony and heart-strain — the ' high-jump ', the ' long-jump ' or the ' hundred yards ' — and, in fact, the solid guarantee of two or three years taken off the end of the life of the boy who won it. . . . Very nice everything looked, she thought, with the silver, and the ferns in green pottery stands. And she felt confident that luncheon to-day would be a success. She had cancelled the soup, made of shredded carrots, barley, egg-powder and bovril, with a lot of pepper added to make it more ' tasty ' — a good, honest, nourishing broth it was, too, though some obstinate little boys refused to touch it — usually the first dish on Thursday, and had substituted for it a dainty little recipe, of chopped ham, parsley and potatoes, all minced and cooked together, with a little curry powder added, served in a scallop, with shrimp sauce all over it, and on the top, an anchovy rolled up as though in a last paroxysm of ptomaine. She had found it, strongly recommended, in the ' Home Cuisine ' page of a ladies' paper, under the heading ' French Food at Home ', and it seemed just the thing for a hot day; not too heavy. . . . And after that they were having chicken, with that nice gluey sauce (chicken impressed the parents), and lots of good trifles and jellies. You really couldn't do more. And Cook was very good at trifles, when she got the chance.

" Miss Prentiss-Pendergrass retraced her steps, turning to the private part of the house again, and entered the drawing-room, a spacious gothic creation, with sham-stone walls, shiny, pale-brown, wooden rafters, and lots of little windows, very high up. There were ferns again, and silver vases, with a few bright-coloured sweet peas struggling through a sort of mosquito-net of gypsophila, and photographs of parents, if of sufficient station, in silver frames, so as to make the place look ' homy ' . . .

Mr. Prentiss-Pendergrass was waiting for her, as she had expected, for they always enjoyed a quiet talk before the fun began. He was one of those very fit-looking schoolmasters, without an ounce of flesh to him, grey-haired and grey-faced, and with very marked lines from nostril to mouth-corner, who resemble a wolf-hound — or, perhaps, a wolf. He could stand any amount of hardship, you would have said, but you would have been wrong : his appearance was most deceptive ; he had been a keen and successful football-player, and had kept it up until rather late in life, so that he was now, at fifty-five, a victim of painful and severe heart-attacks, while a life-time of school food, even in the slightly more palatable and healthy form in which it reached his table, had worked havoc with his digestion. In character, he was somewhat querulous, and always discovering that he had been ' let down ' by someone under him.

" For weeks beforehand, brother and sister had been saying to each other continually, ' I *do* hope we shall have a fine day this year for Paters' Match ! ' : but, now the morning had arrived, they could not but regret the full measure, pressed down and over-flowing, which had been meted out to them. (It was a mistake to *overdo* things : hardly gentleman-like.) Of course a fine day helped the school, but it was going to be *very* hot indeed, and the strain would be considerable. Nor was it so easy to be consistently agreeable to the one hundred and sixty parents odd, and to carry to each pair the conviction that their small and unattractive son, a single unit among eighty, occupied a position in tutorial hearts different from that held by any of his school-fellows. A few years before the war, it had been easier to manage the paters and maters, because they all arrived by train in a herd, hot and tired out, and so you knew, more or less, where they were :

but many of them now reached here on their own, by motor, fresh and quite undisciplined, trampled in from every possible direction, and brought down little brothers and sisters, and even friends, with them. Of course, they were obliged to announce in advance how many, because of the luncheon : but it made a great number to feed, even if, in the end, it always came out of the parents' pockets. . . .

" She sat down, and together they summed up the situation before them. . . . Where the little devils picked up these things, they simply couldn't imagine. Astonishing ! But it was always the same story. However — they could be thankful that the epidemic of German measles had been a light one, the scarlet-fever nothing at all (except for one boy, who, through his own carelessness and disobedience, had lost the sight of an eye): both were finished a month ago. Ringworm was stationary. And the boys in general seemed to be getting over the effects of last term's whooping-cough more rapidly than usual. Unfortunately Pelling Major and Snouty Kendrix wheezed pretty badly still, and were both of them performing to-day : and, it being Paters' Match, they were sure to play up, and run as fast as they could, and that would inevitably bring it on ! You would hear them roaring, like anthracite stoves, all over the playing-fields. . . . Apart from this, however, the Headmaster and his sister felt they could congratulate themselves : it was mid-July, nearly the end of the term, and only two epidemics — unless you counted ringworm ! Later on, of course, one must be prepared for a few mastoid cases. . . . But they must be grateful : so far, they had been wonderfully free ! "

APPENDIX E

THE CAMORRA TRIAL

THE following account of the Camorra trial at Viterbo, and of the crime that caused it, has been extracted from the pages of *The Times*. It has been slightly rearranged and abridged in order to make it easier to follow. For example, the repetitions necessary for day-to-day reading have been omitted. The first instalment appeared in *The Times* on 13th March 1911.

The story unfolded has other, I think, besides intrinsic interest — for example, it possesses implications, constitutes a sort of prophecy of what was to happen politically in the future, as well as affording a parallel to events in Chicago and other American cities during the years of Prohibition.

" *Rome, March 12th.* The Naples Camorra trial began yesterday in the Court at Viterbo. All the prisoners were present and were accommodated in a large cage erected in Court, with the exception of the informer, Abbatemaggio, who was placed in another cage by himself.

" The main business yesterday, the impanelling of the jury, could not be completed, and had to be postponed till Tuesday next. . . . In spite of the marked reluctance of the citizens of Viterbo to serve in a trial of long duration, it is hoped that the panel of 30, from which the ultimate jury will be drawn by lot, will be completed without further difficulty.

" *March 11th.* . . . The number of witnesses is about 600, fairly evenly divided between the prosecution and defence. The President of the Court has rejected already a certain number whose evidence, being merely political, had nothing to do with the case. The number of counsel for the defence is 32, so that, taking into consideration the enormous list of witnesses and the probable determination of every advocate to address the Court, the estimate of three, or even four, months for the duration of the trial hardly seems exaggerated. . . ."

There follows an account of the crime for which the Camorristi were being tried.

" The murder was committed on June 5th, 1906, and though most of the arrests were made within a year, four years and a half have elapsed before the alleged criminals could be brought to justice.

" Both the victims and the persons who are accused of compassing their death were typical figures of the existing Camorra of Naples, which, though greatly fallen away from its old importance, still exercises a very considerable influence in Neapolitan life, especially among the lower classes. A proof of this is afforded in the extraordinary difficulty which the authorities have experienced in getting evidence for a crime of which the true history must have been known to thousands of people. Again, there is the strange story of the antagonistic parts played by the two different branches of the police service.

" The Neapolitan police — *Pubblica Sicurezza* — to whom the first inquiries fell seems to have throughout abandoned obvious clues in favour of false information supplied by the Camorra itself ; not only that, but when the Carabinieri, determined to strike a decisive blow at the Camorra, followed the real track with laudable energy, their conduct of the case was apparently wilfully hampered and interfered with by their colleagues of the other service. When, finally, the case seemed complete, and it was proposed to bring the accused to trial, it was found impossible to hold that trial in Naples, since neither juries nor witnesses could be depended upon in an environment still dominated by the Camorra. The case was first transferred to Rome, but, owing, it is said, to the want of suitable accommodation in the new Palace of Justice, it was finally transferred to Viterbo, distant some two hours by rail north of Rome, where there can be no doubt but that it will be fairly tried.

" The story of the crime is otherwise simple enough, if one can trust the evidence given by the informer, a certain Abbatemaggio, himself one of the accused and a Camorrista. On June 5th, 1906, the body of Gennaro Cuocolo was found on the seashore near Torre del Greco, bearing the marks of 39 wounds inflicted with stabbing instruments, besides other bruises. The same day the body of his wife, Maria, was found in their house in the Via Nardones, also stabbed to death, with at least 14 wounds. The room had been rifled and a watch and some jewelry were missing, but it was evident from the ferocity of the double crime that revenge, and not robbery, was the motive. Gennaro Cuocolo was known as a receiver of stolen goods, his wife was formerly a procuress, and the couple enjoyed the respect and consideration of their neighbours as quiet, well-to-do people, not without influence in Camorra circles. The police, *Pubblica Sicurezza*, began their inquiry, and reported at once that the murder was the result of a Camorra quarrel, naming four men as chiefly implicated, three of whom are now among the number standing their trial. But these men were not then arrested, and, for some unexplained reason, the police abandoned the trial, and, acting on evidence supplied by the Camorra itself, arrested two former convicts who were proved to have nothing to do with the matter. Under the guidance of

Don Ciro Vittozzi the pursuit soon plunged deep into a tortuous maze of perjury and strayed far from the real culprits. Then the Carabinieri took up the running on the original scent, and, in spite of every obstacle put in their way, carried it through to the end.

" According to the evidence upon which the prosecution relies the story is as follows :

" On May 26th, 1906, a meeting of Camorristi was held at a *trattoria* in Bagnoli, at which were present many leaders of the Camorra. Before this tribunal one of these, Enrico Alfano, better known as Ericone, denounced the Cuocolos for the betrayal of a comrade, Arena, who was suffering penal servitude in consequence. The tribunal decided that Cuocolo deserved death and that his wife had better be suppressed also, as, sharing her husband's secrets, she knew too much. A certain Nicolo Morra was told off to make the necessary arrangements. As the result of these Cuocolo was enticed from his house to a spot on the seashore near Torre del Greco, where he was assailed by Morra and three others — Gennaro, Sortino, and Cerrato — with weapons which correspond to the wounds found on the body. The four jumped into a hired carriage, which they had kept waiting, and galloped back to Naples. Here Sortino left the others, and, accompanied by another man, Salvi by name, went to the Cuocolos' house in the Via Nardones, where they murdered the wife, whom they found in bed. . . .

" The Camorra, the union of disputatious persons, is a secret society which for many years dominated Naples. Originally, so far as can be traced, a league of prisoners, formed for good fellowship and mutual aid, it gradually spread through many branches of Neapolitan society. There was a grand master, whose name no one was supposed to know, and a court of judges, picked from the twelve branches of the league. Each branch was composed of a number of semi-independent groups, politicians, blackmailers, smugglers, or thieves. The judges met in secret and sentenced in secret. Those who refused them obedience died, as a long list of unpunished murders testified. The old Camorristi were helped, criminals in its ranks mysteriously escaped punishment ; and respectable citizens submitted to its blackmail rather than fight it. It hung like a shadow over Naples.

" With the coming of popular suffrage the Camorra found a wider field. It entered local politics and carried all before it. Shady contractors became its allies and the local administration of Naples under Camorra influences became notorious throughout Italy. Affairs reached such a pass that the Government appointed a Royal Commission of Inquiry, and the report presented to the Minister of the Interior in 1901 by Senator Sardello bore out the worst that had been feared.

" *Viterbo, March 13th.* The impanelling of a jury for the Camorra trial continues to encounter enormous difficulties. Some of the men on the list have left the town, and are said to be ready to go abroad in order to be out of reach. Strenuous efforts are being made to induce citizens compelled by law to serve to come forward, but, so far, the authorities have only met with obstinate refusal.

" Experts have visited Abbatemaggio, the informer, and declare that his memory is extraordinary. He can quote the minutest details, dates, hours, days, weeks, the appearance of persons, and places in connexion with events that happened years ago. Among his assertions is one that on a certain day in the spring of 1902, Rapi, one of the accused, was in Naples as he (Abbatemaggio) went there to give him his share of the proceeds of a certain theft. It was for this reason that Rapi asked the Court to have the tailor called from England to swear that Rapi was in London at the time and went to his shop to buy a frock-coat.

" *Rome, March 14th.* Abbatemaggio, the informer, speaking with the lawyers to-day, said he was determined to confirm his revelations, first, because he repented of his past bad life, and secondly, because if he remained with the Camorristi he was sure that, knowing too many of their secrets, he would end as Cuocolo did. . . .

" Signor Bianchi, the President of the Court, declared to-day that immediately after the definite formation of the jury several points raised by the defence would be dealt with. The recapitulation of the investigations into the case and the reasons for which the accused had been brought before the Court would be read. These documents occupy 130 printed pages. The Court will then begin the interrogation of the accused in the following order. First, those who are believed to have actually carried out the crime, who number six ; second, the alleged instigators, who are four ; third, the accomplices ; and finally Abbatemaggio, who will endeavour to confute the assertions of the accused, being at the same time one of the accused and a witness.

" The police continue to adopt severe measures against persons who might intimidate the witnesses. They will not allow the relations of the accused who have a criminal record to reside here, and are also sending home those who are without means of subsistence. . . .

" *Rome, March 15th, 1911.* The jury was completed to-day at the Assize Court at Viterbo, to the great satisfaction of the prisoners, who began to fear another postponement of the trial. Twelve jurymen and two supplementary jurors were drawn by lot. All belong to the well-to-do class, and are mainly professional men.

"*Viterbo, March 16th.* The trial of the Camorra leaders was resumed to-day before a crowded Court.

" The efforts of the defence were directed to demonstrating that Abbatemaggio was an abnormal subject, it being argued that he was in an hysteric and epileptic state.

" Before the adjournment a typical Neapolitan Lazzarone appeared among the public in the Court, and was immediately recognised by the accused, who exchanged signs with him. The Lazzarone, approaching the Judge, said that he had just arrived there to proclaim the innocence of all his friends whom he knew perfectly well. The Marshal of the Carabineers recognised him as Domenico Lopez, a dangerous Camorrist who, shortly after the Cuocolo murder, was arrested for another crime and condemned to be imprisoned for four years in the Penitentiary at Trani, from which he came straight to Viterbo, when freed, in the hope of being able to help his comrades. He was arrested and despatched to Naples.

" *Rome, March 22nd.* An extraordinary scene took place at the Camorra trial in Viterbo this morning, provoked by the very unprofessional conduct of the counsel for the defence, who suddenly began to inveigh violently against the advocate of Abbatemaggio, crying shame upon him for defending a spy and an informer. In spite of the calm demeanour of the advocate in question, one after another of the counsel opposed to him took up the cry. The disturbance spread to the prisoners in their cage, who began howling like wild animals against both Abbatemaggio and his advocate, until the whole Court was in a state of pandemonium. It required all the firmness of the President to calm the tumult, in which task he was aided by the diversion afforded by the sudden indisposition of Don Ciro Vitozzi, the Camorra priest. The utter want of control shown by some of the Neapolitan counsel constitutes a serious difficulty in the maintenance of order.

" *Rome, March 25th.* On the conclusion of yesterday's sitting the trial was adjourned until next Tuesday. . . .

" Of course the prisoners who have been so far examined are absolutely innocent according to their own statements. None of them are Camorristi, they do not even know what the Camorra means, except one man who confessed that he did once belong to that association, but left it directly he married, as being inconsistent with married respectability. They also began by denying any criminal antecedents, and, when confronted with lists of previous convictions of sometimes appalling length, protested that they might occasionally have strayed from the path of virtue, being victims of circumstance and the malignant persecution of Carabinieri. One after another of these victims of fate is taken from

the great cage which holds his fellows and invited to tell his story.
He tells it always with much histrionic effect, sometimes with a
passionate sense of the pathos of his situation, and with an extraordinary skill in avoiding any admission which might compromise
his companions in the dock. It is often obvious that the man is
lying ; but, as a rule, the mixture of truth and fiction must be very
puzzling to the jury, who also seem to find it rather difficult sometimes to comprehend exactly the rich Neapolitan dialect in which
the evidence is given.

" The tale is always the same. They are innocent men, who
have unjustly suffered already more than four years' imprisonment
owing to a base conspiracy on the part of the Carabinieri. When,
however, the record of their life is revealed in Court, it is hard
to feel much sympathy even on the supposition of their innocence
of this last crime. Conrado Sortino, for instance, who has the least
black record behind him, should never have been at liberty at all.
He once kicked to death a young girl in revolting circumstances.
He protested then, and he and his friends protest now, that he was
really a *galantuomo* and one of good standing. As he was also
able to plead good service to the State, in the fact that being a
barber he once shaved both the Prime Minister and the Minister
of Justice, his first murder only cost him a few months' imprisonment. Nicolo Morra, another of the alleged actual murderers,
lived by a business which cannot be described in polite language,
in partnership with a woman, Maria Stendardo, who also baffles
description. The story of this worthy pair is almost incredible.
But, in spite of the black list of crime proved against him as a
ruthless trafficker in young girls, to say nothing of minor mis-
demeanours, this man assured the jury : ' My conscience is as
clear as distilled water, I am religious to the hairs of my head.
I love my children, and he who loves his children loves his neighbour.' Salvi, nicknamed ' Peppe o curto ', Antonio Cerrato, di
Gennaro, and di Matteo, all accused of being material agents and
all rejoicing in nicknames within the Camorra circle, proved to
be ruffians of a lesser degree — that is to say, of crime ; but not
one of them had less than three or four previous offences against
his name. It was notable that most of these men disclaimed their
Camorra nicknames, alleging that they belonged rightly to other
men.

" It was during the examination of ' Peppe o curto ' that a
violent scene occurred in Court between the counsel employed, in
which the prisoners joined with imprecations against their accusers,
with sobs, and lamentable cries of ' Siamo povera gente ! ' ' Siamo
assassinati ! ' ' Ci hanno rovinati ! ' ' I carabinieri sono i nostri
assassini,' the while that Don Ciro Vitozzi, the Camorra priest,

called pitifully on his God, and Abbatemaggio sat silent and unmoved in his solitary cage wearing his unchanging sardonic smile.

" Friday's sitting ended with the beginning of Abbatemaggio's examination.

" . . . Yesterday he only got as far as his first connexion with the Camorra. The line taken by the defence is that he is lying in accordance with a carefully invented tale. A number of experts, including Professor Ottolenghi, a well-known alienist, are attending the Court during his evidence in order to form some opinion of his sanity. He certainly showed signs of much personal malice during the first part of his statement, but of insanity none ; and if he is a liar he must have a phenomenal memory.

" *Rome, April 2nd.* The examination of Enrico Alfano, known as ' Ericone ', the alleged chief of the Camorra, occupied two long sittings and came to an end on Friday night.

" Alfano's self-defence was a most masterly performance, revealing a subtle intellect and a real power of rhetoric which fully explain his influence over his fellow Camorristi. His flights of oratory were evidently as often addressed to the prisoners in the cage behind him as to the jury, and, no doubt, will have their effect in the examinations which follow. For Abbatemaggio, the informer, he affected a contemptuous pity, carefully abstaining from any violence of phrase or judgment when rebutting his evidence, and treating him as a poor creature hardly responsible for his actions.

" *Rome, June 27th.* The Camorra trial at Viterbo made distinct progress yesterday, when the advocate for the defence, after speaking for more than four weeks, retired from the case, protesting that the Court insufficiently protected him from the comments of the Press and from the complaints of his own clients.

" *Rome, July 5th.* The Camorra trial at Viterbo reached its last stage yesterday. Inasmuch, however, as the jury has to answer no fewer than 144 questions, the verdict may yet suffer some further delay.

" *Rome, July 8th.* The Viterbo jury this afternoon returned a verdict in the Cuocolo case, finding the prisoners *Guilty* on all counts. Sortino, Morra, Cerrato, di Gennaro, and Mariano were found *Guilty* of the murder of Cuocolo, and Sortino and Salvi of the murder of Cuocolo's wife. Alfano, Fucci, Arena, de Marinis, and Rapi were found *Guilty* of plotting and commanding the crime. The remainder of the prisoners were found *Guilty* of belonging to a criminal association. In short, the whole case of the Carabinieri and the accusations that they have brought against Naples are held by the Viterbo jury to have been fully proved.

" Sentences of 30 years' imprisonment were passed on the six executants of the murders and on Alfano and de Marinis. The other prisoners were sentenced to terms ranging from 20 to four years' imprisonment ; Ciro Vitozzi, a priest, was sentenced to seven years' imprisonment.

" Great confusion was created in Court by an attempt at suicide made by de Marinis."

" The number of people implicated was 41 ; six of these were accused of procuring the murder, five of actually carrying it out, and the rest of complicity in various degrees. The hearing of the case has occupied over 300 sittings of the Assize Court at Viterbo. The taking of the evidence of the 650 witnesses ended in March, and the last three months have been occupied by speeches of counsel.

" There were three advocates for the prosecution and 20 for the defence. One of the latter, Signor Lioy, spoke uninterruptedly for more than four weeks, and might perhaps still be speaking had it not been for an incautious indulgence in bad temper.

" The trial has afforded some interesting studies of character, not the least remarkable among which has been that of Commenda- tore Bianchi, the President of the Court, an admirable example of an Italian Judge. Through all these weary months he has displayed the same patience and imperturbable good temper, and the same quiet determination to hold the scales of justice absolutely even. Considering the nature of the proceedings, the atmosphere of the Court was singularly cheerful. The chief sufferers were the jurymen. The prisoners, well fed, well lodged and with nothing to do but gossip away the idle hours in their own congenial com- pany, enjoyed the *dolce far niente* which, in Naples, makes most for happiness."

INDEX

INDEX

Pare, Stephen, 166
Paris : the Commune, 21 ; the fashions, 161, 286
Parrots, 135-6
Pelham, Hon. Marcus, 160
Pélissier, Henry, 276
Pepys cited, 296
Phillips, Sir Claude, 58 *and n.*
Pianolas, 110, 113, 148
Pilgrims' Way churches, 107
Ping-pong, 19, 162
Poles, 233-4
Portland, 7th Duke of, 264 *n.*
Pourtalès, Mme. de, 115 *and nn.*
Practical jokes, 176-8
Puff-ball, 162
Puglie, 154

Radstock, Lord, 99
Rag and bone man, 5, 61
Ragglesedge, Mr., 163-4, 168, 284, 288 ; his attempted sale of a motor car, 286-287
Religion : tormenting preoccupation with, 27-9, 70, 84-5 ; at school, 127 ; high-church phase, 147
Renishaw : its atmosphere, 1, 118, 208 ; contrasted with Gosden, 33-5 ; its ghosts, 35, 39 ; top floor, 38 ; painted pots, 223 *n.* ; its one bathroom, 281 ; waking dreams of, 139 ; first summer holidays at, 162 ; early morning walk at, 252-4 ; Edith's coming-out party, 279 *et seq.* ; extensive preparations, 280-81
Reresby family, 175
Riding, 19, 162-3
Riviera : towns, 75 ; carnations, 229, 234
Rodin, Auguste, 58
Rolfe, Frederick (Baron Corvo), 243-245
Rome, 7, 8
Rootham, Helen, 145-7, 157, 256
Rossini, 191
Rosslyn, Earl of, 59
Rothenburg, 300
Ruskin, John, 269
Russian ballet, 278

Sacheverell, Henry, 36 *and n.²*, 297
Sacheverell, Katherine, 36 *n.²*
Samoyedes, 107, 113, 118
San Remo, 228, 229-30 ; carnations, 229, 234, 239 ; the old town, 232 ; revisited, 239
Sancha (caricaturist), 270
Sardello, Senator, 308
Sargent portrait group, 3 ; its hanging, 45, 51

Sassoon, Sir Philip, 264 ; visit to, 133-4
Sassoon, Siegfried, 141
Scarborough : charity matinées, 46 ; the stranded whale, 61-2 ; charabanc excursion from, 63-5 ; Pavilion Hotel, 82-3 ; the Coronation celebrations, 82 ; the Jubilee Plunger, 217-218 ; Dumple Street, 218 ; fish for sale, 219 ; visit to, after year at school, 216 ; bombarded (1914), 66
Scrutton, Mr., 286-8
Selby, Mrs., 42-4
Sermoneta, Duchess of, 184
Severini, Gino, 49
Sharp, Cecil James, 128 *and n.*
Shaw, G. B., 268
Sicily, 7, 265
Sickert, Walter Richard, cited, 270
Sitwell, Lady (grandmother), attitude of, to her son as a child, 60 ; her concern for him in his illness, 95-7 ; the Keswick Convention, 98-9 ; her attitude to Camilla, 100-101 ; attitude to Lady Ida, 112 ; relations with Lady Osborn, 101-2 ; in the Indian Room, 107-8, 112 ; first holidays with, 143, 145, 148 ; compared with Aunt Florence, 97 ; her partiality, 109 ; her charm, 112 ; her correspondence, 112 ; letters from, quoted, 194, 269 ; letter to Turnbull, 66 ; visit to her old home, 207-208 ; mentioned, 59, 70, 91, 95
Sitwell, Alice, 36 *n.²*
Sitwell, Cecil, 196
Sitwell, Edith (sister) : her visit to the Tower, 14 ; her education, 17-18, 20; her singing, 111 ; as piano instructress, 113 ; her love of music, 182 ; her sensitiveness, 135, 177, 182 ; her attitude to the U.S.A., 25 ; in the French play, 186 ; in Paris, 217, 225 ; her development in six months, 230-231 ; Italy's effect on, 248 ; at San Remo, 230-31, 237 ; in Venice, 246 ; coming-out party, 279-84 ; her appearance, 157 ; relations with her mother, 22, 81, 135, 146, 182, 283-4 ; with her father, 157, 182, 230, 283 ; "*très difficile*", 283-4 ; her poem quoted, 117 ; her *Collected Poems* cited, 183 *n.* ; letter to, quoted, 16 ; mentioned, 62, 92, 95, 110, 140, 144, 244
Sitwell, Florence (aunt) : her governess, 223 ; at family prayers, 91 ; compared with her mother, 97 ; the Keswick Convention, 98, 99 ; her painting, 113 ; extracts from her Journal, 89, 92, 98 ; mentioned, 84, 87, 109, 117, 147

317

INDEX

END OF VOL. II

Printed in Great Britain by R. & R. CLARK, LIMITED, *Edinburgh.*

8
266

8
66

8
66

THE TIMES BOOK CLUB
42, Wigmore Street,
London, W.1.

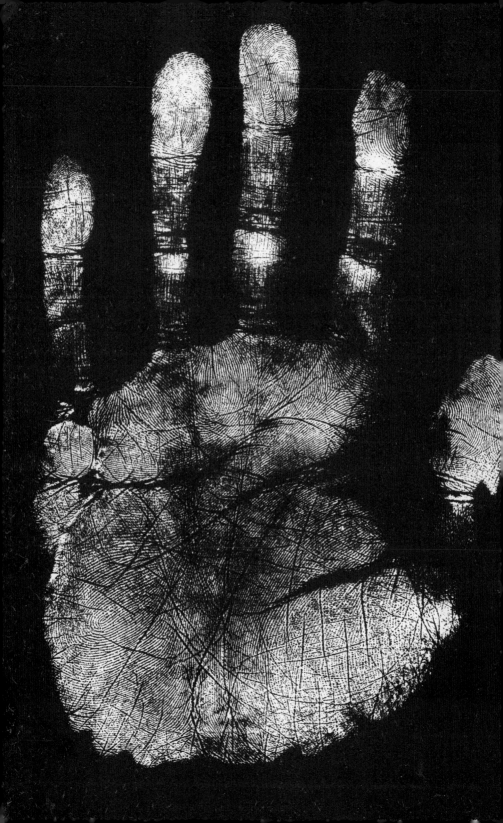